AN INTRODUCTION TO RELIGION AND POLITICS

An Introduction to Religion and Politics offers a comprehensive overview of the many theories of religion and politics, and provides students with an accessible but in-depth account of the most significant debates, issues, and methodologies. Fox examines the ways in which religion influences politics, analyzes the current key issues, and provides a state-of-the-art account of religion and politics, highlighting the diversity in state religion policies around the world.

Topics covered include:

- secularism and secularization;
- religious identity;
- religious worldviews, beliefs, doctrines, and theologies;
- religious legitimacy;
- religious institutions and mobilization;
- rational and functional religion;
- religious fundamentalism;
- conflict, violence, and terror.

This work combines theoretical analysis with data on the religion policies of 177 governments, showing that while most of the world's governments support religion and many restrict it, true neutrality on the issue of religion is extremely rare. Religion is becoming an inescapable issue in politics.

This work will be essential reading for all students of religion and politics, and will also be of great interest to those studying related subjects such as comparative politics, international relations, and war and conflict studies.

Jonathan Fox is Professor of Political Studies at Bar-Ilan University in Ramat Gan, Israel. He has published extensively on religion and politics.

Routledge Studies in Religion and Politics
Edited by Jeffrey Haynes, London Metropolitan University, UK

This series aims to publish high-quality works on the topic of the resurgence of political forms of religion in both national and international contexts. This trend has been especially noticeable in the post-Cold War era (that is, since the late 1980s). It has affected all the "world religions" (including Buddhism, Christianity, Hinduism, Islam, and Judaism) in various parts of the world (such as the Americas, Europe, the Middle East and North Africa, South and Southeast Asia, and sub-Saharan Africa).

The series welcomes books that use a variety of approaches to the subject, drawing on scholarship from political science, international relations, security studies, and contemporary history.

Books in the series explore these religions, regions, and topics both within and beyond the conventional domain of "church–state" relations to include the impact of religion on politics, conflict, and development, including the late Samuel Huntington's controversial—yet influential—thesis about "clashing civilizations."

In sum, the overall purpose of the book series is to provide a comprehensive survey of what is currently happening in relation to the interaction of religion and politics, both domestically and internationally, in relation to a variety of issues.

Politics and the Religious Imagination
Edited by John Dyck, Paul Rowe and Jens Zimmermann

Christianity and Party Politics
Keeping the faith
Martin H. M. Steven

Religion, Politics and International Relations
Selected essays
Jeffrey Haynes

Religion and Democracy
A worldwide comparison
Carsten Anckar

Religious Actors in the Public Sphere
Means, objects and effects
Edited by Jeffrey Haynes and Anja Hennig

Politics and Religion in the United Kingdom
Steve Bruce

Politics, Religion and Gender
Framing and regulating the veil
Edited by Sieglinde Rosenberger and Birgit Sauer

Representing Religion in the European Union
Does God matter?
Edited by Lucian N. Leustean

An Introduction to Religion and Politics
Theory and practice
Jonathan Fox

AN INTRODUCTION TO RELIGION AND POLITICS

Theory and Practice

Jonathan Fox

Routledge
Taylor & Francis Group

LONDON AND NEW YORK

First published 2013
by Routledge
2 Park Square, Milton Park, Abingdon, Oxon OX14 4RN

Simultaneously published in the USA and Canada
by Routledge
711 Third Avenue, New York, NY 10017

Routledge is an imprint of the Taylor & Francis Group, an informa business

British Library Cataloguing in Publication Data
A catalogue record for this book is available from the British Library

Library of Congress Cataloging-in-Publication Data
Fox, Jonathan, 1968–
An introduction to religion and politics: theory & practice / Jonathan Fox.
p. cm. – (Routledge studies in religion and politics)
Includes bibliographical references and index.
Religion and politics. I. Title.
BL65.P7F695 2013
322'.1–dc23

ISBN: 978–0–415–67631–1 (hbk)
ISBN: 978–0–415–67632–8 (pbk)
ISBN: 978–0–203–09441–9 (ebk)

Typeset in Garamond
by Keystroke, Station Road, Codsall, Wolverhampton

Printed and bound in Great Britain by
TJ International Ltd, Padstow, Cornwall

CONTENTS

ILLUSTRATIONS

FIGURES

TABLES

ACKNOWLEDGEMENTS

I would like to thank Jeff Haynes and Nicola Parkin for encouraging me to write this book. I also thank the John Templeton Foundation for supporting the research. The opinions expressed in this study are those of the author and do not necessarily reflect the views of the John Templeton Foundation.

CHAPTER 1

Introduction

Religion and politics have been interconnected throughout history. For every ancient political entity for which we have records, religion was intimately connected to politics. This is true of ancient Egypt and Greece as well as the Mesopotamian, Babylonian, Persian, Greek, and Roman Empires, and it continued in the feudal states that followed the fall of the Roman Empire. It is true even of prehistory. The Old Testament records a time when separation of religion and state was unheard of. Each city or nation had its own god. People sought the approval of their gods when they went to war, and brought these gods, or symbols representing their gods, with them. When one side was victorious, its national religion was often imposed upon the vanquished. The political leaders of some states, such as the Pharaohs of Egypt and the pre-Christian emperors of Rome, were themselves considered gods.

However, even in the countries described in the Bible, theocracies were rare, and while political and religious power were usually interconnected, they were embodied in separate entities. That is, the political class and the priestly class were strongly dependent upon each other and significantly influenced the other's decisions, but they were usually separate classes. The religious authorities would support the legitimacy of the temporal authorities and the temporal authorities would support the religion, both financially and through enforcing the religion's dogma with the power of the state.

In a number of ways, things have not changed. Many states still support official religions but in most cases the state and religious institutions are separate entities. Wars are fought over religion, though in recent decades most of them have been civil wars rather than wars between nations. Also, while leaders no longer demand to be worshiped, except perhaps in North Korea, some do claim to be the representatives of their God on earth. Also, the clergy and religious institutions are often involved in politics, at least at the level of lobbying governments to influence political decisions. While separation of religion and state is prominent in much of the world as an ideology, as demonstrated in Chapters 10–13 it is arguably an ideology that is more often expressed as an ideal than practiced, even in the Western liberal democracies where the concept of separation of religion and state originated. Wars between states are also less often overtly about religion, though religious language is still used to justify war. Whether religion is involved in politics today to the extent it was in the past is a matter of debate but it is certainly still involved sufficiently that the role of religion in politics is worthy of extended discussion, research, and debate.

APPROACHES TO THE STUDY OF RELIGION AND POLITICS

This book is intended to explore the intersection between religion and politics in modern times. I provide a discussion of what I consider to be the most important intersections between religion and politics as well as the important bodies of theory on religion and politics in the political science literature and the relevant literatures from other disciplines. I also provide a more practical description of the nature and roles of specific governments in religious politics. I seek to do so in a comparative global context, both providing examples from the four corners of the earth and providing a theoretical framework that can be applied in a global context.

This book is firmly within the field of comparative politics and places a heavy emphasis on state religion policy. This has two implications: First, the focus is on the actual role religion plays in politics rather than the role it ought to play. For example, political philosophers such as Rawls and de Tocqueville, among many others, discuss the role they believe religion should play in democracy. These philosophies are certainly relevant to questions of how religion influences politics because they influence those who practice politics as well as because they help us theorize about how religion does influence politics. However, the question of how religion ought to influence politics is addressed here only in the context of how these theories can help us understand the actual role of religion in politics.

Second, religion's influence on politics manifests itself through multiple and sometimes overlapping agencies. These include how governments address religion, the political activities of all sorts of religious groups and organizations, and the religion's influence on society in general. While this book addresses all of these, the major comparative focus is on state religion policy. This is not intended to imply that these other influences are less important. Rather, no book can include all possible examples. The book's content simply reflects the author's choice of focus.

There are two possible approaches to the comparative study of religion and politics. The first is to focus on theories and trends—that is, the general ways in which religion can influence politics. This approach is intended to provide a theoretical toolbox that will give a student of religion and politics the means to analyze religion's intersection with politics in any setting. The second is to examine the facts on the ground and explore the connection between religion and politics in particular places. This volume combines both approaches.

In Part 1 of this book I include eight chapters (Chapters 2–9) exploring theories and important literatures in religion and politics. While in these chapters I focus on the theory and trends approach, each of them includes numerous concrete examples that are intended to illustrate these theories and trends. Chapter 2 explores the history of the study of religion and politics—a history that is overshadowed by a large period of time when social scientists mostly ignored religion as a significant political and social factor. I explore how and why this state of affairs occurred and how it influences our understanding of religion and politics today.

Chapters 3–6 explore what I consider to be the four most important avenues through which religion influences politics. Chapter 3 examines religious identity and theories which posit that some religious groups are different, or behave differently, than others. This type of theory, while limited and problematic in many ways, is also the most common in the political science literature. Accordingly, it provides a good starting point for a discussion of how religion influences politics.

Chapter 4 examines how religious beliefs influence political behavior. Its central thesis is that religious worldviews, beliefs, doctrines, and theologies provide a lens through which people can understand the world around them, as well as including explicit instructions on how to behave. All of this can result in a significant influence on political behavior. These qualities of religion, potentially, have profound influences on political behavior.

Chapter 5 looks at how religion is used to justify and legitimize political actions and policies. At its most basic level, religion can lend legitimacy to governments, political parties, opposition movements, institutions, leaders, policies, and just about any other political actor or phenomenon one can list, as well as undermine their legitimacy.

Chapter 6 explores the influence of religious organizations and institutions on how people organize for political activities. While religious institutions are rarely if ever built to organize for political activity, they are commonly put to this use. This chapter explores the dynamics of this phenomenon.

The final three chapters of Part 1 examine literatures and phenomena that I believe can be best understood in the context of the four types of influences I identify in the previous chapters. Chapter 7 examines a body of theories in political science and sociology which posit that religious politics can be understood as the outcome of rational calculations. While arguably this theoretical discussion might be better placed before Chapter 3, I argue that it is best understood in relation to several of religion's influences on politics, and, accordingly, I placed this chapter after my discussion of these influences.

Chapter 8 focuses on the phenomenon of religious fundamentalism. While in many ways a unique manifestation of religion, fundamentalism's influences on politics manifest themselves through the four avenues described in Chapters 3–6.

Finally, Chapter 9 uses the theories of the seven preceding chapters to examine how religion influences conflict, war, violence, and terrorism. Religious conflict is one of the most important current issues in the religion and politics literature. This chapter is intended both to examine how religion can influence conflict and to provide a concrete example of how the theories and literatures on religion and politics can be applied to understand a more specific aspect of religion's influence on politics.

In Part 2 (Chapters 10–13) I emphasize the comparative approach and examine the state religion policies of 177 countries. These chapters look at world trends in government religion policy, focusing on four factors: (1) official religions, (2) government support for religious through legislation and the financing of religions, (3) government regulation and control of the majority religion, and (4) religious discrimination against religious minorities. I discuss in more detail exactly what is meant by these terms later in this chapter.

Finally, Chapter 14 provides some final thoughts on the role of religion and politics. These include discussion of how the issues discussed in Part 1, especially in Chapters 3–6, can be used to build a more comprehensive theory of religion and politics.

Overall, the approach in this volume is intended to give the reader the theoretical tools to understand the intersection between religion and politics anywhere in the world at any point in modern history. I then reinforce this theoretical approach with a strong grounding in examples, case studies, and an examination of how religion and politics works in practice across the globe. Much of this grounding comes from information from the Religion and State (RAS) project, which, as is discussed in more detail later in this chapter, has collected information on government religion policy for 177 countries.

A SOCIAL SCIENCE APPROACH TO RELIGION

There are many possible perspectives that can be applied to the academic study of religion. It is a topic studied by political scientists, sociologists, anthropologists, historians, psychologists, philosophers, and theologians, among others. Each of these disciplines has its own particular set of approaches to understanding the topic of religion, and a particular set of questions around which most research and inquiry revolves. Many of these approaches are not compatible or reconcilable with each other. When studying religion, one must select from them. This book uses a social science approach, relying most heavily on the methodologies of comparative political science and sociology and the questions asked particularly by political scientists, though the insights and queries of other disciplines can also be found in these pages.

What does this mean? Basically, I begin with the assumption that religion is a social institution or phenomenon that strongly influences human behavior. The primary goal of a social scientist is to understand human behavior. Political scientists and sociologists focus on the behavior of groups, with political scientists emphasizing political behavior and sociologists emphasizing social behavior. While the central goal of this book is to understand religion's influence on political behavior, often it is not possible to do so without an understanding of the role of religion in influencing social behavior. In addition, as is seen especially in Chapter 2, the insights of sociologists into religion are essential to understanding its political role because of the inter-connections between the social and political. Furthermore, sociological theory on religion is considerably more developed than that of political science. Be that as it may, the central question asked in this volume is: How does religion intersect with and influence the political?

This approach has some important implications. The first and foremost is that the truth of religious claims is not a question I address. Whether or not a particular religion or belief is true is an important question to theologians, some philosophers, and billions of believers. In contrast, for a social scientist, as long as a belief influences behavior, the truth of the belief is unimportant. That is, social scientists are not equipped to judge which religion is the true religion, and the answer to this question, assuming a definitive answer is even possible in this world, does little to answer the questions we wish to ask. Rather, I limit my inquiry in this volume to the question of how religions influence behavior. For the purposes of answering this question, whether or not a religion is in some existential or epistemological sense the one true religion does not matter as long as a person or group believes that it is. It is this belief that influences their behavior, not the truth or untruth of this belief.

Thus, for the purposes of the exercise of applying a social science perspective to understand religion's influence on politics, we must set aside whatever beliefs we have regarding religion. It is not important whether we believe in a religion or believe all religions are no more than social constructions that have no truth to them. That is, one can believe that one's religion is the one true religion or that all religions are false. However, these beliefs are not relevant to social science inquiry. Rather, we must objectively examine how religion influences political behavior without allowing any of these preconceptions to color the analysis. As has already been noted, this approach is markedly different from that of political philosophy in that it focuses on the observed influences of religion in politics rather than the role many believe it ought to play.

Some of the implications of this perspective can be seen in how social scientists examine religion. For example, let us examine four definitions of religion discussed in Brian Turner's (1991) classic book *Religion and Social Theory*:

- Emile Durkheim's definition: "A unified system of beliefs and practices relative to sacred things, that is to say, things set apart and forbidden—beliefs and practices which unite into one single moral community called a Church, all those who adhere to them."
- Clifford Geertz's definition: "[1] a system of symbols which acts to [2] establish powerful, persuasive, and long-lasting moods and motivations in men by [3] formulating conceptions of a general order of existence and [4] clothing these conceptions with such an aura of factuality that [5] the moods and motivations seem uniquely realistic."
- Daniel Bell's definition: "Religion is a set of coherent answers to the core existential questions that confront every human group, the codification of these answers into a creedal form that has significance for its adherents, the celebration of rites which provide an emotional bond for those who participate, and the establishment of an institutional body to bring into congregation those who share the creed and celebration, and provide for the continuity of these rights from generation to generation."
- Peter Berger's definition: "Religion is the human enterprise by which a sacred cosmos is established. Put differently, religion is cosmization in a sacred mode. By sacred is meant here a quality of mysterious and awesome power, other than

man and yet related to him, which is believed to reside in certain objects of experience. . . . The sacred cosmos is confronted by man as an immensely powerful reality other than himself. Yet this reality addresses itself to him and locates his life in an ultimately meaningful order."

What do all of these definitions have in common? They focus on how religion interacts with human behavior. Durkheim focuses on how beliefs and rituals unite people into a community. He also emphasizes in his works how religious practices are the key to maintaining religion and to understanding its role in society. Geertz focuses on how religion influences man's behavior, beliefs, and understanding of the world. Bell's definition includes religion's role in answering existential questions for man, religion's influence on groups' bonds, and the role of institutions in preserving religion. Berger uses a definition of religion that addresses the sacred without actually taking a stand on the truth of any particular conception of the sacred.

All of these definitions also avoid theological questions such as whether there exists a deity or deities and what these deities, should they exist, want of man. Nor do they address the truth of any religion, or whether religion is good and moral. As sociological definitions, they take no position on these kinds of questions and rather focus on how religion exists as a social phenomenon or institution that influences human behavior. If they did take a stand on the issue of whether a deity or deities exist, they would likely have to exclude religions like Buddhism and Confucianism— which do not include any gods in their theologies—from being considered religions. If they took a position on morality, they would be engaging in questions of whether a behavior is good or bad rather than trying to understand the causes and consequences of that behavior. By focusing on how religion influences human behavior, we can safely set aside this and other theological-philosophical controversies and focus on the questions that are more central to how religion and the political interact.

Political science definitions of religion are rare. Most political scientists who address the issue simply quote one of the existing sociological or philosophical definitions at the beginning of their books or articles, then proceed with their discussions of religion and politics in a manner that does not appear to be heavily influenced by the definitions they quote. Yet it is not difficult to construct one based on the principles discussed so far. For the purposes of this book I define religion as follows: *Religion seeks to understand the origins and nature of reality using a set of answers that include the supernatural. Religion is also a social phenomenon and institution that influences the behavior of human beings both as individuals and in groups. These influences on behavior manifest themselves through the influences of religious identity, religious institutions, religious legitimacy, religious beliefs, and the codification of these beliefs into authoritative dogma, among other avenues of influence.*

I recognize that religion is more than this and that a complete definition of religion would include many of its social functions and influences, as described by the sociological definitions cited above, as well as a theological element describing in more detail the nature of religion's source, be it a monotheistic God, a pantheon of deities, nature, or some other supernatural phenomenon. Yet taking a stand on these issues, especially their existential, epistemological, and theological aspects, would be to enter debates that have continued for millennia without adding significantly to the completion of the task of this book: to understand how religion influences political behavior. Accordingly, this definition should be taken as a definition of religion's political role rather than a comprehensive definition of religion.

Yet there is a need to differentiate religion from other ideologies that influence behavior, such as nationalism, Marxism, and other political ideologies. It is for this reason that I include the first sentence of my definition. It is possible to claim that other political ideologies are the functional equivalent of religion, and to an extent there is truth in this claim. However, religion is something that is different and distinct. Political ideologies are openly attributed to man—that is, no one questions that man created them. Accordingly, man is equipped to reject or revise these ideologies. Religions are attributed to a direct supernatural source such as God. In the minds of believers, this creates an ideology that is not open to question. In addition, most political ideologies do not address a number of the existential issues most religions address. All of this makes religion distinct.

THE RELIGION AND STATE DATASET

Throughout this book, and especially in Chapters 10–13, I use the Religion and State (RAS) dataset as a source of information and insight. This dataset provides a comprehensive look at multiple aspects of government religion policy for 177 countries across the world, including all countries with populations of 250,000 or more as well as a sampling of less populous countries. While the dataset includes information covering the period 1990–2008, this book's use of the dataset focuses mostly on the information from 2008, and, unless otherwise noted, all references to the dataset refer to the information from that year.[1]

The RAS dataset divides government religion policy into four categories, each focusing on a different aspect of religion policy. The first is whether the government has an *official religion*. This is important because it is a formal declaration of intent. It shows whether a government is officially declaring one religion to be the religion that guides the state, including its culture, philosophy, and policy. The manner in which a government declares an official religion or how declares that it has no official religion is more complicated than might seem to be the case at first glance. I discuss this issue in more detail in Chapter 4.

The second aspect is *religious support*. Religious support represents the extent to which governments support a religion in practice. While much of all aspects of government religion policy, including support, comes about through legislation, in practice governments make policy in many ways other than legislation. This is especially true of non-democratic governments. But even in democracies, government policy can be made by non-legislative decisions on policy by leaders, bureaucratic regulations, and the decisions of national and local officials and courts. The RAS dataset includes all of this in the term "religious support."

Government policy on foreign missionaries, while categorized here as a form of religion discrimination (discussed in detail later) rather than religious support, provides a good example of this dynamic. A government can have a law banning foreign missionaries. Whether or not this law is enforced, it remains a law that can be potentially invoked. However, if there is clear evidence a law has not been enforced for decades, it is generally not included in the RAS dataset. Alternatively, a government can have no such law but, in practice, any foreigner who engages in missionary activities is arrested and deported. In practice, the result is the same as if there was a law. Thus, taking the less formal but nonetheless real aspects of government policy into account provides a more accurate picture of what is, in fact, a government's religion policy.

Examining religious support is important. Not all governments that have official religions engage in high levels of support for religion, and many governments without an official religion engage in high levels of religious support. Thus, examining religious support adds to our understanding of a state's religion policy beyond what can be gleaned from the mere presence of an official religion. In essence, the official religious category represents a state's official policy, and religious support represents what a state does in practice. The two are certainly related but levels of support vary considerably among both states with and states without official religions. For example, Iran and the United Kingdom both have official religions, yet clearly their religion policies are not the same. Part of the difference can be found in the extent of religious support in each state.

This support for religion can take several forms. It can include legislating religious precepts as law and financially supporting religious institutions and activities. It can also include other forms of preferences given to religious institutions and activities. The RAS dataset includes 51 types of religious support:

- There are dietary laws (restrictions on the production, import, selling, or consumption of specific foods).
- There are restrictions or prohibitions on the sale of alcoholic beverages.
- Personal status is defined by religion or clergy (i.e. marriage, divorce, and/or burial can only occur under religious auspices).
- Marriages performed by clergy of at least some religions are given automatic civil recognition, even in the absence of a state license.
- There are restrictions on interfaith marriages.
- Laws of inheritance are defined by religion.
- Religious precepts are used to define crimes or set punishment for crimes.
- The charging of interest is illegal or significantly restricted.
- Women may not go out in public unescorted.
- There are restrictions on the public dress of women other than the common restrictions on public nudity. This refers to required dress rather than banned forms of clothing.
- There are general restrictions on public dress or appearance other than those included in the above category. This refers to required dress rather than banned forms of clothing.
- There are restrictions on intimate interactions between unmarried heterosexual couples.
- There are laws that specifically make it illegal to be a homosexual or engage in homosexual intimate interactions.
- There are restrictions on conversions away from the dominant religion.

- There are blasphemy laws or other restrictions on speech about the majority religion or religious figures.
- There are blasphemy laws protecting minority religions or religious figures.
- There is censorship of the press or other publications on grounds of their being anti-religious.
- There are significant restrictions on public music or dancing other than the usual zoning restrictions.
- There is mandatory closing of some or all businesses during religious holidays, including the Sabbath or its equivalent.
- There are other restrictions on activities during religious holidays, including the Sabbath or its equivalent.
- Religious education is present in public schools.
- Official prayer sessions in public schools are held.
- There is government funding of religious primary or secondary schools, or religious educational programs in non-public schools.
- There is government funding of seminary schools.
- There is government funding of religious education in colleges or universities.
- Public schools are segregated by religion, or separate public schools exist for members of some religions.
- There is government funding of religious charitable organizations.
- The government collects taxes on behalf of religious organizations.
- Official government positions, salaries, or other funding are available for clergy, other than salaries for teachers of religious courses.
- Direct general grants are made to religious organizations.
- Funding for building, maintaining, or repairing religious sites is available.
- Free airtime on television or radio is provided to religious organizations on government channels or by government decree.
- Funding or other government support for religious pilgrimages such as the Hajj is provided.
- Funding for religious organizations or activities other than those listed above is made available.
- Some religious leaders are given diplomatic status, diplomatic passports, or immunity from prosecution by virtue of their religious office.
- There is an official government ministry or department dealing with religious affairs.
- There is a police force or other government agency that exists solely to enforce religious laws.
- Certain government officials are also given an official position in the state church by virtue of their political office.
- Certain religious officials become government officials by virtue of their religious position.
- Some or all government officials must meet certain religious requirements in order to hold office. (This excludes positions in religious ministries, head of the state church, or the like.)
- There are religious courts that have jurisdiction over matters of family law and inheritance.

- There are religious courts that have jurisdiction over some matters of law other than family law and matters of inheritance.
- Female testimony in government court is given less weight than male testimony.
- Seats in the legislative branch and/or cabinet are by law or custom granted, at least in part, along religious lines.
- There are restrictions on abortion on demand.
- There are restrictions on access to birth control.
- Religious symbols are present on the state's flag.
- Religion is listed on state identity cards or other government documents that most citizens must possess or fill out.
- A registration process for religious organizations exists which is in some manner different from the registration process for other non-profit organizations.
- There are restrictions on women other than those listed above.
- There are other religious prohibitions or practices that are mandatory.

The third aspect of government religion policy I examine is *religious regulation*. Religious regulation is defined here as all government laws, policies, and practices that limit, regulate, or control the majority religion in a state, or all religions in a state. Thus, unlike religious support, this category of policy represents a desire to keep religion within certain bounds. The motivations for this type of policy are diverse. They can include an ideological animosity towards religion, as is found in communist ideology. The policy can represent a desire to limit religion's political power. It can also represent an attempt to harness religion's political power for the benefit of the state. Especially in the latter case, governments may both support religion and regulate it.

The RAS dataset measures the following 29 types of religious regulation:

- There are restrictions on religious political parties.
- There are restrictions on trade associations or other civil associations being affiliated with a religion.
- There are restrictions on clergy holding political office.
- There is arrest, continued detention, or severe official harassment of religious figures and/or officials, and/or members of religious parties.
- The government restricts or harasses members and organizations that are affiliated with the majority religion but operate outside of the state-sponsored or recognized ecclesiastical framework.
- There are restrictions on formal religious organizations other than political parties.
- There are restrictions on the public observance of religious practices, including religious holidays and the Sabbath.
- There are restrictions on religious activities outside of recognized religious facilities.
- There are restrictions on public religious speech.
- There are restrictions on or monitoring of sermons by clergy.
- There are restrictions on clergy and/or religious organizations engaging in public political speech (other than sermons) or propaganda, or on political activity in or by religious institutions.

- There are restrictions on religious-based hate speech.
- There are restrictions on access to places of worship.
- There are restrictions on the publication or dissemination of written religious material.
- People are arrested for religious activities.
- There are restrictions on religious public gatherings that are not placed on other types of public gathering.
- There are restrictions on the public display by private persons or organizations of religious symbols, including (but not limited to) religious dress, the presence or absence of facial hair, nativity scenes, and icons.
- There are restrictions on or regulation of religious education in public schools. (This variable represents direct government control of teachers and/or curriculum, not a ban on religious education in public schools.)
- There are restrictions on or regulation of religious education outside of public schools, or general government control of religious education.
- There are restrictions on or regulation of religious education at the university level.
- Foreign religious organizations are required to have a local sponsor or affiliation.
- Heads of religious organizations (e.g. bishops) must be citizens of the state.
- All practicing clergy must be citizens of the state.
- The government appoints, or must approve, clerical appointments or somehow takes part in the appointment process.
- Other than appointments, the government legislates or otherwise officially influences the internal workings or organization of religious institutions and organizations.
- Laws governing the state religion are passed by the government or need the government's approval before being put into effect.
- There is state ownership of some religious property or buildings.
- Conscientious objectors to military service are not given alternatives to national service and are prosecuted.
- Other religious restrictions exist.

These diverse types of regulation can be placed into three categories including limitations on religion's political role, controls or limitations placed on religious institutions and clergy, and restrictions on religious practices such as worship.

The final aspect of government religion policy that I examine here is *religious discrimination*. I define religious discrimination as limitations on the religious practices or religious institutions of religious minorities *which are not placed on the majority religion*. This distinction is critical, because limiting minority religions exclusively is the result of motivations that are different from those for limiting all religions or the majority religion. For instance, countries that have a policy of maintaining a secular public space, such as France, might limit the public expression of religion for all religions. France did exactly this when it passed a law in 2004 prohibiting public school students and employees from wearing "conspicuous religious symbols," including headscarves, skullcaps, and large crosses. This law was consciously applied to all religions as part of France's secularist tradition and, accordingly, is considered here to be religious regulation. In contrast, a number of regional governments in Germany and Belgium passed similar laws but applied them only to the head coverings worn by religious Muslim women. This represents a restriction that focuses only on the religious practices of a minority groups and, accordingly, is considered here to be religious discrimination.

Religious discrimination also has several potential motivations. It can represent a desire to maintain the superiority of the majority religion. It can occur in the context of social and political conflicts where the two sides belong to different religions. It can be the result of a policy of protecting the indigenous culture from outside influences, including religions that are considered new to a country. It can also represent a policy of protecting citizens from religions that the government considers dangerous and predatory. For instance, both France and Belgium formed organizations to monitor and limit "cults" in the 1990s after small religious groups orchestrated mass suicides within those countries. However, these organizations quickly evolved into ones that significantly restrict religious minorities that are clearly not a danger to society. I discuss these incidents and the resulting state policies in France and Belgium in more detail in Chapter 10. The RAS dataset includes the following 30 types of religious discrimination:

- There are restrictions on public observance of religious services, festivals, and/or holidays, including the Sabbath.
- There are restrictions on the private observance of religious services, festivals, and/or holidays, including the Sabbath.
- There are restrictions on building, leasing, repairing, and/or maintaining places of worship.
- There are restrictions on access to existing places of worship.
- There is forced observance of religious laws of another group.
- There are restrictions on formal religious organizations.
- There are restrictions on the running of religious schools and/or religious education in general.
- There are restrictions on the ability to make and/or obtain materials necessary for religious rites, customs, and/or ceremonies.
- Education in the majority religion is mandatory.
- Arrest, continued detention, or severe official harassment of religious figures, officials, and/or members of religious parties for activities other than proselytizing takes place.
- State surveillance of minority religious activities is not placed on the activities of the majority.
- There are restrictions on the ability to write, publish, or disseminate religious publications.
- There are restrictions on the ability to import religious publications.
- There are restrictions on access to religious publications for personal use.
- There are restrictions on the observance of religious laws concerning personal status, including marriage, divorce, and burial.
- There are restrictions on the wearing of religious symbols or clothing. This category includes presence or absence of facial hair but does not include weapons, or clothing that covers one's face.

- There are restrictions on the ordination of and/or access to clergy.
- There are restrictions on conversion to minority religions.
- There is forced renunciation of faith by recent converts to minority religions.
- There are forced conversions of people who were never members of the majority religion.
- Efforts or campaigns to convert members of minority religions to the majority religion which fall short of using force take place.
- There are restrictions on proselytizing by permanent residents of the state to members of the majority religion.
- There are restrictions on proselytizing by permanent residents of state to members of minority religions.
- There are restrictions on proselytizing by foreign clergy or missionaries.
- Minority religions (as opposed to all religions) are required to register in order to be legal or receive special tax status.
- Custody of children is granted to members of the majority group solely or in part on the basis of religious affiliation or beliefs.
- Minority clergy have restricted access to hospitals, jails, military bases, and other places where a chaplain may be needed in comparison to chaplains of the majority religion.
- There is a legal provision or policy of declaring some minority religions dangerous or extremist sects.
- Anti-religious propaganda appears in official or semi-official government publications.
- Other restrictions on religious practices or institutions apply.

RELIGIOUS DISCRIMINATION VERSUS RELIGIOUS FREEDOM

While the terms "religious discrimination" and "religious freedom" seem at first glance straightforward, they are not. Each has multiple possible meanings and interpretations. As has already been noted, discrimination implies that different groups are treated differently, so any definition of religious discrimination would include this element. However, the content of this discrimination can have multiple meanings. For example, does it include only restrictions on religion itself or can it include any restrictions on religious minorities even if these restrictions do not in any way limit religious practices or institutions? Political or economic restrictions on a religious minority in a state would be an example of discrimination of this type. In the context of this book the term *religious discrimination* refers specifically to limitations on the religious practices or religious institutions of religious minorities which are not placed on the majority religion.

Religious freedom is an even more ambiguous term. Violations of religious freedom can include all of the various interpretations of religious discrimination discussed above. They can also include any restriction on religious practices or institutions that are placed on everyone in a state. They can include cases when a state enforces aspects of the majority religion's doctrine as state law. Yet would restrictions on abortions, despite being religious doctrine for many major religions, really constitute a limitation on religious freedom? They are certainly an application of religious doctrine that limits freedom in a citizen's personal life and choices. However, I am unaware of any religion that requires its believers to undergo abortions. Thus, from this perspective restrictions on abortion do not in any practical way limit anyone's ability to practice their religion and would, accordingly, not be considered a violation of religious freedom.

There is no correct answer to these questions when defining religious freedom and religious discrimination. The RAS dataset does not include a variable for "religious freedom" and I use the term sparingly in this book because of the ambiguity of the concept. I most often refer to "religious freedom" clauses in constitutions (because constitutions often use this term but rarely define it) or when describing the work of other authors who use this term. As noted already, this book uses a specific definition of religious discrimination, but this definition is specific to the discussion in this book and others can and do use the term differently.

A NOTE ON METHODOLOGY AND CITATIONS

All of these variables were coded (assigned values) on the basis of extensive research by the RAS project, which produced a report for each country. This report used a number of general sources as well as sources specific to each country. Throughout this book I use examples that I draw from these reports. I discuss the procedures for building these variables and data collection in more detail in the Appendix.

In order to avoid repetitive citations, I list the general sources for these reports in the note whose indicator number appears at the end of this paragraph. All subsequent references in this book when discussing the policies of specific governments or specific events refer to sources in addition to these general sources.[2]

CONCLUSIONS

The approach to the study of religion taken in this book can be described as organized and analytical. Religion's influences on politics are divided into neat, well-defined categories, which are discussed individually. Yet the reality is more complex, with the borders of these categories blending and overlapping. Both politics and religion can be "messy" topics and the study of the two together certainly shares in that trait.

This use of a distinct categorization system is not meant to deny the complexity of the topic at hand. Rather, one of the roles of theory and organization is to simplify a complex topic into a format where it becomes more manageable and understandable. I seek to develop and provide a set of tools that can be applied to better understand religion and politics. I realize that these tools are sometimes imperfect and often simplify a complex set of relationships. Nevertheless, I posit that they also enable social scientists to better organize information and better understand how religion and politics interact. I ask that the reader understand my efforts to explain religion's intersection with the political in this light.

PART 1 THEORIES OF RELIGION AND POLITICS

This part of the book is intended to accomplish two goals: First, it describes and examines how the social science literature understands religion and politics. It includes eight chapters, each of which deals with either a specific body of theory or a specific aspect of religion's influence on politics. For example, Chapter 2 deals with a body of theory called secularization theory and how secularism influences politics. Chapter 6 similarly deals with a body of rationalist theory. The other chapters each deal with a more specific phenomenon or relationships. Chapters 3–6 deal with how specific phenomena, including religious identity, beliefs, institutions, and legitimacy, can influence politics. Chapter 8 examines the phenomenon of religious fundamentalism, and Chapter 9 examines how religion can influence conflict.

Second, these chapters provide a framework through which to understand how religion can influence politics. Chapters 3–6 identify what I consider to be the most important ways religion influences politics. Chapter 8 examines how what we learn from Chapters 3–6 can help us explain and understand the phenomenon of religious fundamentalism. Chapter 9 reviews these influences and examines how they can be applied to understand the role of religion in conflict.

CHAPTER 2

Secularization and Secularism

It is impossible to address the academic study of religion and politics without first discussing secularism and secularization. Until the late twentieth century the dominant theory on religion in the social sciences, including political science, was secularization theory. This body of theory is not monolithic and includes a number of variants. Nevertheless, all of these variants predicted that religion would, at the very least, significantly decline in its public role, and some formulations of this paradigm had religion disappearing altogether. One of the more dramatic versions of this argument include Steve Bruce's 2002 book titled *God Is Dead: Secularization in the West*, which borrows its title from Friedrich Nietzsche's famous statement. Similarly, sociologist Peter Berger in 1968 predicted that by "the twenty-first century, religious believers are likely to be found only in small sects, huddled together to resist a worldwide secular culture."[1] Clearly this has not occurred, but secularization theory still has a dramatic influence on our current state of knowledge on religion and politics, both because it discouraged the study of the topic until the past few decades and because it continues to influence the development of theory on the interactions between religion and the political.

While a discussion of secularization theory might seem a dry topic that is mostly of interest to academic historians, nothing could be further from the truth. Secularization theory remains relevant for at least three reasons: First, it heavily influenced how the study of religion and politics evolved to the point where it is not possible to fully understand our current state of knowledge on religion and politics without understanding secularization theory and the extent of this influence. Second, there still remain strong supporters of the theory among those who study religion and politics. Third, despite its serious flaws this body of theory still has much to teach us on the nature of religion and politics, though its insights are likely not those that the theory's creators and advocates might draw from it. In fact, as I discuss in detail later in this chapter, if we focus on secularism, rather than secularization, the predictions of secularization theory can be seen as a guide to understanding the tensions between the secular and the religious in modern times.

It is important to emphasize that there is a significant amount of diversity among those who advocate secularization theory. Predictions range from religion's utter demise to less ambitious claims that religion will somehow decline in importance but not disappear. It is difficult to address all manifestations of the theory in a single chapter but I attempt to identify the major trends.

In this chapter I address the development and influence of secularization theory from its original formulations to its current weakened yet influential formulations. I argue that even though the major prediction of secularization theory—religion's demise—was incorrect, this body of theory successfully and accurately identifies factors that significantly influence the role of religion in politics and, perhaps, even the nature of modern religion. I also argue that the clash between secular and religious ideologies is one of the most important factors in today's religious politics.

Before I begin, it is important to note that while secularization theory had a critical influence on the development of thought on the role of religion and politics, it is a body of theory more clearly articulated among sociologists, or some would say more often discussed among sociologists, than among political scientists. Accordingly, much of this chapter draws from the sociological literature. This is largely because a subset of sociologists directly addressed religion in a way that was until recently uncommon in other branches of the social sciences. Since the sociological discourse reflects the larger influences of secularization theory within the social sciences as a whole, it can, accordingly, inform our understanding of the role it played in the development of today's theories on the role of religion and politics. It is also important to note that this body of theory is based heavily on the Western Christian experience and often assumes that its perception of this Western Christian experience will be repeated elsewhere (Hadden, 1987b: 588–594; Martin, 1978: 2; Sherkat and Ellison, 1999: 364; Stark, 1999: 253).

CLASSIC SECULARIZATION THEORY

While secularization theory was never monolithic and different proponents viewed it differently, in its classic form there is basic agreement over its general parameters. Put simply, secularization theory predicts the decline of religion, and perhaps its disappearance, as a significant social force in the public sphere, owing to a number of processes inherent in modernization.

This prediction has deep roots that go back to some of the most important founding figures in the social sciences and modern social thought. Eighteenth- and nineteenth-century thinkers, including August Comte, Emile Durkheim, Sigmund

Freud, Karl Marx, Friedrich Nietzsche, Ferdinand Tönnies, Voltaire, and Max Weber, all contributed to this expectation. However, it was not until well into the twentieth century that classic secularization theory fully manifested itself in the absolutist form that dominated much of modern social thought on the topic in the post-World War II era (Appleby, 1994; Shupe, 1990; Turner, 1991).

Of course, these thinkers viewed the topic differently but they each articulated at least some aspects of the absolutist views on religion's decline or demise that emerged later. For instance, Nietzsche's concept of the "transvaluation of all values" posited that a crisis in European culture, including a collapse of the credibility of religious belief, created the conditions for generating new forms of moral authenticity but did not "get beyond an announcement of the need for moral reevaluation"[2] (Turner, 1991: 42). Freud considered religion a mass neurosis that would presumably dissipate in modern times, especially with the help of psychologists.[3] Perhaps one of the best-known quotations from Marx is his dismissal of religion as the opiate of the masses. This refers to his argument that those who control the economy control society's dominant ideology, and the purpose of this ideology is social control. While Marx saw religion as an effective means of social control under feudal economic systems, the transition to capitalism was resulting in the collapse of the "religious props of bourgeois political control," which required the development of new secular ideologies to fulfill the same function (Turner, 1991: 40–42, 192). Weber and Durkheim espoused ideas more akin to the classic formulation of secularization theory, basically arguing that modern ideologies would replace religious ones[4] (Turner, 1991: 43, 190–191).

All of these ideas, and others, gelled to form classic secularization theory, which remained clearly dominant in the social sciences through at least the late 1970s and perhaps into the 1990s. The central argument during this era was that "secularization and modernity go hand in hand. With more modernization comes more secularization" (Berger, 1997: 974). Toft *et al.* (2011: 74) express the dominance of classic secularization theory as follows: "By the late 1960s, everyone (a term we do not use lightly) believed that the widespread aspiration for political secularism . . . was rapidly becoming reality in virtually all parts of the world."

While most would not have predicted the utter disappearance of religion, some made exactly this prediction. For example, in 1966 Anthony F. Wallace confidently predicted that the "evolutionary future of religion is extinction. . . . Belief in supernatural powers is doomed to die out, all over the world" (1966: 266–267). While clearly this is extreme, most who addressed the topic during the theory's heyday would have expected at the very least an extreme decline in religion's presence and influence in society. That being said, the specific extent to which religion was expected to decline is not important for our purposes. What is important is the agreement among the theory's supporters on the significant decline of religion as a public force. Without understanding the influence of this expectation on the social sciences as a whole, it is not possible to fully understand the development of current theories of religion and politics.

This body of theory identified a number of social, economic, and political processes associated with modernization which were predicted to lead to religion's decline. These processes include:

- *Urbanization*: As people moved from small rural communities to the city, they moved away from the social structure that supported religion. Small communities in which everyone knows everyone else are better able to enforce social norms, including religion. In contrast, one of the ironies of city life is that the more people there are in one place, the more individuals are able to avoid social contact. While an individual who is different in a small town or community will likely be noticed and suffer social sanctions, such an individual in a large city can avoid notice, or even find like-minded individuals and form their own subculture (Sahliyeh, 1990: 3; Voicu, 2009; Wilson, 1982).

- *Literacy and education*: The ability to read is the key to most knowledge acquisition. In pre-modern times it was often only the clergy who were literate. This monopoly on knowledge was a significant tool that allowed religious elites to maintain the dominance of religion in society. With mass education and literacy, this monopoly was broken. Individuals were better able to access and communicate alternative ideologies and ideas. In addition, individuals were able to read and evaluate religious texts without the mediation of the clergy, making them less dependent on religious institutions for knowledge about religion and about religions' alternatives (Lambert, 1999; Wilson, 1982).

- *Science and technology*: Science provided an alternative way to understand the world. For example, in the Christian world, before science the only way to understand the world's existence came from Genesis, where God created the heavens and the earth. Today, the Big Bang theory and evolution, among other scientific theories, provide alternative explanations, undermining another of religion's monopolies (Gill, 2001: 121; Wilson, 1982).

- *The Enlightenment and rationalism*: The power of ideas is not limited to the presence of alternative explanations for the universe: it also relates to man's role in developing ideas. Rationalism, which can be called the ideology of the Enlightenment, posits that man can create and reveal knowledge and understanding without divine help or guidance. Thus, to a rationalist, religion is no longer the sole source of knowledge, and to some rationalists it is not even a legitimate or useful source. Rationalism is also closely linked to the belief that empirical experience is the only legitimate source of knowledge (Bruce, 2009; Dobbelaere, 1999: 232; Gellner, 1992: 2; Gill, 2008: 34–37; Lambert, 1999; Luttwak, 1994: 8–10; Martin, 1978: 8–9).

- *Competing political ideologies*: In the past, the dominant ideology of state was religion. It was religion that legitimized the state, and God's blessing which gave the rulers their power to rule. However, with the advent of modern political thinkers like Hobbes, Locke, Rousseau, and Marx, among others, the source of a government's legitimacy shifted from the divine to the people. While the specific formulations of this link between the people and their government differ, this basic tenet is common to diverse political ideologies, including liberalism, socialism, communism, and fascism. In addition, the increasing coercive power of the state makes legitimacy less necessary (Wilson, 1982: 54).

- *Growth of the modern state*: Not only are modern states using secular ideologies in place of religious ones as their basis for legitimacy, but the formation of the modern state itself has undermined religion. In the past, religion was an international issue and state governments were subject to overarching religious authority. This ended in the West with the 1648 Treaty of Westphalia, which ended the Thirty Years War and set the precedent that religion was solely an internal state matter. This began the process in which states would be free to choose their religion policy, a precedent that eventually allowed states to choose no religion (Hehir, 1995; Goldewijk, 2007: 29–30; Haynes, 2009: 293; Philpott, 2002, 2009: 187–188; Thomas, 2005: 54–55). In addition, the modern state has begun to take over many of the functions formerly provided exclusively by religion such as medicine, welfare, and education. This has significantly reduced the social influence of religion and people's dependence on services provided by religious institutions (Bruce, 2009; Gill, 2001: 121; 2008: 33; Gorski and Altınordu, 2008: 62; Kaspersen and Lindvall, 2008: 122; Wilson, 1982: 149).

- *Mass participation in politics*: In the past, politics was the domain of elites. With the advent of modern political ideologies, especially those supporting democracy, the masses began to participate in politics. This mass participation undermined the ability of elites of any sort, including religious elites, to dominate individuals (Lambert, 1999).
- *Prosperity*: Economic modernization, as well as capitalism, leads to increased wealth and prosperity. Increased success in this world leads to less of a reliance on the world to come. Studies tend to link economic success with lower levels of individual religious observance (Norris and Inglehart, 2004).
- *Mobility*: The mobility of both people and ideas is increasing. Migration is creating more diverse societies, undermining the ability of one religion to remain dominant (Bruce, 2009). The mobility of ideas and information, especially with the advent of the internet, has accelerated secularization in many ways. It has increased access to knowledge and ideas, which has accelerated the processes noted in nearly every category listed above. It has also created a virtual world community which has influences akin to urbanization on individuals seeking a community of like-minded people. It has further undermined religion's control of knowledge.

As a result of these processes, the world is expected to change. These changes include a number of interrelated characteristics and social processes. However, all of them are in some way related to the basic argument that religion served a social function in the past that is being replaced by modern institutions and phenomena. These include:

- *Legitimacy*: As has already been noted, religion in the past was the only ideology that granted legitimacy to the state. This function is being replaced by modern political ideologies.
- *Knowledge*: As has already been noted, religion is no longer the sole source of knowledge and understanding. Science and rationalism compete with religion and are predicted by secularization theorists to eventually displace it as explanations for the world and as places to seek new knowledge and understanding. Rationalism provides a new philosophy and justification for seeking secular knowledge. The concepts of empirical evidence and the scientific method provide the tools to accomplish this.

- *Social control*: Religion is a form of social control. The belief in an omnipotent, omniscient God who will punish all transgressions is a powerful motivator to adhere to social norms. Today this fear is created by man using science and technology. Science, including surveillance and forensic technology (as popularized by the television series *CSI*), creates a fear of getting caught by human beings and their worldly justice system. Religious rules of behavior are being replaced by rules created by bureaucratic processes that involve scientifically trained experts. For example, the penal system is heavily influenced by the expertise of psychologists and criminologists (Dobbelaere, 1999: 233; Turner, 1991: 109–133; Wilson, 1982).
- *A shift from the public to the private sphere*: While religion may remain present in the world, it is moving out of the public sphere. That is, secularization theorists predict a declining religious influence on public life and institutions, but religion may remain present in people's private behavior and individual beliefs. In addition, public religious institutions decay over time and command declining resources. This process includes both the increasing autonomy of secular institutions—such as government—from religion and the increasing conformity of religious institutions to the secular world (Chaves, 1994; Wilson, 1982: 149). As is discussed in more detail in what follows, this aspect of secularization is arguably a more recent addition to the theory.
- *Secular institutions replace religious institutions*: Functions formerly provided exclusively by religion are now being filled by secular institutions (Chaves, 1994). The modern state is heavily involved in welfare, education, and medicine—all originally the near-exclusive province of religious institutions—and numerous secular private institutions also fulfill these functions. Similarly, while in the past those who were in need of personal counsel when they were troubled would usually seek advice from their clergy, today many seek the help of mental health professionals. While these functions can still be fulfilled by religious institutions, the presence and, in many cases, dominance of the state and other secular institutions in these fields, combined with state regulation of religious institutions serving these functions, has significantly marginalized religion's influence in these spheres.
- *Relativism*: Religion holds to an absolute truth. In modern times, many consider truth to be relative. There is no one truth. Rather, everyone's competing truth or their narrative is legitimate (Almond *et al.*, 2003: 94; Bruce, 2009: 152; Lambert, 1999: 323; Gellner, 1992: 2, 22, 72–73).

While it is clear that these changes represent a decline in religion, there remains a debate over what aspect of religion will decline. There are four possibilities:

1   Religion's role in government. This includes the extent to which governments support religion and are influenced by religion.
2   Religion's role in the public sphere other than government. This includes the extent to which religion is expressed in the public sphere both by private individuals and by public officials.
3   The power and public influence of religious institutions.

4 Personal religiosity—the extent to which people are religious. This includes both religious beliefs, such as the belief in God, and religious practice, such as attendance at places of worship, participation in religious rituals, and the keeping of religious laws and customs.

However, as is discussed in a later section on the evolution of secularization theory, this debate is arguably likely less relevant to classic secularization theory and more relevant to more recent innovations in this body of theory.

RELIGION'S RESURGENCE?

Since the early 1990s there has been increasing discussion of religion's resurgence on the world stage. While the arguments vary as to the causes of this resurgence, they can be placed into five categories

First, the arguments of secularization theory identify real processes that in fact do undermine and threaten traditional religion. However, secularization theorists did not take into account the fact that religion is a dynamic social force that is capable of evolving. Under the pressure of modernity, this is exactly what happened. Religion evolved and transformed in order to revitalize itself and remain socially and politically relevant (Berger, 1999; Eisenstadt, 2000a; Haynes, 1998; Shupe, 1990; Thomas, 2000, 2005). Much of the literature on religious fundamentalism attributes the rise of religious fundamentalism to exactly this sort of process, depicting fundamentalism as a reaction against modernity (Almond *et al.*, 2003; Esposito, 1998; Haynes, 2009: 159). In fact, religious groups are adapting to modernity and using its tools, especially modern organizational, communications, and media tools, to further their aims (Shani, 2009: 311). Toft *et al.* (2011: 7) accurately sum up this train of thought when they point out that not only has religion's political influence been revitalized, but it "has resurged with the help, rather than the opposition, of the very same forces that secularization theorists thought would spell its demise: democracy and open debate, rapid progress in communication and technology, and the unprecedented flow of people, ideas, and commerce around the globe."

Second, secular modernity has failed, especially in the Third World. Governments espousing secular ideologies have failed to produce economic prosperity and social justice. These secular ideologies, and the governments founded upon them, are also perceived as foreign, illegitimate, corrupt, and perhaps the continuation of colonialism by proxy. This crisis of legitimacy has created a power vacuum that religion is filling. It is perceived as legitimate, uncorrupted, and indigenous. Also, as is noted earlier in the chapter, these secular ideologies were intended to fill the social functions of religion, so religion is a natural replacement for them (Haynes, 1997: 714; Juergensmeyer, 1993; 2008; Nasr, 1998: 32; Sahliyeh, 1990: 7–9; Thomas, 2000).

Third, secularization has always been an elite-based process that never was fully accepted by the masses. As the masses became more relevant politically, they brought religion back into the public sphere (Berger, 1996/1997: 9; Rubin, 1994).

Fourth, Samuel Huntington (1993, 1996) argues that the end of the Cold War released religion upon the world as a paradigm-changing international force.

The Cold War was dominated by a clash between Western ideologies. In the post-Cold War era, new groupings called civilizations became the basis of international conflict and politics. Huntington's list of civilizations is based primarily upon religion. While this theory is highly controversial, it has also been highly influential.[5]

Fifth, religion never went away. It has always been a potent political and social force. The dominance of secularization theory took the form of an ideology that blinded academics and their students to the reality on the ground. (Berger, 1996/1997: 9; Thomas, 2005) The extent of religion's continuing influence on state policy is discussed in detail in Chapters 10–13.

Another version of the argument that religion never went away is that secularization is occurring but it is countered by a simultaneous process of sacralization—secularization's opposite. Religion, like any social institution, evolves and changes over time. Various parts of the religious economy decline, while others become stronger and more influential (Barnhart, 1990; Demerath, 2001; Fox, 2008; Gorski and Altınordu, 2008: 65; Hadden and Shupe, 1986). Rodney Stark, in particular, with a number of collaborators, argues that this is the natural process for religious denominations, with denominations tending to become more worldly over time as they become more mainstream and influential. However, owing to a demand for less worldly religions, these denominations produce offshoots that focus more on spirituality (Stark and Bainbridge, 1985; Stark and Finke, 2000; Stark and Iannaccone, 1994).

Assuming there has been a religious resurgence, there is no real agreement on the timing of this resurgence. Many date it back to the late 1970s with the rise of the religious right in the United States and the Iranian Revolution (Thomas, 2005; Roof, 2009; Sahliyeh, 1990). Fox (2007) documents serious civil wars and notes that religious conflicts did not become as common as non-religious ones until the 1990s but the resurgence that led to this increase in the number of religious conflicts began in the late 1970s. That being said, religious conflicts have always been present. So, while there has been an increase of religious conflicts as a proportion of all civil wars, this study also supports the argument that religion never went away, as do other studies of religion and domestic conflict (Toft, 2007).

Others trace this trend back even earlier. Philpott (2009: 190) argues that

> if the Bolshevik Revolution of 1917 was the inaugural ball for the peak period of secularization, the [1967] Six Day War between Israel and Egypt signified the beginning of religion's global resurgence. . . . It both awakened religious conscience among Israeli Jews and crippled the prestige of secular nationalism among Arab Muslims.

This event was complemented by others, including the rise of Hindu nationalist parties in India in the 1960s and the Second Vatican Council of 1962–1965. This process gained momentum in the 1970s with the rise of Islamic nationalism in the Islamic world, Evangelical Protestantism in North and South America, Africa, and parts of East Asia, and "engaged Buddhism" in Asia (Philpott, 2009: 190–191; Toft et al., 2011: 4–7).

While it is unlikely that there will ever be agreement on the exact causes and timing of this resurgence—assuming that religion declined in the first place—there are at least two clear and relevant facts that emerge from this literature. First, currently religion is a potent social, political, and economic factor that cannot be ignored. This has had serious implications for the dominance of secularization theory as well as the development of thought on religion and politics. Second, while the factors secularization theory identified as leading to religion's demise clearly did not accomplish this end, they did have a significant influence over the evolution of religion and its interaction with society and politics in the modern era.

THE EVOLUTION OF SECULARIZATION THEORY

As it became clear that religion was not disappearing, secularization theory began to evolve. It became even more diverse as various strands developed, all of which somehow argued that the world is secularizing but in a way that allows religion to remain present.

The first, and perhaps most popular, strand is the argument that secularization means religion will weaken but not disappear. This has several manifestations, including the view that some aspects of religion will weaken while others will remain strong. This type of argument usually has religion declining in the public sphere but remaining strong in the private sphere—especially with regard to individual religious belief and observance (Chaves, 1994; Dobbelaere, 1999). Stark (1999) attests that the argument described earlier in this chapter that religion will move from the public to the private sphere, with public religion weakening or disappearing, was not originally part of secularization theory. It is, rather, a revision of the theory.

In this vein, some sociologists have redefined secularization to mean "differentiation"—a process where religion was once a dominant influence on all aspects of society but now constitutes one social institution which competes with others (Achterberg *et al.*, 2009; Bruce, 2009; Dobbelaere, 1985, 1999; Kaspersen and Lindval, 2008; Lambert, 1999: 319–320). This redefinition allows religion to remain a potent part of society and politics while still making it possible to claim a decline. Others simply continue to make the same arguments as classic secularization theorists but are careful to note that these processes lead to religion's decline rather than leading to its irrelevance (Beyer, 1999; Bruce, 2009; Chaves, 1994; Davie, 2000; Hallward, 2008; Lambert, 1999; Lechner, 1991; Presser and Chaves, 2007; van der Brug *et al.*, 2009; Voye, 1999; Yamane, 1997).

Many within this trend focus on religion as an individual choice rather than a public choice. The removal of religion's overarching authority unbinds individuals from a major form of social control and allows individuals more free choice. This includes the ability to choose one's own religious beliefs (Bruce, 2009: 147–148; Dobbelaere, 1999: 236–241; Lambert, 1999: 315, 322; Pollack and Pickel, 2007). "Individual religiosity has emancipated itself from the custody of the large religious institutions; religious preferences are increasingly subject to the individual's autonomous choices. Churches no longer define comprehensive belief parameters; individuals instead decide on their own worldviews and spiritual orientations" (Pollack, 2008: 171).

Many of these theorists argue, or at least imply, that this is not a revision of secularization theory but, rather, what it always meant. Stark (1999) strongly disputes this notion, asserting that secularization always meant the decline in individual religiosity. That is, classic secularization theory expected a decline in religion in both the public and private spheres. He accuses many of these theorists of shifting "definitions as needed in order to escape inconvenient facts" (Stark, 1999: 251). He provides a number of direct quotations from prominent secularization theorists, including Peter Berger (who has since mostly recanted his support of secularization theory) and Karel Dobbelaere, to support his claim. He agrees that some aspects of religion have declined, but "the prophets of secularization theory were not and are not writing about something so obvious and limited" (Stark, 1999: 252). Personal piety and religious institutions are linked. If one fades, so will the other. Thus, secularization theory, for Stark, is an all-or-nothing proposition.

A second prominent revision of secularization theory is Norris and Inglehart's (2004) theory of existential security. These authors argue that those who have existential security—being secure in that their personal safety and well-being are not at risk—have less of a need for religion. Through a survey of 76 countries they show that those in wealthy countries are less religious and that wealth is also linked to lower religiosity within countries. Thus, people remain religious, but primarily the poor and those living in underdeveloped countries. However, Thomas (2007) points out that by 2050, 90 percent of the world's population will be living in zones that Norris and Inglehart posit to have existential insecurity, so their theory does not, in practice, predict very much secularization.

Charles Taylor (2007) provides a third revision of secularization theory. He argues, like many others, that religion is declining but will not disappear. However, according to Taylor, this is not the most important aspect of secularization. He argues that secularism itself—the concept that one can find a way to understand the world without reference to the divine—is itself new and constitutes secularization. It represents "a move from a society where belief in God is unchallenged . . . to one in which it is understood to be one option among others" (Taylor, 2007: 3). Society has changed from one where belief is the default option, even for the educated, to one where more and more people consider unbelief the only plausible option. Thus, religion can remain present and even potent, but the fact that there is another option is in and of itself secularization.

This argument rests, to some extent, on the assumption that there was no option other than to accept religion in the past. Stark (1999) calls this type of assertion the "myth of past piety." "Most prominent historians of medieval religion now agree that there never was an 'Age of Faith'" (Stark, 1999: 255) and that there were always people who chose not to participate in religion. Taylor argues that the fact that these people today have an ideology to support that choice is a significant difference which constitutes secularization. I contend, as is discussed in more detail in what follows, that this is in some ways true but in other ways false.

A fourth type of revision has secularization limited to certain geographical regions, usually the West. That is, this group of theorists contends that secularization theory remains accurate, but only for Europe, the West, or some subsection of the West, depending on the particular formulation. For example, Berger (1996/1997, 2009) argues that religion is resurging worldwide but that secularization theory still applies to Western and Central Europe, and certain intellectual circles. Marquand and

Nettler (2000: 2) similarly argue that "Western Europe appears to be an exception. . . . Organized religion almost certainly plays a smaller role in politics in 2000 over most of the territory of the European Union than it did in 1950."[6] While the empirical evidence for religiosity shows a decline in the West (Norris and Inglehart, 2004; Pollack, 2008) it has not disappeared. Müller (2009: 5–6) shows, through a survey of quantitative studies on the topic, that whatever decline occurred in the West, it is at best poorly linked to economic factors. Also, numerous studies, including those provided later in this book, show that religion retains its public influence in the West and is perhaps becoming more important as the region becomes more religiously diverse.

A fifth type is what Toft *et al.* (2011: 8) call "neo-atheists." These writers, including Richard Dawkins (*The God Delusion*, 2008) and Christopher Hitchens (*God Is Not Great: How Religion Poisons Everything*, 2007), accept that religion has not disappeared but fervently wish that it would. They consider all religion primitive, irrational, repressive, and violent. In a similar vein, some non-atheists such as Charles Kimball (*When Religion Becomes Evil*, 2002) differentiate between "true" religion, which supports peace and tolerance, and "corrupted" religion, which shares the traits the neo-atheists attribute to all religion. This body of literature is, perhaps, a successor to secularization theory rather than a revision. It is body of normative theory that paints religion, or for some the misuse and misinterpretation of religion, as the root of all evil. As I discuss below, some consider secularization theory to be an ideology rather than a theory. If this is true, this literature can be considered a successor ideology to secularization theory.

Be that as it may, the most important common point of these redefinitions, revisions, and reformulations of secularization theory is that, while claiming or desiring some form of decline in religion's public influence, all of them acknowledge that religion retains some form of significant influence in the public sphere. This is clearly a retreat from the more absolutist claims made by classic secularization theorists such as Smith (1970, 1971, 1974) and Wilson (1982), among many others. Thus, even if one accepts these weakened forms of secularization theory, there has been a critically important paradigmatic shift within the social sciences—a shift from a dominant theory which argues that religion is irrelevant, or at least sufficiently lacking in importance that it can be ignored, to one where no serious social scientist opposes the principle that religion is an important, relevant, and significant social, political, and economic force that is deserving and worthy of study. They may argue over exactly how much influence religion may possess, but no longer will any serious social scientist deny that it possesses enough influence to be relevant. Perhaps it is because of this that Stark (1999: 252) has criticized these redefinitions as creating versions of secularization theory that are so weak that "if this was all that secularization means, there would be nothing to argue about."

SECULARIZATION AND POLITICAL SCIENCE THEORY

Given that there is now a common recognition that religion remains important in the public sphere—the domain of religion and politics—why is all of this relevant to a textbook on religion and politics? Because secularization theory, whether there be any truth to the theory or not, dominated social science thinking on religion for much of the twentieth century and influenced the development of how social scientists think about religion. It is common wisdom that it is difficult to understand where we are without understanding where we have been and how we got here. This is true of the study of religion and politics. Secularization theory is the single largest element of where the study of religion has been and the largest influence on how we came to be where we are today, to the extent that it easily dwarfs all other factors and influences.

Perhaps the most significant of the consequences of secularization theory is that few devoted any effort to accounting for religion. In some European circles, "religion was more or less a taboo [subject] . . . a scholar speaking 'approvingly' of religion risked a loss of credibility, and the general sentiment was that, in the spirit of progress, religion would be obsolete sooner or later" (Hjelm, 2008: 94). In the United States, academics were recruited from those with a secular worldview, and those who didn't have such a worldview were socialized during the education process (Hadden, 1987b: 595). While both of these descriptions refer specifically to sociologists, they are applicable, at least to some extent, to the social sciences in general, including political science. Also, there are analogous, if less detailed, claims made about political scientists. For example, Hurd (2007: 351) asserts that "political scientists are socialized in the tenets of classical liberalism with its emphasis on the benefits of a strict separation of religion and politics." Similarly, Toft *et al.* (2011: 1) begin their discussion of religion and politics in the twenty-first century by arguing that "had an enterprising fortune-teller predicted four decades ago that in the twenty-first century religion would become a formidable force in global politics, educated people would have considered him a laughingstock."

More importantly, a number of studies examining the presence of articles about religion in journals demonstrate this lack of attention to religion. Wald and Wilcox (2006) found that between 1960 and 2002 the *American Political Science Review*, political science's most prestigious journal, published only 25 articles that included religious terms in their title or abstract, and many of these did not, upon closer examination, treat religion as of central importance. Philpott (2002) similarly examined four major international relations journals between 1980 and 1999 and found that only 4 of 1,600 articles treated religion as a serious influence on international relations. Ver Beek (2002) found no reference to religion in three major development journals between 1982 and 1988.

This does not mean that there were no studies of religion, but they tended to be in journals that focused on narrower issues such as the *Journal of Church and State* and were mostly read only by scholars who focused on religion and politics. Those who published in these journals tended not to be scholars from the top-rated research institutions. Other examples can be found in area study journals that focused on the non-West. Thus, studies of religion and politics have always been present but until recently they were not often to be found within the mainstream of political science. More interestingly, an examination of sociology journals between 1970 and 1985 found that few articles on religion were published by authors who were not themselves personally religious (Hadden, 1987b: 594). If this trend is also accurate for political science, it also means that the authors who chose to work outside the mainstream had strong personal reasons for doing so.

For the mainstream, religion was something that existed but was not normal in a modern society. It was something that existed in the non-West, which had not yet sufficiently modernized. And when it manifested in the West "in a form which is more than a matter of private faith, [it was] defined in most Western societies as disruptive and judged to be marginal and deviant" (Beit-Hallahmi, 2003: 11). When it was taken seriously at all, it was often seen as something that was negative and impeded positive goals and developments (Selinger, 2004: 525–526).

The development of thinking in political science and the social sciences in general regarding religion mirrors the perceived resurgence of religion described above. While sociologists questioned the theory as early as the mid-1960s (Hadden, 1987b: 598), it is arguable that these challenges did not gain considerable attention or popularity until the 1980s, when scholars began to reconsider, challenge, and reformulate secularization theory (Dobbelaere, 1981, 1985, 1987; Hadden, 1987b). This process exploded into a full-scale debate regarding the validity of secularization theory in the 1990s (Berger 1996/1997, 1999; Chaves, 1994; Dobbelaere, 1999; Lambert, 1999; Lechner, 1991; Stark, 1999; Voye, 1999; Yamane, 1997).

Political science was less overt in its reevaluation but the pattern was similar, with small numbers of political scientists addressing the issues of religion until the 1980s. The rise of the religious right in the United States and the Iranian Revolution spurred a reevaluation of the issue in these specific contexts. In the 1990s, many began giving wider consideration to the issue of religion as a serious influence on politics. Religion can be said to have truly hit the mainstream of political science with the publication of two articles in the *American Political Science Review*: Ken Wald and Clyde Wilcox's 2006 article "Getting Religion: Has Political Science Discovered the Faith Factor?" and Daniel Philpott's 2007 article "Explaining the Political Ambivalence of Religion." The first half of Philpott's article and the whole of the Wald and Wilcox article are devoted to the question of why religion had been neglected by political scientists. This is indicative of a wider trend: even after it became clear to many that religion is an important political factor, they still devoted much effort to discussing why religion was ignored and to combating secularization theory. This left less time and fewer resources for engaging in theory development to explain the role of religion in politics.

That serious mainstream attention to religion is a recent development in political science has had a measurable impact upon theorizing about religion and politics. This theorizing can be divided into four categories. First, many of these theories draw upon the existing political science literature on religion and politics from previous decades, which mostly dealt with narrow topics and events, and was not generally intended to be widely applicable. Second, the theorizing draws upon literature from other disciplines, especially sociology, which had more developed theories of religion. Third, it draws upon mainstream political science theories which can be applied to explain religion. Finally, and by far least commonly, it is based on new ideas which form the basis for entirely new theories. All of these types of theories are addressed and integrated into the discussion in the subsequent chapters of this book.

Thus, the current state of the discipline of religion and politics is heavily tied to its past, which was dominated by secularization theory. Secularization theory retarded the development of thinking on the topic of religion and politics, and as a result there is no dominant paradigm on religion and politics which addresses the causal linkages between religion and political behavior, institutions, and phenomena. Rather, what exists is a hodgepodge of observations and attempts at theory building. Nevertheless, what exists can be organized into a more coherent theoretical framework. This book is intended to accomplish such organization.

SECULARIZATION OR SECULARISM?

I have said that Charles Taylor's (2007) contention that the presence of secularism as an ideology in and of itself constitutes secularization has truth in it but is also profoundly wrong. My reason for saying so is because the rise of secularism as an ideology is critically important for understanding the modern era, but it does not in my estimation constitute secularization. Secularization is the decline of religion in the modern era. As Stark (1999) argues, there have always been people who are not religious. That they now have an ideology does not constitute an empirical decline in religion. Rather, it constitutes a change in the nature of those who are not religious. Nevertheless, this alteration does constitute a significant and game-changing development.

This can be seen in the development of secularization theory itself. Jeffrey Hadden (1987b) argues that secularization theory is not a theory but rather a doctrine held by Western intellectuals. "Its moorings are located in presuppositions that have gone unexamined because they represent a taken-for-granted ideology rather than a systematic set of interrelated propositions" (Hadden, 1987b: 588). The Enlightenment ushered in reason and science as competitors for religion in the West. "Reason was king, and science would pave the way to a world that would soon rid itself of superstition and tyrants" (Hadden, 1987b: 589). In this context, those belonging to the founding generation of social scientists were advocates for science and reason and were themselves competing with religion. That is, they wanted religion to go away, and secularization theory is in many ways the intellectual manifestation of that desire. Accordingly, "our heritage, bequeathed by the founding generations, is scarcely a theory at all but, rather, a doctrine of secularization. It has not required careful scrutiny because it is self-evident. We have sacralized our commitment to secularization" (Hadden, 1987b: 594).

This claim of secularization theory as an ideology has been echoed by others. Ebaugh (2002: 387) argues that secularization theory was "so basic to theorizing about religion that it displaced attempts to understand the actual meaning and organizational significance of religion in contemporary society." Thus, an institutionalized "anti-religious bias" was introduced into the study of religion. Gorski and Altınordu (2008: 61) discuss the danger that secularization theory can become

a vehicle for a secularist politics in which religion is aligned with tradition, superstition, and supernaturalism and kindred categories, whereas secularity is aligned with modernity, rationality, and science, with the terms operationalized so as to deliver the most resounding possible verdict on the future of religion.

Sherkat and Ellison (1999: 364) call secularization theory "an ideological impulse strongly rooted in the Western Enlightenment." Thomas (2005) similarly calls secularization a myth created by Western intellectuals based on their desires rather than any empirical reality. Many note that the empirical facts never fit the theory (Gill, 2001; Ebaugh, 2002; Hadden, 1987b), and this can only be explained by an ideological devotion to the theory.[7]

Even given this support, the notion that secularization is an ideology rather than a theory is debatable. However, the presence in the modern world of secularism as an ideology is a fact. "Secularism" is a noun that describes a quasi-religious ideology intended to counter religion (Hallward, 2008: 2–3). In fact, it is not possible to find any interpretation of the term "secular" that does not include some form of negation of religion. That is, the term "secular" cannot be disentangled from its property of being somehow different from or in opposition to religion. For example, Philpott (2009: 185–186) identifies nine ways in which some version of the term "secular" is used in the social science literature, and all of them in some way relate to the "secular" as being something other than religion:

1 *Secular* means pertaining to the world outside the monastic sphere.
2 *Secular* means a concept or use of language that makes no specific reference to religion or revelation but is not necessarily hostile to them.
3 *Secular* means a differentiation between religion and other spheres of society (political, economic, cultural, etc.) but not necessarily the decline of religion's influence.
4 *Secular* describes a social context in which religious faith is one of many options rather than an unproblematic feature of the universe.
5 *Secularization* is a decline in the number of individuals who hold religious beliefs.
6 *Secularization* is a decline in religious practice and community.
7 *Secularization* is a differentiation between religion and other spheres of society (political, economic, cultural, etc.) in a way that entails, and is part and parcel of, a long-term decline in the influence of religion.
8 *Secularization* involves a decline of religious influence on politics, not because of a general long-term decline in religion but rather because of the intentional efforts of regimes to suppress it. This concept does not imply a decline in religious belief or practice.
9 *Secularism* is an ideology or set of beliefs that advocates the marginalization of religion from other spheres of life.

(Philpott, 2009: 185)

Thus, the terms "secular," "secularism," and "secularization" have multiple but related meanings. Many of these nine categories describe a type of argument that can be further subdivided. For example, later in this chapter I discuss several variations in the ninth definition which focus on arguments for the marginalization of religion in politics, itself only one aspect of the ninth argument. "Secular," "secularism," and "secularization" are, accordingly, complex concepts. Yet within this complexity, these concepts cannot be defined without relating to religion.

In this sense, Taylor (2007) is correct. There is secularism in the world and it strongly relates to religion. In many of its manifestations it is an alternative to religion, or even actively opposes religion (Philpott, 2009: 185–186). Put differently, secularism competes with religion on domestic and international political stages to fulfill many of the same functions in society, including guiding our worldviews and legitimizing the state. This competition has become a political struggle that is in many ways central to world politics today. Juergensmeyer (1993, 2008) argues that this competition between religion and secularism—or, as he calls it, secular nationalism— is a central explanation for the emergence of religious challenges to governments in the Third World in the post-Cold War era. These secular governments have failed to provide economic prosperity and social justice, which has created a power vacuum that religion is suited to fill precisely because it is, among other things, an ideology of state.

Given this, it is possible to see the secularization literature in a new light. What this literature was intended to describe was seen as an inevitable process. Its arguments can be transformed to describe an ideological challenge to religion as an ideology that heavily influences both society and government. It is secularism rather than secularization that has challenged religion. All of the processes described earlier in this chapter which are posited to lead to religion's decline are either aspects of the secularist ideology, social, economic, and political processes that strengthened it, or conse- quences of secularism's influence. All of the changes in society and politics described above are descriptions of where secularism has made inroads on religion. This ideology, with its roots in the Enlightenment, has been challenging religion for centuries (Stark, 1999; Taylor, 2007). This existential challenge to religion has shaped much of the politics of the past centuries.

Nevertheless, secularism presents an ideological challenge to religion, especially in the political and social spheres, but it is not an inevitable process. It has changed the shape of society and politics in the modern era but there is nothing deterministic or inevitable about its predicted triumph over religion. In modern times it is arguable that the pervasive influence of secular ideologies has forced everyone to choose among three options: first, to accept modernity and rationalism and reject religion—the secular option; second, to reject rationalism and modernity and embrace religion— the fundamentalist option (more on this in Chapter 8); third, to find some way to accept both modernity and religion. This struggle and set of choices is one that governments cannot avoid. It is possible to argue that until recently, secularism was making steady progress in this struggle. However, with the recent discussion of the resurgence of religion it is possible that the pendulum of this struggle has begun to swing in the other direction. Toft *et al.* (2011), who declare the twenty-first century to be "God's century," certainly believe this to be the case. Whatever the current direction of the pendulum, the struggle between religion and secularism is one that has played out and will most likely continue to play out over generations and centuries. Given this, religion is likely to be a significant element of politics, both domestic and international, for the foreseeable future and it is entirely unclear whether this struggle will end and, if so, which side will win.

POLITICAL SECULARISM

Secularism as a political ideology is not monolithic. Leaving issues of personal religiosity aside, as a political ideology secularism constitutes at a minimum the belief that the state should not endorse a religion. It can include more than this, and there are several identifiable variations. On a most basic level I differentiate between separationism—the concept of state neutrality on the issue of religion—and laicism, which specifically declares that not only does the state not support any religion, it also restricts the presence of religion in the public sphere. These restrictions can include restrictions on public religious activities and on religious institutions, and in extreme cases even bans on religion in the private sphere (Kuru, 2009; Hurd, 2004a, b; Haynes, 1997; Keane, 2000; Stepan, 2000; Durham, 1996: 21–22; Esbeck, 1988). France's 2004 law which restricts the wearing of any overt religious symbols, including head coverings, in public schools is an excellent example of this model. While someone from the US tradition might consider this a restriction on religious liberty, from the French perspective wearing such symbols constitutes aggressively bringing one's religion—which should be a private matter—into the public domain.

The laicist doctrine is a particularly comprehensive political manifestation of secularism in that, at least among secularist ideologies found in democracies, it advocates for the most complete separation of religion and state found in modern democratic states. Many states follow the less extreme separationist policies, which themselves can be divided into three categories. The terms for these categories differ across the literature and we rely here on those developed by Fox (2008), Madeley (2003), and Raz (1986).

The first category is *absolute separationism*. This model requires that the state neither support nor hinder any religion. This is perhaps the most extreme form of separationism, because it allows no government involvement or interference in religion at all, though within this trend, opinions on the proper role of religion in civil society and political discourse differ (Esbeck, 1988; Kuru, 2009). Many consider the United States the archetypical example of this model. While there is a struggle between conservatives and liberals over the exact role religion should play in society and government, both sides support the expression of religion in public life. For example, the use of religious language by politicians is acceptable, but most state support for religion is not (Kuru, 2009; Esbeck, 1988).

The second category, *neutral political concern*, "requires that government action should not help or hinder any life-plan or way of life more than any other and that the consequences of government action should therefore be neutral" (Madeley, 2003: 5–6). This definition allows governments to support or restrict religion as long as the outcome is equal for all religions. Thus, the government can fund religion and support it in other ways as well as restrict it, as long as no religion is treated differently from the others (Kuru, 2009).

The third category, *exclusion of ideals*, requires that "the state be precluded from justifying its actions on the basis of a preference for any particular way of life" (Madeley, 2003: 6). This definition focuses on intent rather than outcome. Thus, religions can in practice be treated differently as long as there is no specific intent to support or hinder a specific religion.[8]

Thus, neither religion nor secularism is monolithic. Just as there are many religions, each with multiple sects and factions, secularists have central disagreements over the nature and application of secularism. That being said, when one looks at the larger picture the struggle between religion and secularism is a defining factor in modern politics. From this perspective, all of the predictions of secularization theory are relevant—not as inevitable political, social, and economic processes but rather as manifestations of a political struggle between two major families of world-spanning ideologies. This gives secularization theory important explanatory value for world politics and society, but not exactly as intended by the theory's originators.

DISCUSSION QUESTIONS

1 How much influence do you think religion has on political life? Do you see this influence as increasing or decreasing in your recent experience?
2 Outside of politics, how much influence does religion have on public life? This can include the setting of public moral standards and the extent to which religious institutions provide public services such as health care and charity.
3 Should religion be a public or a private issue? Is it legitimate for religion to influence public debate over policy issues or is it inappropriate to raise religion in public forums?
4 Do you think people from your generation are as religious as those in your parents' or grandparents' generation? How much of any difference is based on life-stage issues (for example, the argument that people get more religious as they get older)? Do you think that any generational differences in religiosity influence stances on political issues?
5 Do you think religious elements in society are trying to use the government to legislate their religious beliefs? If so, do you think these attempts are due to the mandates of their beliefs or because they feel that they are seeking to defend their way of life and beliefs from the onslaught of secularism?

FURTHER READING

Bruce, Steve "Secularization and Politics" in Jeffrey Haynes, ed. *Routledge Handbook of Religion and Politics*, New York: Routledge, 2009, 145–158.

Calhoun, Craig, Mark Juergensmeyer, and Jonathan VanAntwerpen eds. *Rethinking Secularism*, New York, NY: Oxford University Press, 2012.

Gill, Anthony "Religion and Comparative Politics" *Annual Review of Political Science*, 4, 2001, 117–138.

Gorski, Philip S. and Ateş Altınordu "After Secularization?" *Annual Review of Sociology*, 24, 2008, 55–85.

Hadden, Jeffrey K. "Toward Desacralizing Secularization Theory" *Social Forces*, 65 (3), 1987, 587–611.

Philpott, Daniel "Has the Study of Global Politics Found Religion?" *Annual Review of Political Science*, 12, 2009, 183–202.

Stark, Rodney "Secularization, R.I.P." *Sociology of Religion*, 60 (3), 1999, 249–273.
Taylor, Charles *A Secular Age*, Cambridge, MA: Harvard University Press, 2007.
Wald, Kenneth D. and Clyde Wilcox "Getting Religion: Has Political Science Discovered the Faith Factor?" *American Political Science Review*, 100 (4), 2006, 523–529.
Wilson, Bryan R. *Religion in Sociological Perspective*. Oxford: Oxford University Press, 1982.

CHAPTER 3

Religious Identity

Theories that focus on religious identity are among the most common found in the political science literature on politics. There is no agreed-upon definition of religious identity in the literature. However, it is fair to generalize by saying that religious identity refers to belonging based on beliefs held in common. Individuals belong to a religion, and groups which share that belonging are religious identity groups. For example, one can identify oneself as a Christian, Muslim, Hindu, Buddhist, Jew, or as belonging to one of any number of other religions, as well as a member of a particular denomination of one of those religions. The extent to which members of the same religion actually hold common beliefs varies, as most religions have multiple interpretations and trends, yet they tend to have core beliefs common to all believers, beliefs based on the same core doctrines and sources.

In most cases these religious identity groups maintain religious institutions, which serve a number of purposes. Among them is the preservation and maintenance of religious identity. These institutions help to instill and reinforce identity. They also maintain contacts and common identity between congregations. The role of religious institutions in politics is discussed in more detail in Chapter 6.

Theories of religious identity in politics tend to manifest themselves in one of two ways. First, they can argue that a particular religious identity group is different in some politically significant way from other groups. Second, they can argue that some phenomenon, usually conflict, is somehow different—more or less common, weaker or stronger, etc.—when it occurs between religious identity groups as opposed to within them. This chapter considers both of these types of manifestations of religious identity in politics.

Identity-based theories are among the most problematic in the literature on religion and politics. This is because they provide at best an incomplete understanding of the topic. For example, should one identify a difference in the political behavior of Muslims and Christians respectively, identity provides a poor explanation for that difference. The difference might be due to differences in religious ideologies or differences in the structure of Christian and Muslim religious institutions. It might also be due to some other political, economic, or social factor that happens at least partially to coincide with religious identity. Yet a large proportion of political science research on religion and politics focuses on whether and how members of different identity groups behave differently and does not ask whether there is an underlying reason for this difference, much less set out to discover it. This makes religious identity both a topic that is unavoidable in a serious discussion of the political science literature on religion and one that is from this perspective superficial.

Accordingly, I attempt in this chapter to discuss and critique the concept of religious identity as it exists in the political science literature rather than develop a more comprehensive theoretical framework on religion, politics, and identity. In this context I discuss, first, how religious identity can become involved in politics. Then I discuss several important aspects of politics that religious identity can influence: tolerance, democracy, conflict, and electoral politics.

THE ORIGINS OF RELIGIOUS IDENTITY IN POLITICS

How does religious identity become a relevant issue? It is certainly potentially relevant in nearly every country in the world, as 80 percent of the world's states have religious minorities which make up at least 10 percent of their populations, and all of them have at least some religious minorities.[1] Also, Anthony Smith (1999, 2000) posits that many nationalist ideologies are linked to religious identity. Yet some religious minorities become politically active while others do not, and some governments discriminate against religious minorities while others do not. Similarly, some governments link national identity to religion and others do not. According to an examination of the world's constitutions by the RAS project, 19.7 percent of countries declare an official religion, more than two-fifths (43.0 percent) claim separation of religion and state, and the rest take no official stand on the issue.[2] Yet I demonstrate in Chapters 10–13 that in practice a majority of 66.7 percent favor one religion or some religions over others. Even a number of states that declare in their constitutions separation of religion and state to be their official policy do not follow this in practice.

There are three theories of the origins of politically relevant identity groupings found in the literature on nationalism and ethnicity which can be applied to understand religious identity. These theories are known as *primordialism, instrumentalism*, and *constructivism*. It is important to understand that these theories can be understood as competing theories, but they can also be understood as complementary theories. That is, each of these theories can be seen either as the exclusive path by which all identities become involved in politics or as one among several potential paths by which identities can become involved in politics. In the case of religious identity, I argue that these theories function better as complementary theories that describe three alternative paths in which identity can become relevant in politics.

Primordialism refers to religious issues as being ancient, and culturally embedded within identity groups. This path for religious identity becoming relevant in politics describes cases where religion has been relevant for so long that no one, with the possible exception of historians, can identify when it became relevant or why. These are cases where no one living remembers when religion was not relevant. Essentially, religious identity is relevant today because it was relevant yesterday. Conflicts based on primordial grievances are generally ones that have been continuing for generations, where hatred between the groups is based on perceived injustices and a spiral of violence and retribution that can go for back for centuries. Conflicts that have been fought nearly continuously for generations, such as the Israeli–Arab conflict and the conflict in Northern Ireland, fit into this category.

The *instrumentalist* path to religious identity becoming relevant in politics points to a more recent origin for this relevance. In this type of case, religious identities have existed in society but for some time have not been particularly relevant to politics. Then a political entrepreneur seeks to activate religious identity, making it politically salient. There are any number of reasons this can occur. In most cases it involves a politician or political party seeing religious identity as an untapped resource that can provide an effective path to power and influence. Such a development is particularly likely in times of power transition, when an old regime is falling and is going to be replaced by a new one. The redivision of the political pie is a high-stakes game in which new tactics are used and new alliances often form. Religion can easily become the basis for such a new alliance. It is also common in times of crisis, such as after losing a war, or during and after serious economic downturns. Governments, among other political entities, often seek scapegoats, people to blame for the crisis. Minorities, including religious minorities, are potential scapegoats. It is important to note that the instrumentalist path does not mean religious identity was never salient in politics. Rather, it is meant to explain cases where it has not been salient in recent times. Thus, it can apply to cases where old but dormant religious divisions are awakened as well as to cases where they are made politically relevant for the first time.

For example, while many attribute the violent ethnic war in the former Yugoslavia after the fall of the Soviet Union to religious tensions, this is arguably a classic case of instrumentalism. De Juan (2008: 1121) argues that

[t]he antagonisms between Orthodox Serbs, Catholic Croats, and Muslim Bosnians are interpreted as the cause of the war in 1992. Recent studies, however, contradict this view: before the outbreak of the hostilities, religious identifications did not play a central role for the majority of the population. Discrimination was hardly practiced and there were many instances of mixed marriages: both indications that all three religious groups lived side by side in relative amity, not enmity. Hence it is not "ancient hatred" that is responsible for the religious dimension of the Bosnian conflict. Rather, [O]rthodox clerics and nationalistic political elites have cooperated to mutually support each other in the realization of their respective aims. Slobodan Milosevic needed the Orthodox Church to legitimize his

claim for power as well as his nationalistic and expansionist agenda. Orthodox clerics supported him with the aim to regain their former influence in the Serbian society.

Thus, in this case political entrepreneurs activated politically dormant religious identities in a time of transition in order to further their political goals.

Constructivism is similar to instrumentalism in that it refers to political entrepreneurs using religious identity as a path to power and influence. However, in this case, rather than activating an already existing identity, the constructivist path creates a new one. Within the nationalism literature this refers to creating a new narrative which, in effect, brings into existence a new national or ethnic identity. Gurr (1993: 9) and Horowitz (1985: 64–69) call this ethnogenesis. Gurr argues that it can be a result of recent shared experiences such as repression by a dominant group. In this case it constitutes the linking of a number of local identities into a larger ethnic identity. Horowitz uses this term to refer to any shifts in group boundaries where groups assimilate new members or divide into separate groups. Thus, constructivism is about shifting boundaries of identity. Few identities are constructed from scratch, though it is certainly possible for them to be. Rather, in most cases existing identities are altered.

Given this, constructivism begins with identities, or at least shared traits, that already exist but uses them to construct new identities that are somehow different from what existed in the past. While it is certainly possible to construct a religion from scratch, this process is slow and often unsuccessful. If it is successful, it usually takes decades or more before the group is large enough to be politically powerful. Thus, political entrepreneurs who use constructivist tactics on religion tend to remake existing traditions to suit their needs. While some might consider this concept— that religion is constructed—to be a radical one, it actually has a long history in the social sciences, dating back to at least Sigmund Freud and Karl Marx in the late nineteenth and early twentieth centuries. Freud argued that human beings construct a mass neurosis consisting of religious fictions for their psychological self-protection (Wilson, 1982: 4). Marx argued that religion was constructed as a tool by the ruling classes to maintain order among the masses. This is what Marx meant when he claimed that religion is the opiate of the masses. It was a tool used by the ruling classes—in this case the capitalists—to keep the masses from rebelling (Westhus, 1976: 299; Kowalewski and Greil, 1990: 511; Lincoln, 1985: 267; Lynch, 2000: 742; Martin, 1989: 352–353).

The literature on religion repeatedly refers to at least some religious identities and ideologies as being constructed. For example, Appleby (2002: 498), among many others, argues that modern religious fundamentalism is a constructed religious identity:

> The mentality of fundamentalists is shaped by a tortured vision of the past— a construction of history that casts the long and otherwise dispiriting record of humiliation, persecution, and exile, of the true believers . . . as a necessary prelude to the decisive intervention of God and the final vanquishing of the apostates.

Memories of the past are reconstructed into new forms and interpretations to fit modern needs[3] (Soloveitchik, 1994: 82).

While fundamentalism is not necessarily political or violent, many argue that new militant sects, in particular, are constructed. Leaders harness alienation and use it to build new interpretations of religious ideology which can justify violence and killing (Juergensmeyer, 1997, 1998; Minkenberg, 2003: 151–152; Stern, 2003: 30–31). Constructivism can also be applied to other political purposes. For example, many argue that constructivist tactics can be useful in conflict resolution. Specifically, trends within religious texts which support peace, cooperation, and reconciliation should be sought out and emphasized as more mainstream within the religious traditions in question (Appleby, 2000; Gopin, 2000, 2002)—though, to be clear, milder forms of these reinterpretations of religious texts which do not lead to the formation of new identity groups are better understood as instrumentalist.

While the above examples refer to sub-state groups, the argument that religious identity can be constructed is not limited to this type of group. States often construct and support their own version of the national religion to prevent the political mobilization of religion against the state, or to support the legitimacy of the state (Demerath, 2001: 197). For example, four post-Soviet Sunni Muslim states—Kyrgyzstan, Tajikistan, Turkmenistan, and Uzbekistan—did exactly this. All of them were in similar positions with the fall of the Soviet Union. They had Muslim populations which were relatively non-religious after decades of Soviet repression of religion. They were in search of a legitimating state ideology. Also, they began experiencing movements within their populations, often supported from the outside, preaching radical forms of Islam which these governments worried could undermine their rule.

All of these states adopted similar policies in the 1990s which they have continued to follow since then. These policies can be divided into seven distinct but interrelated elements. (1) They declare the separation of religion and the state. (2) The state bans religion or religious organizations from influencing politics or the state. (3) The state establishes official or semi-official Islamic organizations that are fully controlled by the state. These organizations control all aspects of officially recognized Islam in the state. (4) The state uses religious registration laws to ban, monitor, or limit religious organizations other than the one controlled by the state. (5) The state bans religious education in public schools and strictly controls or monitors all other religious education. (6) Mosques are heavily limited, controlled, and monitored by the government. (7) Radical Muslim organizations are banned and anyone engaging in Islamic religious activity that is perceived as outside of the state-controlled system is harassed and sometimes arrested by the government. For details of these policies, see Table 3.1.

In these cases, the constructed religious identity and ideology is designed primarily to allow religious expression, but in a way that does not threaten the state. Official institutions are intended first to keep religion politically benign and second to support the state's legitimacy. In one of these cases, Turkmenistan, President Niyazov produced a book called *The Rukhnama*. This book is best described as a "spiritual guidebook" on Turkmen culture and heritage, which also incorporates history, religious morality, and the autobiography of the president. Until after his death in 2006, all religious education centered on his book.[4]

Table 3.1 State control of religion in four post-Soviet Sunni Muslim republics

Type of regulation	Kyrgyzstan	Tajikistan	Turkmenistan	Uzbekistan
Official separation of religion and state	1993 constitution article 8: "Religion and all cults are separate from the state"	1994 constitution article 8: "No state ideology or religion may be established.... Religious organizations are separate from the state and may not interfere in governmental affairs."	1994 constitution, article 11: "Religious organizations are separate from the government, and may not perform governmental functions."	1992 constitution article 61: "Religious organizations and associations are separate from the state and equal before the law."
State control of Islamic organizations	State Commission on Religious Affairs (SCRA) and Muftiate	State Committee for Religious Affairs (SCRA)	Council of Religious Affairs (CRA)	Muftiate
Ban on religion or religious organizations influencing politics or government	1993 Constitution article 8: "... it is unlawful ... to form political parties on the basis of religion. Religious organizations should not pursue political goals and objectives; for the clergy of religions and cults to interfere with the operations of state agencies; ..."	1994 constitution (see above). Law on religious organizations: "The State does not entrust religious organizations with exercise of any State functions ... religious organizations cannot be part of the state apparatus."	1994 constitution (see above)	1992 constitution article 57: "It is forbidden to form or operate political parties, as well as other social associations, that have as their goal ... religious animosity ... religiously based political parties."
Registration laws	All religions must register	SCRA monitors all religious organizations for compliance with the law	Government-controlled Muslim organizations allowed. Religious activity by an unregistered organization is a criminal offense	All non-government-controlled Muslim organizations banned. Religious activities by unregistered organizations prohibited

Continued

Table 3.1 Continued

Type of regulation	Kyrgyzstan	Tajikistan	Turkmenistan	Uzbekistan
Religious education in public schools	Banned	Banned	Banned (article 11 of Constitution)	Banned, 1998 law
Private religious education	SCRA and Mufiate control all Islamic education	Official Islamic education controlled by government. Private instruction officially banned but in practice allowed	Banned except in mosques for a few hours a week by CRA-approved teachers. Ban on receiving Islamic education abroad	Allowed only in religious schools but not in private. Religious schools and teachers require government license. State controls training of clerics
Mosques	Most regulated by government and controlled by Mufiate	Must register with SCRA	One allowed per city. Attendees monitored by government. Imams appointed by government	State-controlled mosques allowed. Some private mosques allowed but they are run by state-appointed imams
Ban on radical Muslim organizations	Several organizations banned	Hizb ut-Tahrir banned	All unofficial organizations banned	Several organizations banned

These cases show that the political relevance of religious identity has multiple sources and that states, among others, can manipulate religious identities for political purposes. However, religious identity is more than a tool of state policy. It is also significantly correlated with political behavior at multiple levels. In the rest of this chapter I consider some important examples of this influence.

RELIGIOUS IDENTITY AND TOLERANCE

Tolerance is putting up with those things that one disagrees with, dislikes, rejects, or opposes. Those individuals and groups who fit into these categories are tolerated if they are treated fairly and equally (Eisenstein, 2008: 15). In the case of religion, this fair and equal treatment potentially applies on two levels.

The first is equal civil and economic rights in the context of state policy. Equal rights of this kind can include a wide range of issues, including fairness in employment, in both the public and the private sectors; freedom from violations of general civil rights, such as the right to free speech; and equal treatment in the justice system, among many. However, of particular importance in this concept are the right to practice one's religion freely and a state of affairs in which religious institutions are free of government interference or limitations that do not apply to all religions.[5]

The second level is the societal level. Even in societies where minority religions *de jure* have equality, prejudices and intolerance at the societal level can result in *de facto* discrimination.

While the issue of tolerance is not solely one of identity, much of the literature on the topic views it through the lens of identity. In fact, there is a significant debate in the literature over the link between religious identity and the linked concepts of democracy and tolerance for minority religions. Specifically, this debate revolves around the question of whether Islam is notably intolerant. The basic argument which contends that Islam is correlated with intolerance is that many Muslims, especially Islamists, consider Islamic law to be the only legitimate basis for governing, so there is little room for "Western" concepts such as democracy and human rights (Jaggers and Gurr, 1995: 478; Lewis, 1993: 96–98). In the words of Bernard Lewis (1987: xvi–xvii), "The true and sole sovereign in the Muslim view was God, from whose mandate the Prophet derived his authority and whose will, made known by revelation, was the sole source of law."

Most studies of human rights records which address the issue show that most Muslim-majority states have a poor human rights record—though, as is discussed in more detail in Chapter 12, there are certainly exceptions to this general pattern. While this link between Islam and discrimination has multiple and complex origins, one aspect of these origins that is particularly relevant in the context of a discussion of religious identity is Sharia law: Muslim religious law. This body of law influences legislation in many Muslim states either directly or through its influences on Muslim culture. In practice, it results in discrimination against members of other religions (van der Vyver, 1996). In fact, Islamic law formally addresses the status of religious minorities. In effect, in Islam there are three categories of religious minorities:

1   *Peoples of the Book*: This phrase refers to followers of those religions that are believed to be based on valid divine revelations previous to the revelation that Allah gave to the prophet Muhammad, but the messages of those revelations are said to have been corrupted and are therefore flawed and incomplete. It is considered legitimate for those who have never been Muslims to follow these religions. However, members of these religions are accorded a second-class status. On a strict reading of the doctrine, this includes the right for these religious communities to live by their religious laws and govern their own internal affairs. However, it also includes restrictions, including limits on constructing or renovating places of worship—typically that a church, for example, may not be built close to a mosque or in a fashion that is larger and more opulent than that of local mosques. In addition, the community must pay a special tax to its Muslim rulers. On a strict interpretation of Islamic doctrine, these religions include Judaism and Christianity, the monotheistic religions that predate Islam, but historically they have also sometimes included other minorities living under Muslim rule, such as Hindus, Buddhists, and Zoroastrians.

2   *Apostate religions*: These are religions that have developed from their roots in Islam into new forms which are not recognized by most Muslims as authentically Islamic. Consequently, they are considered heretical and typically suffer from the most severe restrictions in Muslim countries. Religious groups in this category include the Baha'is, Druze, and Ahmadis.

3   *All other religions*: These religions are neither heretical offshoots of Islam nor those of peoples of the Book. Their treatment has varied greatly over time and location.[6]

This Muslim concept of doctrinally mandated tolerance of some minority religions influences tolerance in a complex and crosscutting manner. On the one hand it involves doctrinal instructions for limiting the rights of adherents of minority religions on the basis of their religious identity. On the other hand it creates a set of rights for at least some minority religions which limit discrimination against them. That being said, these instructions have been interpreted differently, with some countries following harsh interpretations of these concepts while other countries appear to ignore them altogether. For example, today Saudi Arabia officially bans all religions other than Islam. On the other hand, some Muslim-majority countries, such as Burkina Faso, Gambia, Senegal, and Sierra Leone, place absolutely no restrictions on the practices or institutions of minority religions.

While this discussion has focused on Islam, there is no Muslim monopoly on religious intolerance. For example, as is discussed in detail in Chapters 10 and 11, many Christian states place restrictions on Muslim and other religious minorities.

More importantly, religions, by their very nature, tend to be exclusive. That is, they generally claim to have a monopoly on divine truth to the exclusion of all other religions. As Stark (2003: 32) puts it, "Those who believe there is only One True God are offended by worship directed toward other Gods." Such an attitude has the potential to lead to extreme intolerance of all other religions, and there is no shortage of historical examples of this occurring. Yet Islam has a built-in mechanism that dictates a certain level of tolerance for some religions. From this perspective, Islam has a set of checks and balances that limits intolerance. Jewish religious doctrine has a similar mechanism recognizing the legitimacy of any religion that follows certain basic precepts, including monotheism and the requirement that they include just laws such as bans on murder, theft, and adultery.

Also, there is a significant literature arguing that Islam is compatible with tolerance and democracy. I outline this literature in detail in the "Religious identity and democracy" section of this chapter.

MUSLIMS IN THE WEST AND CHRISTIANS IN THE MIDDLE EAST[7]

A comparison between the treatment of Christians in Muslim-majority Middle Eastern countries and Muslims in Western democracies brings out both the variety and the potential complexity of religious tolerance. This section is intended to demonstrate how perceptions that are aligned to religious identity are often inaccurate when examined more closely. This is true both because identity-based descriptions often give the impression of monolithic relationships that in reality contain a considerable level of diversity and because descriptions focusing on a single identity group can lead to significantly different conclusions than descriptions which view this identity group in comparison to others.

The treatment of Muslim minorities in Western Christian states has become a high-profile issue in world politics. Three recent laws embody the nature of these issues in the West. First, a 2004 French law prohibited public school students and employees from wearing "conspicuous religious symbols," including headscarves, skullcaps, and large crosses. While this law technically applies to all religions, Muslims perceive the law as directed primarily against the wearing of head coverings by devout Muslim women. Second, in 2010 France banned the wearing of full face coverings in public. Like the 2004 law, this one is perceived to be targeted against Muslims, though it is written to apply to all citizens. It also contains exceptions for safety gear and, more importantly, when worshiping in a religious place. Third, in 2009 a Swiss referendum banned the building of minarets—the prayer towers that are an integral part of mosques.

All of these laws have been accurately portrayed as religious discrimination against Muslims. More importantly, these are not isolated incidents, with similar practices occurring in other Western democratic states. Yet while it is a lower-profile issue, many ignore the treatment of Christian minorities in many Muslim states. In this section I compare the treatment of Muslims in 26 Western democracies to the treatment of Christians in 17 Middle Eastern Muslim-majority states. (Lebanon is not included, because of substantial participation by non-Muslims in its government.) This comparison demonstrates that when examined in a comparative context, the isolated discussions of Muslims in the West can be seen as an example of a wider world trend.

Mosques, minarets, and churches

The Swiss minarets referendum of 2009 did not occur in a vacuum. Calls for such bans had previously occurred and were rejected in the legislative bodies of several of Switzerland's cantons, including Solothurn, Bern, and Zurich. In practice, however, minarets could not be built because local governments denied building permits on technical and bureaucratic grounds.

This type of behavior is common in Western democracies. However, it occurs at the local level, with some, but not all, local governments in some countries restricting mosques. Local governments in Austria, Australia, Denmark, Germany, Greece, Italy, Malta, Norway, and Spain have all used tactics similar to those in Switzerland to restrict the building of mosques. Switzerland remains unique among Western countries in that there is a national-level restriction on mosques, though it limits only the construction of minarets, not that of the entire mosque.

Restrictions on the building and maintaining of churches in the Middle East are both more common and more severe. Ten of 17 Muslim-majority Middle Eastern states (58.8 percent) place some form of restriction on churches, most of which go well beyond local governments using indirect tactics to block construction. Saudi Arabia bans houses of worship of all religions other than Islam. In Egypt, which has one of the Middle East's largest indigenous Christian populations, Ministry of Interior regulations specify a set of ten conditions that must be met for a new church to be built. For instance, a church may not be within 100 meters of a mosque and it must be approved by the neighboring Muslim community, essentially giving locals an absolute veto over church construction. In addition, any repairs to a church, no matter how minor, require the approval of the regional government, and before 2005 such repairs required presidential approval. In Tunisia, operational churches generally date back to the nineteenth century or earlier. The government has rarely permitted the building of a new church since then. While not all of the restrictions on churches in the Middle East are this severe, they are distinct from those in the West in that they are all based on national, rather than local, policy.[8]

Head coverings and Bibles

The head covering issue raised by France's 2004 law is becoming more pervasive across Europe. France's law is distinct from that of other European countries in that it was enacted nationally and consciously applied to all religions. In all other cases the bans on head coverings were by local or regional governments and apply specifically to Muslims. For example, in 2003, Germany's Federal Constitutional Court upheld a state-level ban on headscarves for civil servants. By the end of 2008 at least eight of Germany's states had enacted such a ban. Similarly, several municipalities in Belgium, including Antwerp and Brussels, enacted bans on head covering by municipal employees.

As Christians have no overt dress code, it is hard to compare this issue directly to the policies of Middle Eastern states but it is arguable that the Bible, like a Muslim woman's head covering, is a potent religious symbol and a necessary possession for a practicing Christian. Six Middle Eastern states (35.3 percent) place restrictions on Bibles. In most cases these are not outright bans on Bibles but, rather, heavy regulation. For example, Kuwait officially bans the publishing of Bibles but in practice allows recognized churches (as opposed to the many unrecognized churches) to print religious literature for their congregations and permits one company to import Bibles. Sometimes these bans are unofficial yet pervasive. For example, Morocco has no law banning non-Muslim religious literature; however, in practice the government bars Arabic-language versions of the Bible. Outright bans exist as well. For instance, in Saudi Arabia any non-Islamic religious literature is banned, although foreigners may bring Bibles with them for personal use.

Other forms of religious discrimination

While a total of 16 of the 30 types of religious discrimination tracked by the Religion and State project are present against Muslims in at least one Western democracy, only three of them exist against Muslims in more than two or three Western states. These include head covering bans and limitations on mosques, as already discussed. As well, many Western governments require all minority religions to register with the government in order to gain official recognition in some way not incumbent on the majority religion. In most cases this registration is a bureaucratic formality, and failure to register does not influence freedom of religion, though it may influence a religion's ability to gain tax-free status, open a bank account, and rent or buy space.

In contrast, 28 of these types of discrimination exist in at least one Middle Eastern state against Christians, and 18 exist in four or more states. While discussing all of these forms of discrimination is beyond the scope of this discussion, some examples highlight their seriousness. In 14 countries, Christians are not allowed to proselytize, and in 12, Muslims are restricted from converting to Christianity. In 11 countries, Christians attending public schools are required to take courses in Islam. In six countries Muslims are given preference in child custody arrangements upon divorce. All of these types of discrimination are discussed in a broader context in Chapters 10–13.

Overall, when viewed in the context of how religious minorities are treated elsewhere, the treatment of Muslim minorities in the West seems less severe. Clearly, any religious discrimination is wrong. There is a worldwide consensus on this, at least in theory, enshrined in international treaties and evidenced by the fact that over 90 percent of the world's constitutions have religious freedom clauses—though these clauses in practice are often not fully observed. Yet it is an interesting example of a not at all uncommon quirk in the tolerance and human rights literature that more attention is focused on some identity groups rather than others and that this attention does not correlate with the identity groups which experience the highest levels of intolerance.

RELIGIOUS IDENTITY AND DEMOCRACY

As with the tolerance debate, there is significant discussion over whether religious identity is linked to democracy. This debate also revolves to a great extent around Islam and involves two different and contradictory sets of interpretation of Islamic law.

The first body of literature interprets Islamic law and practice to argue that Islam and democracy are incompatible. This literature makes three basic arguments: First, Islamic doctrine makes no separation between religion and state. That is, there is no equivalent of the concepts that exist in other religions that there are areas of policy reserved for temporal powers. In Christianity this manifests itself in a well-known quotation from Matthew 22:21: "Render unto Caesar the things which are Caesar's; and unto God the things that are God's." In Judaism this concept manifests itself as "*dina dimalhuta dina*"—the laws of the kingdom are the laws. There is no analogous concept in Islam which gives secular authority any independent base of power. Yet while Islam does in fact differ from other religions in this respect, this argument in the literature is problematic because, technically, separation of religion and state does not in and of itself define democracy.

Second, since Islamic law is the divinely decreed law of the land, there is no room for public participation in lawmaking. Third, as already noted, not all citizens have the same rights, as non-Muslims are not accorded the same rights as Muslims and women are not accorded the same rights as men (Dalacoura, 2000: 879; Lewis, 1993: 86–98). On an empirical level, several studies have shown a strong correlation between autocracy in the world today and Islam (Fisch, 2002; Midlarsky, 1998).

The second body of literature disagrees with this characterization of Islam and argues that Islam and democracy are compatible. It views Islamic laws and doctrines very differently from the first body of literature and makes four basic arguments.

First, as with other religions there are many diverse interpretations of Islam, many of which are compatible with democracy. The advocates of this argument acknowledge that anti-democratic trends are present in Islamic doctrine but note that they are balanced by other democracy-friendly principles. These interpretations focus on Islamic principles like consultation, consensus, the equality of all men, the rule of law, and independent reasoning as a basis for Islamic democracy (Esposito and Piscatori, 1991; Fuller, 2002). While the non-democratic tendencies in Islam are often linked to Islamist or fundamentalist versions of Islam, most religions are sufficiently diverse that they include sects, interpretations, and doctrines that can be just as easily linked with democratic tendencies. Scott Appleby (2000) calls this "the ambivalence of the sacred" and argues that religious individuals and leaders have choices that allow them to choose democracy or autocracy as well as tolerance or intolerance, as all of this and more can be justified by religious ideologies. Thus, current links between religious identity and any form of government represent current choices rather than deterministic links.

Second, Islamic parties have successfully used parliamentary systems to their benefit and even pushed for democratic reforms (Esposito and Piscatori, 1991). Third, even if Islamic doctrine inhibits democracy, in practice there has rarely, if ever, been true unity between Islam and ruling regimes (Haynes, 1998: 128; Hefner, 2001: 494).

Fourth, many argue that Islam's link to non-democratic government is happenstance. That is, there is technically such a correlation but the reason for this correlation has to do with factors not related to Islam. For instance, Alfred Stepan (Stepan, 2000; Stepan and Robinson, 2003) argues that any link between Islam and autocracy is a link that is particular to the Middle East and not Islam in general. For a variety of cultural, political, economic, and historical reasons, the Middle East is a very non-democratic region, but when other factors are taken into account, Muslim-majority states outside of the Middle East, such as Indonesia, meet or exceed expectations for democracies based on world averages. Other factors linked to democracy, or the lack thereof, such as economic development, a history of colonial rule and the specific nature of that rule, rentier statism, patriarchal societies, tribalism, ethnically divided societies, and natural resource wealth are also offered as explanations for why many Muslim-majority states are authoritarian.

Scott Appleby (2000: 256) notes that many Muslims and scholars of Islam strongly dispute this set of arguments call it "apologetics":

That is false Islam ... claims 'Umar 'Abdel Rahman, the Egyptian shaykh convicted of conspiracy in the bombing of the World Trade Center; it points to "the shameful predilection of our religious establishment towards apologetics; they wish to endow Islam with a face-lift, lest they be accused of being reactionary." Surveying the messages contained in audiotapes of thirty popular Arabic-speaking Islamic preachers, Emmanuel Sivan finds abundant evidence that Rahman's suspicion of and disdain for Western-style democracy is widely shared by many thousands of Muslims who are "neither theologians and jurists splitting hairs in erudite treatises, nor journalists writing for external consumption." Similarly, Max Stackhouse's comparative study of human rights in three cultures concluded that Islam has no basic concept of inalienable rights and does not permit the individual to enjoy the freedoms of action and association characteristic of a democracy.

This debate over the compatibility of a particular religious identity and democracy must be placed in the context of the debate over whether religion in general is compatible with democracy. Many argue that no religion is compatible with democracy. For example, Rawls (1993: 151) argues that we must "take the truths of religion off the political agenda." Demerath (2001: 2) similarly argues that while separating religion from *politics* is often not desirable or possible, "separating religion from *the state* is both possible and desirable." Some would go so far as to argue that liberalism was at least in part a response to the European religious conflicts of the sixteenth and seventeenth centuries and specifically includes separation of religion and state in the ideology in order to alleviate this type of conflict (Shah, 2000). This belief is taken by some to the extreme position that "religion, any religion, is the enemy of liberal democracy as long as it has not been defanged and privatized" (Beit-Hallahmi, 2003: 32). Many of these arguments are based on the assertion that religion often does not tolerate dissent from its dictates, which makes it incompatible with democracy.

The normative argument that democracy and religion are incompatible is by no means universally accepted. De Tocqueville argues that "successful political democracy will inevitably require moral instruction grounded in religious faith"

(Fradkin, 2000: 90–91). He understands that religious energy is important for democracy (Tocqueville, 1863: 22–32). However, he does not advocate a religious state. Greenawalt (1988: 49, 55) argues that liberal democracy tolerates people who want to impose their religious convictions on others, "just as it tolerates people who wish to establish a dictatorship of the proletariat," and that without resort to religion there are often no "ample grounds for citizens to resolve many political issues."

The normative debate is complicated by an empirical examination of the links between religion and democracy. That is, discussions in the abstract of what role religion should play in democracy cannot ignore the role it plays in fact. On the one hand, many posit that democracy is unstable and finds it difficult to maintain religiously plural societies (Mill, 1951: 46; Horowitz, 1985: 86–86). The literature on consociationalism and power sharing reflects this by implicitly arguing that heterogeneous societies can only maintain democracy through complex power-sharing arrangements.[9] On the other hand, many note that there are numerous examples of religion and democracy coexisting, including the existence of established churches in several Western European states and widespread government support in Europe for religion, especially religious education (Stepan, 2000: 41–43). The discussion in Chapter 10 of this book provides detailed evidence that this assessment is correct. Anthony Smith (2000) links many particular nationalist ideologies in democratic states to religious origins, including the national ideologies of France, Greece, Ireland, the United States, and the United Kingdom. Research suggests that when there is a strategic interest in their doing so, religious groups often support democracy (Kalyvas, 1998, 2000; Linz, 1978).

Thus, normative arguments that democracies should avoid religion discuss a type of democracy that is considerably rarer than one would suspect solely on the basis of the normative discourse. On one level this does not influence the validity of arguments that discuss how the world ought to be. However, on another level the empirical results tend to demonstrate that either democracies can support religion and remain liberal democracies or many countries widely considered liberal democracies are in fact not liberal democracies.

Mazie (2004, 2006) takes an intermediate approach in both the normative and the empirical debates and argues that some elements of religion are compatible with democracy while others are not. Religious holidays are common to most states and do not undermine democracy as long as observance is not mandatory and religious minorities can observe their own holidays. Funding of religion is possible because democratic checks and balances and an effective judicial system can prevent reasonable levels of support for religion from turning into religious tyranny. He also points out that most states fund policies and institutions that have no link with religion and are unpopular with large segments of society, but that such funding is not considered to undermine democracy. However, imposing religious values or behavior is in most cases incompatible with democracy.

Mazie's differentiation between different types of government involvement in religion brings out more clearly something that is inherent in the arguments of all of those who posit that religion and democracy are compatible: that religion can be compatible with democracy but that there are clearly intolerant forms of religion which are not compatible with the concept of pluralism and some that are not tolerant even of any diversity within their own traditions. Put differently, states can support a religion and remain democratic as long as this support is combined with tolerance of other religions. Thus, democracy can be compatible only with manifestations of religion that are willing to tolerate democracy and religious freedom or whose followers do not have the ability to oppose it.

In practice, one can find many incidences of religious support for democracy. For example, Künkler and Leininger (2009) found that among 82 cases of transition to democracy between 1972 and 2000, in about a third, "religious actors played a significant and constructive role toward democratization." Gill (2008) argues that support by religious organizations for tolerance and democracy depends upon political calculations. If a religion is in a position to gain and benefit from a religious monopoly, it tends to support intolerance and authoritarianism. In all other cases, religious institutions tend to support tolerance and democracy, because when religions cannot become a monopoly, they thrive best in free societies. When combined with Appleby's (2000) concept of the ambivalence of the sacred, this suggests that religious doctrine can be used to support or inhibit democracy, and the major factor that determines which interpretation of a religion will prevail is not doctrinal but, rather, a basic cost–benefit calculation. The role of cost–benefit calculations in religious politics is discussed in more detail in Chapter 7.

RELIGIOUS IDENTITY AND CONFLICT

Perhaps one of the most common uses of religious identity in the political science literature is to explain the dynamics of conflict. This type of argument comes in two general forms: (1) the argument that some religions are more prone to conflict than others, and (2) the argument that inter-religious conflict is more common, likely, or violent than intra-religious conflict.

It is impossible to discuss this topic without first referring to the most prominent version of this type of argument in the past two decades. Samuel Huntington's (1993, 1996) widely cited "clash of civilizations" argument is perhaps the best-known example of both of these types of arguments. He divides the world into seven or eight civilizations (depending on how one counts them)—Western, Slavic-Orthodox, Sino-Confucian, Latin American, Japanese, Hindu, Buddhist, and (possibly) African—which are, for the most part, congruous with religious identity. He posits that after the end of the Cold War, most conflict will be between civilizations, rather than within them, and that the Islamic civilization will be particularly violent toward other civilizations.

This theory has been highly controversial.[10] However, if we limit the discussion to actual analyses of Huntington's arguments focusing on whether (1) Islam is more violent than other religions, and (2) whether inter-civilization conflict is in fact more common, the results show that with, some important qualifications, neither of these propositions is supported by the evidence. Studies that have actually accumulated lists of conflicts across the world and tested Huntington's predictions against reality found inter-civilizational conflicts to be less common than conflicts within civilizations (Chiozza, 2002; Fox, 2004, 2005, 2007; Gurr, 1994; Russett *et al.*, 2000; Svensson,

2007; Tusicisny, 2004), that civilization is not a good predictor of conflict (Fox, 2004; Ellingsen, 2002; Henderson, 1997, 1998, 2004, 2005; Henderson and Tucker, 2001), and that most violence by Muslims is directed against other Muslims. This higher incidence of intra-religious conflict as opposed to inter-religious conflict is also true of conflicts involving Christians (Fox, 2004; Tusicisny, 2004). The part of Huntington's arguments which can be confirmed is that terrorism in recent years has been carried out primarily by Muslim groups. Yet, as terrorism is one tactic among many that are available to those engaged in violent conflict, when one looks at this in the larger context, which includes all types of conflict, this indicates a tendency of Muslim groups that use violence to select terrorism as a tactic—a topic discussed in more detail in Chapter 9—but not any particular tendency to being more violent.

That being said, Huntington's arguments, while prominent in the literature, are arguably overambitious but not completely false. Specifically, Huntington claims that inter-civilizational conflict will be the most common form of conflict and that civilizational identity will be the most important predictor of conflict. If these claims are toned down to the claims that civilizational identity can be an important aspect of conflict—that is, it has an impact but not necessarily the most important and prominent impact—they can be supported by the evidence. While Huntington focuses on civilizations, the large overlap between his concept of civilization and religious identity links his arguments to religious identity. Thus, the conclusions regarding the role of civilizational identities in conflict are directly applicable to the role of religious identities in conflict. Nevertheless, a bit of caution is in order when one is deriving any conclusions regarding religion based on tests using civilization as variable. This is because, while highly correlated, religious identity and civiliza-tional identity—as defined by Huntington—are not identical.

Religious identity conflict—conflicts between two groups of different religions—has always been present and constitutes a large proportion, though usually a minority, of all conflict in the world in any given year (Fox, 2004, 2007; Toft, 2007; Toft *et al.*, 2011). Also, one can find a limited impact of religious identity on conflict when one looks both at the conflict patterns of specific religions and at whether conflicts between different religions are more violent than intra-religious conflicts. Yet the impact of both these factors is limited and tends to fade when other factors such as regime, economic development, the spread of conflict across borders, and inter-national support for rebel organizations are taken into account (Fox, 2004).

Even if one accepts the argument that some religions are more conflict-prone than others—and again the evidence for this is at best weak—religious identity can never provide a Huntingtonian all-encompassing explanation for conflict. This is because of two simple facts: First, there is no religious group all of whose members have always been engaged in conflicts at all times. That is, even the religions that allegedly have the most violent tendencies are not always associated with violence. Second, religions are universally capable of justifying both violence and peace.

Many Muslim states, to take Huntington's example of the most violent religion, have been in a state of peace for most of their histories, and for the purpose of this discussion I define peace as not being engaged in violent international or domestic conflict. Second, most religious traditions, even those that are doctrinally pacifist, have been used to justify violence and had members engage in violence that was legitimized by those justifications. Also, as is discussed earlier in this chapter, Islamic doctrine includes a number of concepts that support peace and tolerance.

That religion can justify violence is an easy concept to demonstrate. Christianity, Judaism, and Islam all have versions of holy war within at least some interpretations of their doctrines. Even Buddhists, adherents of a classically pacifist religion, have used Buddhism to justify violence. For example, a form of Buddhist doctrine supports the violence by the Buddhist majority in Sri Lanka against its Hindu, ethnic Tamil minority. Some Sri Lankan Buddhist monks and nationalists believe that the Buddha charged them with preserving the true Buddhism—Theravada Buddhism—and gave the island of Lanka to the Sinhalese Buddhist majority to create a "citadel of pure Buddhism." Accordingly, violence is justified in support of that goal (Manor, 1994). Another example of Buddhist justifications for violence is that used by Asahara, the Tokyo subway killer, who believes that since souls are transferred upon death, some people are better off dead, especially people living in evil situations that will cause damage to their karmas (Juergensmeyer, 2000). While clearly many Buddhists dispute these interpretations, and this second example is not recognized by any mainstream version of Buddhism, it demonstrates that even in a doctrinally peaceful religion, interpretations of doctrine that support violence are possible and do in fact occur.

Thus, all religions are capable of supporting and justifying both peace and violence. This means that even if some religious doctrines are more easily interpreted to support conflict than others, none of them universally does so. Consequently, at most religious identity can be linked to the likelihood that one's religion will be a motivation for violence, but there always remains a possibility that it will support peace, even if this possibility is less likely than might be found in other religious traditions.

Overall, the current state of the evidence is not sufficient for us to reach a full conclusion regarding religious identity and conflict. However, it is clear that to the extent that religious identity is a factor in conflict, it is clearly not the dominant factor that Huntington predicted it would be. Thus, the usefulness of religious identity as a predictor of conflict is at best limited. In addition, the question of under what circumstances any particular religion will support violence and under what circumstances it will support violence remains open. In later chapters of this book, especially Chapter 9, I attempt to answer this pivotal question, among others.

POLITICAL OPINIONS, VOTING, AND BEYOND

While the above discussion has focused on tolerance, democracy, and conflict, one should note that religious identity has been linked to a wide variety of politically relevant factors and behavior. These include party affiliation, voting behavior (Jelen, 1993; van der Brug *et al.*, 2009), the extent to which a country militarizes (De Soysa and Neumayer, 2008), and voting patterns in national legislative bodies (Oldmixion and Hudson, 2008; Oldmixion *et al.*, 2005). Religious identity also influences political opinions on a wide variety of topics, including foreign policy (Baumgartner *et al.*, 2008; Froese and Mencken, 2009; Wuthnow and Lewis, 2008), abortion (Minkenberg, 2002), embryo and stem cell research (Fink, 2008), the desirability of democracy (Kim, 2008; Norris and Inglehart, 2004; Patterson, 2004; Wink *et al.*, 2007), support for political institutions (Nelsen *et al.*, 2001), national identity (Kunovich, 2006), and support for the use of violence in politics (Canetti *et al.*, 2010; Polkinghorn and Byrne, 2001; Zaidise *et al.*, 2007). Religious identity has also been linked to factors that are less overtly political but still politically relevant, such as people's ability to trust and forgive (Fox and Thomas, 2008; Welch *et al.*, 2004), and economic performance (Barro and McCleary, 2003; Cavalcanti *et al.*, 2007; McCleary and Barro, 2006a).

This listing, combined with the more detailed discussion of tolerance, democracy, and conflict above, is likely an incomplete listing of all the actual links between religious identity and political phenomena that have been researched by social scientists. However, it is sufficient to demonstrate that these links are numerous, cover a wide variety of phenomena, and should be taken seriously.

That being said, limiting one's understanding of religion and politics to religious identity will result in at best an incomplete understanding of the role of religion and politics. As already argued, there is considerable ambivalence in the sacred, as Appleby (2000) calls it, as most religions have diverse traditions that can support a wide variety of contradictory political behaviors. For example, many link Islam to intolerance and conflict today. Yet even if this view is correct, at the time Europe was experiencing feudalism it was considerably less tolerant of minority religions than was the Islamic world. Similarly, during the period of the Reformation, Christians were considerably more involved in violent conflict than were Muslims.

These facts imply that other factors beyond identity are at work. Put differently, the most relevant question is not "what is your religion?" but rather "what factors are influencing members of your religion today which impact on your interpretations of that religion which in turn influence your political behavior?" As is noted earlier in the chapter, Anthony Gill argues that the key factor is the political interests of politicians. Elsewhere, he argues that the interests of religious institutions also play a significant role (Gill, 1998, 2008). Others point to significant cultural, historical, and economic phenomena which can change over time.

More importantly, as I note at the beginning of this chapter, I posit that the identity literature is both the most common and most problematic of the religion and politics literature. While it is not possible to fully discount identity, I believe that the most useful answers to the question of religion's role in politics can be found in other aspects of religion.

In the next several chapters I survey religious phenomena common to all religions which can impact on how the religious interacts with the political. These include religious worldviews, laws, institutions, legitimacy, and fundamentalism, as well as the argument that it is rational calculations that are behind most religious politics. I examine how and why these phenomena become relevant in politics, as well as how they can potentially impact on the political realm. In any given time, the configuration of these influences can differ across religious identity but in the larger picture I argue that the political relevance of all religions can be understood through using these principles. Thus, they can both explain why different religions are currently interacting with the political in different ways and, at the same time, provide a more holistic understanding of the role of religion in politics.

DISCUSSION QUESTIONS

1 Can you think of any current political issues that are influenced by religious identity? That is, are there political issues where opinions are significantly influenced by one's religious identity?

2 In the early 1990s Samuel Huntington predicted that all conflict after 1990 would be between different religious identity groupings, and especially between Islam and other identity groups. Do you think his prediction proved to be an accurate one?

3 Do you think that when religious identity becomes relevant in politics or conflict it is because (1) these religious groups have always differed over political issues or have always been in conflict, or (2) because politicians and other leaders are using religious divisions for political gain?

4 Do you think it is legitimate of a state to officially or unofficially associate itself with a specific religion? Does the dominance of a single religion undermine the quality of democracy for members of minority religions?

FURTHER READING

Eisenstein, Marie A. *Religion and the Politics of Tolerance: How Christianity Builds Democracy*, Waco, TX: Baylor University Press, 2008.

Fisch, M. Steven "Islam and Authoritarianism" *World Politics*, 55 (1), 2002, 4–37.

Hasenclever, Andreas and Volker Rittberger "Does Religion Make a Difference? Theoretical Approaches to the Impact of Faith on Political Conflict" *Millennium*, 29 (3), 2000, 641—674.

Huntington, Samuel P. "The Clash of Civilizations?" *Foreign Affairs*, 72 (3), 1993, 22–49.

Huntington, Samuel P. *The Clash of Civilizations and the Remaking of the World Order*, New York: Simon & Schuster, 1996.

Kunovich, Robert M. "An Exploration of the Salience of Christianity for National Identity in Europe" *Sociological Perspectives*, 49 (4), 2006, 435–460.

Spohn, Willfried "Europeanization, Religion, and Collective Identities in Enlarging Europe: A Multiple Modernities Perspective" *European Journal of Social Theory*, 12 (3), 2009, 358–374.

CHAPTER 4

Religious Worldviews, Beliefs, Doctrines, and Theologies

As is noted in Chapter 1, social scientists study human behavior and political scientists focus on political behavior. In this chapter I focus on some of the most important religious influences on human behavior: religious worldviews, beliefs, doctrines, and theologies. These aspects of religion provide a lens through which people can understand the world around them. Religions also include explicit instructions on how to behave. These qualities of religion potentially have profound influences on political behavior.

RELIGION AS A BASIS FOR UNDERSTANDING THE WORLD

Human beings process huge amounts of information brought to them by their senses. However, they do not do so in a vacuum. They use belief systems or some other framework to help them interpret, comprehend, and process the information brought to them by their senses. This includes the need to understand the physical universe in which we live and how we relate to it.

Essentially we have a need to answer a series of questions: How do we understand the world around us? How do we understand day-to-day events? Is there a will behind the world around us and the events that take place in it and, if so, what is the nature of that will? It also includes more existential questions, such as: Who are we? Where do we come from? Why are we here? What is our place in the world? Finally, we also strive to understand the unknowable and un-understandable: What happens after death? Why is there evil in the world?

Religion can provide a set of answers to these questions, as well as many others. I argue that every human being has a framework of belief that helps them grapple with these issues, among others. Religion is clearly not the only source for these frameworks, but it is significant one. Political ideologies such as liberalism, fascism, communism, socialism, and nationalism, among many others, can all play a role in people's frameworks of belief. Yet religious beliefs are common. Surveys show that most of the world's population have some level of religious belief (Norris and Inglehart, 2004), which implies that the majority of people in the world have frameworks of belief that are, at the very least, influenced by religion.

These beliefs can be powerful and significant influences on behavior. When someone bases their belief system completely on religion, that religion can influence everything they perceive and every action they take. For example, Ammerman (1994: 150) describes the belief system of a true believer as follows:

> This conviction that the world is best knowable and livable through the lens of divine revelation is coupled with the . . . conviction that their revelation is one that radically reframes all of life. All other knowledge, all other rules for living are placed in submission to the images of the world found in sacred texts and traditions. All other authorities and credentials are de-legitimized, or at least put in their place.

For someone who bases their belief system on religion to this extent, all that matters is religion. The world's events are seen from this perspective, as are the actions that are to be taken in response to these events. Clearly, not everyone's belief system is totally dominated by religion, but to the extent that religion is an influence on someone's belief system, it influences their perceptions and actions, including their perceptions of politics and their political actions.

More importantly for the political context, these frameworks of belief are not purely an individual phenomenon. That is, while each individual's experiences make them and their frameworks of belief unique, these frameworks nevertheless have significant shared elements. Religious ideologies and doctrines can create shared beliefs within a religious community that bridge individual frameworks of belief into a community-based framework of belief. In fact, as is discussed in more detail in Chapter 6, building and maintaining shared religious belief systems is one of the major tasks of religious institutions. This shared framework can create collective motivations and behaviors. Religious

> collective meaning systems enable groups and group members to interpret their shared experiences including their historical and recent relations with other groups and group members to interpret their shared experiences. . . . They can influence the goals and the behaviors of groups on both national and international levels.

> (Silberman, 2005: 649)

Awareness of such shared frameworks is key to understanding religion's role in motivating political behavior, because politics is primarily a group-level phenomenon.

When a politician or a state bases a policy on religion, there is an inevitable political consequence: intractability. "[O]nce they are constructed collective meaning systems tend to be viewed within a given group as basic undisputable truths. Accordingly, they are usually held with confidence, and their change or redirection can be very challenging" (Silberman, 2005: 649). When one bases a policy on what one believes to be an absolute, divinely inspired truth, there is little room for compromise. Demerath (2001: 202) points this out when he argues that

[a]bsolute religious principles do not fit well in the compromise world of statecraft. Theological constraints on state actions do not sit well with officials who seek to preserve a capacity for flexible policy responses to changing circumstances. And if religion must be incorporated into law or state policy, most officials prefer very brief and very general codifications that can be variously interpreted as conditions warrant.

Laustsen and Wæver (2000: 719) similarly argue that "religion deals with the constitution of being as such. Hence, one cannot be pragmatic on concerns challenging this being." Given this, making political promises based on religion has potentially negative consequences. On the one hand, if a politician makes such promises and is unable to deliver, their political career can be seriously undermined. On the other hand, if a politician manages to deliver, the inability to compromise can also create high political costs in maintaining such a policy. This is why Demerath argues that politicians tend to avoid religious-based policies.

Yet as is demonstrated in Chapters 10–13, the policy makers of most of the world's states do not fully heed Demerath's advice, and allow religion to influence state policy. There are a number of reasons why that is the case. First, as is discussed in more detail in Chapter 5, religion is a strong source of legitimacy. It can legitimate states and their policies. Inflexibility on certain issues can certainly be considered a reasonable price for such a useful tool. Second, if a policy maker does have a religious belief system, deviating from it may simply not be an option. People who believe in a divine truth are extremely reluctant, at best, to violate the tenets of this truth. Third, whatever a politician's personal beliefs, if their constituency holds to a set of beliefs with sufficient strength, violating those beliefs can easily end the politician's political career. Thus, assuming that politicians place a high priority on maintaining their power and influence, in a pure cost–benefit calculation any price short of losing this power and influence is rational.

Thus, it is easy to hypothesize that the more religious the people in a particular country are, the more strongly will policy and politics in that country be linked to religion. While this is certainly an important factor in the equation, as I discuss in Chapter 7, the equation is not so simple and there are other crosscutting factors that make the link between individual belief and state religion policy considerably more complicated.

RELIGIOUS AND SECULAR PERCEPTIONS OF INTERNATIONAL RELATIONS

The history of international relations between the West and Islam provides a good illustration of how secular and religious worldviews can perceive the same events differently. Most intellectuals and policy makers in the West, at least until recently, viewed international relations as secular. The 1648 Treaty of Westphalia explicitly ended the era when religion was considered an international issue by designating it as an issue that is included within the right of sovereignty. That is, a state's religion policy, by international agreement, was not the business of other states. The Muslim threat to the West ended in 1683 with the defeat of the Ottomans at the gates of Vienna. Major international relations theories, including realism, liberalism, and Marxist-based theories, among others, rarely addressed religion at all. The world was seen as one where power, economics, the structure of the international system, nationalism, and perhaps ethnicity, among other secular factors, dominated international relations (Hehir, 1995; Fox and Sandler, 2004; Philpott, 2000, 2002; Thomas, 2005). Furthermore, secular political ideologies supporting separation of religion and state gained increasing popularity. These ideologies relating to domestic politics crossed over into international relations through the ideologies of individual policy makers (Farr, 2008; Hurd, 2007; Kuru, 2009).

Farr (2008) describes this confusion about religion among the US foreign policy community as follows:

> The problem is rooted in the secularist habits of thought pervasive within the U.S. foreign policy community. Most analysts lack the vocabulary and the imagination to fashion remedies that draw on religion, a shortcoming common to all the major schools of foreign policy. Modern realists see authoritarian regimes as partners in keeping the lid on radical Islam and have nothing to say about religion except to describe it as an instrument of power. Liberal internationalists are generally suspicious of religion's role in public life, viewing religion as antithetical to human rights and too divisive to contribute to democratic stability. Neoconservatives emphasize American exceptionalism and the value of democracy, but most have paid little serious attention to religious actors or their beliefs. . . .
>
> There is widespread confusion over the proper role of religion in public policy. The persistent belief that religion is inherently emotive and irrational, and thus opposed to modernity, precludes clear thinking about the relationship between religion and democracy.

However, in the Muslim world the religious view of the world was never lost and many Muslims perceived history and international relations differently. Most Muslims never accepted the Westphalian concept of religion being irrelevant to world politics. Nor do they believe that the religious war with the Christian West ended in 1683. Rather, they see 1683 as the beginning of centuries of defeat and humiliation at Christian hands. Christians have, since then, been winning a war for the control of the world, with Russia's conquest of Muslim Central Asia, European colonialism's success in controlling large parts of Muslim South Asia and North Africa, and the conquest of the Muslim Balkans by Greece, Bulgaria, and Serbia. The continuing influence of Western Christian states in the Muslim world, including several recent military interventions, like those in Iraq, Afghanistan, and Somalia, underscores this humiliation of Muslims at Christian hands. Thus, from this perspective the recent resurgence of Islamic violence against the West and regimes perceived as being influenced by the West is not a resurgence of religion. Rather, it is a shift in the tides of a centuries-old war (Miles, 2004).

If US policy makers had been more attuned to religion, they might have paid more attention to a 1998 declaration published on February 23, 1998 in *Al-Quds al-Arabi*, a London Arabic-language newspaper, titled "Declaration of the World Islamic Front for Jihad against the Jews and the Crusaders" and signed by, among others, Usama bin Laden. This declaration represents an extreme religious-based view on foreign policy and, while not representative of all Muslims, is representative of a segment that became politically significant on the international scene shortly after it was published. It includes a very religious perspective on international relations, repeatedly calling the United States and the "Jews" Crusader invaders of the Arabian Peninsula. It sees the First Gulf War as US aggression against Iraq and part of a "Crusader" plot to keep Arabs divided in order to ensure "the survival of Israel and the continuation of the calamitous Crusader occupation of the lands of Arabia." These actions are "a clear declaration of war by the Americans against God, his Prophet, and the Muslims." Accordingly,

> to kill Americans and their allies, both civil and military, is an individual duty of every Muslim who is able, in any country where this is possible, until the Aqsa Mosque [in Jerusalem] and the Haram Mosque [in Mecca] are freed from their grip and until their armies, shattered and broken-winged, depart from all the lands of Islam, incapable of threatening any Muslim.
>
> (Lewis, 1998)

Clearly, the writers of this declaration, including Al-Qaeda founder Usama bin Laden, see US foreign policy in the Middle East and elsewhere in religious terms and respond to it in that manner. This view of the world is so different from that of the US foreign policy makers of the time of this declaration and afterwards that the depth of the devotion of this group to attacking the United States was grossly underestimated. Madeleine Albright (2007) laments that when she was Secretary of State under Bill Clinton she had access to expert advisers on all issues other than religion. Religion was simply not on the radar at the US State Department in the 1990s. This secular perception of the world likely hindered the State Department's ability to take seriously and understand the religious worldviews of those like Usama bin Laden.

RELIGIOUS RULES AND STANDARDS OF BEHAVIOR

Religions generally include some sort of instructions guiding the behavior of their adherents. The content, scope, and complexity of these instructions can vary across religions but their presence is near-universal.

Jewish laws, known as *halacha*, include a complex and voluminous set of laws found in both the Old Testament and what was originally an oral tradition, but for the past two millennia the oral law has been written into hundreds, perhaps thousands, of authoritative volumes. This includes the Talmud—itself a multivolume work with over 60 tractates which includes 517 chapters each with wide-ranging discussions on major Jewish legal issues. There are multiple authoritative and important commentaries on the Talmud and volumes which distill the Talmud into a more practical listings of laws. In addition, numerous commentaries have been written on these volumes listing the laws. On top of all of this there is a large set of *responsa*: collections of answers to questions that rabbis have written over the ages to various questions posed to them, answers based on the Talmud and all these subsequent works.

This body of authoritative religious literature is not limited to rules regarding religious ceremonies. It includes laws regarding all aspects of life, including marriage, divorce, inheritance, criminal law, morality, and torts (laws for civil damages and contracts). It also includes more overtly political topics, including relationships with governments and laws regarding warfare.

While not all religions have a set of rules that is quite as complex and extensive as those found in Jewish tractates, such rules are present in most religions. Among Muslims these laws are called Sharia and are similar to those found in the Jewish tradition, with regard both to their complexity and to the extensive legal literature which embodies them. Most Christian denominations, by comparison, have less of a legalistic literature, yet they certainly include instructions on behaviors that are required and those that are forbidden.

Religious laws, whether they manifest themselves as actual laws or as ideologies or doctrines, can have several potential influences on political behavior. While these influences are interrelated and overlapping, for purposes of clarity I treat them here as separate.

POLITICAL MANIFESTATIONS OF RELIGIOUS WORLDVIEWS, BELIEFS, AND IDEOLOGIES

Religions tend to contain universal values and truths. By this, I mean values and beliefs that a religion's believers consider to be universally true. Put differently, religions claim a monopoly on the truth. This certainty as to what is right and what is wrong can lead to two types of political activity.

The first is a desire to use the government to enforce religious precepts either as law or policy, as well as generally support religion. As is discussed in more detail in Chapters 10–13, the majority of governments do this to at least a limited extent. They can enforce religious precepts in three ways:

1 They can enforce religious laws only on members of the majority religion of the state. In effect, religious precepts are legislated as state law but applied only to those who are members of the religion whose precepts have been legislated for. For example, Brunei, a Muslim-majority state, has incorporated Sharia (Islamic) family and inheritance law as the national law on the topic and established special Sharia courts to enforce these laws.[1] In addition, Brunei's government has legislated for a number of additional Islamic principles, including mandatory attendance at Friday prayer services.[2] However, none of these laws are enforced on non-Muslims. In fact, there is a completely separate set of legislation on issues of family law and inheritance for non-Muslims in Brunei.[3] This type of legislation has significant political implications because it makes following religious laws mandatory, removing an individual's freedom of choice as to whether or not to be religious. Family and inheritance law are by no means trivial issues. They determine who may get married, how people can obtain divorces, who can inherit, and how much they inherit. These are all issues that will at one time or another significantly influence nearly everyone's lives. In the case of Sharia law, women typically are placed at a significant disadvantage with regard to both divorce and inheritance. The treatment of women under Sharia law is discussed in more detail in Chapter 12.

2 Religious laws can be enforced on the entire population of a state regardless of whether or not they are members of the majority religion. A typical example is a state's abortion policy. While abortion is not solely a religious issue, it is one with a significant religious content. For example, an analysis of the Religion and State dataset shows that states with official religions are 31 percent more likely to have restrictive abortion policies. Also, the presence of bans on abortion is correlated with religious identity (Minkenberg, 2002). Among the 177 countries included in the RAS dataset, in 121 (68.4 percent) abortion is not available on demand, in 24 (13.6 percent) it is available only in order to save the life of the woman, and in six (3.4 percent) it is sometimes restricted even when the mother's life is at risk. Abortion is an intensely political issue, and in nearly every country where abortion policy is debated, religious institutions and leaders take public positions on the issue and often use their political clout to influence the outcome of the debate.

3 It is not only majority-group governments that seek to enforce religious laws. Often, minority groups in a state seek to enforce religious laws on members of their own religion. For example, in the United Kingdom Muslims have lobbied to have the right to apply Sharia law within their community. In 2008 they succeeded in getting the government to recognize five Sharia courts as having authority as arbitration courts on matters including divorce, inheritance, domestic violence, and financial disputes. While both parties must voluntarily agree to use these courts, the judgments of these courts are enforceable in the United Kingdom's secular courts. There is concern that social pressure may be used to force people to use these courts even if they would prefer the secular courts. By 2009 as many as 85 Sharia courts were operating in the United Kingdom.[4]

A second political manifestation of religious beliefs is the desire to create religious exclusivity. That is, religious groups often seek to maintain a monopoly of religion, or at least a privileged status in a state. Such monopolies exist when the state officially endorses a religion and limits the ability to practice any other religion. While 42 of the 177 states in the RAS dataset endorse an official religion, only Saudi Arabia and the Maldives go as far as to officially ban all other religions. Yet even these states have minority religions. Saudi Arabia, a Wahhabi Sunni Muslim state, still *de facto* tolerates some minority religions, including Shia Islam. Both Saudi Arabia and the Maldives sometimes allow other denominations to practice their religion if they are foreigners and practice in private. However, in both states public space is dominated by the state religion.

Other states with official religions allow at least some religious minorities to practice, but among the states with official religions included in the RAS dataset, only Andorra places no restrictions on the religious practices and institutions of any minority group. In very few cases are these restrictions trivial, and they are present even in Western democracies with official religions. For example, Greece, which declares in article 3 of its constitution that "the prevailing religion in Greece is that of the Eastern Orthodox Church of Christ," engages in all of the following restrictions on the practices and institutions of minority religions: Minority religious groups are required to fill out lengthy applications for renovating or moving official houses of worship. This requirement is not applied to the majority religion. Minority religious groups are often rejected for house-of-prayer permits, and those operating houses of worship without a permit are subject to prosecution. Muslims in Athens, for example, have been prevented from building a mosque and are forced to worship in unofficial mosques and prayer rooms. Until 2007, minority religious groups were taxed, while the Orthodox Church was and continues to be subsidized by the government. The government is in a dispute with the Muslim community of Thrace because the government seeks to appoint Muslim religious officials on the grounds that they perform civil judicial functions—for which they are paid by the state—in addition to religious functions. While the government has agreed to consider recommendations by the community, it is not obligated to do so. As a result, the community has elected "unofficial" religious leaders whom the government has prosecuted for usurping the functions of the appointed religious leader. In July 2007 the European Council for Human Rights ruled that these prosecutions violate the rights of the elected muftis.[5]

This trend toward religious exclusivity is not limited to states with official religions. In addition to the 42 (23.7 percent) states with official religions, another 42 (23.7 percent), despite having no official religion, clearly support one religion more than another. Another 33 (18.6 percent) favor several religions over all others. As discussed already, this government support for one or some religions can include the enactment of religious precepts as law or policy. It can also manifest itself as financial support for religion. States also maintain exclusivity by engaging in religious discrimination against minority religions. Both support for religion and religious discrimination are discussed in more detail in Chapters 10–13.

GOVERNMENT RELIGION POLICIES: SUPPORT FOR AND HOSTILITY TO RELIGION

This concept of implementing religious beliefs and rules through state policy and providing exclusivity and privileges to some religions is a highly political issue, one that states cannot avoid. Effectively, every government must decide on a religion policy that has two dimensions: the extent of support for religion and how to treat religious minorities. In theory, the decision regarding support can range from a ban on all religions to maintaining exclusive support for a single religion. This support for religion also involves support for religious institutions. While the role of religious institutions in politics is the topic of Chapter 6, this discussion of state religion policy focuses on the link between religious beliefs and state policy. A state's options with regard to religion policy include the following:

- *Banning all religions*: Since the fall of the Soviet Union, this option has been rare and exists currently only in North Korea.
- *Hostility to religion*: Policies in this category do not ban religion outright but look at religion as something negative that should be limited and controlled. Such a view is often motivated by a fear of any organization that is capable of providing an alternative basis for organization to the state. For example, China's explicit policy is to eventually eliminate religion in favor of atheism. One Chinese policy document states, "we Communists are atheists and must unremittingly propagate atheism. Yet at the same time we must understand that it will be fruitless and extremely harmful to use simple coercion in dealing with the people's ideological and spiritual questions—and this includes religious questions."[6] China sets up legal "patriotic religious organizations" that are controlled by the state. They are closely monitored and the clergy are appointed by the state. Religion is legal within the context of these organizations. All other religious organizations in China are officially illegal but are often allowed in practice as long as they are not too large and are not seen as posing any risk to the state. Members of the Communist Party are required to be atheist. Most leadership positions in China are open only to members of the party (Fox, 2008).
- *Laicism*: Policies in this category provide no support for religion and tend to ban religion from the public sphere. However, religious practices that do not impinge upon the public sphere are not restricted. France is often considered an archetypical example of this type of policy.
- *Neutrality toward religion*: Policies in this category neither support nor hinder religion. Whether the government considers religion as a positive or negative social or cultural phenomenon, it maintains a policy of not intervening in religious affairs beyond the minimal regulation necessary. The United States and its policy of maintaining a "wall of separation" between religion and the state is a classic example of this type of policy. It does not preclude religion from influencing political discourse but it does limit the government's ability to regulate or support religion in general, much less any religion in particular.
- *Support for all religions*: The government considers religion a positive factor in society but treats all religions equally. It therefore supports all religions. This is a

relatively rare policy, one followed only by eight states: Brazil, Gambia, Jamaica, Nepal, New Zealand, Senegal, Suriname, and Trinidad and Tobago. Senegal, for example, is a Muslim-majority country with a substantial Christian minority but it defines itself as a secular state in its constitution.[7] The country does not in any way seem to favor Islam over Christianity and supports religion in general. It provides financial assistance to religious groups to preserve their places of worship or carry out special events, as well as to religious charities. It also provides encouragement and assistance for an annual Muslim participation in the Hajj and a Catholic pilgrimage to the Vatican. Optional religious education in both Christianity and Islam has been available in public schools since 2002.

- *Support for some religions*: This type of policy divides religions into two or more categories. In most cases this type of policy privileges well-established religions with a history of presence in the state. Religions that are small and new to the state tend to be those left out of the state support system for religion. In a simple case, such as Belgium, there are two categories: religions that receive state support and those that do not. In Belgium, "recognized religions"—including Catholicism, Protestantism, Anglicanism, Judaism, Islam, and Christian Orthodoxy, as well as "*Laïcité*", which is an organization of secular humanism that for all practical purposes is considered the seventh recognized religion—enjoy benefits such as direct government subsidies, government salaries for clergy, and funds for the building and upkeep of places of worship. Other religions receive no such support. In less common cases, such as those of Austria, Bosnia, the Czech Republic, Cyprus, Hungary, Latvia, and Lithuania, the state creates a multiple-tier system where each tier has different types of support and privileges. In Lithuania, for example, there are four classifications of religious groups. "Traditional communities" are those that have a history of 300 years or more in the country, and include Roman Catholics, Evangelical Lutherans, Orthodox Christians, Sunni Muslims, and Jews, all of whom are recognized in Lithuania's constitution. These religions receive annual government grants and subsidies, provide religious instruction in public schools, and maintain chaplains in the military. Their clergy and theological students are exempt from military service, and the highest-ranking clergy are eligible for diplomatic passports. They may register marriages, establish subsidiary institutions, and do not have to pay social and health insurance. "State-recognized religious groups" are those that have been registered in the country for at least 25 years. They receive privileges, but not as many as traditional religious groups receive. They are entitled to perform marriages and are entitled to certain tax breaks, but do not receive subsidies from the government or exemptions from military service. Since 2005, both state-recognized and traditional religious groups have received social security and healthcare subsidies for spiritual leaders and employees. "Registered communities" can act as legal entities, open bank accounts, act in a legal capacity, and own property for constructing religious buildings. Unregistered religions have no privileges, but are not prevented from worshiping.
- *Support for a single religion*: In addition to the official religion category, many states do not officially endorse a single religion but in practice support a single religion. Such a policy is particularly common in Latin America, including Belize, Chile,

El Salvador, Guatemala, Honduras, Nicaragua, Panama, and Venezuela. In all of these cases the Catholic Church, while not the official religion, is clearly favored by the state. For instance, in Guatemala the Catholic Church is the only religion explicitly recognized in the constitution, though not as the state's official religion. In Nicaragua the government funds private Catholic education but not similar institutions run by other religions. It pays teachers' salaries at a number of primary and secondary schools owned and directed by the Catholic Church and funds several Catholic universities.

- *Official religions*: This category includes a wide variety of states, including those described earlier, which enforce the official religion on all or a portion of their population. However, others, while supporting the official religion, do not make it mandatory. This is true of the nine Western democracies with official religions: Andorra, Denmark, Finland, Greece, Iceland, Liechtenstein, Malta, Norway, and the United Kingdom.

GOVERNMENT RELIGION POLICY: TREATMENT OF MINORITY RELIGIONS

All of the above categories apply to the extent to which a state supports one or more religions or limits religion in general. With the exception of states that make a religion mandatory for everyone, these categories do not address directly the second aspect of state religion policy: treatment of religious minorities. The most important aspect of this type of policy is religious discrimination, which is a term that is more complicated than one might think at first because it can have multiple potential meanings and can get confused with terms like "religious freedom," which potentially has a different meaning.

As is noted in Chapter 1, the RAS project defines the term *religious discrimination* with a focus on how religious minorities are treated. Specifically, in the context of the discussion in this book, religious discrimination is defined as a situation where a state limits the religious institutions or right to practice one's religion for minority groups in a way that is not applied to the majority religion. To "discriminate" means to treat differently. Restrictions placed on all religious groups can certainly be considered a violation of religious freedom, but in the context used here they are not considered discrimination. That is, *religious freedom* usually refers to the ability to practice one's religion and support religious institutions in a state for all religions, including the majority religion as well as minority religions, though, as is noted in Chapter 1, it can be defined even more broadly. Religious discrimination, as the term is used in this book, more narrowly focuses on restrictions that are placed on a minority religion that are not placed on the majority religion.

This distinction between restrictions placed on minority religions exclusively and restrictions placed on all religions is critical to understanding government religion policy. Restrictions placed on all religions represent a hostility toward, or at least a wariness of, religion in general. Restrictions placed exclusively on minority religions represent a different set of motivations. I discuss this distinction in more detail in Chapter 1.

An additional conceptual distinction is between religious discrimination and a form of support for the majority religion that is not also granted to the minority religion. For the purposes of the discussion in this book, when a government supports a majority religion in a manner in which it does not support minority religions, this is not considered religious discrimination. This aspect of the definition of religious discrimination is not universally accepted. Some, such as Stark and Finke (2000), would argue that such an uneven playing field puts such religions at a disadvantage for maintaining membership. Nevertheless, lack of government funding and support does not in and of itself prevent members of minority religions from practicing their religions and supporting their religion's institutions, be they churches, synagogues, mosques, temples, or some other form of institution. That is, if no restrictions are placed on a minority religion, its members can practice it freely, even though the material costs for doing so will most likely be higher than for practicing a state-supported religion. This is not to say that exclusive support for one religion is unimportant. Rather, it is a centrally important issue in state religion policy. I simply place it in a different conceptual category than religious discrimination.

Wide-scale restrictions on most or all minority religions, especially in combination with a policy of supporting one or a few religions more than others, can be considered prima facie evidence that the state is engaging in a policy to maintain the dominance of one or a few religions. The motivations for maintaining this dominance can be religious, political, or cultural. Religious motivations include the theological imperative to maintain the dominance of the "true" religion. Cultural motivations can simply be based on maintaining the purity and integrity of a nation's culture, which includes religion. In such cases, governments often support several indigenous religions and suppress or disadvantage religions considered non-indigenous. Finally, in many cases religious identity overlaps with political cleavages, especially in ethnically divided societies. In these cases, restrictions on minority religions can be part of a campaign to maintain political dominance.

Another source of religious discrimination is the desire by governments to protect their citizens from religions perceived as "cults." In theory the government needs to protect citizens from these cults because they are dangerous. It is a certainty that such dangerous cults exist. For example, there have been several instances of mass suicides by religious groups such as the Order of the Solar Temple in France, which committed mass suicide in 1996. There are also cults that are dangerous to others, such as the Aum Shinrikyo cult in Japan, which perpetrated a series of attacks with poisonous gas in 1994 and 1995. However, instances like these are rare. More common are limitations on non-mainstream religious groups which place high demands on their members, to the extent that some governments consider them predatory. Many governments consider the Unification Church and Scientologists to fall into this category.

However, limitations on "cults" in most cases are directed at groups that are small and relatively new to the country in question. In some cases these religions can be considered mainstream in other countries. For example, a 1996 French parliamentary commission identified 173 groups as cults. This list includes groups considered mainstream elsewhere, such as Mormons, Seventh-Day Adventists, and Pentecostals.[8] The defining criteria for inclusion on the list appear to be size and a lack of an extensive history in France. These groups, while not banned, are subject to intense scrutiny. In 1998 the government created the "Inter-ministerial Mission in the Fight against Sects/Cults" (MILS), which was dissolved in 2002 and replaced in 2003 by a similar organization called MIVILUDES (Fox, 2008; Kuru, 2009).[9]

Similarly, in 1999 Belgium created the "Belgian Sect Observatory," which maintains a list of over 600 sects and cults and has been accused of targeting some of them for slander and discrimination. Like the French list, this one includes groups considered mainstream, or at least benign, elsewhere, including Seventh-Day Adventists, Zen Buddhists, Mormons, Hassidic Jews, and the YWCA. In extreme cases, discrimination against these groups can include police surveillance, loss of jobs, denial of citizenship, and loss of child custody.[10] Thus, both the Belgian and the French policies seem to be targeted primarily against groups that are small and different rather than against dangerous groups.

In sum, a state's religion policy is a highly political issue. It is driven in large part by people who wish to use the state to enforce their belief systems, both religious and secular. As Anthony Gill (2008) points out, whatever the status quo, there are constituencies that benefit from it and those that seek change. Religious minorities tend to benefit from policies that treat all religions equally while religious majorities often seek to use their numerical advantages to gain preferential treatment and, perhaps, restrictions on some or all religious minorities. In some cases, minorities also seek exclusive privileges for their religions, such as religious courts with jurisdiction over matters such as family law. Secularists often seek to ban all religion from the public sphere and perhaps the private sphere. Most countries have all of these elements within their body politics, though the specifics of their religious or anti-religious ideologies vary, as does the proportional distribution of these groups.

The one thing that is certain is that no policy can fully satisfy all of these constituencies, and most policies satisfy none of them. This means that no matter what a state's policy on religion, there will be constituencies unsatisfied with the status quo, and most likely these constituencies will constitute a majority of the country's population and include elements pushing for both more and less religion in a state's policy. While there is little agreement among these competing constituencies whether there is too much or too little religion in government, they can agree that the government does not have it right. Except perhaps in highly repressive states, these unsatisfied constituencies tend to try to alter the status quo to make it more in conformity with their belief systems and interests.

This is likely a political problem that cannot be avoided, short of massive repression. This is because the one option a state does not have is to have no policy at all. Having no policy is essentially taking a strictly neutral policy toward religion by neither supporting nor restricting religion in any way, which is also a policy choice. Thus, even if by default, religion is an issue that is inextricably intertwined with politics.

As Philpott (2007: 506) notes, this inevitable relationship between religion and state can be difficult because on the one hand religion

> professes truths about the moral order of the universe, whereas the [state] asserts sovereignty, or supreme authority within a territory, and has succeeded in becom-

ing the only form of polity ever to replicate itself across the entire land surface of the globe.

Thus, the state and religion cohabit the same space, which makes entwinement and friction inevitable.

RELIGIOUS ACTORS

Toft *et al.* (2011: 23) define a religious actor as "any individual, group, or organization that espouses religious beliefs and that articulates a reasonably consistent and coherent message about the relationship of religion to politics." This concept is useful in understanding how religious beliefs influence politics for at least three reasons.

First, it gives a name and definition to the entities that seek to apply their religious beliefs to the political arena. One type of religious actor is an individual who acts upon their religious beliefs in the political arena. This can be a politician who holds an elected office, such as Iranian president Mahmoud Ahmadinejad, or US presidents including George W. Bush and Jimmy Carter, who both claimed that their religious beliefs guided their actions. Individual religious actors do not need to be politicians. A private citizen who makes use of all the avenues open to a private citizen to influence the political arena, including voting, lobbying, and participating in protests, can be a religious actor.

Religious leaders also fit within this category. Diverse actors, including the Pope, the Dalai Lama, and the Taliban leader Mohammed Omar are all religious leaders who are also religious actors. They share in common that they are recognized by many followers as spiritual leaders and have actively used this position to follow a political agenda, though the specific agendas of these three actors are extremely different. Religious leaders do not need national or international prominence to be religious political actors. Leaders of local congregations, for example, can be politically active in their local communities.

Another type of religious actor is religious organizations of all stripes. This category includes political organizations guided by religious beliefs as well as traditional religious institutions which take on a political agenda. I discuss these types of entities in more detail in Chapter 6. The category can also include religious political parties.

Second, this concept emphasizes that religious identity is not sufficient to understand religion's role in politics. Motivations and beliefs are also important (Toft *et al.*, 2011: 24).

Third, this concept highlights that not everything is about government religion policy. While governments play a critical role in the relationship between religion and the political, much of religion's political power comes from other parts of society. This power is largely wielded by religious actors.

CONCLUSIONS

Religious worldviews, beliefs, doctrines, and theologies are an important element of religion's influence on politics. These concepts emphasize how religion can cause and motivate political behavior. However, they constitute just one of several ways religion can influence political behavior. In subsequent chapters I discuss other influences, including the impact of religious legitimacy and religious institutions on politics.

DISCUSSION QUESTIONS

1   To what extent do you think religious beliefs influence the political behavior of local and national politicians in your country? If to a certain extent they do, how do those beliefs influence their behavior? Do they influence the language they use, or their policy choices? If so, how? Is any religious influence because of the politicians' own personal beliefs or because they feel the need to take into account the religious beliefs of their constituents?

2   To what extent do religious beliefs influence your own political decisions? Such decisions can include which party and politicians you support as well as decisions on specific policy issues.

3   Using the categories described in this chapter, how would you describe your country's religion policy? How does this compare to the religion policies of other countries with which you are familiar?

4   Using the categories described in this chapter, what role do you think religion should play in government? How does this compare to the role religion does play in your government?

5   Do you think discrimination against religious minorities is motivated by religious beliefs or by the same factors that cause discrimination against racial and ethnic minorities?

FURTHER READING

Durham, W. Cole Jr. "Perspectives on Religious Liberty: A Comparative Framework" in John D. van der Vyver and John Witte Jr. *Religious Human Rights in Global Perspective: Legal Perspectives*, Boston: Martinus Nijhoff, 1996, 1–44.

Fox, Jonathan *A World Survey of Religion and the State*, New York: Cambridge University Press, 2008.

Kuru, Ahmet T. "Passive and Assertive Secularism: Historical Conditions, Ideological Struggles, and State Policies toward Religion" *World Politics*, 59 (4), 2006, 568–594.

Kuru, Ahmet T. *Secularism and State policies toward Religion: The United States, France, and Turkey*, New York: Cambridge University Press, 2009.

Philpott, Daniel "Explaining the Political Ambivalence of Religion" *American Political Science Review*, 101 (3), 2007, 505–525.

Silberman, Israella "Religion as a Meaning System: Implications for the New Millennium" *Journal of Social Issues*, 61 (4), 2005, 641–663.

Wentz, Richard *Why People Do Bad Things in the Name of Religion*, Macon, GA: Mercer, 1987.

CHAPTER 5

Religious Legitimacy

Legitimacy is a central aspect of politics. It can be defined as "the normative belief by an actor that a rule or institution ought to be obeyed" (Hurd, 1999: 381). Put differently, a government's legitimacy is based on creating a feeling among its constituents that it is correct and proper to follow its laws. As such, it is one of the key reasons people obey rules and consider governments worthy of ruling. Of course, other factors such as force and self-interest can provide similar results, but legitimacy is something that nearly all governments and political actors covet. It allows them to achieve their goals and maintain their power more easily. Robert Dahl (1971) considers legitimacy an essential element of government, without which it would likely collapse. Even in autocratic regimes that rule primarily through force, the government must maintain legitimacy among a small number of elites who hold the power in society. This is because even a dictator has no power if no one will follow his orders. He needs at least a small core of people to whom he entrusts the means of coercion who will obey him.

Given this, legitimacy is essentially located in the mind and in collective beliefs. It is based on what people think. If citizens think a government is legitimate, then it is. That is why it is such a powerful tool for rulers. If people consider a government, leader, policy, or institution legitimate, they will choose to follow it. This reduces the resources governments must invest in enforcement and perhaps repression. Put differently, legitimacy is perhaps the most powerful, efficient, and inexpensive method for a government to maintain order and compliance.

This chapter considers the role of religion in supporting and undermining religious legitimacy. The discussion here should not be taken to mean that religion is the only source of legitimacy. Other important factors include:

- *Success in accomplishing goals*: Governments that achieve what is expected of them by their constituents achieve significant legitimacy by doing so. These tasks can range from a local government making sure the garbage is picked up on time to a national government maintaining a free public space, and a prosperous economy from which all benefit.
- *Tradition*: Following long-standing traditions and basing government on institutions that have been recognized for generations can generate considerable legitimacy. The preservation of the monarchy in the United Kingdom is an excellent example of this type of legitimacy.
- *Popular consent*: People are more likely to consider a government legitimate if they feel they have a say in it. Usually, having a say takes the form of the ability to decide or at least influence the choice of who governs.
- *Democracy*: Democratic government has become one of the most legitimate forms of government in the modern world. That many autocratic governments still adhere to the appearance of democracy through elections and other institutions of democracy testifies to this. Democracy can be considered a more specific example of the concept that legitimacy derives from popular consent.
- *Revolutions*: Governments that come to power through popular revolution often claim legitimacy because the revolution expressed the will of the people. This form of legitimacy is also linked to popular consent.
- *Indigenous-ness*: People tend to prefer forms of government and leaders that are perceived as indigenous or native and appropriate to their culture, society, and state. Perceived foreign influences can often undermine legitimacy.
- *Charisma*: Charismatic leaders can generate legitimacy through their ability to influence people. Also, many offices come with what is called a charisma of office. This is when a position, such as that of the US president, lends a feeling of charisma to the person who holds it.
- *Rule of law*: Governments that are perceived as faithfully following their declared rules and procedures and that enforce their laws equally on all, including the powerful, are perceived as more legitimate.
- *International recognition*: The international community, both through the recognition of individual governments and through acceptance by international institutions such as the United Nations, can bolster the legitimacy of a government. However, this form of legitimacy is, perhaps, most conspicuous when it is absent.
- *Ethnicity and nationalism*: In relatively homogeneous countries, linking a state to ethnic or national identity can bolster its legitimacy. In some cases this nationalism can be built even in heterogeneous societies.

The ability of religion to both enhance and undermine the legitimacy of a government, a policy, political actors, and political institutions, among many other things, is arguably among the most uncontroversial propositions in political science. Accordingly, the rest of this chapter focuses on the nature of religious legitimacy, rather than demonstrating its existence.

RELIGION AS A JUSTIFICATION FOR ANYTHING

For all of recorded history, religion has been present in human society and has been a potential source of legitimacy. Religion is one of the few things that can legitimate nearly anything. It has clearly been used on numerous occasions to legitimate governments, opposition movements, policies, and institutions.

It can be used to legitimate even those acts and institutions that are considered beyond the pale in other circumstances. For example, the Dutch Reformed Church, a prominent church in South Africa, provided religious justifications for South Africa's apartheid regime—a system of enforced racial separation that existed between 1948 and 1994, though many discriminatory laws which were the basis for this regime predate 1948.

The Dutch Reformed Church has a Calvinist orientation. An essential element of Calvinism is predestination, which is the belief that people are destined from birth to go either to heaven or to hell. This creates a theological system where some people are by God's decision superior to others. This concept was used to justify the superiority of whites over blacks, though there is some debate over whether this belief contributed to the formation of the apartheid regime or was used to justify it after the fact. However, elements within the church called for separate services for whites and blacks as early as 1857, justifying this as the will of God (Johnston, 1994).

Other biblical quotations were used in this context. For example, blacks were said to be the descendants of Noah's son Ham, whose sexual violation of Noah caused Noah to curse Ham, declaring he would be "a servant unto his brethren."[1] Similarly, the separation of peoples at the Tower of Babel was also a popular analogy. As is discussed later in this chapter, the Dutch Reformed Church has since abandoned this ideology (Johnston, 1994).

Apartheid is certainly not the only example of the use of religion to justify racial superiority. George Fitzhugh's infamous 1857 defense of slavery in the United States in his book *Cannibals All!* also shows the ability to use religion to justify what is now considered to be one of the most despicable institutions in human history. Fitzhugh repeatedly argues that the Bible "recognizes" and "guarantees" slavery and justifies it as God's will.

The ability to use the Bible as a justification for slavery is not surprising. Scott Appleby (2000) argues that most long-standing traditions contain complex doctrines and source documents which leave much room open for interpretation. Furthermore, it is the nature of the sacred to be ambiguous and ambivalent because of man's distance from God and the difficulty in perceiving his true will. As a result, religions and their texts can be used to justify nearly anything. Appleby focuses on the ability of religion to justify both peace and violence, but this principle, which, as noted in previous chapters, he calls the "ambivalence of the sacred," is much more widely applicable. Religion can be used to justify apartheid and slavery even as many who opposed these institutions used religion to call these same institutions evil. It can also be used to justify acts that are universally considered abhorrent, such as genocide (Fein, 1990).

In sum, religion can be used to legitimize anything. Whether doing so is an appropriate use or interpretation of the religion in question can be a matter of debate among theologians. However, from a political science perspective the truth or accuracy of these interpretations is less important. What is important from this perspective is whether these interpretations are used in the political arena and are successful at influencing political behavior, in this case whether a regime, policy, political actor, or institution is considered legitimate.

THE EVOLVING ROLE OF RELIGIOUS LEGITIMACY IN GOVERNMENT

Religion has always been linked to legitimacy. In fact, for much of Western history religious legitimacy was a prerequisite to rule. Until the past few centuries, in the West the church was a central basis for legitimating the government. It was believed that the king ruled through divine right. This "descending" theory of political legitimacy has it that power descends from God and is granted to the king. This is why the clergy played a central role in coronation ceremonies. By placing the crown on the king's head, they were stating that the king's right to rule came from God. Under such a theory of legitimacy, people have no right to oppose their rulers, because to do so is to oppose God (Turner, 1991: 178–183; Toft *et al.*, 2011: 55–56).

Today, religion competes with an "ascending" theory of political legitimacy. This means that legitimacy comes from the people, who must consent to their government. The need for consent gives the people the right to choose and replace their government. While examples of this theory of political legitimacy can be found earlier, in modern times, the political relevance of the "ascending" theory of political legitimacy dates to political thinkers such as Hobbes, Locke, and Rousseau. While the specifics of their theories differed, all of them argued that the ruler and the ruled have a social contact which defines the power of the ruler and which, if violated by the ruler, can result in the ruler's replacement.

The US constitution was written on the basis of these ideals and is among the first practical expressions of a social contract that grants power to a government on the basis of the consent of the governed. Thus, for its time it was a radical document that redefined the nature of government. It was the first among many such documents.

Yet while it heralded an age in which religion was less often a source of "descending" legitimacy for the state, religion still remains an important potential source of legitimacy for governments. This can be seen in the world's constitutions—perhaps the most basic and definitive expressions of the social contracts between the rulers and the ruled.

The Religion and State dataset includes information on 172 constitutions that were active in 2008. Many of them contain reference to religion. Thirty-four declare an official religion. However, 74 declare official separation of religion and state. One country, Bulgaria, declares both in its constitution. This leaves 63 that do not address the issue. In Table 5.1, I examine the extent of religion in constitutions (other than Bulgaria's) on the basis of these three categories.

This table looks at six common clauses in constitutions, all of which support religion or draw legitimacy from religion. If we combine the first two categories, 29.7 percent of constitutions (taking the overlap between the two categories into

Table 5.1 Religious legitimacy in constitutions, 2008

	Official religion	*Separation of religion and state*	*No reference in constitution*
A symbolic mention of God	50.0%	24.3%	39.7%
Other symbolic mention of religion	42.7%	13.5%	17.5%
Official oath of office in constitution mentions God or religion	61.8%	24.3%	33.3%
Religion has a special place in the country's history or culture	17.6%	5.4%	7.9%
Establishment of religious courts or judges	14.7%	4.1%	4.8%
Support for religious education	29.4%	10.8%	6.3%
Any of the above	79.4%	39.2%	54.0%

account) that declare separation of religion and state symbolically make reference to religion or God. Thus, even among secular states, calling upon God or religion to bless a social contract is not uncommon. Of these constitutionally secular states, 24.3 percent also make reference to God or religion in oaths of office mandated in their constitution. When we combine this with the other categories in Table 5.1, a large minority of 39.2 percent of constitutionally secular states still either rely on religious legitimacy or substantially support religion in their constitutions.

Take, for example, Germany's 1949 constitution, which, with amendments, remains in effect today. Article 140 incorporates several articles of the 1919 constitution into the current one, including the statement that "there is no state church." Yet the preamble of the 1949 constitution begins, "Conscious of their responsibility before God." Article 7 states that "religion classes form part of the ordinary curriculum in state schools." Also, the oath of office for the president in Article 56 ends in "so help me God," though this portion of the oath is optional.[2]

Poland's 1997 constitution similarly declares in article 25 that "the relationship between the State and churches and other religious organizations shall be based on the principle of respect for their autonomy and the mutual independence of each in its own sphere." Yet the preamble makes several religious references, including the following: "Beholden to our ancestors for . . . culture rooted in the Christian heritage of the Nation," "recognizing our responsibility before God or our own consciences," and "Both those who believe in God as the source of truth, justice, good and beauty, As well as those not sharing such faith but respecting those universal values as arising from other sources." Article 53 states that "the religion of a church or other legally recognized religious organization may be taught in schools." Articles 130 and 151 contain oaths for officials, including the president, the prime minister, deputy prime minister, and ministers, all of which include an optional "so help me God" at the end.[3]

Given this, it is clear that Nikos Kokosalakis (1985: 371) was more correct than he knew when he stated that a "strong residual element of religion, which clearly exists even in western societies, can still perform basic legitimizing or oppositional functions within such ideologies."

In fact, many would argue that religion is making a comeback. In a classic version of this argument, Mark Juergensmeyer (1993, 2008) argues that the "descending" theory of legitimacy is making a comeback against the "ascending" theory, though he does not use precisely that terminology. He argues that, especially in the Third World, though also in the West, secular ideologies such as secular nationalism, liberalism (the combination of democracy and capitalism), socialism, fascism, and communism are suffering from a crisis of legitimacy. The reason for this is because many governments are failing to maintain the legitimacy-based criteria Juergensmeyer describes, which substantially overlap with several of the bases for legitimacy outlined at the beginning of this chapter.

He argues that governments, especially in the postcolonial Third World, have based their structure and legitimacy on these secular ideologies. However, these ideologies are seen as having failed and are perceived as being corrupt and inefficient. They have been unable to deliver on promises of prosperity, freedom, and social justice—essentially, the equitable distribution of wealth and power. Furthermore, these ideologies and the leaders who espouse them are seen as non-indigenous and even a continuation of colonialism by proxy—as many of these leaders have been educated in the West and have significant connections to the West.

As a result, people are seeking an alternative ideology as the basis for government, and religion is a popular option. Religious leaders and organizations are seen as non-corrupt and indigenous. They promise social justice and blame the corruption and inefficient government on a lack of morals and grounding in indigenous culture. Thus, religion's inherent legitimacy combines with the illegitimacy of the existing governments to create movements for the return of religion not only as a way to legitimate governments but also as an alternative basis for government.

As yet, few governments, with some notable exceptions, such as that of Iran, have converted from governments based on Western ideologies to theocracies. However, there are a growing number of religious opposition movements seeking to make governments do just that.[4]

Mark Juergensmeyer's arguments are not unopposed in the literature. Charles Taylor (2007) argues that the processes of modernization and secularization discussed in more detail in Chapter 2 have inextricably changed the world. We now live in a world where the secular option exists and it is not possible to return to the times when religion dominated unchallenged. While his arguments focus on individual religiosity, they are applicable to the sources of religious legitimacy. This aspect of his argument is likely correct. As I note in Chapter 2, for the foreseeable future religion and secularism will likely coexist and be in conflict to fill the same roles in society, including being a source of legitimacy.

However, Taylor (2007: 1) takes his arguments a step further, arguing that

the modern Western state is free from this connection . . . with a couple of exceptions, in Britain and the Scandinavian countries, which are so low-key and undemanding as not really to constitute exceptions . . . in our "secular" societies you can engage fully in politics without ever encountering God.

As I demonstrate in Chapter 10, if Taylor is not seeing God in the West, it is because he is not looking hard enough. Religious laws and policies are ubiquitous in Western countries. Returning to my analysis of constitutions, if Taylor were to look, he would find God mentioned in the constitutions of Canada, Germany, Greece, and Ireland, all of them Western democracies. Also, even if this was not the case, Taylor purposely limits his arguments to the West and makes no claims regarding the rest of the world. This is most likely because religion is clearly important in non-Western states. Yet the non-West, where most people are religious (Norris and Inglehart, 2004), is encroaching on the West. Immigrants from the non-West are flocking to the West. Thus, even if religion and religious legitimacy were becoming scarce among Westerners—an argument I dispute—the West's changing demographics is clearly altering this situation.

THE POLITICAL USES OF RELIGIOUS LEGITIMACY

Simply put, religion can lend legitimacy to governments, political parties, opposition movements, institutions, leaders, policies, and just about any other political actor or phenomenon one can list. It can also be used to undermine the legitimacy of all of the above. Everything else that can be said about the political uses of religious legitimacy is an elaboration upon or an example of this basic concept. Accordingly, in this section I provide some important elaborations and examples.

Governments

Most states either seek religious legitimacy or fear its use against the state. In many cases this legitimacy manifests itself in what is an archetypical and stable act of mutual support in which the state supports a religion and, in return, the religion supports the government. A classic example of this type of pact is the relationship between the Catholic Church and the state in medieval Europe. The Catholic Church was granted a monopoly of religion in a country, with all subjects automatically being members of the church and subject to its laws. Many, including Gill (2008) and Stark and Finke (2000), argue that this form of religious monopoly is what many religions consider the ideal situation. In return, the church supported the legitimacy of the temporal rulers, declaring that their rule as well as the hierarchical feudal system was the will of God. Thus, opposing that system or rejecting one's place in it was tantamount to opposing and rejecting the will of God. Furthermore, the higher-level church officials were often the younger brothers of the temporal feudal lords, creating an additional bond between religious and temporal elites.

In such cases there remains the question of who is in charge of this relationship. When the state is totally dependent upon religion as a basis for legitimacy, the withdrawal of that legitimacy can cripple or even destroy a government. Put differently, if the king rules by the will of God, then if God's representatives claim that that will has changed, the king has no legitimacy at all. On the other hand, when a religion is dependent upon the state apparatus to enforce its tenets, the withdrawal of that support can seriously harm that religion's status in society. Given this, these relationships can be accurately described as co-dependent.

In modern times most of these mutual support pacts are not quite so comprehensive, both in that they often do not provide a religious monopoly and in that the religion's support for the state is present but not so all-encompassing. Also, in most cases the state is firmly in control but still could be harmed by a withdrawal of religious legitimacy.

Yet examples exist of the more comprehensive relationship, mostly in the Muslim world in states such as Iran and Saudi Arabia. Iran is a theocratic state where the clergy control the government. Saudi Arabia has a system more similar to the medieval European feudal system, where the monarchy supports the religious monopoly of the Wahhabi Muslim sect and the Wahhabi clergy support the government.

More typical among states that support a single religion are countries such as Denmark. Denmark's constitution states that "the Evangelical Lutheran Church shall be the Established Church of Denmark, and, as such, it shall be supported by the State."[5] And the Danish government supports its national church in practice in a number of ways. The government provides a number of direct subsidies to the state church and, in addition, collects a tax paid only by church members to support the church. The state church is the only one to receive such support, and these two sources of funding provide nearly all of its funds. The government also provides funds to seminaries and Christian Theological University programs. The Church of Denmark is responsible for registering all civil births, deaths, marriages, and divorces, and for the management of cemeteries (including secular ones). Also, the law stipulates that "Christian studies" be taught in public schools; the class focuses on the Evangelical Lutheran faith but also covers world religions and philosophy, while promoting tolerance and respect for all religions. Despite all this support, the state religion is not mandatory and the law specifically grants religious freedom and states that non-members are not required to pay the religious tax. Thus, Denmark strongly supports the Evangelical Lutheran Church and derives legitimacy from doing so but does not grant the church a religious monopoly.

Even in states without official religions, a weaker version of this relationship can exist. For example, among the 26 Western democracies included in the Religion and State dataset, only two—the United States and France—do not support religious education in public schools. This includes countries that declare a separation of religion and state in their constitutions, such as Australia, Germany, Ireland, Italy, Portugal, and Spain. In five of these six countries—Germany being the exception— the religion teachers in public schools are themselves clergy or appointed by religious institutions. While none of these courses is mandatory, this means that in five Western European countries that declare separation of religion and state, the government nevertheless supports religious education in public schools taught by clergy, or by teachers appointed or approved by the clergy. This is a significant benefit given to religion.

While the ability of a religion to bolster a state's legitimacy is clear, it is also clear that religions can bolster the legitimacy of opposition movements. This is precisely the dilemma, or at least an aspect of the dilemma, faced by China in its rule in Tibet. The opposition includes many Buddhist monks and is headed by a venerable religious figure with a worldwide reputation: the Dalai Lama. It is arguable that the aura of legitimacy and the ability of the Dalai Lama to use this aura to get his message out is, in large part, responsible for the high profile of the movement to free Tibet from China.

It is clear that the Chinese government recognizes this power of religious legitimacy. The Dalai Lama is traditionally the most important Lama in Tibet. The second most important is the Panchen Lama. Tibetan Buddhists believe in reincarnation and that the reincarnations of important spiritual leaders can be identified. Several years after the previous Panchen Lama's 1989 death, the Dalai Lama identified a 5-year-old boy as the reincarnation of the Panchen Lama. The Chinese government arrested the boy and his parents and named another boy as the true reincarnation of the Panchen Lama. In doing so, the Chinese government is trying to gain the legitimacy of support of a major traditional Tibetan Buddhist leader or, at the very least, neutralize the potential use of this type of legitimacy against it.[6] It is also important to note that traditionally the Panchen Lama plays an important role in discovering the Dalai Lama's reincarnation. In 2007 the Chinese government formalized this issue by passing a law that requires government approval for any recognition of reincarnation.[7] Thus, even a militantly secular state recognizes and manipulates the power of religious legitimacy.

Even the most religious of states can be vulnerable to this type of challenge. Saudi Arabia, which, at least according to the RAS measures, supports the state religion more strongly than any other state currently in existence, is challenged internally by religious radicals who consider the government insufficiently religious. States like Saudi Arabia, which depend in large part upon religion to support the legitimacy of their rule, are particularly vulnerable to this type of challenge.

When a state is challenged by a religious opposition that is successful at portraying the state as illegitimate at least in part because it is insufficiently religious, the state has few options. Ignoring this opposition is an option only if the opposition is insufficiently strong to seriously threaten the state. Otherwise, the state has two practical options. First, it can repress this opposition. Second, it can co-opt religion in order to both render it less dangerous and at the same time bolster the legitimacy of the state. As is noted in more detail in Chapter 3, the Muslim-majority former Soviet states of Kyrgyzstan, Tajikistan, Turkmenistan, and Uzbekistan engaged in a combination of both of these policies in the face of opposition movements calling for a theocratic state in the region. They created state institutions that are loyal to the government and repress all expressions of Islam that fall outside the purview of these institutions. It is arguable that the increased religious support found in many Muslim states since 1990, as discussed in more detail in Chapter 12, is a similar attempt to co-opt Islam in support of the state in an era of rising Islamic militancy. While these efforts will unlikely be sufficient to satisfy militant radicals, they may be enough to blunt the legitimacy-based challenges of such groups in the eyes of the majority of the population of these states or, rather, bolster the state's Islamic credentials enough for the majority of the population to consider it sufficiently Islamic.

Politicians and policies

In addition to influencing the legitimacy of a regime or government in general, religion can also be used to legitimate specific politicians, policies, and political agendas. As an inherent source of legitimacy, religion is a powerful tool of persuasion. Political actors can use it either to support their agenda or to undermine the agenda of their opponents. This is because convincing others that your policy agenda is legitimate is a significant step in gaining their support. In this context, to claim that a policy is legitimate and supported by religious precepts is to argue that others are morally obligated to support your policies. While it would be naive to argue that all political actors act morally, few politicians want to be perceived as immoral. Thus, successful appeals to religious legitimacy are potentially powerful tools of persuasion.

For example, US presidents have repeatedly used religious language to legitimate efforts to go to war. Froese and Mencken (2009: 103–104) argue that this is the case with regard to George W. Bush and the Iraq War:

> Throughout the course of the Iraq War, the Bush Administration has consistently framed its war policy in decidedly religious language. . . . Bush's chief speech writer from 1999 to 2004, Michael Gerson, affirms that he inserted religious language and biblical quotes into nearly all Bush's speeches, literary references understood by millions of religious Americans.

This resort to religious language can be found at all levels of the Bush administration. For example, General William Boykin, Deputy Undersecretary for Defense Intelligence, in a 2003 public lecture stated that

> the battle this nation is in is a spiritual battle, it is a battle for our soul. And the enemy is a guy called Satan. . . . Satan wants to destroy us as a nation and he wants to destroy us as a Christian army.
>
> (cited in Froese and Mencken, 2009: 103)

This is part of a larger set of beliefs that legitimate US foreign policies, including the effort to spread democracy around the world. Roof (2009) identifies two elements of this legitimating ideology. The first is the "myth of the chosen nation." This ideology suggests that Americans have a covenant with God and are, accordingly, the "new Israel." The second is the idea that "Nature's Nation, emerging out of the Enlightenment and Deism—gave rise to the notion that the United States arose out of the natural order, and that the country reflects the way God had intended things to be from the beginning of time" (Roof, 2009: 288). These foundational myths combine to imply that "God chose America to bless the nations of the world with the unfolding of a golden age" (Roof, 2009: 288) based on American ideals. Thus, any effort to spread American ideals to the world is inherently legitimate to those who believe this ideology. It is an ideology that is popular in the United States with members of both parties, but a significant number of Americans, including many religious Protestants, are uncomfortable with this linking of state policy to religious ideologies (Froese and Mencken, 2009; Wuthnow and Lewis, 2008).

Religious legitimacy of this nature is important with respect to two constituencies: other policy makers and constituents. In order to successfully enact and implement a policy, it is generally important to convince other policy makers to work with you. Even in non-democratic governments, decisions made by the ruling elites often involve negotiations and compromises. In addition, if a policy is widely popular or unpopular among constituents, this can have a significant influence on its success. While the reasons for this being true are obvious for democracies, even in autocratic states, following a policy that is widely unpopular and seen as being against the religious sensibilities of the population is a practice that is best avoided.

Religious legitimacy can be a powerful tool in politics, sometimes to the extent that it can allow the side that is weaker in material power to nevertheless persevere in battles over policy. The fall of South Africa's apartheid regime, discussed earlier in this chapter, is an example of this. The regime, which, as noted above, was supported by church ideology, was also attacked from religious quarters, specifically by the World Council of Churches (WCC). The WCC represents hundreds of Christian denominations encompassing hundreds of millions of Christians worldwide. In 1970 it decided to devote half of its program to combat racism and opposing apartheid. The funds devoted to this effort never exceeded a few hundred thousand dollars a year, but the symbolic value of this effort contributed to the downfall of the apartheid regime in several ways.

First, the monetary commitment by the WCC, however small, was a serious one to the extent that it was willing to financially support a liberation movement. This gave the contributions significant symbolic value.

Second, the legitimacy granted by the WCC to the opposition movements gave many blacks in South Africa the courage to "make their voices heard" within their own churches, which in turn influenced the thinking of those churches (Warr, 1999: 499–504). As I discuss later in this chapter, these developments contributed to causing the Dutch Reformed Church to change its stance on apartheid.

Third, the public opposition of an organization that represents hundreds of millions of Christians posed a significant legitimacy problem to South Africa's government, which thought of itself as ruling a Christian nation. The WCC also advocated and catalyzed international sanctions against South Africa. This advocacy was instrumental in a divestment campaign in which hundreds of businesses and numerous individuals stopped supporting companies that did business with South Africa. The campaign cost South Africa almost $10 billion from 1984 to 1989 (Warr, 1999: 504–506). Thus, an organization with no political power inside of South Africa but with significant amounts of religious legitimacy used that legitimacy to help cause the downfall of an entrenched regime.

THE LIMITS OF RELIGIOUS LEGITIMACY

While religious legitimacy is a potentially powerful political tool, it has several important limitations. First, it is a double-edged sword. That is, while religion can bolster the legitimacy of a government, policy, institution, or political actor, it can also be used to undermine them. In fact, to the extent that one relies on religious legitimacy, one can be hurt by it. Consider a hypothetical politician who is caught with a woman other than his wife in a compromising position. While such a circumstance is rarely good for a political career, it is more harmful if that politician has used religion to bolster his legitimacy. That is, a politician who bases his political appeal in part on being moral is more vulnerable to harm when he is proven to be immoral. Similarly, states that rely upon religion for legitimacy are more vulnerable to being influenced by religious actors and are more vulnerable to the withdrawal of that legitimacy.

There are almost always other political and religious actors that can invoke religious legitimacy. Given this, religion's "double-edged sword" is always in play. Put differently, it is difficult to monopolize religious legitimacy; it can always be invoked against those who invoke it.

Second, religious legitimacy does not easily cross denominational borders. That is, invoking religious legitimacy can be effective among those whose religious beliefs are similar to yours, to the extent that these beliefs are different, religious legitimacy loses its effectiveness. For example, invoking Jesus is as likely to sway a Buddhist as invoking Muhammad is likely to influence a Christian. There are certainly religious themes that cross religions, but they are limited in comparison to the forms of legitimacy that can be invoked within a religious tradition. Thus, the Dalai Lama can invoke calls for peace and reconciliation that cross religious borders from Buddhism to other religions, but if you want to convince a Catholic, it might be more effective to quote the Pope.

Third, religious legitimacy is effective only to the extent that its audience is religious. Some people are more religious than others and more swayed by religious arguments than others. Furthermore, a significant segment of the world's population is secular and is unlikely to be swayed by religion. Among people like this, especially militant secularists, invoking religion can have an effect opposite to the desired one and cause them to oppose a policy.

Fourth, the religious legitimacy is often reliant upon the religious credentials of the one invoking it. Put differently, a politician who has a well-known reputation for being personally religious, moral, and pious will be more easily able to use religious legitimacy than would a politician without such a reputation.

Fifth, in some cases religious legitimacy follows public opinion rather than the other way around. That is, sometimes religious organizations can be considered irrelevant if they do not adhere to widely popular opinions. Liz Fawcett (2000) argues that this is what happened within the Dutch Reformed Church in South Africa. As is noted earlier in the chapter, this church ideologically supported South Africa's racist apartheid regime. However, in the last years of the regime the church changed its stance and began to oppose apartheid. Why? Fawcett argues it was because public opinion in South Africa had changed and apartheid was becoming less and less popular. Supporting the regime, which in the past had been popular among large segments of the church's congregants, was becoming a liability and causing congregants to begin to question the church's legitimacy and even leave the church. In order to remain relevant and maintain its congregation, the church had to come in line with what was already considered legitimate among the population. Thus, in this case the tail wagged the dog.

Finally, this discussion can be seen as treating religion as a tool that politicians cynically manipulate to their benefit. As is discussed in more detail in Chapter 7, this certainly occurs. However, religious legitimacy is more than just a tool. It is also a reflection of religious beliefs and sensibilities which, while subject to manipulation, as discussed in Chapters 4 and 7 have an independent basis in society and can only be pushed so far. Religion can legitimate anything, but in order for it to do so, this legitimacy must resonate with the audience it is intended to convince. While in theory anything can be justified by religion, in practice most populations and individuals have lines that cannot be crossed.

DISCUSSION QUESTIONS

1   To what extent do you think your government's legitimacy rests on religion as compared to the other factors listed at the beginning of this chapter? If not the government, are there any political parties, politicians, or other political actors who rely on religious legitimacy? To what extent do you think this use of religious legitimacy is effective?
2   When political actors in your country use religion to justify and support their actions, to what extent do you believe they are doing so on the basis of a genuine and sincere religious belief and to what extent are they cynically using religious legitimacy to justify an agenda that doesn't really have much to do with religion?

FURTHER READING

Appleby, R. Scott, *The Ambivalence of the Sacred: Religion, Violence, and Reconciliation*, Lanham, MD: Rowman & Littlefield, 2000.

Bellah, Robert N. "Religion and Legitimation in the American Republic" *Society*, May–June 1978, 16–23.

Fawcett, Liz *Religion, Ethnicity, and Social Change*, Basingstoke, UK: Palgrave Macmillan, 2000.

Froese, Paul and F. Carson Mencken "A U.S. Holy War? The Effects of Religion on Iraq War Policy Attitudes" *Social Science Quarterly*, 90 (1), 2009, 103–116.

Juergensmeyer, Mark *The New Cold War?*, Berkeley: University of California, 1993.

Lincoln, Bruce *Holy Terrors: Thinking about Religion after September 11*, Chicago: University of Chicago Press, 2003, chapter 6.

Roof, Wade C. "American Presidential Rhetoric from Ronald Regan to George W. Bush: Another Look at Civil Religion" *Social Compass*, 56 (2), 2009, 286–301.

Religious Institutions and Political Mobilization

Imagine you want to organize a political event such as a rally in support of the state of Israel. How would you go about it? Would you contact your friends and ask them to come? Use social media such as Facebook to advertise the event? Perhaps look up people with Jewish-sounding names and contact them, asking them to join your rally? Or, rather than building everything from scratch, would you contact all the synagogues in your area and ask them to support your effort and urge their congregants to come?

On April 15, 2002, the largest-ever rally in the United States in support of Israel was organized precisely by contacting all synagogues in the United States via national Jewish organizations. Held in Washington, DC, on the Mall, it attracted over 100,000 supporters of Israel. The rally took only a week to plan and attracted supporters from diverse places in the United States, including California, Georgia, Indiana, Massachusetts, Michigan, Missouri, New Jersey, New York, Ohio, Tennessee, and Texas. It attracted important public figures, including then former Israeli prime minister Benjamin Netanyahu, Nobel Prize laureate Elie Wiesel, former New York City mayor Rudolph W. Giuliani, New York governor George E. Pataki, Deputy Secretary of Defense Paul D. Wolfowitz, and several members of Congress and senators, both Republicans and Democrats.[1]

This is an example of a more common phenomenon where religious institutions are used to organize for political actions, both peaceful and violent. "All of the major world religions include organizations of believers who advocate for political issues" (Toft *et al.*, 2011: 22). This type of organization is called political mobilization. "Religious institutions are neither designed nor intended to mobilize political action.

Yet, across the globe, they seem to have done precisely that" (Wald *et al.*, 2005: 121). This chapter examines this significant religious influence on politics.

RELIGIOUS INSTITUTIONS AND POLITICAL RESOURCE MOBILIZATION

A huge branch of political science literature is devoted to how people organize for political action. While a full evaluation of this literature is worthy of a book in and of itself, for our purposes a brief overview is sufficient. This literature does not focus on the causes of conflict and assumes that groups have collective interests or common goods which they pursue in the political arena. The literature focuses on how these groups go about attaining these goals (Rule, 1988). The most important variables in this literature are opportunity structure and resources. Opportunity structure deals with the opportunities for political action. For example, peaceful protest movements are more likely in democracies than in autocratic states because the latter repress such tactics and the former encourage them. I first discuss the resources element of this literature and address opportunity structure later in the chapter in the context of explaining when religious organizations choose to engage in political mobilization.

The resource mobilization literature posits that the ability to organize for political action is heavily influenced by the resources that are available for mobilization and the success of a political movement in finding a way to mobilize these resources.[2] My basic argument is that religious institutions have access to significant resources, are able to mobilize them efficiently, and are in and of themselves potentially powerful resources for political resource mobilization.

It is clear that traditional religious organizations such as churches, mosques, and synagogues were not created in order to organize for political activity but, rather, to defend and protect a religion and its believers, organize religious activities, to formalize and maintain religious doctrine, to transmit the religion from one generation to the next, to provide religious services for congregants, and to train clergy and develop their leadership skills, among other activities. Yet the resources and skills necessary for political mobilization strongly overlap with the resources needed to perform these religious tasks. They include:

- *A public pulpit*: Religious institutions and clergy are often publicly recognized and high-profile. Thus, when they publicly address an issue it is very likely that it will be noticed by both political leaders and the media. In fact, religious organizations often have direct access to the media, and even have their own media outlets. This can help them to publicize an issue or political event (Hadden, 1987a: 5–6; Harris, 1994: 45; Johnston and Figa, 1988: 36–37; Martin, 2005: 831; Minkenberg, 2009: 1195). For example, high-profile US televangelists have used their public pulpits to organize influential political movements. Jerry Farwell organized the Moral Majority in 1979 and Pat Robertson organized the Christian Coalition in 1989. Both of these organizations had significant influences on political discourse and even elections in the United States (Penning, 1994; Shields, 2007; Wilcox *et al.*, 1991).

- *Political connections*: As influential social organizations, religious institutions and clergy often have significant political connections. In both democratic and non-democratic countries, religious institutional support is valuable to politicians and governments. These connections can be translated into political influence on behalf of a cause, as can a religious organization's ability to influence the votes and opinions of its congregants. Often, religious institutions have international connections that can also be tapped to support a cause or are themselves international, increasing their connections and resources (Rubin, 1994: 31; Martin, 2005: 831; Minkenberg, 2009: 1195). Johnston and Figa (1988: 42–43) argue that in hierarchical religious organizations these connections have an interesting dynamic. The higher ranked the clergy member, the better the political connections but also the higher the chance that he will support the government rather than protesters against it. Some religious figures such as the Pope and the Dalai Lama are so influential that they nearly automatically attract the attention of high-ranking politicians, and their visits are treated as diplomatic visits. While these are exceptional examples, they represent a more widespread political influence that is common among clergy members.
- *A place to meet and organize*: Religious institutions generally include a meeting room where services are held, as well as smaller rooms for meetings and conferences. These rooms are just as useful for political meetings.
- *Organizational resources*: Like any organization that organizes people, a religious institution usually has basic office and organizational resources, including an office with basic resources such as phones, faxes, an internet connection, and computers. They also have internal communication resources such as mailing and e-mail lists, pages on social networks such as Facebook, and the simple ability to make announcements in newsletters and religious services. All of these resources can be mobilized to inform congregants about a political cause (Harris, 1994: 48; Minkenberg, 2009: 1195; Wald *et al.*, 2005: 135–136).
- *Financial resources*: While money is not absolutely necessary for political resource mobilization, it certainly helps. Religious institutions often have significant financial resources and access to potential donors (Minkenberg, 2009: 1195).
- *Leadership and civic skills*: Religious institutions develop leadership skills in both clergy and laypersons. Participation in religious organizations beyond simply attending services can develop both leadership and civic skills. For instance, running the women's auxiliary, organizing a clothing donation drive, and the many other charitable, social, and civic activities that occur under the auspices of a religious institution develop leadership and civic skills. A pool of people with these skills who are active in a religious institution and, accordingly, likely to become involved if called upon is thus created. These leadership and civic skills can be tapped for political purposes (Ayers and Hofstetter, 2008: 5–6; Harris, 1994: 48; Hill and Matsubayashi, 2008: 571). However, religious leaders are used to talking to homogeneous audiences, so these skills can be limited when dealing with those who are not members of their congregations or similar congregations (Wald *et al.*, 2005: 133–134).
- *Congregants*: The congregants of a religious institution can be a resource in and of themselves. On a mass level they can provide the basic human resources for a

movement and, if mobilized, increase the numbers attending political rallies and protests. They can spread awareness of issues among their own social networks. They also often include skilled professionals with skills relevant to political activities such as public relations, advertising, and logistics, among many others.

In addition to the tangible resources associated with religious institutions, there are several less tangible resources that also can facilitate mobilization:

- *Legitimacy*: As is discussed in detail in Chapter 5, religion can lend legitimacy to nearly any cause. Religious institutions are significant arbiters of religious legitimacy. This resource makes people more willing to participate and support political action (De Juan, 2008; Johnston and Figa, 1988: 37; Wald *et al.*, 2005: 132).
- *Ideology and symbols*: Beyond lending legitimacy to a political movement, religious institutions can link religious beliefs, ideologies, and symbols to a movement. If a political cause is supported by religious beliefs, it is easier to motivate believers to participate. Also, as is noted in Chapter 4, religious belief systems filter information and help us understand reality. Such a religious understanding can have a significant influence on how people relate to political issues (Ayers and Hofstetter, 2008: 5; De Juan, 2008: 1123).
- *Motivation*: While this category could be placed under legitimacy or ideology and symbols, it is related to both of these, yet in a way separate. Certainly the legitimacy of a cause and its connection to religious beliefs can motivate individuals to participate, and strengthen their levels of participation. However, beyond this, "whereas individuals tend to be risk-averse about challenging the government in general, a sense of belonging to a sacred community can . . . embolden individuals to act in ways that may appear individually irrational outside the religio-cultural context" (Wald *et al.*, 2005: 132).
- *Bridging effect*: In societies that are religiously homogeneous but fragmented along political, social, or class lines, religion can be a bridge between factions. It can frame an issue as transcendental and beyond a country's divisive politics. Hence, it can create alliances and coalitions that might not otherwise be possible. Thus, support of religious institutions for a cause can create this effect (De Juan, 2008: 1122–1123; Hadden, 1987a: 5–6; Johnston and Figa, 1988: 38). Glynn (1988: 835) argues that this occurred in the 1990s to bridge racial differences in the United States:

> Several Evangelical organizations, including the Southern Baptist Convention and the National Association of Evangelicals, have launched fresh initiatives on race during the decade. But the backbone of the new reconciliation effort is the Promise Keepers organization—American Evangelism's new fast-expanding, all-male crusade—which has made racial reconciliation a major theme of its revival. Founded in 1990 by former Colorado University football coach Bill McCartney and targeted at Protestant men, the movement has by now drawn more than 2 million to its revival rallies, typically held in major sports stadiums around the country.

Interestingly, this bridging effect can also bridge between religions. When two religious groups have similar political interests, the result can be a political alliance between them, which in turn can strengthen ties between the religious groups.

- *Protected status*: While religious organizations are not invulnerable, their popularity, high profile, and legitimacy make governments reluctant to challenge them. Accordingly, in societies that are less free, religious institutions can provide a safe place to organize, or at least a relatively less dangerous place. As is discussed in detail in Chapters 10–13, governments can and do attack and shut down religious organizations they consider to be political threats. However, they are often less willing to do so than they are with political organizations meeting under other auspices. The willingness of a repressive government to attack a religious institution is dependent on several factors, including popular support for the institution (which if present increases the price of attacking it), the perceived level of threat from the political movement the religious organization supports, and the extent to which the government is dependent upon that religious institution for its legitimacy (Fox, 2008; Johnston and Figa, 1988: 35; Rubin, 1994: 31). A high-profile example was the Solidarity movement in Poland in the 1980s. This movement, which led a successful movement against Poland's Communist regime in the 1980s, was aided by the organizational resources of the Catholic Church (Piekalkiewiez, 1991). In contrast, in response to a 1999 protest in Beijing by the Falun Gong—a spiritual movement that combines Buddhism and Taoism—the Chinese government banned and severely repressed the organization because it considers the movement a political threat.

There have been numerous studies of the role of religious organizations in political processes. They tend to find that membership in religious organizations influences voting, stands on political issues, and the likelihood that an individual will participate in other forms of political activities (e.g. Peterson, 1992; Beyerlein and Chaves, 2003; Jones-Correa and Leal, 2001).

RELIGION AND THE "FREE RIDER" PROBLEM

Another branch of the resource mobilization literature, developed by Mancur Olson (1971), argues that the types of resources really necessary for political mobilization are different than one would expect. This is because of what Olson classically termed the "free rider" problem. Essentially, all political movements tend to seek what Olson calls a "collective good," which he defines as any resource that has value but cannot be denied to those who do not participate in a movement. For example, the civil rights movement in the United States in the 1960s and 1970s succeeded in increasing civil rights in that country, especially for minorities. However, those who did not participate in the movement benefited just as much from this collective good of civil rights as those who participated. These non-participators are the free riders.

This brings up the question: Why participate? If I get the same collective good whether I participate or not, why should I participate? Participation has costs in time, personal resources, and in some cases personal risk. If I stay home, essentially I get something for nothing. Yet people do participate in political movements. Olson argues that this is because of "selective incentives"—a benefit beyond the collective good that only those who participate get. Religious institutions can provide some of these selective incentives, thus facilitating political mobilization.

These religious selective incentives overlap with the list of religious resources for mobilization described earlier. Religious beliefs, legitimacy, and motivation can create a religious benefit for those who participate. They have done a good deed, one for which they can gain a spiritual reward. Participating through a religious institution can also increase one's social status within that institution. This enhanced status is especially attractive to those whose social lives are strongly connected to their congregation. Thus, in this branch of mobilization theory too, the ability to mobilize for political action can be significantly facilitated by religious institutions.

THE DOWNSIDE OF RELIGIOUS-BASED MOBILIZATION

From the above description one would think that all political movements would use religious institutions to organize, and all religious institutions would be involved in political movements all the time. Yet this is clearly not the case. That is because there are a number of factors that place pressure on religious institutions to avoid this kind of participation.

First, devoting time and resources to political issues takes time and resources away from religious ones. Religious institutions are rarely if ever created to engage in politics, but rather to serve the religious community. If clergy are away at a protest, they are not around to provide spiritual guidance to their congregants, lead services, console mourners, and all the many other functions of the clergy. Similarly, to the extent that resources are devoted to a political issue, they are less available for the day-to-day functioning of the organization, which can undermine the organization's ability to function.

Second, political issues can be divisive. While studies show that religion can influence stands on political issues, I am aware of no study which shows that belonging to a particular religious denomination creates unanimity on political issues, though it is possible that religion can create near-unanimity if the issue is directly related to a core belief or doctrine, an issue I discuss in more detail later in the chapter. Taking a political stance can upset or even alienate congregation members who disagree with this stance. The result can be to lower their participation in, and even loyalty to, the institution. As religious institutions have a tendency to desire more members rather than fewer, this is a serious consideration. However, an interesting study shows that congregants are less troubled by clergy with whom they disagree on political issues if they believe their clergy are doing a good job. That is, "when church members are satisfied with the religious and spiritual benefits the church offers to them, clergy then have more latitude to pursue political action" (Djupe and Gilbert, 2008: 49).

Third, organizers of political action in some cases may not want the endorsement of religious figures and institutions. This occurs when an institution in and of itself is perceived as being outside the mainstream or is otherwise disliked. In these cases the public involvement of a religious institution in a political movement can actually push away more followers than it attracts. Jerry Falwell's infamous comments after 9/11 are a good example of this.

> Used to speaking in terms of good and evil to a like-minded audience, the charismatic Falwell used the tragedy of September 11 to reiterate his familiar political mantra, namely that people who are not conservative Christians are ruining America. He held liberals, gays, prolife groups, civil libertarians, and others to blame for God's decision to withdraw the cloak of protection surrounding the United States, permitting the hijackers to do their work.
>
> (Wald *et al.*, 2005: 133)

Fourth, there can be costs to the institution itself for participation in political movements, especially those that are against the government. Religious institutions commonly receive funding and support from governments. The RAS dataset shows that in 147 of 177 (83.1 percent) of countries the government provides some sort of financial support for at least some religious institutions. Protesting against the government can in some cases put this funding at risk. In autocratic societies, and even occasionally in democratic ones, the participation of religious institutions in opposition movements can lead to government reprisals against these religious institutions.

In recent years the Catholic Church's opposition to President Chávez of Venezuela has led to such a situation. President Chávez's government has continually clashed with the Catholic Church. Chávez believes that the Catholic Church disregards the poor while siding with the oligarchy intent on ousting him from power.[3] In 2008 some priests left the mainstream Catholic Church to form the Reformed Catholic Church—a breakaway church openly supportive of President Chávez.[4] Many claim that this church is funded by the government, though church officials deny this. They claim to share the humanistic and socialist goals of helping the Venezuelan masses.[5] The Catholic Church condemned the Reform Catholic Venezuelan Church for "usurping its rites." Nevertheless, the Catholic Church's perceived support for Chávez's opponents led to an unwanted schism and competing institutions.

Fifth, this issue of state reprisals against religious institutions becomes more complicated when the state and religion are mutually dependent. A mutually dependent relationship, in this case, is defined as one in which the state and religious institutions provide mutual support and legitimacy to each other. As is described in more detail in Chapter 5, the state grants the religion privileges which can range from financial support to enforcing the religion among the populace. In return, the religion ideologically supports the state's right to rule. There are often additional entanglements, including that the government plays a role in the appointment of religious officials and religious officials play a role in government, usually as policy advisers. While this relationship was more common in premodern times, to the extent that it exists today the religious institutions in question are unlikely to facilitate mobilization against the state precisely because they are so closely intertwined with the state (Toft *et al.*, 2011: 48–58). For example, 37 (20.9 percent) of the states in the RAS dataset are involved in the process of appointing the clergy of the dominant religion in the state. Since their jobs are dependent, at least in part, on government approval, this arguably makes them less likely to support protests against the government.

Sixth, states will often restrict the rights of religious organizations to participate in politics, precisely to prevent mobilization against the state. For example, according to the RAS dataset, 24.9 percent restrict the ability of clergy or religious institutions to engage in political activity, 23.2 percent monitor or restrict clerical sermons, mostly for political content, and 13.4 percent restrict clergy from holding political office. A total of 42.4 percent of countries limit religious participation in political activities in at least one of these ways.

For example, article 28 of Costa Rica's constitution states that "clergymen or secular individuals cannot make political propaganda in any way invoking religious motives or making use of religious beliefs." Articles 131, 142, and 159 specifically state that the president, vice president, members of the cabinet, and justices must be laypeople.[6] Article 82 of El Salvador's constitution similarly states that "no ministers of any religion . . . may belong to political parties [or are] eligible for elective office. They may not make political propaganda in any form."[7]

Seventh, often governments will even go so far as to create their own state version of the majority religion in order to make sure that political organization against the state via religious institutions is not possible (Fox, 2008). The state-supported versions of Islam in Kyrgyzstan, Tajikistan, Turkmenistan, and Uzbekistan (discussed in Chapter 3) are a good example of this phenomenon. In all of these cases the state supports, officially or unofficially, a state version of Islam and represses all other Islamic institutions precisely in order to avoid a religious threat to the state. In such situations, religious institutional support and facilitation of political movements other than those desired by the state is extremely unlikely.

Eighth, while this overlaps with several of the above categories, it is important to emphasize that there are states, usually autocratic ones, that do not tolerate opposition at all, even from religious institutions.

WHEN DO RELIGIOUS INSTITUTIONS MOBILIZE?

Given these crosscutting pressures on religious institutions on the issue of political mobilization, can we predict when an institution will or will not support political activities? Exact prediction is not possible but we can identify a number of factors that will contribute to this decision.

Perhaps the most basic issue is opportunity structure. As has already been noted, in some situations the costs of participation can be extremely high and even threaten the existence of an institution. A simple example is that protest movements tend to be more acceptable in democracies than in autocracies. In some cases, government control is sufficiently high that no real opportunity to engage in political activity exists, at least not without prohibitively high costs. As is noted earlier, the Falun Gong discovered that protesting against the Chinese government had an extremely high cost.

The concept of opportunity structure can be expanded into a more basic question of costs and benefits. Mobilization has costs. In addition to the costs described in the "Downside of religious-based mobilization" section of this chapter, these costs can include political resources such as the using of political currency or the loss of influence that occurs when one mobilizes against a government, especially if the religious institution and government are former allies. It can include material resources such as money and time. These costs can involve loss of congregants, institutional legitimacy, and future monetary donations if the cause is unpopular.

Potential benefits include the collective good sought by the movement, though this potential is realized only if the movement is successful. For this reason, the probability of the movement's success is also a consideration. Other benefits include the fact that engaging in political movements can attract congregants and, if the cause is popular, increase the legitimacy of a religious institution. Successful political actions can also lead to political influence.

Religious ideology has two influences on this decision. First, "It has long been understood, first, that different religious faiths have different orientations toward social and political problems and how such problems—of individuals or the community at large—should be addressed" (Hill and Matsubayashi, 2008: 571). That is, religious ideologies often have something to say about the desirability of political involvement. Yet the level of support within a religion for political action is not fixed and can vary over time (Toft *et al.*, 2011).

Second, when a core religious value is at stake, mobilization via religious institutions is more likely than when it is not. That is, religious institutions are more likely to organize politically in support of a core religious value than for some cause, no matter how worthy and otherwise important, in which no such value is at stake.

Similarly, though distinctly, religious institutions are likely to mobilize when they see a threat to institutional survival. Bellin (2008: 320–321) argues that

> the differential development of confessional parties across Europe was a consequence of church and lay leaders responding to two conditions:(1) liberal attack, and (2) the political resources available to parry that liberal attack. Where liberal attack was absent (for example, in Ireland and Spain) no mobilization of confessional parties was motivated, no matter how Catholic the populace. Where liberal attack was present, the church proved willing to support confessional parties, but only as a last resort when no alternative political strategies were available.

Gill (1998) similarly argues that the political mobilization of the Catholic Church against Latin American governments was guided by institutional survival. He argues that such opposition occurred only in countries where the church was losing members to Protestant denominations because of being associated with unpopular governments. Otherwise, the church did not oppose a government and chose to maintain its preferential treatment by those governments.

The interests of an institution's congregants are also important. When a cause is popular among congregants, supporting that cause can be a way to mobilize congregants into a political institution or maintain their existing support (Fawcett, 2000). Put differently, not only can religious institutions facilitate political mobilization, but political mobilization can strengthen religious institutions.

CONCLUSIONS

Religious institutions are central to organized religion. Their central purposes include organizing religious activities, providing religious services to members, maintaining religious doctrine and transmitting it from generation to generation, training clergy, and defending the religion and its believers. Yet religious institutions are also suited to facilitating political mobilization, to the extent that it can seem as if they were created for exactly that purpose. They are high-profile organizations that often have political connections. They have the physical resources for mobilization, including a place to meet, organizational and financial resources, an experienced leadership, and human resources. They have a status in society that gives efforts supported by them legitimacy, allows them to be a bridge between different elements of society, and makes governments reluctant to challenge them. Furthermore, religious institutions often have political interests and agendas. This dynamic has often resulted in religious institutions playing a central role in politics. It is also the reason that the facilitation of political mobilization by religious institutions is likely among the most common and certainly among the most important avenues for religion to influence politics.

DISCUSSION QUESTIONS

1 Can you think of an example of a religious institution organizing a political event or supporting a political movement? Were its efforts effective? If so, were they more effective than might have been the case if the organization had been handled by a secular political organization? Why?
2 How much influence do you think religious institutions have on the political process? To what extent does each of the resources of religious institutions that can be applied to mobilization that are listed in this chapter contribute to this influence?
3 Do you think the advantages of using religious institutions for mobilization outweigh the disadvantages? If so, is this under all circumstances or only some circumstances? If only under some circumstances, what are those circumstances?

FURTHER READING

Harris, Fredrick C. "Something Within: Religion as a Mobilizer of African-American Political Activism" *Journal of Politics*, 56 (1), 1994, 42–68.
Hill, Kim Q. and Tetsuya Matsubayashi "Church Engagement, Religious Values, and Mass–Elite Policy Agenda Agreement in Local Communities" *American Journal of Political Science*, 52 (3), 2008, 570–584.
Johnston, Hank and Jozef Figa "The Church and Political Opposition: Comparative Perspectives on Mobilization against Authoritarian Regimes" *Journal for the Scientific Study of Religion*, 27 (1), 1988, 32–47.
Wald, Kenneth D., Adam L. Silverman, and Kevin S. Fridy "Making Sense of Religion in Political Life" *Annual Review of Political Science*, 8, 2005, 121–143.

CHAPTER 7

Rational and Functional Religion

While elements of this perspective have already been addressed in the first six chapters of this book, the argument that religion is a potential tool for policy makers has been treated as part of a larger picture where religion also has an independent influence. The theoretical perspectives discussed in this chapter perceive religion as a dependent variable rather than an independent one. That is, they look at religion primarily as something that is not an independent influence on society and politics.

Until this point in the book, religion has been addressed primarily as a significant influence on politics in and of its own right. Even Chapter 5's analysis of religious legitimacy considers religion as a phenomenon that exists independently, even if it is sometimes used as a tool for persuasion. That is, while religion can be used as a tool, this is only one aspect of its political and social significance, and it retains an independent influence.

However, there are several schools of thought that dispute this perspective. This chapter examines bodies of theory that look at religion as mostly a consequence of secular, rational actors and forces in society and politics. Some of these bodies of theory take this perspective to the point that they contend that religion is no more than a tool of other social and political actors and that religion policy is the outcome of purely secular and political calculations.

These perspectives are important because they provide insight into important elements of religion's interaction with other social and political forces. However, restricting one's understanding of religion and politics to the insights of this type of perspective is limiting because it represents only a portion of religion's interactions with the political.

FUNCTIONALISM

Functionalism is a sociological school of thought that focuses on the functions religion and religious institutions perform in society. It is not a monolithic school of thought but as a body of theory its proponents are in general agreement on two central arguments that are relevant to our purposes: First, religion can be socially understood through the functions it performs in society. That is, the only aspect of religion that is relevant socially—and by implication politically—is what it does to and for society. Second, these functions are determined not by religious institutions, leaders, and theology but rather by other social institutions and forces that use religion to perform these functions.

To be clear, this means that from a functionalist perspective, religious theologies and institutions are created and manipulated by other forces in society solely for the benefit of these secular forces. Religion is a tool that serves a function. The identity of these other forces varies depending on the version of functionalism in question. For example, the Marxist argument that religion is the opiate of the masses has religion as a tool of the ruling class (feudal lords or capitalists, depending on the era) to keep the masses satiated and in line. When Marx referred to opium, he was referring to religion as a drug that placates and pacifies the masses. Had he been writing today, he might have referred to religion as the crack cocaine, heroin, crystal meth, or ecstasy of the masses. This theme of social control is one that can be found in many versions of functionalism (Beckford, 1985; Friedrichs, 1985: 361).

This perspective of religion as a tool is critically important. If religion is nothing more than a tool, it becomes a secondary factor at best in politics. Why? Because if religion is simply a tool used by other social forces and institutions, true understanding of what is really occurring can be found only in the motivations of and influences on these more central institutions and forces. That they chose to use religion to accomplish these goals is as about as relevant as whether a murderer chooses a 9-millimeter automatic gun or a .44 Magnum to shoot his victim. It is the person who holds, points, and shoots the gun who has the answers to why they fired the gun, not the gun itself.

The following social functions of religion overlap somewhat, but each describes a distinct function of religion that can be found in the functionalist literature:

- *Social control*: As has already been noted, social control is an oft-cited function of religion. As is discussed in Chapter 4, religion provides rules and standards of behavior. It also provides a fear of divine punishment for those who do not abide by the rules. Religious institutions transmit and, to varying extents, enforce those rules. The rules can be an effective and efficient tool for social control. They maintain norms of behavior that are useful to society, including bans on antisocial and criminal behavior, as well as respect for authority and the existing political and socials hierarchy (Martin, 1989: 352–353; Pickering, 1984: 307–312; Schoenfeld, 1992: 111).
- *Social stability and social change*: Lewy (1974: 3) argues that

> religion has often been a force upholding the status quo, reinforcing the stability of society and enhancing political quietism. . . . And yet, religion

has also been an important force for facilitating radical political and social change, providing the motivation, ideological justification, and social cohesion for rebellions and revolutions.

This speaks to religion's ability to form, maintain, and change social structures.

- *Morality and values*: Religion provides a basis for what is moral and for what values a society holds. That is, it can help determine what is considered acceptable behavior and what is not, what goals are desirable and what goals are not. This function overlaps with the previous two but deserves separate mention because it goes beyond social control and stability. Morality can influence and even determine a wide variety of types of behavior, which can go beyond social control and serve other purposes. For example, the morality of wealth accumulation and a religion's work ethic can significantly influence a country's economy as well as its social hierarchy (Wilson, 1982: 38–42). This is precisely the argument Max Weber (1930) makes in his classic work *The Protestant Ethic and the Spirit of Capitalism*.
- *Understanding*: We human beings have a need to understand the world we live in and our place in it. We also have a need to understand the un-understandable. This includes questions like: Who are we? Where do we come from? What is our purpose on this earth? What happens after we die? And why is there evil in this world? Religions provide answers for these questions. Religions also often explain the physical universe. Durkheim classically addresses this, arguing that primitive man had a religious explanation for everything. Why does the sun rise in the morning? In Greek mythology, it's the wheel of Apollo's chariot. Durkheim's distinction between modern man and primitive man is that modern man distinguishes between the natural—what he can understand through science and reason—and the supernatural, which is everything else (Durkheim, 1964; Geertz, 1973: 123; Pickering, 1975: 77–78, 1984: 303; Spiro, 1966: 109). Psychologists argue that this function of religion can be essential for humans to function because it gives stability and coherence to our conceptual system (Silberman, 2005: 645).
- *Solace*: Human suffering is inevitable and people need sources of solace for that suffering. Religion provides this solace, in part through its role in providing understanding, but it also goes beyond that. In its role in providing understanding, it can provide explanations for events, and beliefs that bad things such as death are truly the beginning of a wonderful experience for the departed. In addition, it provides rituals of mourning to deal with death and other rituals to deal with other forms of suffering as well as a social support structure to help those who suffer. This function also supports social solidarity and stability (Lincoln, 1985: 267; Silberman, 2005: 645). When combined, solace and understanding form what Wilson (1982: 26–32) called religion's manifest function: its ability to offer reassurance and salvation.
- *Identity and social solidarity*: As is discussed in detail in Chapter 3, religion creates links between people. People who share religious beliefs feel they are similar and belong to the same community. These feelings strengthen social solidarity and facilitate cooperation in a society. They can even bind people who might otherwise be antagonistic, and suppress conflict among social groups. This function

of religion is especially associated with Durkheim's theories on religion (Apter, 1964: 17–20; Mol, 1976; Turner, 1991: 109).

- *Legitimacy*: As is discussed in detail in Chapter 5, religion can legitimate governments. Geertz (1977: 267–278) argues that this function is still relevant today when he states that "thrones may be out of fashion and pageantry too; but political authority still requires a cultural framework in which to define itself and advance its claims, and so does opposition to it." Kokosalakis (1985: 371) similarly argues that the "strong residual element of religion, which clearly exists even in western societies, can still perform basic legitimizing or oppositional functions within such ideologies." Wilson (1982: 33–34) goes beyond this and argues that religion legitimizes the purposes and procedures of society as a whole.
- *Family*: Most religions strongly support another central social institution: the family. The family is essential to social stability. Religion is linked to marriage, child rearing, and inheritance, among other factors that are essential to defining and maintaining the family (Turner, 1991: 110–114).

Of course, these functions overlap. For the purposes of religion and politics, social control and stability are perhaps the most important, followed by legitimacy and identity. Be that as it may, if religion is a tool that serves all of these functions, it is a powerful tool indeed.

This theory is intimately linked to secularization theory. As is discussed in Chapter 2, a central argument of secularization theory is that secular institutions are replacing religious institutions in serving these functions in society. However, unlike secularization theory, functionalism cannot be disproven by showing that religion still influences society and politics. A functionalist can answer that of course it does, but that does not matter because religion is a tool. It is used by other social institutions and forces, and it is these institutions and forces that we should be studying.

Critiques of functionalism

Functionalism has its critics. Perhaps one of the most cutting criticisms is what Chaves (1994: 751) and Coleman (1990: 336) call "the functionalist fallacy." They point out that sociologists successfully document the fact that religious institutions serve a social function but do not prove that these institutions exist because of that function. To prove functionalism, sociologists would have to show that the need for a social function directly caused the establishment of an institution that satisfies that need. The critics contend that this has not been proven.

It is completely possible, even likely, that religion exists for other reasons and, once in existence, adapted to fulfill social functions, in addition to its primary purposes. If this is the case, the fact that religion serves social functions does not preclude it from having an independent influence on society. It is not unexpected that various social forces and institutions will interact, often influencing each other to attain desired goals. But just as these institutions use religion, they are also used by it. Religion and religious institutions are not just tools, though certainly they can be. They are also independent actors. Thus, if religion is sometimes the weapon that another hand wields, it is also sometimes the hand that wields other social and political institutions that it uses to serve its own interests.

Most serious critiques of functionalism are in some way related to the functionalist fallacy argument. For example, Francis Fukuyama (2001: 16–17) makes a similar argument:

> It is, of course, possible to try to give economic or rational explanations for religious and cultural phenomena, and thus to try to fit them into some larger theory of social behavior based on rational choice. There was for some time a school of "functionalist" sociology and anthropology that tried to find rational utilitarian reasons for the most bizarre social rules. The Hindu ban on eating cows was ascribed, for example, to the fact that cows were resources that had to be protected for other uses like plowing and dairy-farming. Similarly, one could try to explain the Protestant Reformation in terms of the economic conditions prevailing in central Europe in the 16th century that led people to respond to religious reformers like Luther, Calvin and Melanchthon. But ultimately, these accounts prove to be unsatisfying because they are too reductionist; all such historical developments usually incorporate a substantial measure of chance, genius, accident or creativity that cannot be explained in terms of prior conditions.

While he does not call this the functionalist fallacy, he is also essentially arguing that religion exists of its own accord and cannot be attributed to being cynically created to serve a rational social purpose.

Some, like Robertson (1985: 356–357), in addition to making this type of argument, declare functionalism to be damaging to our understanding of religion. He considered functionalism a legitimating mythos of sociologists of religion. While it can provide some useful perspective, to focus on it exclusively would be "throwing out the baby with the bath water." Pickering (1984: 300–301) similarly argues that functionalism is a useful perspective but one that must be balanced with other perspectives because "one must not reduce social phenomena to their utilitarian ends."

Thus, functionalism is a useful perspective for understanding some of the roles religion can play in society and politics, especially those roles that involve supporting other social and political actors and goals. However, to reduce religion to only its functionalist aspects would essentially limit our understanding of religion's role in politics and society to only a portion of its actual influence.

RELIGION AS A TOOL VERSUS AS AN INDEPENDENT FORCE IN POLITICAL SCIENCE THEORY

The debate referred to in the previous section is primarily among sociologists and, while relevant to political phenomena, rarely directly addresses them. Yet parallel functionalist-type arguments can be found in the political science literature regarding religion. For example, the instrumentalist and constructivist perspectives on religious identity discussed in Chapter 3 are essentially functionalist. Both argue that political entrepreneurs use religion to attain goals that often have little to do with religion. The arguments in Chapter 5 regarding religious legitimacy similarly have religion as a tool used by policy makers to support or oppose policies. In the same vein, in Chapter 6 I describe how religious institutions can be potent tools of political mobilization.

This role of religion as a political tool is real. It is not simply a theoretical attempt to explain away religion, though some who make this type of argument certainly have this goal in mind. Religion is commonly and cynically used as a political tool, and much political science theorizing on religion and comparative study of religion focuses on this aspect of religion.

Yet assuming that religion's only political influence is as a tool is essentially to commit the "sin" of the functionalist fallacy. Just because religion is used as a tool does not mean that it is only a tool and nothing else. For example, in Chapter 4 I discuss how religious frameworks of belief and religious rules and standards for behavior motivate behavior. While it is possible to argue that all such motivations were created for a social purpose, this argument is unconvincing when examined closely.

For example, if Al-Qaeda's radical ideology is a tool, who is using it? Certainly there are those who find an entity that attacks the West useful. However, it is hard to find any serious political actor which feels that way which is not also subject to attack by Al-Qaeda. Any secular or non-Islamic state is also in the crosshairs of Al-Qaeda and its allies, leaving just religious Islamic states as the possible forces using Al-Qaeda as a weapon against the West. Yet Saudi Arabia, perhaps the most fundamentalist of all Muslim states, has also been in Al-Qaeda's crosshairs. Saudi Arabia has arrested and issued additional warrants for the arrest of hundreds of suspected Al-Qaeda members who are accused of setting up terror cells to attack the country.[1] Iran has also arrested Al-Qaeda suspects for similar reasons.[2] Even if one argues that the Saudis and Iranians in the past created and supported Al-Qaeda, then lost control, a tool that stops following orders and bites the hand that once fed it is not at all consistent with the argument that religious forces are solely tools with no capability of independent action.

Furthermore, the political science theories that describe religion as a tool themselves contain evidence of religion as an independent actor. For instance, the discussion on religious institutions as tools for mobilizing for political action in Chapter 6 shows that a number of factors influence the decision by religious institutions on whether or not to facilitate political mobilization. These include how the action would influence institutional survival and the extent to which core religious issues are at stake. An institution that was simply a tool might take institutional survival into account in order to remain a good tool. However, that the religious content of an issue influences the institution's role in mobilization runs directly counter to the perspective that these institutions are no more than tools with no independent influence on their actions. In fact, this adherence by religious institutions to core religious beliefs whether or not this is convenient for other societal and political actors is perhaps the clearest evidence that religious institutions, no matter how entangled with other social and political forces they may be, usually retain an essential element of independence.

There are certainly exceptions to this independence in some repressive regimes that maintain high levels of control of religious institutions. However, even in most repressive states (North Korea, perhaps the world's most repressive state, possibly being an exception) there exist underground religious institutions that are not under state control. China, for example, while maintaining strict control of the official "mainstream" religious institutions, has numerous unofficial Muslim and Christian religious institutions. China's house church movement is one such movement and involves millions of Chinese people participating in Protestant religious institutions outside the government-controlled framework, despite significant repression of this movement by the government.[3]

Even the instrumentalist and constructivist perspectives, which specifically look at religious political action as a manifestation of religion being used by political actors, have within them elements that question whether religion is no more than a tool. Both the instrumentalist and the constructivist perspectives have it that political entrepreneurs activate religion in order to attain a political goal. This is true even of constructivist perspectives because these perspectives, with regard to religion, usually involve the remaking of existing religions, rather than creating religions from scratch.

This has two important implications. First, both of these perspectives are based on the assumption that religion is capable of motivating political behavior. This is, in and of itself, not incompatible with the argument that religion is a political tool. It just means religion is a useful tool. The second implication is that religion had not been a political tool in at least the recent past. Otherwise, it would not need to be activated. If religion is in fact nothing more than a potent social and political tool, why would it be dormant politically? Religion requires a considerable amount of resources and effort to maintain and it seems odd that that this effort would be invested in maintaining a tool that is not used for years, or even for decades or centuries, until some political entrepreneur comes along to activate it.

Take the case of the former Yugoslavia. Former president Milosevic certainly activated Serbian identity, including the Serbian Orthodox Church, for his own political gain. Yet prior to this, the church was to a large extent not merely politically dormant but just emerging from decades of repression and limitations under Yugoslavia's Communist regime. Yugoslavia's Communist government certainly had other tools to achieve the social functions served by religion, and in addition followed an ideology that was expressly and militantly anti-religious. Yet the Serbian Orthodox Church survived, as did its belief system, which it utilized to motivate its followers. This is considerably more consistent with the argument that this institution and the belief system it supports have an independent social and political basis than with the argument that they are no more than tools.

RELIGION AND RATIONAL ACTORS

The supply side theory

The "rational actor" approach to understanding religion first appeared in the 1990s as a school of thought in sociology also known as the "supply side" theory of religion.

This theory does not focus on political questions but on the question of why people are religious, though it does include some significant political elements. It uses economic logic and terminology to answer this question. The basic theory is that government policy on religion has a deep influence on whether people are religious, but not the relationship one would assume. One would assume that government support for religion would make a population more religious. However, supply side theory predicts that the more a government supports religion, the less religious the nation's population will be.[4]

Why is that the case? There are three major reasons found in this literature. The first, and perhaps primary, argument is that to the extent that a government retains a religious monopoly, there is less freedom of choice in the religious market. A religious market is defined as the interaction between religious denominations or institutions, known as religious "producers," on the one hand and potential con-gregants, or religious "consumers," on the other. In cases where all other denominations are repressed, the choice of religious producers is limited to one. Even in cases where the government only supports the state religion and does not limit or repress other religions, this creates an uneven playing field where the barriers to entry are higher for other religious producers. These minority religions must be supported privately while the state religion is supported by everyone's tax money, thus creating a higher financial barrier to participating in non-state religions. Essentially, minority religious consumers must pay twice for their product: once in the form of taxes and once in the private costs of supporting a religious institution.

When such a monopoly exists, religious consumers have limited choices. This means they are less likely to find a religious producer they like and, accordingly, are less likely to participate in religion. If this participation, usually measured in the literature through attendance at religious services, is defined as being religious, in a monopoly situation people become less religious.

In comparison, in a free religious market religions compete on a level playing field. In order to succeed, they need to make themselves attractive to religious consumers. As a result, there are more choices of religious producers, and empty niches get filled. This means religious consumers are more likely to find a choice that suits them.

It is important to note that all of this influences religious *participation* rather than religious *belief*. Belief—or the demand for religion—is not influenced by government religion policy, according to supply-siders, but participation varies depending on the ability of religious producers to fill that demand. Thus, the demand for religious product is not influenced by this dynamic, but when there is a religious monopoly, some of this demand is not met—that is, some potential consumers find no religious product they wish to "purchase."

Second, state-supported religions and their clergy provide relatively poor service to their communities in comparison to free religious markets. State-supported religions are less reliant on the goodwill of congregants for institutional survival. They are funded by the government, which also often gives them privileged access to religious consumers. This privileged access can include the teaching of religious courses in public schools and a visible presence at government functions. It can also include the enforcement of religious laws. Success within the clerical hierarchy is often more related to politics than to popularity among congregants. In fact, a job in the clergy can been seen as a path to political power, which can attract a different sort of job entrant as compared with a job that focuses on community service.

In contrast, in a free religious market only those producers that provide quality religious goods will survive the competition. Thus, not only is there an incentive to meet a congregation's needs, but it is essential to do so. In addition, clergy will be motivated to provide the best religious product possible because their jobs depend upon it. Thus, in a free religious market religious goods will tend to be superior and attract more congregants. Marginal consumers who may be unwilling to invest their time and efforts in a religion that provides a poor product will be more likely to consume a superior one.

Third, people resent being told what to do. States with official religions often enforce these religions through state law and policy. This causes resentment toward the state religion and a decrease in participation.

Critiques of the supply side theory

The supply side theory is very controversial and has many critics. A basic argument of these critics is that it does not fit the facts. The empirical literature testing the theory is problematic, for two reasons. First, the results of the studies are mixed, with some supporting and some contradicting the theory. Second, many of the studies that purport to test the theory do not actually do so. They actually test how religiosity is different in societies that are religiously diverse as opposed to societies that are religiously homogeneous. These studies assume that diversity means a lack of a state monopoly, which is often not the case (Fox, 2008; Fox and Tabory, 2008). This shortcoming in the empirical literature can be attributed to the fact that until recently, good data on state religion policy were not available.[5]

A second type of critique is that the theory does not take into account the non-Western experience. Most studies of the topic focus on the West, or a portion of the West, where there is state support for religion but the state religion has not been mandatory for generations. In contrast, in many non-Western societies, such as Saudi Arabia, state support for religion makes the religion, or aspects of it, mandatory, and these states have highly religious populations. Thus, this theory, to the extent that it is applicable, likely best describes the dynamics in free Western societies and is less relevant to less free and non-Western societies.

Third, the theory assumes that religious monopolies influence religiosity. Yet it is just as logical to assume that religiosity in a state influences the presence of religious monopolies. Religious pressure groups seeking to get a state to create and/or enforce a religious monopoly are not at all uncommon. Pressure to create a religious monopoly can also occur when people are becoming less religious and religious reactionaries want to use the government to enforce what was once common societal practice. Thus, this theory has a serious issue of directions of causality, or, if put more colloquially, a serious chicken-or-egg issue.

Fourth, the theory has a number of practical caveats. For instance, true religious monopolies cannot exist without the use of state coercion. To the extent that such coercion can be said to exist in the West, where the theory has primarily been tested, it is weak. Also, the religious market is not fully fluid. People who shift denominations rarely do so more than once in a lifetime, usually shift in the context of mixed marriages, and most often shift denominations within the same religion rather than leaving one religion for another. Thus, to the extent that the supply side theory is true, the dynamics require generations to play out. Even more importantly, the theory does not take into account that there are strong social benefits for staying within the religion into which one was born and there can be severe social sanctions for leaving it. For example, converting to another religion can cause resentment among family members and friends who belong to the religion that one is leaving.[6]

While this theory deals primarily with sociological phenomena, it is relevant to politics for two reasons. First, it postulates that a political decision regarding religion—whether a state supports a religious monopoly or not—has considerable social implications. Second, it pioneered a methodology of applying rational and economic theoretical thinking to the study of religion that is beginning to become popular among those who study religion and politics.

Religious liberty and rational calculation

In what is perhaps the most prominent application of rational actor reasoning to a clearly political issue, Anthony Gill (2005, 2008) argues that religious liberty—which he defines as both whether there is a state religion and whether minority religions are restricted—is purely the result of political calculations by politicians and religious institutions. His theory can be described in the following six propositions:

1   Religious majorities favor a religious monopoly, and religious minorities favor religious freedom. This is because religions make universal claims and want them to be believed universally. However, when they are in the minority, enforcing their claims is impractical and the best option for institutional survival is religious freedom. Thus, religious freedom will be dependent to a great extent on religious demography. Gill (2008: 45–46) argues persuasively that the Catholic Church's policy of sometimes pushing for a Catholic monopoly and sometimes pushing for religious freedom follows this model. That is, in countries where Catholics are a majority, the church tends to push for a privileged position, and in countries where Catholics are a minority, the church supports policies of religious freedom.
2   Politicians have the following goals in the following order: (1) political survival; (2) maximizing government revenue on the one hand and minimizing the costs of governing on the other. Their decisions on religion policy are based on these factors.
3   Where possible, politicians will try to co-opt religion to support the state and are willing to give privileges up to and including a religious monopoly to accomplish this. A state religion that supports the government costs government revenues, but these costs are less than those of coercion, so it is an efficient means to secure the compliance of the population. As a state–religion relationship can create a stable society, it also benefits politician's political survival.

4 "To the extent that political survival, revenue collection, economic growth and social stability are hindered by restrictions on religious freedom or subsidies to a dominant church, religious regulation will be liberalized or not enforced. . . . In other words, when restrictions on religious liberty have a high opportunity cost . . . deregulation of the religious market results" (Gill, 2008: 52).

5 The bargaining power of religious organizations is dependent upon the extent to which they are unchallenged by other religions and secular forces. To the extent this is true, there is a higher likelihood of a religious monopoly.

6 To the extent that political competition is limited, the government has less need of religious assistance in maintaining control and is, accordingly, less likely to grant and enforce a religious monopoly.

This model constitutes a perspective where both religious and political actors engage in a practical, even cold-blooded, cost–benefit analysis based purely on their political interests, the most important of which is survival. It also happens to be a good explanation for the variation in state support for religion (Guillermo, 2009).

Rational actor theories in perspective

This type of model for understanding religion is beginning to become more popular among political scientists and is crossing over from sociology precisely because it provides a useful perspective that helps us understand why important religious factors vary from place to place. However, this type of model, while not denying that religion is an independent force in society, does tend to bury this insight.

To return to Gill's model, religious institutions clearly have political interests that they pursue in the political arena, one of these being ideological hegemony: that their belief system be the only one to which people subscribe. Yet the desire for this ideological hegemony is based on religious motivations. Many religious people believe that they have access to the one and only truth and that it is their mission to spread this truth to the world. They may use rational and pragmatic calculations to achieve this end but their ultimate goal is guided by religious beliefs. Thus, the driving force behind much of Gill's model is religious belief. Yet at first glance it is difficult to see this in the model.

Given this, rational actor models can be useful for understanding religion's role in politics. However, it is necessary to place this type of model in the proper perspective, which balances rational calculations with an understanding of religion as an independent actor in society and politics. Toft *et al.* (2011: 34–39) provide six dimensions to measure this independence: First, and perhaps most obviously, the extent to which a state establishes a religion as the state's official religion limits independence. Second, protections for freedom of religion enhance independence. Third, independence is reduced when the state has a say in the appointment of religious leaders. Fourth, independence is lower when the religious leadership has a formal say in policy. While this is not religious discrimination, because it does not necessarily limit the religious institutions or practices of minority religions, it is a significant entanglement between religion and state. Fifth, when a state finances religion, this gives it a measure of control over the religious institutions it finances. Finally, religious institutions that are transnational, such as the Catholic Church, have a greater independence.

The RAS dataset has measures for the first five of these dimensions of independence: 24.3 percent of states have an official religion and an additional 23.7 percent unofficially support one religion more than others (which means that 48.0 percent of states either officially or unofficially establish a religion); 82.5 percent of discriminate against at least some minorities; 20.9 percent of states take part in the appointment process for religious leaders (this variable is part of the religious regulation index, which includes 29 types of government control over the majority religion or all religions); 82.5 percent of states engage in at least one of the actions included in this index; 4.0 percent of countries give religious officials government positions by virtue of their religious offices; and finally, 83.1 percent provide financing of some sort to religion. Only three countries fail to do any of the above: Burkina Faso, Namibia, and South Africa. This is not to say that religions have no measure of independence in the other 174 countries in the RAS dataset. But it does show that full and complete independence of religious institutions from the state is a rarer commodity than many believe.

Independence for religion has additional consequences. Toft *et al.* (2011) argue that giving religious actors independence has several positive consequences for society. It gives them the freedom and capacity to perform many positive functions in society, one of which is peacemaking between rival groups. It also includes a range of social services. In fact, the competition between religions for members makes it almost inevitable that religions will provide these special services to attract members. Also, the best strategy to attract members is to appeal to the majority, which tends to be in the middle of the spectrum, a fact which guarantees that mainstream religion will be moderate.

However, religious freedom is a double-edged sword. It can be beneficial to religion and society but it also makes room for more extremist niche religions. Religious freedom can also protect intolerant and extremist religions that seek to gain dominance and undermine the very religious freedom which nurtures them. Religious freedom can allow a sect to preach intolerance, hate, racism, and the overthrow of the government, and even set up schools where these principles are taught to children. This is most likely why 36.7 percent of states in the RAS dataset qualify religious freedom by limiting religious hate speech. It is also probably one of the reasons why 72.8 percent of the 158 countries with religious freedom clauses in their constitutions qualify that religious freedom in some manner.

RELIGION AND THE ECONOMY

While the supply side debate discussed earlier uses economic terminology to describe how religion functions in society, there is a long-standing tradition of arguing that religion has a direct impact on the economy. Most discussion of this issue dates back to Max Weber's (1930) classic work *The Protestant Ethic and the Spirit of Capitalism.*

Weber argues that economic development varies according to religious denomination. He posits that values inherent in Protestantism, especially Calvinism, helped develop capitalism more quickly in societies which followed these doctrines. For example, the Calvinist doctrine of predestination posits that people's place in the afterlife is predestined. That is, from birth it is already determined who will be going to heaven and who will be going to hell. Those who are predestined for heaven are also successful on this earth, which creates a motivation for economic success on this earth to demonstrate that one is destined for heaven in the afterlife. More generally, roughly to the extent that a religion focuses on this life rather than the next one, its believers will tend to be more economically successful. This is especially true of religions that encourage values of hard work and discourage laziness. Thus, charity would be limited because it encourages laziness. As a result, more funds would be available for reinvestment, creating further economic success.

For many decades this theory, while discussed, did not spur a large research program among social scientists. However, recently the question of the impact of religion on the economy has been attracting increasing interest. One aspect of this literature has been to test whether the differences Weber predicted between Protestant and Catholic economies have proven to be correct. The results are mixed. Cavalcanti *et al.* (2007: 105) find that differences between Protestants and Catholics "may possibly explain why Northern Europe developed before Southern Europe, but they cannot explain why Europe developed before Latin America." Norris and Inglehart (2004: 159–178) find that Catholics currently display more of a work ethic than do Protestants. Stulz and Williamson (2003) find that Protestant countries do a better job of protecting the rights of creditors than do Catholic countries.

Others have been asking how Islam influences the economy. Many see this impact as a negative one. Berger (2009: 72), for example, argues that Islam retards economic development: It discourages women from participating in the workforce. It ties social institutions to religion, limiting their flexibility and ability to adapt. It also encourages a conservative education which is less suited to a modern economy. Lewis (2003) argues that the support for state religion in the Islamic world has retarded economic growth, especially because it limits the growth of civil society, an essential requirement for economic growth, and a reliance on Islamic doctrine limits economic reform. Kuran (1991) argues that Muslim fundamentalists seek to curb demand with morality. Wong (2006) finds that religious freedom has a "positive impact on economic well-being when the majority religion of a country is Christian or Other and a negative impact on economic well-being when the majority religion of a country is Islam."

However, some dispute the notion that Islam retards the economy. Norris and Inglehart (2004: 167–168) find that Muslims have the strongest work ethic of any religious denomination. Other studies find that economic growth is higher in countries with larger Muslim populations (Noland, 2007; Sala-i-Martin *et al.*, 2004).

Another research program has asked whether religious beliefs in general influence the economy. Here too the results are mixed. Some studies find that religiosity or religious beliefs undermine the economy. For example, Barro and McCleary (2003) find that church attendance reduces economic growth but religious beliefs such as believing in hell increase it. Hilary and Hui (2009: 455) find that "firms located in counties with higher levels of religiosity display lower degrees of risk exposure." Kuran (1991) argues that fundamentalism is linked to a poorer economy because it leads to less economic flexibility. Mendelsohn (1993) similarly argues that the fundamentalists place moral restraints on aspects of scientific and technological development. In contrast, Guiso *et al.* (2003) find that religious beliefs are linked with attitudes conducive to higher per capita income and growth.

With some notable exceptions, this literature largely ignores the question of whether religion's impact on the economy, whatever that may be, is or is not functionalist—in that religion was designed to have this effect. Yet many of those who argue in favor of functionalism rely heavily on the writings of Max Weber. Also, the theoretical links between religion and the economy are strongly associated with the functions of religion discussed in the functionalist literature, especially social control, morality, and values. A functionalist view of religion's impact on the economy could argue that religion was designed to have an impact on the economy. It could also argue that this impact is an unintended consequence of a tool which was created for a different purpose.

CONCLUSIONS

Rational choice theory has been extremely influential in political science in general for the past several decades. Given this, it is not surprising that it is beginning to be applied to explain religion's role in politics. Both the rational choice and functionalist approaches can certainly provide insight into the interactions between religion and the political. Yet limiting oneself to this type of approach exclusively would likely lead to an imperfect understanding of the topic. Religious actors and political actors who interact with religious actors and institutions certainly can include rational calculations in their decision-making process. Religion can be a tool for other forces in society and politics. However, not all religious influences on politics are based on rationality, and secular actors manipulating religion for their benefit. As I argue in Chapter 4, religious belief systems motivate political behavior. While the agenda that is set by religious beliefs may be pursued rationally, the process for creating that agenda is influenced by elements of religious belief systems which are outside the universe that rational actor or functionalist theory can explain. Religious legitimacy may be a tool that rational actors can use, but the tool itself is based on a foundation that is more akin to religious beliefs than to rational calculations.

It is probably an understanding that combines an awareness of religion's non-rational elements with an understanding of rational actor approaches which will achieve the best explanation of religion's influence on politics and vice versa.

DISCUSSION QUESTIONS

1 Do you think religion performs necessary social and political functions? If so, does it do so better or worse than secular institutions? Please keep in mind that the answer can vary from function to function.

2   Do you think that freedom of religion would make you more or less likely to be religious than you would be in the following circumstances: (a) you live in a state which supports an official religion but does not make that religion mandatory; (b) you live in a state which obligates its citizens to observe an official religion through legislating that religion's laws as state law, which is enforced strictly?

3   Do you think policy makers decide on religion policy purely on the basis of their own political interests or do you think their religious beliefs also play a role?

FURTHER READING

Gill, Anthony "The Political Origins of Religious Liberty: A Theoretical Outline" *Interdisciplinary Journal of Research on Religion*, 1 (1), 2005, 1–35.

Gill, Anthony *The Political Origins of Religious Liberty*, New York: Cambridge University Press, 2008.

Guillermo, Trejo "Religious Competition and Ethnic Mobilization in Latin America: Why the Catholic Church Promotes Indigenous Movements" *American Political Science Review*, 103 (3), 2009, 323–342.

Iannaccone, Laurence R. "Voodoo Economics? Reviewing the Rational Choice Approach to Religion" *Journal for the Scientific Study of Religion*, 34 (1), 1995, 76–89.

Stark, Rodney and Roger Finke *Acts of Faith: Explaining the Human Side of Religion*, Berkeley, CA: University of California Press, 2000.

CHAPTER 8

Religious Fundamentalism

I am aware of at least two claims as to the origin of the term "fundamentalism," though these claims attribute the term to similar origins. Almond *et al.* (2003: 1–2) trace it back to a

> 1920 edition of the Northern Baptist (USA) periodical, The Watchman-Examiner, whose editor described himself and a group of conservative evangelical Protestants as militants willing to do "battle royal" to preserve the "fundamentals" of the Christian faith from the evolutionists and biblical critics infecting mainline seminaries and colleges.

Others trace it to similar US Protestant groups who published a series of paperbacks between 1910 and 1915 called *The Fundamentals*, which consisted of edited essays written by leading US conservative theologians who defended biblical inerrancy and attacked what they perceived as the evils of secular, theistic modernism (Barkun, 2003: 57; Emerson and Hartman, 2006: 131–132; Misztal and Shupe, 1992: 7).

As we will see in this chapter, basing the modern term "fundamentalism" on an early-twentieth-century group of US religious conservatives who sought to preserve the fundamentals of their faith against the onslaught of modern criticism, modernism, and secularism is quite appropriate. These characteristics are relevant to the core of what is today called fundamentalism. In this chapter I seek to define fundamentalism, outline its characteristics, comprehend its origins, and understand how fundamentalists and fundamentalist movements interact with the political.[1]

WHAT IS FUNDAMENTALISM?

In order to understand fundamentalism, it is essential to understand its causes. Essentially, fundamentalism is a reaction against modernity. As I discuss in more detail in Chapter 2, modernity has created a number of challenges to religion. These challenges are unavoidable and all religious movements must react to them. As I also note in Chapter 2, there are only three viable reactions to the challenges of modernity. The first is to accept modernity and rationalism and reject religion—the secular option. The second is to find some way to accept both modernity and religion. The third is to reject rationalism and modernity but embrace religion—the fundamentalist option.

Thus, fundamentalism, at its most basic, is a type of a religious framework of belief designed or evolved to defend religion against modernity through the rejection of modernity. Fundamentalists see modernity and secularism as a threat to religion. As discussed in Chapter 2, this is arguably an accurate assessment. Elements of modernity do undermine traditional religion, and secularism clearly competes with religion. Given this, it is not surprising that most of the unique, as well as the not so unique, characteristics of fundamentalism are geared toward protecting religion from modernity and secularism. Almond *et al.* (2003: 17) recognize this when they define fundamentalism as "a discernible pattern of religious militancy by which self-styled 'true believers' attempt to arrest the erosion of religious identity, fortify the borders of the religious community, and create viable alternatives to secular institutions and behaviors."

While there is no agreement in the literature as to the exact mix of characteristics associated with fundamentalism, the following characteristics are associated with fundamentalism in the literature.

Anti-modernity

As already noted, fundamentalism is a reaction against secularism, rationalism, and modernity. As a result, fundamentalist movements tend to oppose many aspects of modernity and, in fact, feel threatened by it. While these aspects can include technology, they usually do not unless the technology itself contradicts some basic religious principle. Contraceptives, for example, contradict many fundamentalist interpretations of Judeo-Christian values and are, accordingly, opposed by many fundamentalist groups. The science related to the theory of evolution is also often opposed by many Christian fundamentalists because it contradicts their interpretation of the first part of the book of Genesis.

Yet most fundamentalists drive or ride in cars, use modern medicine, and otherwise use and benefit from modern science and technology. More importantly, fundamentalists use modern communications technology and organizational techniques to further their movements (Eisenstadt, 2000b: 601; Esposito, 1998: 22; Lawrence, 1989: 232). Fundamentalist objections to science most often occur when the "decoupling" of religion and science has removed the normative restraints from modern technology. For a fundamentalist, technology and science must be subordinated to religious principles. They can be useful, but only with the proper moral guidance (Mendelsohn, 1993).

The primary focus of this opposition to modernity is against the ideas, philosophies, and theologies of modernity. A central aspect of these ideas, philosophies, and theologies is the proposition that rationalism and the sciences can replace religion's central role in guiding society and its values. Thus, television and the internet as technologies are not the central issue. What is an issue is much of the content transmitted through television and the internet. It is this content that undermines traditional values such as modesty and chastity. It is this content which promotes value systems that are in contrast with religious values (Emerson and Hartman, 2006: 134; Woodhead and Heelas, 2000: 32; Lawrence, 1989: 106–108; Lechner, 1993: 20–24; Marty and Appleby, 1991: 620). Put differently, most fundamentalists would not object to television and the internet if their content were consistent with their values. However, Western entertainment television shows are seen as promoting sexual promiscuity, among many other values that are in contrast with those of many fundamentalist belief systems. The internet's content is even more problematic for fundamentalists because it provides space for any and all ideas, not to mention pornography and gambling.

Fundamentalists go beyond rejecting modernity. They claim to be the solution to its problems. That is, they identify the weak points and dislocation caused by modernity and seek out those who have become alienated by modernity. They offer these people religion as a solution for these problems (Esposito, 1998: 21).

Boundaries

Fundamentalist groups erect boundaries between those who are members and those who are not. These barriers can be physical, in that some communities retreat from the world, building their own sealed communities. More often, these barriers are social, psychological, and behavioral. Members try to associate only with other members and avoid outsiders as much as possible. They develop particular modes of dress, behavior, and speech which distinguish them from non-members (Almond *et al.*, 2003: 52–54; Marty and Appleby, 1991: 4; Piscatori, 1994: 363–365). These modes of behavior are enforced within fundamentalist communities, sometimes violently (Sprinzak, 1991: 463–465). Many of these modes of behavior have similarities across many or even most religious movements. For example, emphasizing traditional family roles and personal modesty is a common mode of behavior in most fundamentalist movements.

Jewish ultra-Orthodox sects with their distinctive dress code are a good, if extreme, example of this. Many of them also make a point of speaking the Yiddish language among themselves, which currently is used as a day-to-day language practically exclusively among such sects. These are just two of the more obvious of many modes of behavior among these sects that make it clear to members who are insiders and who are not.

In addition, they often have their own independent social institutions. These include traditional religious institutions but also include schools, community centers, businesses, and burial societies. An individual born to this society can live their entire life with minimal contact with outside institutions or outsiders. All of this is designed to provide clear boundaries between the threatening and dangerous outside world and the protected and sheltered world created by fundamentalism (Emerson and Hartman, 2006: 134).

Black-and-white view of the world

Fundamentalists view the world as simple. There are right and wrong, good and evil, insiders and outsiders, and salvation and damnation. Boundaries are clear. There is no room for shades of gray (Almond *et al.*, 2003: 95–96; Ammerman, 1994: 150).

Elect membership

The members of fundamentalist groups consider themselves the elect or the chosen. They have exclusive access to the truth and hence are favored by God. This feeling supports boundary maintenance (Emerson and Hartman, 2006: 134; Almond *et al.*, 2003: 97; Frykenberg, 1994: 594).

Inerrancy of and focus on the texts

Inerrancy of and focus on the texts is the first among three sometimes contradictory characteristics that describe fundamentalist ideology and its relationship to religious texts. The overall social goal of fundamentalist ideology is to develop an ideology that allows the fundamental, essential, and authentic aspects of religion to survive in the modern era. In the search for authenticity, the sacred texts are emphasized. They are considered the inerrant and infallible sources for religious authenticity and are to be taken literally.

Theological innovation

As religion in its old format is seriously challenged by modernity, some theological innovation is necessary. Accordingly, a religion's central texts and ideologies are reinterpreted with a mind toward emphasizing a society that can meet the challenge of modernity. While this seemingly contradicts the concept of literal interpretation of the texts, these innovations are presented and understood within fundamentalist communities as proper and literal interpretations of these texts. That is, funda-mentalists reject outright the idea that these innovations are anything new (Almond *et al.*, 2003: 17–18, 49, 92; Esposito, 1998: 21; Gellner, 1992: 2; Don-Yehiyah, 1994: 268–269).

Selective emphasis

One of the methods of theological innovation is a selective emphasis on doctrines. Appleby (2000) argues that most religions have multiple and often contradictory doctrines, and which ones receive the emphasis can have a significant influence on which beliefs and doctrines guide behavior. Fundamentalists select specific aspects of doctrines that are most suited to protecting religious traditions from the threats of modernity and secularism (Marty and Appleby, 1994: 6).

Haym Soloveitchik (1994: 64–67) describes a shift in the understanding of religion by ultra-Orthodox strands of Orthodox Judaism during his lifetime which has all three of these characteristics. He describes traditional Judaism as being based on two equally important sources: (1) religious texts, and (2) Jewish tradition as transmitted from generation to generation by community practice and in the home. Traditionally, saying, "I do it this way because this is how my parents did it and how their parents did it before them" was a legitimate claim even when one was confronting religious texts. However, in modern times the community and the home are no longer considered authentic sources of religious authority. The emphasis now rests solely on the texts as taught in the yeshivas—religious seminary schools. "Common practice . . . has lost its independent status and needs to be squared with the written word." If a long-standing traditional practice is seen as contradicting the texts, the texts are considered authoritative and the traditional practice is abandoned.

These texts are being

> scoured, new doctrines discovered and elicited, old ones given new prominence, and the results collated and published. Abruptly and within a generation, a rich literature of religious observance has been created . . . [which] focuses on performances Jews have engaged in and articles they have used for thousands of years.

Yet the forms of practices emerging from this literature are innovative and new in that standards of religious practice are being created that had never before existed. "Religious observance is being both amplified and raised to new, rigorous heights." Practices that had been the norm for generations no longer suffice and are replaced with new, more rigorous practices that have a basis in the texts but had never before been applied in this manner (Soloveitchik, 1994: 67–73).

For example, Jewish religious practice has a concept called *humra*. A *humra* is a practice which intentionally meets a standard that is more stringent than the minimum standard for fulfilling a Jewish law or practice. In theory, an observant Jew is not required to abide by the standard of a *humra* to fulfill his religious obligation. Rather, observing the *humra*'s standard is only for those who choose to go the extra step when observing a law. Yet among the ultra-Orthodox, observing this more stringent standard has often become the minimum accepted practice, and in many cases new *humras* are created which then are considered obligatory.

This can be seen in the standards for kosher food in Israel. Jewish laws include dietary laws that limit what foods can be eaten and how food can be prepared. Food that meets these dietary requirements is called kosher. The application of *humras* to what food is considered kosher in Israel reflects this tendency to seek stricter standards. Traditionally, when food producers, such as companies that prepare food products, or restaurants, want recognition as producing kosher food, they seek a rabbinical certification that they observe the required practices. In Israel, the official rabbinate—which is supported by the government—maintains two standards: a normal certification and a certification known as a *mehadrin* certification, which meets a stricter set of standards. In essence, the standard certification certifies that the food meets the minimum standard for being considered kosher and the *mehadrin* certification certifies that the food meets standards that include several *humras*. For many ultra-Orthodox Jews in Israel, even the *mehadrin* certification is insufficiently strict. As a result, a number of private rabbinical organizations such as Badatz Edut HaHaredi, and the *mehadrin* certification of Rabbi Rubin, among many others, provide certifications that meet even stricter standards involving more *humras*. While the concept of the *humra* has always existed in Jewish law, in the past those who observed these *humras* were the exceptions. In most ultra-Orthodox Jewish communities today, these *humras* are the new standard. Arguably, these stricter standards serve to maintain borders between the ultra Orthodox Jewish community and other observant Jews whom the ultra-Orthodox consider too influenced by the modern world.

Soloveitchik (1994: 71–73) argues that this shift occurred because modernity undermined the traditional community to the extent that it no longer was capable of maintaining religious tradition. In the traditional community, adherence to religion was not just mandatory, there was no other option. This was simply how people lived, and there was no point in questioning it, and little inclination to do so. Religion as practiced in the community was what set the standard for behavior. In modern times, alternatives exist and

> adherence is voluntary. A traditional society has been transformed into an orthodox one, and religious conduct is less the product of social custom than of conscious reflexive behavior. . . . Behavior once governed by habit is now governed by rule. If accuracy is now sought, indeed deemed critical, it can be found only in texts.

This has resulted in "a tireless quest for absolute accuracy, for 'perfect fit'—faultless congruence between conception and performance—is the hallmark of contemporary religiosity. The search is dedicated and unremitting; yet it invariably falls short of success." The tools for this quest are the inerrancy of and focus on the texts, theological innovation, and selective reading of the texts.

As a result, among Orthodox Jews religious institutions replaced the home as the primary means for preserving the religious tradition. Yeshivas, which were once institutions for the elite and primarily trained the Jewish religious leadership, have become mass institutions. Jewishness, which was once taken for granted, has to be instilled. Among ultra-Orthodox Jewish sects, nearly all men now attend yeshivas until they are well into their twenties, and often considerably longer, in order to shore up their ability to maintain their Jewishness (Soloveitchik, 1994: 85–97).

The myth of the golden age

Fundamentalists tend to focus on a utopian golden age of religion where the religion was pure and perfect. Since then, there has been a decline in the religion's purity and perfection. Much of this decline is due to the purposeful and treacherous dilution of the religion by co-religionists. Much of their effort described here regarding theological change is designed to return to this mythical golden age of the past (Almond *et al.*, 2003: 55–62; Appleby, 2002: 503). "This 'history' filters untoward facts and glosses over the darker aspects of the past. Indeed, it often portrays events as they did not happen" (Soloveitchik, 1994: 82).

Authoritarianism

Fundamentalist leaders have taken authority over political, economic, and personal issues which in the past were under the purview of laity. Their opinion is sought and followed in all major life decisions (Almond *et al.*, 2003: 18, 78–83; Emerson and Hartman, 2006: 134; Hunsberger and Jackson, 2005: 809–810; Kuran, 1991). Among Israel's ultra-Orthodox Jews this authority is considerable. Rabbis are consulted regularly on issues of daily life, including where to live, where to send children to school, whom to marry, what names to give one's children, and where to work. Ultra-Orthodox rabbinical leaders instruct their congregants on whom to vote for in political elections and receive nearly universal compliance from their followers. Ultra-Orthodox political parties are guided by councils of highly regarded rabbis, and in some cases, such as the case of the Rabbi Ovadia Yosef and the Shas party, a single religious leader can direct the policy of major ultra-Orthodox political parties with multiple seats in Israel's legislative body as well as choose and remove its leaders (Kamil, 2000; Willis, 1995).

Absence of distinction between the public and private spheres

All aspects of life are important to fundamentalists and no aspect is private. Religious authority guides all aspects of life and behavior, including private and intimate zones such as sex and the family. While the family may no longer be a sufficient medium to transmit religious traditions, it is still the center of religious life and, accordingly, cannot be a wholly private matter (Garvey, 1991: 13; Hardacre, 1993).

> Fundamentalists have expended the greater portion of their energies, and have enjoyed greater success, in reclaiming the intimate zones of life in their own religious communities than in remaking the political or economic order according to the revealed norms of the traditional religion.
>
> (Marty and Appleby, 1993: 5)

Hierarchical and patriarchal relations between the genders

Fundamentalism is often associated with male-dominated societies where women are expected to defer to men (Hardacre, 1993; Woodhead and Heelas, 2000: 32). In fact, one of the main complaints of many fundamentalist movements regarding secularism and modernity is the undermining of traditional gender roles (Almond *et al.*, 2003: 28–30).

This list of traits should not be taken as absolute. Rather, it is a list of various traits attributed to fundamentalism in the literature. Few definitions and listings of the traits of fundamentalism include all of them, and there is little agreement over which among these traits is the most important. More importantly, while movements considered fundamentalist tend to conform to varying extents to most of these traits, few such movements strictly conform to all of them.

When comparing different fundamentalist movements across religions, it is arguable that these movements in many ways have more in common with each other than they do with their non-fundamentalist co-religionists. That is, these shared traits, when combined together, are so distinctive that fundamentalists constitute a brand of religion that is fundamentally different from previous manifestations of their religion tradition—so different, in fact, that fundamentalists can often share more with fundamentalists from other traditions than they do with other members of their own religion (Marty and Appleby, 1993: 5). Thus, while the examples I used here focus on ultra-Orthodox Judaism, similar traits are also present in Christian and Muslim fundamentalist movements.

Given all of this, religious fundamentalism is a modern phenomenon. It is built on the foundation of "old-time" religion, yet what has been built or has evolved is something distinctly new and modern. It would not exist without the threats posed to religion in modern times. Put differently, only a modern movement could reject modernity. Also, significant elements of fundamentalist movements, especially their organizational, communications, and recruitment techniques, rely on modern technology and methods. Thus, in trying to go back to a golden age of religion, fundamentalists have instead succeeded in going back to the future (Marty and Appleby, 1991: 3).

WHY IS FUNDAMENTALISM POLITICALLY RELEVANT?

Religious fundamentalists are politically relevant because they usually have a political agenda that matters deeply to them, one which they are strongly motivated to pursue. Any answer to the question of fundamentalism's political relevance is simply an elaboration upon this basic fact. In this section I discuss the nature of fundamentalist political agendas and how they manifest themselves in the political arena.

While the political agendas of fundamentalist groups are by no means monolithic, they all come from similar motivations. Essentially, fundamentalists believe something is not right in the world; the world does not conform to their religious ideology. Specifically, the religious utopia they seek does not exist on this earth. While some fundamentalists are more versed in their religion's texts than others, all of them have a notion of how the world ought to be. Modernity, secularism, and the corruption of their non-fundamentalist co-religionists have profaned the world. Things are not at all in order. Fundamentalists are strongly motivated to rectify this situation.

This leaves them with two options. The first is to withdraw from the world, to form a closed community in which they can create and preserve the environment they seek. These groups tend to be politically active only in support of their ability to maintain the independence and integrity of their closed communities. If they are left alone, they tend to pursue no further political agenda (Almond *et al.*, 2003: 146–187). Almond *et al.* (2003: 185–187) call these groups "world renouncers." They tend to be small and less well known unless they run afoul of secular authorities, as happened with the Branch Davidians in Waco, Texas, in 1993.

It is the second option that has had a serious impact on politics across the world. This option is to pursue an agenda of being active in the world in order to change the world to conform to the standards set out in their ideologies (Almond *et al.*, 2003: 146–187). Groups that fit this category are easily identified. They range from groups that support active political parties, such as the Shas party in Israel, to Al-Qaeda. These two groups have political agendas that are quite similar. Both groups seek to increase compliance within society and politics to religious doctrines. However, the tactics they use to achieve these ends are quite different, with Shas using tactics common to most political parties, such as running for political office and influencing policy from within the system, and Al-Qaeda using violence to create change.

The tactics used to pursue the agenda of a fundamentalist movement are the same as those available to any group with a political agenda. This includes peaceful methods such as lobbying, the use of pressure groups, and forming political parties, as well as violent tactics such as terrorism and civil war. Which tactic is chosen has more to do with opportunity structures and resources than political ideology, and for each possible tactic it is possible to find fundamentalist groups that use it. I address the question of why groups select certain types of tactics in Chapter 9, which focuses on the causes of religious violence. I focus here on the content of fundamentalist political agendas.

The most important political consideration for setting the immediate agenda of a fundamentalist group is whether a fundamentalist group is part of a country's religious majority. That is, when dealing with a Christian fundamentalist group, for example, the most pertinent issue is whether most of the country in question is Christian. If it is, then the agenda is usually to transform society as a whole, to make it more in line with the fundamentalists' ideologies. The long-term agenda is often a religious state. However, in the short term this aim is often politically unrealistic, and more modest short-term goals are set.

In the United States, for example, the likelihood of a religious state in the fore-seeable future is remote. The US political ideology with regard to religion is to maintain separation of religion and state. This policy is widely popular and is likely to remain so in the near future. Despite this, fundamentalists believe they can make inroads on specific issues. These issues include banning abortions, limitations on homosexuals, and promoting prayer in schools. These issues themselves cannot garner the support of a majority of Americans, but those who oppose these agendas tend to be less dedicated and less organized, so successes on these issues are politically possible for an organized, focused, and motivated group. More importantly, the relative popularity of these issues compared to imposing a religious state is an excellent tool to politically mobilize people into fundamentalist political movements and to find non-fundamentalist allies to support them in these specific agendas.

When following this type of agenda, fundamentalist groups tend to use a coherent strategy. They capture the terms of political debate, defining the issues in a manner that makes it difficult to oppose them. When opposing abortion, they do not call themselves anti-abortion but, rather, "pro-life." They use religious symbols and legitimacy to support both their groups and their agenda. God is against murder, including the murder of unborn babies. Their control over religious authority makes it difficult to come up with a legitimate response to their agenda, at least among believers. In fact, this moral authority allows those who use it to align themselves with all that is good and moral and to present themselves as disinterested parties "involved in politics only out of a sense of righteousness, not personal gain." This moral authority is often acknowledged even by those who oppose them. It may be easy to disagree with the Pope but it is considerably more difficult to deny that he has legitimate religious authority (Williams, 1994: 792–796).

More ambitious agendas also exist. Fundamentalist movements in multiple Muslim countries, including Algeria and Egypt, seek to create a religious state. In both of these countries attempts have been made at doing so through the ballot box—that is, by organizing political parties and running candidates for office. In both Algeria and Egypt, until 2011 these attempts failed, but not because of electoral weakness. Rather, in both cases the government created an uneven playing field where, despite popular support, these movements could not succeed. In the case of Algeria they were poised to win elections in 1992 but the military engineered a *coup d'état* to prevent this. As a result, many fundamentalists in Algeria turned to violence, a course of action that resulted in one of the bloodiest civil wars of the 1990s. Until 2011, the failure of fundamentalists in Egypt to overcome government limitations and repression on their political wings also resulted in periodic violence, but not on the scale of what occurred in Algeria. The 2011–2012 parliamentary elections in Egypt were the first to be free of government repression against fundamentalist political groups. Two fundamentalist Muslim parties combined to win just over two-thirds of the parliamentary seats. However, at the time of this writing it is unclear whether Egypt's military will allow these parties to take power.

Despite the significant differences between the political situations and opportunity structures in Algeria, Egypt, and the United States, not to mention the theological differences between Islam and Christianity, the long-term agenda of creating a society that is more in conformity with religious ideals is common to the fundamentalist groups in these countries. However, this can be said to be true of many religious groups that are not fundamentalist. What differentiates fundamentalists from other groups?

One answer to this is the perceived level of threat. A major distinction between fundamentalism and other forms of religion in the modern era is fundamentalists' attitude toward modernity. Fundamentalists are those who reject modernity and choose religion exclusively. Other religious groups seek to find an accommodation between modernity and religion. Thus, fundamentalists are precisely those who feel that modernity and secularism are a threat to their way of life. This means that the fundamentalist perception of the threat of modernity is fundamentally different than the perception of other religious groups.

Accordingly, while many non-fundamentalist religious groups feel that society could use more religion, non-fundamentalists are simply not as motivated by threat perception as are fundamentalists. Also, unlike fundamentalists, they are often willing to balance this desire with other considerations, such as the benefits of a regime that separates religion and state and supports religious freedom. Thus, while non-fundamentalist religious organizations and individuals are often politically active, other things being equal, fundamentalist groups tend to be more active and have more ambitious goals.

The success of their agenda is dependent upon a number of factors, most of which are similar to the factors for success of any political movement and are discussed in more detail in Chapter 6. However, it is important to highlight that recently the few examples of outright victory by fundamentalists—the establishment of a religious state—occurred in states with severe legitimacy problems and/or weak states (Juergensmeyer, 1993, 2008). This is certainly the case for the successful Islamic revolutions in Iran and Afghanistan.

When fundamentalists belong to a religious group that is a minority in a state, their short-term goals change. Their long-term goal sometimes remains that of changing the entire country into a religious state, but doing so would involve converting the country's population to their religion. The short-term goal is similar to that of fundamentalists from the majority denomination, who seek to withdraw from society and create their own separate space which is protected from the threats of modernity, secularism, and any ideas that contradict their beliefs. Some groups do exactly this; ultra-Orthodox Jewish sects outside of Israel are a good example. However, these groups remain politically active to the extent necessary to politically support their right and ability to maintain these closed communities.

Some fundamentalist minorities take a more active approach by maintaining a separate community but one that actively interacts with the rest of the country. They organize politically, seeking to pursue an agenda that can include the following: First, they seek to gain whatever level of government support and privileges are given to the majority religion. If the government funds the majority religion, they seek similar funding. If it allows or supports religious education in the schools, they will seek to have classes in their religion added to the curriculum. Second, they sometimes seek privileges that are not given to the majority religion. For example, as is noted in Chapter 4, Muslims in the United Kingdom have succeeded in gaining government recognition for Sharia (Islamic law) courts to handle matters of personal status, including marriage and divorce for Muslims. Third, they sometimes seek to proselytize and spread the religion, though, as is noted in Chapters 10–13, many countries, even democracies, limit this type of activity.

Fundamentalists of both the majority and minority variety who are not "world renouncers" are also active in building up grassroots support and becoming influential within their religious community. Doing so involves becoming active in mainstream religious institutions and trying to take them over from within. It also often involves charity work in the community, providing services such as education and welfare in places where the government provides inadequate resources. This kind of activity can mobilize a large number of recruits and sympathizers. Such tactics have proven effective in increasing numbers and political influence. This community organization tactic is used by the Islamic Brotherhood, Israel's ultra-Orthodox Shas party, and Christian missionaries in the Third World, among many other groups.

One should note that many fundamentalist movements are international. Religion does not recognize state boundaries. The truth remains the truth everywhere. Thus, at least in theory, if not always in practice, the fundamentalist agenda also knows no state boundaries. Many movements are explicitly international, Al-Qaeda perhaps being the most notorious of these. However, many movements have an international presence which they often seek to expand through missionary work.

To the extent that like-minded groups exist in multiple countries, they tend to be in contact, or at the very least aware of each other's activities. They often help each other out in various ways such as by providing training, expertise, and perhaps funds.

CONCLUSIONS

Religious fundamentalism has been among the most visible political manifestations of religion in recent decades. Fundamentalist groups have engaged in sensational acts of violence, organized powerful political parties, and otherwise had a measurable impact on politics across the world. However, it is important to put fundamentalism into proper context. Not all people who are religious are fundamentalists, and not all of religion's influences on politics involve fundamentalists.

While such things are difficult to measure precisely, it is almost certain that the religion's greatest overall influence on politics comes from non-fundamentalist religion. Influences such as religious beliefs and legitimacy are common to all manifestations of religion. Most studies show that the majority of religious people (however this is measured) are not fundamentalists. Even taking into account that fundamentalists have a higher likelihood of linking religion and politics, the collective weight of the non-fundamentalist majority likely outweighs the impact of fundamentalists on politics.

This is not to say that fundamentalists have had a trivial influence on politics. I would argue that their impact has been substantial and will likely continue to be important for the foreseeable future. This influence is focused and easy to identify. For that reason, many perceive fundamentalists to be the primary, or perhaps only, religious political actors. Without downplaying fundamentalist participation in politics, it is important to place this phenomenon into the proper context.

Also, while fundamentalists tend to have a different type of agenda than non-fundamentalists and are likely to pursue this agenda more intensely, the dynamics between religion and politics for fundamentalists follow the same general principles as other types of religion. That is, religious worldviews influence their political opinions. They use religious legitimacy as a political tool but at the same time are influenced by religious legitimacy. Their religious organizations are used for political mobilization. Put differently, all the factors that influence the dynamics between religion and politics described earlier in this book apply to fundamentalists. In this, fundamentalists are not different from non-fundamentalists.

DISCUSSION QUESTIONS

1 Do you think religion can survive as a viable social institution in the modern era unless religious believers and institutions take positive actions to defend their beliefs and institutions against modernity? If not, why not? If you answer yes, is the fundamentalist form of defense described in this chapter the only form of defense that can work? Why, or why not?

2 Do you think there are religious fundamentalists in your country and/or locality who have a political agenda? If so, is this political agenda to protect their right to live within their community as they wish or to enforce their religious views on everyone?

FURTHER READING

Almond, Gabriel, R. Scott Appleby, and Emmanuel Sivan *Strong Religion: The Rise of Fundamentalism around the World*, Chicago: University of Chicago Press, 2003.

Emerson, Michael O. and David Hartman "The Rise of Religious Fundamentalism" *Annual Review of Sociology*, 32, 2006, 127–144.

CHAPTER 9

Religion and Conflict

In recent decades, much of the increase in religion's rising political profile has been due to the violent conflicts and events attributed to religion. These include the Iranian Revolution, which was followed by violent Islamic opposition movements in many Muslim countries, including some particularly violent civil wars such as the civil wars in Algeria and Afghanistan during the 1990s. They also include the events of 9/11, which eventually led to the continual clashes between Western, primarily US, forces and Muslim militant groups in Afghanistan and Iraq as well as continued terrorist activities by Al-Qaeda and other militant Muslim groups worldwide.

While many of the most prominent violent religious conflicts in recent decades have involved Muslims (Fox, 2007; Toft, 2007; Toft *et al.*, 2011), religious violence is certainly not limited to Muslims. As is discussed in Chapter 3, all major religions have the potential to inspire violence. The conflict between the Sri Lankan government and the Tamil Tigers, one of the bloodiest civil wars in recent years, was between Buddhists and Hindus. The Ku Klux Klan and many other white supremacist groups in the United States and Europe are inspired by Christian ideologies (Stern, 2003).

This chapter is intended to serve two goals: First, it examines the links between religion and conflict, which is in and of itself a topic of considerable importance. While I discuss the link between religious identity and conflict in Chapter 3, I focus here on how religion can cause, or significantly influence, a conflict. The discussion follows the categories and theories discussed in Chapter 4–6 and 8: (1) religious worldviews, beliefs, doctrines, and ideologies; (2) religious legitimacy; (3) religious institutions and mobilization; and (4) religious fundamentalism. It also includes elements of a rational choice approach, though not those specifically discussed in

Chapter 7. Second, this use of the theories and approaches from previous chapters is intended to provide an example of how to apply these theories to a more specific political context, in this case conflict.

This use of theories and approaches to religion and politics to understand religion's influence on conflict is straightforward. This is because the link between religion and politics defines religion's influence on conflict. The nineteenth-century military theorist Carl von Clausewitz famously and correctly stated that war is the continuation of politics through other means. This is a basic and extremely useful theory for the causes of political violence. Essentially, from this perspective politics is about different groups competing for resources and control. The rules of the political game may vary over time and location, but this truth remains. Often, political goals can be obtained through normal political channels. However, sometimes there are individuals, groups, and even countries that do not succeed in obtaining their goals through normal and non-violent political processes. When this occurs, political actors have limited choices. The first is to accept the outcome, at least for the time being, and continue to play the game in the hope that the outcome will be more favorable in the future. The second is to move into the world defined by Carl von Clausewitz and use violence to attain these political goals. While this perspective likely simplifies a more complex reality, it is useful for understanding the choice to use violence to achieve political goals.

From this perspective, violence is simply a political tactic. Religious groups, like any other political groups, choose violence when they are unable to attain their goals through normal political means such as party politics, lobbying, etc. and are unwilling to accept this outcome—sufficiently unwilling that they are willing to pay the costs of using violence. These costs include the fact that violence is often unpopular. It can bring serious reprisals and other consequences. It is also one of the most effective ways to get a divided opposition to unite against you. This is to say nothing of the moral implications of using violence, perhaps even killing, to attain one's goals.

Very few cases of religious violence are violence for the sake of violence. Religious violence is almost always instrumental—designed to attain a goal—though the goal itself is often inspired by religious ideology. Exceptions to this tend to be exotic and rare. For example, the Thugs were a sect in India who believed that at a certain time of year they were commanded by their deity to kill people with a garrote (strangulation wire or rope), then dismember the corpse. Some estimate that during their existence they killed over 1 million people this way over a 2,500-year period. The sect is currently believed to be extinct (Rapoport, 1984: 660–664).

Yet most religious violence today follows the pattern set out by Clausewitz: violence to further a significant political goal. However, it can differ in one respect: Religion can strongly influence emotions. Accordingly, it can inspire violence, which, while clearly serving an instrumental purpose, may not necessarily be the most effective tactic to achieve the goal in question. This is especially the case with spontaneous violence and violence perpetrated by small groups. When violence is larger-scale and planned, it is more often the result of rational cost–benefit calculations.

Despite this, religious ideologies still play a significant role in violence. As noted in Chapters 3, 4 and 5, all religious ideologies are capable of justifying violence. It is also undoubtedly true that some religious doctrines are more conducive than others to justifying violence, but it is rare that a religious doctrine will demand violence to achieve a political purpose in cases where non-violent activity will achieve a goal.

Nevertheless, it is likely that a religious tradition of political violence makes the use of political violence in the present more likely, for two reasons: First, a standing tradition of justifying political violence may make it more likely that religious actors will consider it in the present. That is, when a religion's adherents are engaging in a cost–benefit analysis, the existence of an ideology that justifies violence will make the violence seem less costly. Similarly, a pacifist tradition may consider the use of violence to be more costly because it would be a direct contradiction of religious doctrine. Second, it has been demonstrated that governments which have successfully used violence in the past are more likely to use it in the present (Fein, 1990; Gurr, 1988). Basically, past success and the existence of a procedure to use violence facilitate its use. This argument is applicable to religious institutions and traditions.

This is consistent with how the political science literature views cost–benefit calculations. In politics, cost–benefit calculations are not universal mathematical formulas that result in exactly the same behavior no matter who is making the calculation. Rather, different political actors place different values on different things. They also make different evaluations of the likelihood of success of different tactics. In this case, a religious tradition that more easily supports violence can lower the perceived costs of violence, enhance its perceived benefits, and enhance the perceived likelihood of the success of violent tactics. However, from this perspective the cost–benefit analysis is the dominant factor in the decision to use violence. The content of a religion's theology and a history of using violence are simply variables, among many other variables, that influence the outcome of this calculation.

It is also important to emphasize that despite the focus here on rational calculations, I am not claiming that religious violence is merely religion being used to justify secular goals, though this certainly occurs. As I discuss in detail in Chapter 4, religion can and does motivate political activity. I am simply arguing that, given the presence of a political goal, whatever its motivation, the choice of how to achieve that goal is heavily influenced by a rational cost–benefit process. That being said, the rational choice approach does not address how goals are formed, and, as is noted in Chapter 4 and in the next section of this chapter, religion can play an important role in forming political goals.

RELIGIOUS WORLDVIEWS, BELIEFS, DOCTRINES, AND IDEOLOGIES

Violence that is caused by religion is usually connected to a religious worldview, belief, doctrine, or ideology. Religious causes of violence can be divided into four overlapping and interrelated but distinct categories.

Instrumental violence

The first is instrumental violence. Religious ideologies can include a political component and, like any political ideology, it can be translated into a political agenda.

This agenda can include the establishment of a religious state, the passing of laws protecting or privileging a religion, the legislation of religious precepts as law, maintaining the dominance of the religion by the restricting of other religions, or any number of other agendas. As is noted earlier in the chapter, there are numerous tactics available to pursuing any political agenda, one of which includes violence. Instrumental violence tends to occur mostly in cases where peaceful means of pursuing a political agenda have failed or when it is believed that they will fail (Gurr, 1993). That is, politically it is generally preferable to work within the system rather than challenge it with violence. Violence is a last resort when all other tactics have failed. While there are certainly exceptions to this statement, in general, rational political actors, including religious political actors, prefer peaceful and legal means to attain their goals when possible. Of course, as noted already, since ideology can influence cost–benefit calculations, some actors will come to the conclusion that violence is the most efficient means to achieve a political goal sooner than others.

As is noted briefly in Chapter 8, this is what occurred in Algeria. A religious party, the Islamic Salvation Front, was poised to win national elections in 1992 until the military closed off that option by taking over the government, precisely to prevent the more religious state that the Islamic Salvation Front would have created. When the option was available, these religious actors used peaceful and legal means to attain their goals. However, once this was no longer an option, one of the most violent civil wars of the 1990s erupted in Algeria. In this case, the goals remain the same but the tactics changed, owing to a change in the opportunity structure. To be clear, not all supporters of the Islamic Salvation Front chose violence. Many of them did not consider this a good option and chose peace over violent means for attaining their goal. However, the minority who did opt for violence were sufficient to cause a bloody civil war.

Anti-abortion violence in the United States has followed a similar path. The *Roe v. Wade* decision by the US Supreme Court, which banned limitations on abortions in the first trimester, occurred in 1973. Political opposition to the ruling came almost immediately, but the first arson attack against an abortion clinic did not occur until 1976, the first bombing until 1978, the first butyric acid attack in 1992, and the first murder of an abortion provider in 1993, two decades after the original decision.[1] To be clear, most of those who are politically opposed to abortion in the United States do not support the use of violence. However, a small minority believe that nothing other than violence will achieve their goal of stopping abortion. The escalation of this violence over time demonstrates that as political efforts and lower levels of violence failed, some political actors felt that this failure justified more violent tactics.

In non-democratic countries, peaceful means of protest are often unavailable. In these cases the options for peacefully pursuing social and political change are often limited. Accordingly, violence is usually the only viable option in non-democracies, other than inaction.

Defending the religion

The second way religious worldviews, beliefs, doctrines, and ideologies can lead to violence is based on their potential centrality to individual and group identities, as discussed in Chapter 4. Religion is not simply an intellectual framework through which to understand the world and answer epistemological and metaphysical questions. It is central to how believers see themselves, their community, and the world. It is part of their individual and collective psyche and, to someone who believes in them, their souls. It resides at least in part in the non-rational portion of a believer's mind.

Accordingly, if a believer or community of believers perceives a threat to their religion, or something that runs counter to their beliefs, this threat is a serious one. It is not merely some challenge that must be dealt with rationally. Rather, it is a threat to their identity, to the way the world ought to be, to everything that is pure and good, to their very being. It is a threat that is felt at least in part on an unconscious level. It cannot be denied, and ignoring it is difficult, if not impossible. In cases like this, both rationality and instinct tell believers to respond to defend their religion. This defense can often be violent.

It is important to emphasize that the threat is defined by those who perceive it. If they feel that it is a threat, they will respond accordingly. That is, actions or events which provoke such a reaction are based on how the believers in question see those actions, not on how those who take these actions see them. This means that acts which many would consider benign can still be considered otherwise by believers and provoke a defensive response.

For example, in Israel the simple act of driving a car in the wrong place at the wrong time can lead to violent protests. A central tenet of Orthodox Judaism is that the Sabbath is a day of rest, and work is forbidden. There is general agreement among Orthodox rabbis that driving a car involves work and violates the Sabbath. Consequently, in certain Israeli ultra-Orthodox neighborhoods, which are often located along main thoroughfares, driving a car on the Sabbath can provoke protests, which can include violent actions such as stone throwing. For instance, in September 2009 the city of Jerusalem opened a new public parking lot that was located near an ultra-Orthodox neighborhood and open on the Sabbath. This resulted in violent clashes between ultra-Orthodox residents and the police.[2]

Other actions that have sparked spontaneous religious protests have included the publication of unflattering images of Muhammad in newspaper editorial cartoons by a Danish newspaper in 2005. This sparked global protests by Muslims, which included the storming of embassies and burning of buildings associated with Denmark. Non-flattering depictions of Jesus or other Christian figures in movies such as *The Life of Brian* and *Dogma* have sparked protests, though these protests were generally not violent. In Saudi Arabia, normal acts of expression of faith can be perceived as a threat. This is a description in the *New York Times*[3] of instructions to US soldiers stationed in Saudi Arabia in December 1990:

"As the guardians of Islam's holy places, the Saudis restrict the overt practice of proselytizing of any religion other than Islam," the Pentagon said in a statement outlining its policy on religious worship. "Our personnel, whether Jewish, Christian or any other faith, are free to practice their religion as long as they do so in a discreet manner." That means that while there is a full range of religious services on American military installations in Saudi Arabia, soldiers who wear a cross or a Star of David around their necks must keep the symbol hidden beneath their uniforms. There are reports of some Army commanders who limit the display of religious symbols even at private gatherings. American soldiers are being warned not to discuss their religious beliefs with Saudis and not to take Bibles outside their compound. They are told that in public settings, their religious services should be described as "fellowship meetings," and their chaplains identified only as "morale officers." On Christmas Day, soldiers will have church services and a full Christmas feast with turkey and the trimmings. But all of it will take place on military installations, away from the Saudi public.

Thus, the US government feared that simple actions such as the carrying of Bibles, wearing of religious symbols, and praying, as well as the presence of clergy, could provoke a response from Saudi Muslims.

Sometimes even the simple presence of another religious group is enough to provoke a response. Manor (1994) argues that, at least in part, the civil war between Buddhists and Tamils in Sri Lanka was provoked by a chauvinistic interpretation by Buddhism which has it that the Buddha charged them with preserving the true Buddhism—Theravada Buddhism—and gave the island of Lanka to the Sinhalese to create a "citadel of pure Buddhism." As a result, the presence of large a non-Buddhist population on the island was enough to provoke a defensive response. This response included murderous riots in 1956, 1958, 1977, 1981, and 1983, and massacres of Tamils by extremists within Sri Lanka security forces. These events prompted the Tamils to respond with force, resulting in a bloody civil war.

This instinct to defend one's religion is widely recognized in the literature. Wentz (1987) calls this instinct the "walls of religion." People will do anything to preserve their religious frameworks. These frameworks make people feel they are part of something larger and more important than themselves. "Fanatics," according to Wentz, are not worried about themselves, but are, rather, willing to sacrifice themselves to defend the collective identity and social solidarity that they find essential to their very being. They build walls around them, usually psychological but sometimes physical, and defend those walls at all costs. Geertz (1966: 13–14) similarly states that

> man depends upon symbols and symbol systems with a dependence so great as to be decisive for his creational viability and, as a result, his sensitivity to even the remotest indication that they may prove unable to cope with one or another aspect of experience raises within him the gravest sort of anxiety.

These and other scholars[4] are essentially describing how individuals and communities of religious believers react to events or actions they consider unthinkable in the context of their belief systems. Such events and actions can create extreme anxiety and usually provoke a reaction. In the eyes of the believer, this reaction is rational and normal, though it is often not perceived in this manner by outside observers. However, if one wants to understand the motivations for conflict, one needs to examine the point of view of the participants.

Doctrines and ideologies mandating violence

The third way religious worldviews, beliefs, doctrines, and ideologies can lead to violence focuses on religious laws and doctrines. These laws and doctrines often have explicit instructions on when to go to war. For example, Christianity, Islam, and Judaism all have concepts of holy war. These wars are usually justified to defend the religion but can also, historically, include conquering members of other religions in certain circumstances. In Islam, the laws of war are more specific for *jus in bello* (behavior during a war) than for *jus ad bellum* (when to go to war), but it is generally accepted that wars to defend Islam are mandated and wars to expand Islam are allowed at the discretion of the rulers (El Fadal, 1999; Hashimi, 1999; Kennedy, 1999). In recent years the Muslim concept of *jihad*, holy war, has been used by radical elements to mandate a war against all non-Muslims. This is based on the argument that Islam is challenged with an existential threat that justifies actions which otherwise might not be justified (Charters, 2007; Dalacoura, 2000; Juergensmeyer, 2008; Kramer, 1991). To be clear, this is not the only interpretation of the concept of *jihad*, and many Muslims consider it a distortion of Islam, but it is one that exists and is followed by many other Muslims (Lewis, 1998; Lincoln, 2003: 33–34). I discuss this topic in more detail later in the chapter under the heading "Religious legitimacy."

While the potential for holy war exists in other religions, in recent times it has been observed most often among Muslims. Toft (2007: 11) argues that

> [t]his external defense-of-the-faith component of Islam has parallels in other religions, including Christianity. In contemporary states whose histories include participation in the Thirty Years' War, however, this component has remained dormant for centuries. In the Islamic world, the external aspect of jihad was revived during the Soviet Union's ill-fated attempt in the 1980s to preserve an unpopular Marxist regime in Afghanistan. It gave license to young men to travel great distances to Afghanistan to defend Islam by killing Soviet troops and the Soviet Union's local allies. This effort was thus characterized by a sense of religious obligation; and combined with a never-ending stream of cash and weapons.

The concept of *jus ad bellum* was also mostly dormant in Jewish thought until the establishment of the state of Israel. Currently, there is still little discussion of the holy war aspects of *jus ad bellum* among Orthodox rabbis, and the discussion has focused more on when a defensive war is allowed (Cohen, 2005).

This third path between religious laws and conflicts is related to the second one (responses to perceived threats). Laws regarding defending the religion are most likely to be invoked when there is a threat that mandates such a defense. Nevertheless, this path is distinct in that it provides a more formalized basis for such a defense and for a legalistic and philosophical discussion that is less associated with the more distinctive and spontaneous nature of the second path. It is also important to point out that this type of law rarely mandates violence for the sake of violence. Rather, such laws tend to mandate violence in specific circumstances to achieve a specific purpose.

"Benign" religious activities and violence

The fourth way in which religious worldviews, beliefs, doctrines, and ideologies can lead to violence also focuses on religious laws and is related to the second path. There are many religious activities that are in and of themselves benign but can still provoke religious conflict. They can do so because, as described above, seemingly benign religious actions can be seen as a threat in the eyes of members of another religious group. As is discussed in more detail in Chapter 3, in Western countries the building of mosques is often seen as such a threat and is sometimes restricted, just as the building of non-Muslim places of worship is seen in many Middle Eastern countries as a threat and is, accordingly, restricted. In fact, this type of behavior is common across religions. According to the RAS dataset, 40.6 percent of countries place limitations on minority places of worship. Those doing so include 36.5 percent of Christian countries and 61.7 percent of Muslim countries.

In some cases the mere presence of a religion within a state can be enough. This is true of the Baha'is in many Muslim countries, because they are considered apostates. It is also true of US Protestant denominations in many former Soviet-bloc Christian countries because they are considered to be encroaching on the traditional culture and religions of these states (Fox, 2008). While in many ways this is a reiteration of an aspect of the second path to conflict described here, it is important to emphasize it separately in order to fully understand how even normal religious activities that are mandated by the laws of religions can provoke a violent or discriminatory response.

RELIGIOUS LEGITIMACY

As is discussed in detail in Chapter 5, religion is capable of legitimating just about any government, policy, or action. This certainly applies to conflict and violence. As this concept is self-evident, in this section I focus here on the circumstances under which religion is more likely to legitimate this type of behavior.

When a conflict is a religious one, religious legitimacy is almost automatically in play. Religious conflicts can include conflicts between groups which belong to different religions and it can include conflicts in which a substantial portion of the issues at stake are religious. The former category can be a difficult one to analyze. The mere fact that a conflict is between two groups which belong to different religions does not necessarily mean that there is any other religious content to the conflict. It is completely possible that such a conflict is little different from any ethnic conflict between groups that belong to the same religion.

However, there is, at a minimum, one difference between religious identity conflicts and other types of identity conflicts: the fact that religion has a significantly larger potential to come into play. It is possible that this potential will never be realized and will remain dormant. Yet this is a potential that is often realized even when conflicts have little to do with religious issues. As is noted in Chapter 6, religious institutions are so useful at mobilization that using them will always be a temptation, and the more central the conflict to the groups involved, the more likely it is that religious institutions will feel they need to participate in order to remain relevant and popular with their congregations.

When a conflict involves religious issues, the issue of religious legitimacy is more straightforward. Fighting on the side of religion automatically invokes religious legitimacy. How could it not be legitimate in the eyes of a religion to side with it in a conflict?

Religious legitimacy becomes especially potent in cases of what Mark Juergensmeyer (1991, 2000, 2008) calls "cosmic war." A cosmic war occurs when believers perceive there to be an existential threat to a religion. This is not simply a threat to the religion locally, or some occurrence that violates the religion's tenets. Rather, it is a case where the religion itself is in danger of being extinguished, or at least severely harmed. The former case would most likely provoke a defensive response, but the nature of the response to a cosmic threat is more extreme. Juergensmeyer (2000: 148–149) describes this response as

> an all-or-nothing struggle against an enemy one assumes to be determined to destroy. No compromise is deemed possible. The very existence of the opponent is a threat, and until the enemy is either crushed or contained, one's own existence cannot be secure. What is striking about a martial attitude is the certainty of one's position and the willingness to defend it, or impose it on others, to the end.

This situation can be differently described as living in exceptional times. When such a threat exists, actions that might not otherwise be allowed can be legitimated by religion. Exceptional times require exceptional measures.

The tactic of suicide bombers is case in point. Islamic laws ban suicide, and Islamic laws of war clearly ban the attacking of civilians (El Fadal, 1999; Hashimi, 1999; Kennedy, 1999). Thus, any religious Muslim should refuse both to be a suicide bomber and to attack civilians. Yet many Muslim terrorist groups, including groups guided by religious ideologies, encourage suicide bombers who target civilians. Dating back to the first modern use of suicide bombing in Lebanon by Hezbollah in the 1980s, this necessity justification has been used among Muslim extremists to justify what otherwise would not be allowed (Kramer, 1991). The Sunni Islam ideology which was developed by Al-Qaeda in parallel to Hezbollah's Shiite Islamic ideology to justify suicide terrorism can be attributed to Abdullah Azzam, a twentieth-century Palestinian Islamic scholar. "More than any other individual, Azzam persuaded *jihadis* in Afghanistan and beyond that those who die for the sake of God (*fi sabil Allah*) will be rewarded in paradise" (Moghadam, 2008–2009: 59). While Azzam focused on sacrifice and not suicide bombing specifically, this ideology evolved into the concept that "the suicide attacker does not kill himself for personal reasons, but sacrifices himself for God. He is therefore not committing suicide, but achieving martyrdom" (Moghadam, 2008–2009: 60). Furthermore, the great power of the enemy, whose numbers and weapons so greatly threaten Islam, justifies extreme and normally unjustifiable tactics (Moghadam, 2008–2009: 61).

In a discussion of the Crusades, Horowitz (2009: 168) similarly attributes to religion the power to legitimate extraordinary actions:

> Religious beliefs make a higher-order claim on behavior than do claims by groups organized along purely ethnic, linguistic, or cultural lines. It is hard to argue with the messenger of God telling you what to do—the behavioral demands are absolute compared to the sometimes ambiguous behavioral norms of citizenship. The inherent truth of religious logic, therefore, can theoretically justify the pursuit of certain ends through any means necessary, legitimizing warfare in some cases. . . . The ability of religion to make claims about eternity is a powerful motivator. Religious beliefs elucidate how to weigh costs and benefits. In some cases, they can de-emphasize physical survival in favor of spiritual reward.

There is considerable empirical proof that this relationship between religion and exceptional or extraordinary violence exists. Most studies that compare levels of violence between religious and non-religious conflict find the religious conflicts to be more violent (Fox, 2004; Toft *et al.*, 2011).

While most of this discussion focuses on religious legitimacy in religious conflicts, it is important to emphasize that religion can also be used to legitimize conflicts that do not have a religious basis, in that they involve no significant religious issues. The Abolition movement which opposed slavery in the pre-Civil War United States is a case in point. Religious organizations were heavily involved in this movement and delegitimized slavery on religious grounds. Yet the conflict over slavery itself did not involve issues of religious freedom, nor was it between different religious identity groups.

RELIGIOUS INSTITUTIONS

As is discussed in Chapter 6, religious institutions are well suited for political mobilization, including mobilization for conflict. In democratic settings, religious institutions are less easily used for violent conflict than for open political mobilization. This is due to the fact that mobilization for violence in a democratic setting is more difficult in general than is mobilization for peaceful and legal political actions. While democratic governments generally allow protest activities, they repress violent opposition. Also, in democratic settings peaceful mobilization has a high probability of at least partial success. In a cost–benefit analysis, this makes violence an unattractive option.

In non-democratic settings, any political involvement by religious groups is often repressed, so the secretive nature of mobilization for violent opposition is relatively easier. Many of the resources available to religious institutions discussed in Chapter 6 are still useful when organizing a clandestine opposition group. Religious institutions can be a safe place to meet and organize. The protected status of these organizations makes governments more reluctant to use the tools of repression on them. However, this protection is not absolute, and repressive governments often do repress religious institutions, especially when these are seen as a threat to the regime.

Religious institutions can also provide a cover, as it is expected that people will congregate in houses of prayer. Organizational, financial, and leadership resources can also be tapped for these purposes. The leadership is in a good position to identify congregants who have the necessary skills and are willing to participate. Finally, the legitimacy, ideology, symbols, and motivation associated with religious institutions can also serve this type of movement.

FUNDAMENTALISTS AND VIOLENT CONFLICT

It is important to emphasize that not all religious conflict involves fundamentalists. All of the dynamics described up to this point in the chapter can apply to any religious movement or organization. There has been no systematic study of how much of the world's religious conflict can be attributed to fundamentalist groups, yet anecdotally it is clear that much of recent religious violence can be attributed to such groups.

Why is that the case? Fundamentalists draw their ideologies from the same religious traditions as non-fundamentalists, so the letter of the law is not the answer. Yet fundamentalists are more likely to activate those aspects of religious law doctrine, and ideology that justify violence.

I argue that the answer to this question is directly structural but indirectly ideological. As is discussed in more detail in Chapter 8, fundamentalist ideologies include a rejection of modernity. This leads to their having a political agenda that is more generally radical than those of non-fundamentalist groups. Fundamentalists who choose political activity over retreat from the world seek to make changes in society that are profound and generally unpopular among non-fundamentalists. In some cases, fundamentalists have the political power to enact these changes, or at least some of them, through normal political means. In these cases, fundamentalists are less likely to initiate violent conflict, though, as is discussed in more detail in what follows, there may be some enforcement violence—violence intended to enforce the fundamentalist lifestyle within that community (Sprinzak, 1991). Violent responses against these changes are also a possibility.

However, in most cases fundamentalists are in the minority and do not have the political power to make the changes they desire. This puts them in the quandary defined by Carl von Clausewitz: either give up on their goals for the time being, or pursue them through violence. As fundamentalists often fervently believe in their agenda, to the point where it is unthinkable not to pursue it, they are more likely to choose the violent option.

Thus, ideology has a component in fundamentalist violence, but it is not an ideological impetus to use violence. Rather, it is an ideology that (1) is so important and so central that any means are justified in pursuing it, (2) demands changes that are so radical that in most cases they cannot be accomplished peacefully, and (3) is the word of God, which leaves little or no room for compromise. These facts set up a structural situation where, when peaceful means are not sufficient to achieve this agenda, which is often the case, violence is easily and often justified.

For example, Juergensmeyer (1998: 88) explains Christian political violence in the United States as an example of this dynamic:

In the United States, attacks on abortion clinics, the killing of abortion clinic staff, and the destructive acts of members of Christian militia movements are chilling examples of assaults on the legitimacy of modern social and political institutions, based on the theological frameworks of reconstruction theology and Christian Identity thinking. These examples of Christian militancy present a religious perception of warfare and struggle in what is perhaps the most modern of twentieth-century societies. The secular political order of America is imagined to be trapped in vast satanic conspiracies involving spiritual and personal control. This perception provides Christian activists with both the justification and the obligation to use violent means to fulfill their understanding of the country's Christian mission—and at the same time offers a formidable critique of Enlightenment society and a reassertion of the primacy of religion in public life.

Juergensmeyer (2000: 218–220) argues that these movements, and others, which justify and use political violence tend to be marginal within their own traditions. This is logical, because if they were not marginal, most of their societies would agree with their goals and they would be able to use this majority to achieve peaceful change.

A less extreme but nevertheless important form of violence associated with fundamentalism is enforcement violence. As is noted earlier in the chapter, this type of violence is present in the more closed fundamentalist communities and is intended to enforce the fundamentalist lifestyle within that community (Sprinzak, 1991).

RELIGIOUS TERROR

While religion is not the only justification for terror, it is a classic justification for terror (Hoffman, 1995; Rapoport, 1984; Toft *et al.*, 2011). In recent decades, most new terror groups have been religious ones, and most terror incidents have been perpetrated by these groups (Ben Dor and Pedahzur, 2003; Juergensmeyer, 2000; Ransler and Thompson, 2009).

The explanation for this religious terror is related to the structural explanation for fundamentalist violence. Consider a religious group that meets the following two criteria: (1) Its members have a political goal inspired by their religious ideology which they consider critically important, to the extent that even in the absence of peaceful means to achieve them, the goals must be pursued. (2) They are not politically powerful enough to create the political and social changes they desire through peaceful and legal means. In these situations the use of terrorism becomes likely. This is because such groups are, by definition, weaker than the states they oppose. They simply do not have the means and resources to meet a state's military power head-on. Few opposition movements have this magnitude of power. Opposition groups with this kind of power and resources usually occur only in particularly weak and failing states.

Accordingly, if one wishes to use violence under these circumstances, the most effective option in this situation is terror. It is a tactic that is designed specifically for asymmetric conflict against a more powerful state. Thus, terror is chosen as a practical option, not an ideological one.

That being said, religious terror is distinguishable from terror motivated by other ideologies in that it is often more violent and extreme. Religious terror groups are more likely to use suicide bombers (Ben Dor and Pedahzur, 2003: 85; Ransler and Thompson, 2009) and to create more casualties (Enders and Sandler, 2006; Ransler and Thompson, 2009). This is attributed to the religious legitimacy, which removes moral restraints on violence, and to the fact that religious terrorists are often more interested in teaching a lesson than engaging in measured terror intended to achieve a political goal but not overly outrage their intended audience. That is, secular terrorists are more likely to fear the use of more violence than is necessary to achieve their goals because of the negative impact this may have on their long-term agenda. In contrast, some have described religious terror as being symbolic to the point of being ritualistic (Hoffman, 1995; Juergensmeyer, 2000: 119–132).

While this is true of terrorism in general, one should note that terror tends to be a tactic used against democracies. This is because it is easier to organize in a freer society. Also, the most effective tool in stopping terror is repression, which democracies are more reluctant to use, and when they do use it, use less extreme versions than autocratic states (Pape, 2003: 349–350; Rapoport and Alexander, 1989: 16–17).

MESSIANIC VIOLENCE

A final form of religious violence that is significant, though less common, is messianic violence. Messianism is the "faith that there will be a day in which history or life on this earth will be transformed totally and irreversibly from the condition of perpetual strife which we have all experienced to one of perfect harmony that many dream about" (Rapoport, 1988: 197). It is a particular form of religious framework that can mandate violence in two circumstances.

The first is violence to bring about the messianic event. When believers think that the day of the messianic event is imminent, they often become violent. This violence is often theologically central to the messianic event. For example, some Jews and Christians believe that the Messiah will come only after an apocalyptic war. Believers who think this event is imminent may seek to provoke this war.

> Once a sense of imminence takes root, some believers must find it psychologically impossible to regard their actions as irrelevant. . . . At the very least, they will act to secure their own salvation. And, once the initial barrier in action has been overcome, it will only be a matter of time before different kinds of action make sense too. Soon they may think they can shape the speed or timing of the process.
> (Rapoport, 1988: 201)

As the messianic event is imminent, it becomes more important to demonstrate one's faith, often through violent actions. As the violence is mandated by God, it is justified and has no moral restraint. Violent action will also be taken no matter the odds against success. When God is on your side, odds are irrelevant. When the world as we know it is coming to an end, consequences can also be irrelevant (Rapoport, 1988; Juergensmeyer, 2000: 44–59).

The second is when the predicted messianic event fails to occur, which historically has generally been the case. When this occurs, the religious groups in question often come to the conclusion that they were mistaken, or find some biblical excuse for the failure, and revert to pacifism. But sometimes they need to find someone to blame for the failure of the messianic event to occur. This can result in violence against group members as well as violence against "unbelievers" whose impurity prevented the messianic event from occurring (Rapoport, 1988; Sprinzak, 1998).

For example, Sprinzak (1998) argues that in the wake of the 1967 war in Israel, the Gush Emonim and Kach movements—both Orthodox Jewish Zionist movements—were essentially messianic movements. These movements believed that the military victory was the beginning of God's redemption of the Jewish people and would usher in an age of unchallenged Jewish sovereignty and an end to the Arab threat against Israel. At first, this belief inspired violence to bring this messianic age faster, including a plot in the 1980s by extremists within the Gush Emonim movement to blow up the Al-Aqsa Mosque on the Temple Mount in Jerusalem—a plot condemned, along with any terrorism, by many of the movement's most prominent rabbis. Rabbi Meir Kahane, the leader of the Kach movement, was more extreme: "While he never instructed his followers to actually kill innocent Palestinians, Rabbi Kahane welcomed and praised every individual who committed such crimes" (Sprinzak, 1998: 121). This in large part is why the Kach movement was eventually banned in Israel.

Eventually, these movements began to realize that the messianic event was not occurring.

> The realities of the peace process have since 1992 created for Gush Emunim and Kach a devastating predicament. Both movements have believed since their establishment that redemption, which is currently imminent, could only take place within the biblical boundaries of the Land of Israel, which include the occupied territories. They also have come to believe that redemption is irreversible.
>
> (Sprinzak, 1998: 121)

The disappointment over this failed redemption resulted in some significant violence. According to Sprinzak (1998: 123), the 1994 massacre in Hebron's Cave of the Patriarchs, which killed 29 Muslims and wounded over 100, and the "1995 assassination of [Israeli Prime Minister] Yitzhak Rabin were, in my judgment, clear expressions of messianism in an acute crisis."

RELIGION AND PEACE

While this chapter focuses on religion and conflict, it is important to reiterate that, as I discuss in Chapter 3, in addition to supporting violence and conflict, religion can also support peace and tolerance. Scott Appleby's (2000) *ambivalence of the sacred* concept highlights this. Appleby points out that most major religions have large and complex theologies which include elements that support both violence and peace.[5] Christianity, Judaism, and Islam all have concepts of holy war. Yet Judaism also contains the concept of the lion lying down with the lamb and prayers for peace that are part of daily services. For example, a prayer included in multiple parts of Jewish services, called the *Kaddesh*, ends with the phrase "He who makes peace in His height, may He make peace upon us, and upon all Israel." A central concept in Christianity is to turn the other cheek. In fact, Christianity began its history as a pacifist religion. Many Muslims interpret *jihad*, Islam's concept of holy war, not as a call to violence but as a personal struggle with oneself to be a better Muslim.

It is also clear that many religious actors actively engage in inter-religious dialogue, efforts to mediate between combatants, and grassroots efforts to alleviate the suffering caused by war. If one could count all such acts of peace and compare them to the number of acts of violence in the name of religion, it is not inconceivable that the acts of peace would outnumber the acts of violence. Thus, this is a substantial political influence of religion which receives less attention than religion's involvement in violence.

It is possible to understand these acts of peace through the same lenses we use to understand religion and violence. As I note above, religious belief systems include support for peace and can clearly provide a motivation to support peace. Religious leaders and institutions can clearly lend legitimacy to peace. Religious institutions can mobilize members to support peace.

DISCUSSION QUESTIONS

1 Do you think there are any political goals sufficiently important that violence is justified and legitimate? Are any of these goals at least in part inspired by religious worldviews?
2 Can you think of any instances of religious violence not intended to attain a political goal or defensive violence? Can you think of any instances of religious violence clearly intended to attain a goal that would have been more easily attained through peaceful means?
3 How important are your core beliefs (religious or otherwise) to you? What would it take for you to perceive a serious threat to these beliefs? What are you willing to do to defend them?

FURTHER READING

Appleby, R. Scott *The Ambivalence of the Sacred: Religion, Violence, and Reconciliation*, Lanham, MD: Rowman & Littlefield, 2000.

Fox, Jonathan *Ethnoreligious Conflict in the Late Twentieth Century: A General Theory*, Lanham, MD: Lexington Books, 2002.

Juergensmeyer, Mark *Global Rebellion: Religious Challenges to the Secular State, from Christian Militias to Al Qaeda*, Berkeley: University of California Press, 2008.

Wentz, Richard *Why People Do Bad Things in the Name of Religion*, Macon, GA: Mercer, 1987.

PART 2 THE RELIGION POLICIES OF 177 GOVERNMENTS

Part 1 of this book focuses on how social scientists have understood the role of religion in politics. Part 2 focuses on religion and politics in practice. More specifically, it focuses on state religion policy. While this is clearly only one aspect of religion and politics, it is an important one. It is not possible to provide in a text such as this one an in-depth empirical analysis of every possible manifestation of religious politics. I selected state religion policy, for three reasons. First, it is a topic that is among the most central to religion and politics. A major goal of religious political actors in society is to influence state religion policy. Thus, even though I do not examine these actors in depth, from this perspective the results of their successes and failures can be seen in state religion policy.

Second, this is the topic with which I am most familiar. Third, using the RAS dataset as the basis for the discussion in these chapters allows a comparison across 177 governments and provides a wealth of examples. Arguably it provides a resource for an analysis that is broader and more detailed than any other single source of information. This means that while I may focus on one aspect of religion and politics, I discuss this aspect thoroughly. This discussion involves 111 specific types of policy, which, as is discussed in Appendix A, cover all state religion policies that exist in these 177 states.

Covering all of these countries in a few chapters is a difficult task because each country's religion policy is unique. No two of these 177 countries have identical policies. For that reason, it is not possible to delve into detail on all of these countries. Rather, I discuss the general trends in state religion policy, emphasizing the more common practices while delving into more detail into a few representative countries.

This methodology is intended to provide an understanding of the multiple ways governments intervene in religion while placing these larger patterns into context by examining in detail the policies of a few countries.

In order to accomplish this, I rely heavily on the RAS dataset's categorization of state religion policy. Unless otherwise noted, all information in these chapters is from the most recent year available, 2008. The RAS dataset identifies four major aspects of policy, all of which are discussed in detail in Chapter 1:

1 *Does a state have an official religion?* The RAS dataset divides a state's official relationship with religion into 14 categories, including 5 for states with official religions and 9 for those with no official religion. These categories are discussed in more detail in Chapters 1 and 4. In this analysis, these categories are simplified in order to ease discussion of this topic. This category measures the formal relationship between religion and state in a country.

2 *Religious support*: Governments support religion in many ways. The RAS dataset measures 51 categories of these laws. These laws can include legislation of religious law as state law, funding religion, or otherwise giving privileges to some religions over others. I discuss the most common types of religious support present in the states in the countries covered in each chapter.

3 *Religious regulation*: Governments also regulate religion. They limit it and often ban religious activities. This category examines how governments restrict and limit the majority religion or all religions in a country. The motives for this type of activity can range from an ideological dislike of religion, fear of religion's political power, or attempts by the state to use religion for its own political benefit. The RAS dataset examines 29 types of religious regulation. These chapters examine the most common types present in the states in the countries covered in each chapter.

4 *Religious discrimination*: Most governments place limits on the religious practices or institutions of minority religions *that are not placed on those of the majority religion*. Thus, this category focuses on the repression of minority religions exclusively. While these actions are often similar to those in the previous category, the decision to place these limitations only on minority religions is evidence of very different motivations. These motivations can include wanting to maintain the dominance of the majority religion and fear or distrust of religions new to a country. The RAS dataset examines 30 types of religious discrimination. These chapters examine the most common types present in the states in the countries covered in each chapter.

An advantage of this approach is that all of the policies discussed can be analyzed as empirical facts. That is, for example, either a state has an official religion or it does not. Similarly, it either funds religious education in private schools or it does not. This means the discussion of state religion policy in this section focuses on revealing the worldwide landscape of state religion policy. The results and trends I identify reveal a complicated landscape where no two states have the same religion policy and all of them other than South Africa either support or restrict religion in at least some small way. Most of them do so at a level that few would call "small" or "insignificant."

While the focus of this part of the book is to describe the state of government religion policy around the world, it is still linked to the theoretical perspectives discussed in Part 1. As is discussed in Chapter 2, all of these types of policy are a potential source of contention. Each of these 177 states has secular elements that would like less government involvement in religion as well as elements who seek to have the state support religion more strongly. Religious fundamentalists, the topic of Chapter 8, are particularly likely to desire more state support for religion. Those who wish to support religion more, whether they are fundamentalist or not, may mobilize for this cause through religious institutions, as discussed in Chapter 5. States often associate themselves with a religious identity, a topic covered in Chapter 3. This association is correlated with stronger support for a single religion. Religious belief systems, worldviews, doctrines, and theologies, discussed in Chapter 4, can certainly motivate both the supporting of religion and the restricting of religious minorities. Doing so can also bolster the religious legitimacy of a government, as discussed in Chapter 5. Of course, as is discussed in Chapter 7, all of this is influenced by cost–benefit analyses by both politicians and religious actors.

That being said, this part of the book focuses less on the motivation behind policies than on the policies themselves. It is possible to measure policies empirically. Until such time as we can see into the minds and hearts of human beings, motivations will always be a matter of speculation, dispute, and controversy. The theoretical framework developed in Part 1 of this book is a good tool with which to understand these policies but it is still a theoretical framework intended to simplify, and thereby understand, reality. In this sense, like any theoretical framework in the social sciences, it is imperfect. Nevertheless in Chapter 14 I discuss in more detail how this theoretical framework can help us understand the empirical realities revealed in Part 2 of this book.

For the purposes of this analysis, I divide the world's states into four chapters based on world religion. This is because, as is discussed in Chapter 3, religion policy is strongly associated with religious traditions—though, as I demonstrate in these chapters, there is a huge diversity in religion policies within each religious tradition. Accordingly, in these chapters I discuss the commonalities among countries while also pointing out some of the sources of diversity and difference among them.

I begin with Christian-majority countries: states in which Christians are the majority of the population. As Christian-majority countries include 97 of the 177 states examined here I divide Christian-majority countries into two categories. Western democracies and the former Soviet bloc make up the first, and the second is Christian-majority countries in the Third World (non-Soviet Asia, Africa, and Latin America).

A note on methodology and citations: As I note in Chapter 1, the RAS project used a number of standard sources for all cases that are listed in Chapter 1. The citations throughout this book, and especially in Part 2, do not list these standard sources and cite only country-specific sources.

CHAPTER 10

Christian-Majority States 1

Western democracies and the former Soviet bloc

This is the first of two chapters examining Christian-majority countries.[1] I divide Christian majority countries into two chapters because of the sheer number of such countries. The reasoning behind this specific division is that Third World and non-Third World countries are likely to have substantial differences in state policy, which in fact proves to be the case. In this chapter I focus on Western Democracies and the former Soviet bloc, and in Chapter 11 I focus on the Third World, but also compare the two groups of countries.

While there are no countries among Western democracies without Christian majorities, several in the former Soviet bloc have Muslim majorities. This chapter examines only those 46 countries in these world regions that are included in the RAS dataset and have Christian majorities. While these countries include all Christian countries outside of the Third World, they have diverse histories and traditions. In this chapter I focus on three political and cultural factors that help to categorize these countries into more similar subsets of countries.

The first is religious tradition. As is discussed in more detail in Chapter 2, many posit that religious identity has an impact on politics. I account for this by dividing the countries into three categories: Catholic majority, Orthodox Christian majority, and all other Christian states. While the states in the last category mostly have Protestant majorities, there is some dispute over exactly how that term is defined. This disagreement centers on theological and historical distinctions that are beyond the scope of this analysis. Accordingly, I avoid that label.

The second is whether the country is a Western democracy or a former Soviet-bloc state. The histories of these countries in the twentieth century, especially after

World War II, are substantially different. While Western democracies have been, at least in theory, liberal democracies, for most of the post-World War II era those in the former Soviet bloc were under the rule of anti-religious Communist regimes, which repressed all religion, until 1990. Thus, religion in these countries has, as of 2008, had less than two decades to recover from this repression. This is perhaps the most significant political factor that differentiates these states for many policy areas, including religion.

The final category is EU membership in 2008. Membership in the European Union has significant influences, including a centralized mechanism for protection of human rights, including religious freedom. This includes a central set of principles in the European Convention for Human Rights which are enforced by the European Court of Human Rights. Article 9 specifically protects religious freedom.

As I demonstrate in this chapter, while these categorizations do help to differentiate between these states, overall there are many commonalities among them. Perhaps the most important commonality is that religious support and discrimination are ubiquitous in these states. All of them, without exception, have at least some religious support, and the vast majority of them restrict the religious practices or institutions of religious minorities. There are variations in some of the specifics within this general finding but the overall finding holds for all categories of states examined in this chapter.

OFFICIAL RELIGIONS

The pattern of official support for religion reveals these commonalities and differences (Table 10.1). In general, 84.8 percent of these states support some religions, or one religion, more than others. This means that in most of these countries, religions do not compete on a level playing field, with one or more religions receiving benefits not shared by all. That a majority of states behave in this manner is consistent across categorizations. The least support for some religions more than others is among "other" Christian states, 62.5 percent of which favor at least some religions over others.

The presence of an official religion is important because it indicates a formal designation of a single religion (or, in the case of the United Kingdom, two related religions) as having a special place in the country. Nearly one in five (19.6 percent) of these states declare an official religion, and all categorizations of states include at least one state that does so. Official religions are most common in "other" Christian Western democratic states. Five of the nine states with official religions—Denmark, Finland, Iceland, Norway, and the United Kingdom—fit into this category. This listing also demonstrates that official religions are common in the Nordic states, especially when one considers that Sweden eliminated its official religion in 2000. Official religions are rarest among former Soviet Christian states, with only Armenia having an official religion.

Over a third (34.8 percent) of these states favor one religion over all others without designating it as an official religion. There is some diversity in this result. For instance, no "other" Christian states are in this category. All such states which favor a single

Table 10.1 Official religions in Western democracies and former Soviet-bloc Christian states

	Denomination			Region		European Union 2008		All cases
	Catholic	Orthodox	Other Christian	Western democracy	Former Soviet	No	Yes	
Official religion	11.8%	15.4%	31.3%	30.8%	5.0%	21.1%	18.5%	19.6%
One religion supported more than others	47.1%	61.5%	0.0%	19.2%	55.0%	42.1%	29.6%	34.8%
Some religions supported more than others	35.3%	23.1%	31.3%	26.9%	35.0%	15.8%	40.7%	30.4%
No unequal treatment	5.9%	0.0%	37.5%	23.1%	5.0%	21.1%	11.1%	15.2%
N	17	13	16	26	20	19	27	46

religion do so through an official religion. This category is also less common among Western democracies. On the other side of the coin, a clear majority of all Orthodox majority states and states in the former Soviet bloc fit into this category. Among Orthodox states, only Cyprus, Montenegro, and Ukraine do not support Orthodox Christianity more than all other religions, either as an official religion or unofficially. Overall, combined with the previous category this means that a majority of 54.4 percent of these states support one religion more than all others.

Most of these states that do not favor one religion over all others give preference to some religions over others. This sometimes occurs in complicated multiple-tier systems of recognition and benefits. Hungary, for example, has three tiers: The first comprises four "historical" religions, which receive most state funding. In the second are other religions, which can register and receive some funding. The third, non-registered religions, are not officially limited but receive no state support, and, since they are not registered entities, do not get the tax benefits of registered and historical religions (Schanda, 2002). As is described in more detail in Chapter 4, Lithuania is a particularly complicated case, with four tiers.

States that treat all religions equally—Australia, Canada, Estonia, France, the Netherlands, New Zealand, and the United States—are mostly Western, "other" Christian-majority states, with France and Estonia being the exceptions. While most of these states maintain relatively strict separation of religion and state, France is somewhat hostile to religion in the public sphere. France's 2004 law which restricts the wearing of any overt religious symbols, including head coverings, in public schools is an example of this, as is its 2011 law banning face coverings in public. Despite the variations in policy, the most striking result is that these seven states, among all Christian states in the West and former Soviet bloc, are the only ones that give equal treatment to all religions; the other 39—84.8 percent of these states—favor one or a few religions over all others.

RELIGIOUS SUPPORT

Like nearly all states in the RAS dataset, all of the countries discussed in this chapter engage in at least some religious support. The average country has about 7½ of the 51 types of religious support included in the RAS dataset, and 33 of these types are present in at least one of these countries. The countries with the fewest types are Liechtenstein and Macedonia, with 2, and the countries with the most are the Czech Republic and Greece, with 13. While there is some variation across categorizations of countries, it is not large, with EU countries averaging less than one law above the overall average being an example of the largest deviation.

In this section, I discuss ten of the most common types of religious support in Western democracies and former Soviet Christian-majority states.

Religious education

The most common form of support in these countries is the presence of religious education in public schools, which is present in a large majority of these states no matter what categorization of states is used. Only Belarus, France, Macedonia, Montenegro, Slovenia, Ukraine, and the United States do not allow religious education in public schools. However, such education is rarely coercive. In 37 of the 39 countries with religious education in public schools, the education is optional, or there is a mechanism for those who do not want it to opt out. In Cyprus it is mandatory only for members of the majority religion. In Russia, while religious education is by law not mandatory, a number of schools have instituted courses in the "fundamentals of Orthodox culture" which are mandatory and include religious content. Interestingly, in 19, nearly half, of these 39 countries the religion teachers are clergy or appointed by clergy. This is particularly common in Catholic countries, such as Belgium, Croatia, Italy, Poland, and Spain. Thus, in many cases these classes are religious classes taught by clergy.

This widespread presence of religious education in public schools is likely a surprising fact to those living in the United States and taught in the US tradition of the Jeffersonian wall between religion and state. In the United States, many consider religious education in public schools a prime example of something that should not be allowed in a liberal democracy. Yet among Western liberal democracies, it is only France and the United States that do not allow religion to be taught in public schools. Even most of the former Soviet-bloc Christian-majority states, where religion itself was repressed until 1990, now have religious education in public schools. I discuss some of the implications for this in liberal political thought later in this chapter.

Another common category of religious support also relates to education. Among these states, 65.2 percent financially support religious private schools. This is true of a majority of these states in all subcategories examined here. For example, six of Canada's ten provinces finance religious schools, though the extent of this funding varies from none to 75 percent. The province of Ontario is the only one that

Table 10.2 Religious support in Western democracies and former Soviet-bloc Christian states

	Denomination			Region		European Union 2008		All cases
	Catholic	Orthodox	Other Christian	Western democracy	Former Soviet	No	Yes	
Average number of types of religious support	7.12	7.38	8.25	7.46	7.75	6.32[a]	8.48[a]	7.59
Engage in at least some religious support (%)	100%	100%	100.0%	100%	100%	100%	100%	100%
Common types of religious support (%)								
Marriages performed by clergy are given automatic civil recognition	41.2%	23.1%	25.0%	34.6%	25.0%	10.5%	44.4%	30.4%
Religious education is present in public schools	88.2%	69.2%	93.8%	92.3%	75.0%	73.7%	92.6%	84.8%
Government funding of religious primary or secondary schools or religious educational programs in non-public schools	70.6%	38.5%	81.3%	69.2%	60.0%	52.6%	74.1%	65.2%
Government collects taxes on behalf of religious organizations	35.3%	0.0%	37.5%	42.3%	5.0%	10.5%	37.0%	26.1%
Official government positions, salaries, or other funding for clergy	58.8%	30.8%	43.8%	46.2%	45.0%	26.3%	59.3%	45.7%
Direct general grants to religious organizations	41.2%	61.5%	43.8%	42.3%	55.0%	42.1%	51.9%	45.7%
Funding for building, maintaining, or repairing religious sites	29.4%	84.6%	31.3%	26.9%	70.0%	42.1%	48.1%	45.7%
Free airtime on television or radio is provided to religious organizations on government channels or by government decree	35.3%	46.2%	25.0%	19.2%	55.0%	31.6%	37.0%	34.8%
Presence of an official government ministry or department dealing with religious affairs	47.1%	61.5%	43.8%	23.1%	85.0%	57.9%	44.4%	50.0%
A registration process for religious organizations exists which is in some manner different from the registration process for other non-profit organizations	64.7%	92.3%	62.5%	53.8%	95.0%	63.2%	77.8%	71.7%

Notes
a   Significance of marked mean as compared to means for groups in other categories <0.05.
b   Significance of marked mean as compared to means for groups in other categories <0.01.
c   Significance of marked mean as compared to means for groups in other categories <0 0001.

continues to fund Catholic education by classifying it as "public education," while not providing funding for other types of religious schools.

Even the United States is beginning to partially fund private religious schools. As most funding for schools in the United States comes from state and local governments, the major issue in that country is what sort of funding is allowed. Until the 1980s the US Supreme Court barred religious schools from receiving any sort of government subsidy. During the 1980s, however, the courts began to allow religious schools to receive indirect aid. In 2002 a landmark ruling (*Zelman* v. *Simmons-Harris*) allowed religious schools in Cleveland, Ohio, to receive financial aid in the form of government vouchers. In 2000 the Supreme Court ruled in *Mitchell* v. *Helms* that using tax dollars to pay for "instructional equipment" for parochial schools did not violate the constitution.[2]

New Zealand and Belgium provide more typical examples of education. New Zealand's 1964 Education Act states that teaching within public primary schools "shall be entirely of a secular character." However, it also allows religious instruction and observances in public schools within certain parameters. Schools may, at their discretion, close any class at any time of the school day within specified limits for the purposes of religious instruction given by voluntary instructors as long as attendance at religious instruction or observances is not compulsory.[3]

Article 24 of Belgium's constitution guarantees "non-denominational education. This implies in particular the respect of the philosophical, ideological or religious beliefs of parents and pupils." However, it also states that "all pupils of school age have the right to moral or religious education at the community's expense."[4] In practice, all public schools require religious or moral education as part of the curriculum. The students may choose between instruction in one of Belgium's recognized religions or, for the non-religious, a course in morals and ethics. The instructors of the religious courses are nominated by their religious group but appointed by the minister of education of the community government and paid for by the government. Private religious schools of religions recognized by the government, known as "free" schools, receive government subsidies for building and operating expenses. Their teachers are paid by the regional government.

Funding religion

The funding of religious private schools is one of 12 types of funding for religion examined by the RAS dataset. The average state examined in this chapter engages in 3.52 of these 12 types of financing, and only Estonia engages in none of them. This makes the funding of religion the most common form of support for religion in Western and former Soviet Christian-majority countries. In addition to the financing of religious education in public schools, which I discuss in the previous subsection, in this subsection I examine in more detail an additional four types of government financial support for religion.

Twelve of these states collect taxes on behalf of religions. This method of funding is different from all other types of funding where governments fund religions out of the general budget. Here, governments collect a separate tax that specifically funds religious institutions. In some cases this tax is compulsory. In Austria there is a tax of 1.1 percent of income for the country's 13 officially recognized religions. It is compulsory for Catholics. In Belgium the tax is mandatory but taxpayers can direct their tax to a designated religion. In Germany and Finland the tax is compulsory only for members of recognized religious communities. One must officially leave the religious community to be exempt from the tax.

In some countries the tax is voluntary. In Italy, taxpayers can designate some of their taxes to be sent to certain recognized religions. In Portugal and Spain, taxpayers can designate a portion of their income taxes to be paid to the Catholic Church. In Hungary they can do so for any registered religion. In Sweden, taxpayers may choose to divert the tax to the religious group of their choice or receive a tax reduction.[5] In Switzerland the issue is decided by the canton's government. In some cantons the church tax is voluntary; in others, a person opting to not pay the church tax is forced to leave the church, or the tax may be non-negotiable (Robbers, 2001).

Twenty-one of these states provide general funding for religious institutions out of the state budget. For example, the Bulgarian government supports the Bulgarian Orthodox Church as well as a few other "historical" religious groups, including the Muslim, Jewish, Armenian Apostolic, and Protestant communities. But most of the funding goes to the Bulgarian Orthodox Church. In Denmark, 12 percent of the budget of the Evangelical Lutheran Church comes from state subsidies, which are above and beyond the compulsory tax collected from church members by the government on behalf of the church. Hungary similarly allocates money to religious groups in addition to the funds that come from religious taxes.

Twenty-one of these states provide funds specifically for clergy. For example, in Belgium the federal government pays the salaries, pensions, and other expenses of ministers from recognized religions. Romania funds the salaries of ministers of recognized religions as well as subsidizing their housing costs. Hungary funds the clergy for its four "historical" religions in small towns. In Portugal, chaplaincies for the military, prisons, and hospitals are state-funded positions open to Catholics only.

Twenty-one of these states fund the building, maintenance, or repairing of places of worship. For example, in Latvia, religious groups recognized as "traditional" can receive funds to repair and renovate places of worship.[6] In Sweden, recognized religions can similarly request financial help beyond the religious tax. For instance, in 2006 the government funded the rebuilding and repairing of a mosque in Malmö that had been the victim of several arson attacks.[7]

While these five types of funding of religion are the most widespread, governments of these states also fund seminary schools, religious education in universities, religious charitable organizations, and religious pilgrimages, among other types of funding. As is indicated in many of the examples above, funding preference is almost always given to one or a few religions. This practice is sufficiently widespread that it is arguable that it is in this way, more than any other, that governments in Christian majority states in the West and the former Soviet bloc show their support for religion.

Other types of support for religion

With a few exceptions such as blasphemy laws, which are rarely enforced, these states rarely legislate religious laws as state law. Perhaps the most common exception is a relatively benign one. Fourteen states give religious marriages civil recognition. This means that marrying under the auspices of a religion brings automatic civil recognition without any necessity to take extra steps to register the marriage with the civil authorities. In some cases, such as those of Finland and Georgia, this privilege is given only to the majority church. In some other countries, such as Germany and Portugal, it is granted to most registered religions.

Sixteen countries provide free airtime on public television or radio for religious institutions. For example, in 2006, senior Georgian government officials intervened when public television decided not to broadcast a live Christmas Eve service; the service was broadcast after the intervention. In France, public television features programming from all major religions in the country (Bowen, 2007). In Poland, public radio and television broadcast the Catholic Mass under license granted by the National Radio and Television Broadcasting Council.

Twenty-three states have official government ministries or departments dealing with religion. As is indicated in Table 10.2, this is far more common in the former Soviet-bloc states, but Western countries such as Iceland, Sweden, and Spain have government departments, commissions, or offices dealing specifically with religion.

Thirty-three states have some form of registration process for religions. This means religious organizations must register in some manner that is unique to religious organizations. In most cases this registration is not required, but organizations that do not register do not get certain benefits or are not considered legal entities. In Iceland, Malta, and Montenegro, registration is technically required but it is never denied and is rarely enforced. However, in seven former Soviet-bloc countries, including Belarus and Russia, unregistered religions are restricted and registration is sometimes denied. In many cases there are legal barriers to registration. Twenty-three states require a minimum membership threshold for registration and 12 require a minimum period of presence in the country before a group can register. Austria, Belarus, Belgium, Croatia, Estonia, Germany, Russia, Slovenia, and Sweden all have both of these types of requirement.

REGULATION OF THE MAJORITY RELIGION

Religious regulation involves limitations placed on the majority religion or all religions. In Western democracies and the former Soviet bloc, the overwhelming majority of states engage in at least some religious regulation. However, as is shown in Table 10.3, except in Orthodox Christian-majority states, levels of regulation are relatively low. As will be recalled, each of the 29 items on the religious regulation scale can be coded as high as 3, depending on the severity of the regulation. The average Orthodox Christian state engages in almost five types of regulation, with many of them coded as higher than 1. This indicates a significant amount of regulation of the religion. The average non-Orthodox state engages in less than two types

Table 10.3 Regulation of the majority religion or all religions in Western democracies and former Soviet-bloc Christian states

	Denomination			Region		European Union 2008		All cases
	Catholic	*Orthodox*	*Other Christian*	*Western democracy*	*Former Soviet*	*No*	*Yes*	
Average number of types of religious regulation	1.35[c]	4.85[b]	2.19	1.85[a]	3.65[a]	3.16	2.19	2.63
Average religious regulation score	2.35[c]	9.54[b]	3.94	3.38[a]	6.95[a]	6.21	4.04	4.93
Engages in at least some religious regulation (%)	82.4%	92.3%	87.5%	88.5%	85.0%	84.2%	88.9%	87.0%
Most common types of religious regulation								
Restrictions on religious political parties	5.9%	46.2%	0.0%	3.8%	30.0%	26.3%	7.4%	15.2%
Restrictions on clergy and/or religious organizations engaging in public political speech	0.0%	38.5%	6.3%	3.8%	25.0%	26.3%	3.7%	13.0%
Restrictions on religious-based hate speech	70.6%	61.5%	75.0%	65.4%	75.0%	63.2%	74.1%	69.6%
The government appoints or must approve clerical appointments, or somehow takes part in the appointment process.	17.6%	30.8%	12.5%	19.2%	20.0%	15.8%	22.2%	19.6%
Other than appointments, the government legislates or otherwise officially influences the internal workings or organization of religious institutions and organizations	0.0%	38.5%	6.2%	7.7%	20.0%	15.8%	10.1%	13.0%
State ownership of some religious property or buildings	5.9%	30.8%	18.7%	15.4%	20.0%	21.1%	17.4%	17.4%

Notes

a Significance of marked mean as compared to means for groups in other categories <0.05.

b Significance of marked mean as compared to means for groups in other categories <0.01.

c Significance of marked mean as compared to means for groups in other categories <0.001.

of regulation, of which one is coded as higher than 1. This indicates that regulation is present but relatively minor.

Of the 29 types of religious regulation included in the RAS dataset, 24 are present in at least one of these states but very few are present in many of them. Table 10.3 lists the six types of regulation that are present in at least six of these states. The most common is restrictions on religious-based hate speech, which are present in 32 states. These laws, which are common in all categories of states examined here, are often found in constitutions and are often parts of general bans on hate speech which are also applied to religion.

The other five types of restrictions discussed here, while found in all categories of states, are most common by far in states with Orthodox Christian majorities. In nine countries, four of them with Orthodox majorities, the government plays a role in appointing clergy. For example, in the United Kingdom the monarch, in consultation with the prime minister and the Crown Appointments Commission (lay and clergy representatives), appoints Church of England officials.

Six countries, five of them with Orthodox Christian majorities, influence the internal workings of religious organizations in some manner other than appointing religious leaders. In Greece the government has the right to modify the Greek Orthodox Church charter, introduce regulations, and suspend non-compliant synods.[8] A 2002 Bulgarian law designates the Metropolitan of Sofia as the seat of the patriarch of the Bulgarian Orthodox Church.[9]

In eight states, four of them with Orthodox Christian majorities, the government owns or controls a significant amount of the religious properties. For example, in France all religious buildings built before 1905, when the law separating religion and state was passed, are owned and maintained by the government (Kuru, 2009). In former Soviet-bloc states such as Russia and Ukraine this refers to property seized during the communist era that has yet to be returned.

In seven countries, six of them with Orthodox Christian majorities, the government restricts religious political parties. In Bulgaria and Portugal the ban is constitutional. In other countries it is based on law. For example, the 1992 Moldovan Law on Denominations states that "[t]he organization of political parties on the basis of religion is forbidden."[10]

Six countries, five of them with Orthodox Christian majorities, limit the participation of clergy and religious organizations in politics. In the United States, tax laws do not allow tax-exempt status for churches that endorse candidates for elections or otherwise engage in electoral political activities. Bulgaria's 1992 Law on Freedom of Confessions and Religious Organizations states that "religious organizations do not participate in the activity of political parties and other public associations which pursue political aims, and do not render them any financial and other support." The 1997 Russian Law on Freedom of Conscience and Religious Associations states that religious associations may not participate in elections to state agencies, or participate in or contribute to political parties.

RELIGIOUS DISCRIMINATION

Religious discrimination involves restrictions placed only on minority religions. I discuss how I define religious discrimination in more detail in Chapter 1 and the introduction to Part 2 of this book. It is common among Western democracies and the Christian states of the former Soviet bloc. Only seven (15.2 percent) of these states (Andorra, Canada, Estonia, Ireland, New Zealand, Portugal, and Slovenia), five of them Western democracies, engage in no religious discrimination. As is shown in Table 10.4, while this discrimination is most common and most intense among the former Soviet states, especially those with Orthodox Christian majorities, it is common in all categories of state examined here. The average country engages in 6 types of religious discrimination, several of them coded as higher than 1. Among Orthodox Christian-majority states this rises to almost 12 types, as opposed to a little less than 4 types for Catholic and other Christian-majority states. The levels of religious discrimination in even those categories of states with comparatively low levels are sufficiently high that they are by no means trivial, and constitute noticeable limitations on minority religions.

Table 10.4 lists ten of the most common types of religious discrimination in the states covered in this chapter. However, 27 of the 30 types included in the RAS dataset are to be found in at least some of these states. The only types not present involve bans on conversion to minority religions and forced conversions to the majority religion.

While these states rarely make religious practices of the majority religion mandatory, they often restrict the religious practices of minority religions. The most common restriction on religious practices is limitations on proselytizing. This type of limitation is common in the West, though usually not particularly severe. For example, Austria, Belgium, Denmark, Switzerland, and the United Kingdom require special visas for missionaries and/or religious workers, and/or have denied entry to some missionaries or religious workers.

In Belarus the restrictions are more severe. Although proselytizing is technically legal, individuals who proselytize are followed by the authorities, detained, and punished. Foreign charity workers, clergy and missionaries, even those with valid visas, faced numerous government obstacles, such as deportation, visa revocation, and harassment. In January 2008, Belarus introduced new, more restrictive guidelines for foreign clergy which authorize the government to deny a visa request without explanation. Only registered national religious associations may apply to invite foreign clergy. Approval is required before the foreign workers can carry out any work or study related to the organization. Foreign missionaries are also forbidden from engaging in religious activities outside of their host institution without prior state permission.[11]

Thirteen countries, eight of them with Orthodox Christian majorities, restrict the public observance of religion. For example, Russia has severely harassed Jehovah's Witnesses, repeatedly breaking up meetings and disrupting religious services. While much of this is done by local authorities, there is a clear pattern. Two typical incidents of this type of harassment include the following. In 2006 the Moscow police disrupted a religious meeting of Jehovah's Witnesses on their most important religious

Table 10.4 Religious discrimination against minority religions in Western democracies and former Soviet-bloc Christian states

	Denomination			Region		European Union 2008		All cases
	Catholic	Orthodox	Other Christian	Western democracy	Former Soviet	No	Yes	
Average number of types of religious discrimination	3.82[a]	11.77[b]	3.88[a]	4.19[a]	8.55[a]	7.63	5.00	6.09
Average religious discrimination score	5.65[a]	19.84[a]	5.69[a]	6.04[a]	14.40[a]	12.52	7.67	10.88
Engages in at least some religious discrimination (%)	76.5%	100%	81.2%	80.8%	90.0%	85.2%	84.2%	84.8%
Most common types of religious discrimination								
Restrictions on public observance of religious services, festivals and/or holidays, including the Sabbath	11.8%	61.5%	0.0%	11.5%	35.0%	26.3%	18.5%	21.7%
Restrictions on building, leasing, repairing and/or maintaining places of worship	47.1	76.9%	43.7%	46.2%	65.0%	57.9%	51.9%	54.3%
Arrest, continued detention, or severe official harassment of religious figures, officials, or members of religious parties for activities other than proselytizing	23.5%	69.2%	6.2%	23.1%	40.0%	26.8%	25.9%	30.4%
State surveillance of minority religious activities not placed on the majority	29.6%	53.8%	12.5%	19.2%	45.0%	26.3%	33.3%	30.4%
Restrictions on the wearing of religious symbols or clothing	17.6%	23.1%	31.2%	23.1%	25.0%	26.3%	22.2%	23.9%
Restrictions on proselytizing	17.6%	76.9%	37.5%	34.6%	50.0%	47.4%	37.0%	41.3%
Requirement for minority religions (as opposed to all religions) to register in order to be legal or receive special tax status	47.1%	84.6%	43.8%	50.0%	75.0%	63.2%	59.3%	60.9%
Restricted access of minority clergy to hospitals, jails, military bases, etc. in comparison to chaplains of the majority religion	35.3%	61.5%	25.0%	23.1%	60.0%	40.3%	36.8%	39.1%
There is a legal provision or policy of declaring some minority religions dangerous or extremist sects, or a government that monitors cults or sects	52.9%	38.5%	12.5%	26.9%	45.0%	44.4%	21.1%	34.8%
Anti-religious propaganda in official or semi-official government publications	29.4%	76.9%	12.5%	24.1%	55.0%	42.1%	33.3%	37.0%

Notes
a Significance of marked mean as compared to means for groups in other categories <0.05.
b Significance of marked mean as compared to means for groups in other categories <0.01.
c Significance of marked mean as compared to means for groups in other categories <0.001.

holiday. Fourteen leaders were detained and interrogated, and had their passports forcibly taken. In 2009, officials in St. Petersburg prevented 68 people from leaving a religious meeting; all worshipers were forced to give out personal information and were interrogated.[12] In Austria, small, non-recognized religious groups are often subject to discrimination and harassment. The Church of Scientology, for example, reported problems in obtaining concessions for staging public events in downtown Vienna.

One of the few types of religious discrimination that is more common in non-Orthodox-majority states are restrictions on the wearing of religious symbols. In the West these exclusively involve restrictions on Muslim women's head coverings. In most cases these restrictions are on public employees and teachers, and are often the result of local government policies. For instance, in 2003 Germany's Federal Constitutional Court upheld a state-level ban on headscarves for civil servants. By the end of 2008 at least eight German states had enacted such a ban. Similarly, several municipalities in Belgium, including Antwerp and Brussels, enacted bans on head coverings by municipal employees. Such bans are different from the 2004 French law banning the wearing of "conspicuous religious symbols" in schools because the French law, while likely targeted at Muslims, applies to all religions and, accordingly, is considered in this book to be a restriction on all religions rather than a form of discrimination that applies only to minority religions.

Another set of common forms of restrictions include limitations placed on religious organizations and their members. Perhaps the most serious category is the arrest, severe official harassment, and detention of members of the minority religion because of their religious activities. Fourteen countries, including five Western democracies, engage in this type of restriction. As already noted, Belarus's limitations on proselytizing result in the arrest and harassment of members of minority religions even when they are not proselytizing. In Armenia the government harasses members of minority religions. For example, in May 2009 government security services detained and interrogated members of a group called "International Services of Christian Culture" for hours without reason and without proper legal procedures. In April 2009 over half the concerts of a visiting American Baptist Church choir were cancelled after the Armenian Church and government accused the choir of being "out to steal souls" during their visit. The group was hassled by national security services during its visit.

In a rapidly increasing form of restriction, 14 of these countries engage in surveillance of minority religious activities. Between 1990 and 2008, Belgium, France, Macedonia, Poland, Russia, and the United Kingdom all began or increased the intensity of this type of activity. This surveillance is to some extent against Muslims in the post-9/11 era but it is mostly against those perceived as "sects" or "cults." In both Belgium and France this is surveillance of cults in the wake of a mass suicide by a cult, discussed in more detail in Chapter 4. Austria similarly monitors groups such as Jehovah's Witnesses, Scientologists, and the Unification Church. This variable was coded only if the surveillance was of religious activities and beyond what would be expected for basic security concerns.

In Macedonia this surveillance is primarily against a specific denomination, the "Orthodox Archbishopric of Ohrid," which is a schismatic group of the Serbian

Orthodox Church that has refused to acknowledge the independence of the Macedonian Orthodox Church and in doing so has incurred the wrath of the Macedonian government and public. This group has suffered from a range of measures by the government, including surveillance of the group's members, repeated arrests and harassment of its leader, Zoran Vraniškovski, denial of legal recognition by the state, and the destruction of one of the group's monasteries. The harassment includes harassment of church officials as they reenter Macedonia based solely on their affiliation with the church, and police questioning of members of the group and their family members. In one case, officials questioned the students of a teacher who belongs to the group. Also, the police refuse to investigate or deter violent incidents against church members and officials.[13] This is a particularly interesting example because it is a clear example of the government repressing a breakaway sect of the dominant religion in order to maintain the institutional dominance of the majority religion.

Seventeen of these countries engage in propaganda against specific minority religions. For example, Poland has declared the Unification Church a "dangerous society" and disseminates literature attacking it. In Austria, "the Society against Sect and Cult Dangers" distributes information to schools and the public, and actively works against any non-recognized religion. While technically an NGO, it is funded by the state, and the government appoints and supervises its head.

A large portion of this harassment, propaganda, and surveillance overlaps with another category, the declaration and monitoring of "dangerous" cults and sects, which is present in 16 countries. This type of law is rapidly increasing, with Belgium, Belarus, France, Germany, Hungary, Italy, Lithuania, Poland, Russia, Spain, and Sweden all adding or increasing the intensity of this type of law or practice between 1990 and 2008. As is discussed in more detail in Chapter 4, both France and Belgium began this practice after mass suicides by cults. However, the targets of these policies are often groups that are not dangerous. Both the Belgian and the French policies seem to be targeted against groups that are small and different rather than against dangerous groups, and groups on the list can potentially suffer from serious discrimination.

By far the most common form of limitations on minority religions are those placed on places of worship. Twenty-five of the states examined here engage in this practice, including 12 Western democracies. This type of discrimination is increasing. Between 1990 and 2008, Austria, Bulgaria, France, Macedonia, Malta, Russia, Spain, Switzerland, and Serbia all either began engaging in this type of restriction or increased the intensity of existing restrictions. In almost all cases these restrictions are the denial of building permits by local governments, but these denials are often widespread across local governments. As is noted in Chapter 3, in the West this type of restriction is mostly against mosques but is also common against religions considered cults. For example, several local governments in France refuse to rent space or grant building permits to Jehovah's Witnesses. In Austria, several provinces have used zoning laws to restrict the building of mosques or minarets. In Switzerland the codings, which end in 2008, predate the national law against minarets passed by referendum in 2009 and, as in Austria, are due to the use of local zoning laws to deny permits for building mosques or minarets. This pattern indicates the possibility that national government policies of restrictions on religious minorities can be fore-shadowed by the actions of local and regional governments.

In the former Soviet bloc and former Yugoslavia, this practice is more widespread and often more severe. In Macedonia, for example, most minority religions are regu-larly denied permission to build places of worship and are often prevented from using existing places of worship. Religious communities including Baptists, Evangelicals, Seventh-day Adventists, Jehovah's Witnesses, and Muslims have complained that the authorities deny them permission either to build new houses of worship or to extend existing ones. In Russia a Moscow court ruled in 2004 that a local group of Jehovah's Witnesses should be banned for being a "threat to society," marking the first time that such a ban was implemented under a 1997 law which includes a clause allowing the banning of "totalitarian sects." Although the ban applied only to Moscow, local organizations of Jehovah's Witnesses throughout Russia reported that their rental contracts on their buildings were cancelled. Numerous local governments across Russia have also restricted building places of worship by Catholics, Evangelical Christians, the Hare Krishna movement, Unitarians, and Muslims.

As is discussed earlier in the chapter, many governments require religious orga-nizations to register. These registration requirements are often applied only to minority religions, as the majority religion is already recognized. In the West this registration is rarely mandatory, and failure to register has few consequences other than a lack of recognition as a legal entity. However, in several former Soviet-bloc states registration is sometimes denied, with significant legal consequences. For example, Bulgaria's 2002 Confessions Act bans all religious activity, including public worship, by unregistered organizations. Similarly, Belarus's 2002 Law on Freedom of Conscience and Religious Organizations bans all religious activity by unregistered groups. In Armenia, unregistered groups may not publish more than 1,000 copies of newspapers or magazines, rent meeting places, broadcast programs on television or radio, or officially sponsor visitors' visas.

Finally, 18 states, including 6 Western states, do not give equal access to chaplains of minority religions. For example, Germany has no Muslim military chaplains. In Greece the restrictions are more severe, as non-Orthodox Christian faiths are not entitled to have official chaplains in the armed forces, hospitals, or prisons.

IMPLICATIONS FOR LIBERAL THOUGHT ON DEMOCRACY

This ubiquitous presence of religious support, regulation, and discrimination in Christian states, many of which are liberal democracies, runs counter to the normative standards set for democracy by many liberal thinkers. Stepan (2000: 39–40), in his classic study of religion and toleration, describes this school of thought as follows:

> Democratic institutions must be free, within the bounds of the constitution and human rights, to generate policies. Religious institutions should not have con-stitutionally privileged prerogatives that allow them to mandate public policy to democratically elected governments. At the same time, individuals and religious communities . . . must have complete freedom to worship privately. In addition,

as individuals and groups, they must be able to advance their values publicly in civil society and to sponsor organizations and movements in political society, as long as their actions do not impinge negatively on the liberties of other citizens or violate democracy and the law.

Perhaps the best-known version of this normative plea can be attributed to Rawls (1993: 151), who argues that we must "take the truths of religion off the political agenda."[14]

As is discussed in more detail in Chapter 2, there are several versions of ideologies that require some form of separation of religion and state. However, all of them require that either the state support no religion or all religions be supported equally. They all require that minority religions have at least as much freedom of religion as the majority religion. Yet the evidence presented here shows that Western democracies, which are generally considered to be the most liberal of the liberal democracies, substantially support religion and limit the freedom of religious minorities. This finding implies that liberal democratic theory on religion is an ideal that is rarely met rather than a description of what actually occurs in most liberal democratic states.

RELIGION AND STATE IN THREE WESTERN DEMOCRACIES

In order to further illustrate the range of religion policies in Western democracies, I briefly discuss three of them, intended to represent the low to middle levels of the spectrum.

The United States

The Western country with the highest level of separation of religion and state in practice is the United States. The first amendment of the US constitution is one of the shortest constitutional clauses on religion of any country in the world. It very briefly declares that "Congress shall make no law respecting an establishment of religion, or prohibiting the free exercise thereof." Through a legal doctrine called the "incorporation doctrine" the US Supreme Court has made this also obligatory for state and local governments. With a few notable exceptions, these clauses are strictly followed and the government does not fund, support, or limit religion. There is some minor funding of religious charitable organizations, which are allowed to compete for government contracts to provide social services, and for religious private schools by local governments, which provide vouchers to students who want to study in private schools. A number of states and local governments also ban the sale of alcohol or require that businesses close on Sundays and certain Christian holidays. The only incidence of religious discrimination in the United States that met the level of influencing the RAS codings is a refusal by the US military to provide Wiccan chaplains. The levels of religious support and discrimination in the United States are extremely minor compared to those in most other Western democracies.

Spain

Spain is a typical mid-level country. Article 16 of its constitution guarantees religious freedom and states that "no religion shall have a state character." However, it also states that "the public authorities shall take into account the religious beliefs of Spanish society and shall consequently maintain appropriate cooperation relations with the Catholic Church and other confessions."[15] This ambivalence, where the government declares separation of religion and state on one hand but gives preference to one or a few religions on the other, is the most common policy among Western democracies.

While recently the government has tried to distance itself from it, the Catholic Church maintains a special relationship with the government. It receives financing and tax benefits not given to other religions, including the funding of salaries of the clergy, Catholic schools, and prison and hospital chaplains. Also, taxpayers can contribute up to 0.7 percent of their taxes to the Catholic Church through a voluntary check-off on their tax forms.[16]

Jewish, Protestant, and Muslim groups receive a status known as *notorio arraigo*: "well-known, deeply-rooted beliefs." This involves benefits based on bilateral agreements between the governments and these religions which grant tax benefits, civil validity to religious weddings performed, and allow chaplains and teachers of each religion to be placed in hospitals, schools, and prisons. Mormons, Buddhists, and Jehovah's Witnesses have also recently been granted this status but are not granted the same privileges as the three religions that originally received the status. All other religions must register to gain legal recognition. The process is cumbersome, so some religions choose to register with regional governments as cultural associations. In rare cases, such as that of the Church of Scientology, registration is sometimes denied. This, in effect, creates a hierarchical system of recognition, with each tier having a different status and receiving different benefits.

Since 2003 a yearly course on Catholicism, given by priests, or teachers appointed by the Catholic Church, has been taught in all public schools. The curriculum for the courses on Catholicism contains the church's position on sex, divorce, abortion, and basic theology. However, students may opt to take a "non-confessional" general religious facts course, which has been criticized for content that is similar to the courses on Catholicism. In 2004 the government allowed courses in Judaism, Protestantism, and Islam.[17] However, recent changes have weakened government support for Catholicism. Since the 2004 election of a socialist government, laws have been passed to legalize same-sex marriage, make divorce easier, and legalize stem cell research.[18]

Discrimination against religious minorities in Spain is lower than average but present. They include the registration issue noted above. Chaplains who are not Catholic, Jewish, Protestant, or Muslim have less access to hospitals, prisons, and the military. Also, some local governments have denied permits for the building of places of worship by minority religions.

Spain is about average for a Western democracy. As is noted earlier in the chapter, eight Western democracies have official religions. Others, such as Germany, Sweden, and Switzerland, despite having no official religions, engage in levels of support for religion and levels of religious discrimination higher than Spain's. Many additional countries score higher on at least one of the RAS variables religious support, religious regulation, and religious discrimination.

Greece

Greece has what is perhaps the strongest connection between religion and state among Western democracies. Article 3 of Greece's constitution not only establishes the Greek Orthodox Church as the state religion but discusses the composition of the church's leadership and church doctrine:

> The prevailing religion in Greece is that of the Eastern Orthodox Church of Christ. The Orthodox Church of Greece, acknowledging our Lord Jesus Christ as its head, is inseparably united in doctrine with the Great Church of Christ in Constantinople and with every other Church of Christ of the same doctrine, observing unwaveringly, as they do, the holy apostolic and synodal canons and sacred traditions. It is autocephalous and is administered by the Holy Synod of serving Bishops and the Permanent Holy Synod originating thereof and assembled as specified by the Statutory Charter of the Church . . . [19]

However, article 13 protects religious freedom.

The government pays the salaries of all officially recognized Greek Orthodox and Muslim religious officials, and finances the maintenance of church buildings. The government has the right to modify the Orthodox Church charter, introduce regulations, and suspend non-compliant synods. Greek Orthodox canon law is recognized by the government for matters of religious and civil law. Most shops must be closed on Sunday but in practice there are legal means for stores to remain open. Religious education in the state religion, as well as Greek Orthodox morning prayers, is present in public schools. It is mandatory for members of the Orthodox Church, but members of other religions may opt out. Non-Orthodox faiths are referred to disparagingly in school textbooks. Only the Orthodox Church, Islam, and Judaism have the status of "Legal Entities of Public Law," which entitles them to own property and appear in court as religious organizations. All other religions must register as "Legal Entities of Private Law." They cannot own property and must create legal entities in order to own land or appear in court. Catholic churches can gain legal recognition only if they were established before 1946.[20]

All elected and government officials are required to take religious oaths of office. In February 2008, Greece was found by the European Court of Human Rights to be in violation of article 9 of the European Convention on Human Rights in the case of a lawyer who was forced to publicly state that he was not an Orthodox Christian before being permitted to take a non-religious oath.[21]

In addition, minority religions with legal status must apply for "house of prayer" permits from the Ministry of Education and Religion to build each place of worship. Until 2006 the approval process included consulting the local Greek Orthodox bishop, which resulted in the denial of most permits. Operating a place of worship without a permit can result in prosecution. Minorities without legal status, such as the Baha'is, are not eligible for these permits. They may operate as civil associations but their beliefs have no legal status as religions. According to Greek law, private religious schools may not function in buildings owned by non-Orthodox religious faiths, but this law is not enforced. Until 2007, minority religious organizations were taxed. Until 2006, cremation was illegal, which made it impossible for Buddhists to observe burial rites. Although it is now legal, cremation facilities are generally unavailable in Greece.[22]

Although Jehovah's Witnesses are officially a "known" religious group, members are routinely harassed by arbitrary identity checks. They are regularly denied "house of prayer" permits, or, more often, the government does not respond to requests. This is often used as an excuse not to register marriages among Jehovah's Witnesses because they were not performed in recognized houses of prayer. In 1999 and 2001 a tax office repeatedly refused to recognize a Jehovah's Witnesses group as a non-profit organization and imposed an inheritance tax on property willed to the Jehovah's Witnesses (Anderson, 2003).

Article 13 of Greece's constitution prohibits all proselytizing. This ban is enforced selectively. Mormons and Jehovah's Witnesses engaged in proselytizing are regularly detained by police, but members of most other religions are left alone.[23]

The Muslim community of Thrace has a special status under the 1923 Treaty of Lausanne. The treaty allows Muslims to maintain charitable organizations and have muftis (Muslim judges) render decisions on Muslim family and civil law. Accordingly, Sharia family and civil law is recognized in Thrace. However, civil courts can overrule Sharia law, which happens on occasion, especially in cases in which it is believed that the Sharia courts have discriminated against women. The government appoints these muftis despite opposition to this practice by Thrace's Muslim community, which has elected its own muftis. On several occasions the government has prosecuted the elected muftis for usurping the functions of the appointed mufti. The European Council for Human Rights ruled that these prosecutions violate the rights of the elected muftis.[24]

Muslims outside of Thrace have a more difficult time. For example, in Athens there is no mosque, despite the existence of a 250,000-member community. Muslims in Athens and elsewhere are forced to worship in unrecognized mosques, technically an illegal act. Greek law requires the exhumation of remains after three years, a practice that is problematic for Muslims, as Islamic law prohibits exhumation of remains. Moreover, there is no Islamic cemetery in Athens.[25]

CONCLUSIONS

State support for religion and discrimination against religious minorities is the norm in both Western democracies and former Soviet Christian states. While the specific policies vary greatly from state to state, exceptions to this more general rule are rare. In fact, several Western democratic states significantly discriminate against many religious minorities. Such discrimination runs counter to notions held by many of what ought to be occurring in liberal democracies and emphasizes that examination of the facts on the ground should be an important element of theoretical discussions of religion and politics.

CHAPTER 11

Christian-Majority States 2

The Third World

This chapter examines the 52 Christian states not included in the previous chapter.[1] These include 6 Christian states in Asia which are not part of the former Soviet bloc (called here non-former Soviet Asia), 21 in sub-Saharan Africa, and 25 Latin American states. Like the countries examined in the previous chapter, these countries have diverse histories and traditions. Yet they also share at least one commonality: that Christianity was brought to them with colonization from the West. The colonizers have officially left, and these countries are now independent, but Christianity remains the majority religion in all of these states. These states are similar in some respects to Western and former Soviet Christian states but different in others.

In order to take into account the diverse traditions and histories of these countries, I categorize these countries based on two factors. The first is world region. As is noted above, the countries can be found in three world regions. The second is religious tradition. As there are no Orthodox Christian states in the Third World, I differentiate between Catholic and non-Catholic states. As I note in Chapter 10, while the states in the last category mostly have Protestant majorities, there is some dispute over exactly how that term is defined, so I avoid that label.

In this chapter I also introduce a third point of comparison. I compare the results from this chapter with those from the previous chapter in order to highlight the overall differences between Christian states in the Third World and Christian states in the West and the former Soviet bloc. To simplify matters, I will call the Third World Christian states TWCs and those of the West and former Soviet-bloc WFSBCs.

Overall, the TWCs have considerably less government involvement in religion in all four categories examined here than do the WFSBCs. More importantly, levels of official support for religion, religious support, and religious discrimination are lower in the TWCs than in Western democracies. This fact directly contradicts a large body of literature discussed in more detail in Chapter 2 which argues that the West is secular, and religion is experiencing a resurgence in the Third World. The TWCs engage in more regulation of the majority religion than do the WFSBCs, but much of this regulation is about limiting religion's role in politics rather than limiting religious practice or institutions.

That being said, government involvement in religion remains the norm for these states. I discuss potential explanations for this finding later in the chapter.

OFFICIAL RELIGIONS

Table 11.1 shows the prevalence of official religions in Third World Christian countries. Six of the 52 TWCs have official religions. Five of these states—Cape Verde, Argentina, Bolivia, Costa Rica, and the Dominican Republic—are Catholic-majority countries. Among these states, all but Cape Verde are in Latin America. An additional 14 support one religion more than others. Thus, a minority of 38.4 percent states, all but three of them with Catholic majorities, single out one religion for support, as compared to a majority of 54.4 percent of the WFSBCs. While the proportion of Catholic states supporting a single religion (as either an official religion or an unofficially preferred religion) is similar among both the TWCs and the WFSBCs, there is a dramatic difference in the proportion of non-Catholic states supporting a single religion. In the TWCs it is 3 of 25 (12 percent), while in the WFSBCs it is 10 of 13 (76.9 percent) Orthodox Christian states, and 5 of 16 (31.3 percent) of "other" Christian states, support one religion more than others. Thus, the practices of Catholic states in this respect remain consistent across world regions but the behavior of non-Catholic Christian states is markedly different.

Most of the states that do not favor one religion tend to treat all religions equally. While the highest concentration of these states is in non-Catholic states and in sub-Saharan Africa, a large proportion of states in all regions, as well as a large proportion of Catholic states, fit into this category. These states include some that are among the most restrictive of religion, such as Eritrea and Mexico, and those that are among the most uninvolved in religion, such as Namibia, South Africa, and Uruguay.

RELIGIOUS SUPPORT

Other than South Africa, all of the TWCs engage in some form of support for religion. In fact, South Africa is the only state in the entire RAS dataset that did not engage in any of the 51 categories of religious support included in the RAS dataset in 2008.

As is presented in Table 11.2, the average TWC country has about 5 of the 51 types of religious support included in the RAS dataset, and this is consistent across world religions and true of both Catholic and other Christian countries. Thirty of these types are present in at least one of these TWCs. However, as common as religious

Table 11.1 Official religions in Third World Christian countries

	Denomination		Region			All cases	Western democracies and former Soviet
	Catholic	Other Christian	Asia	Sub-Saharan Africa	Latin America		
Official religion	18.5%	4.0%	0.0%	9.5%	16.0%	11.5%	19.6%
One religion supported more than others	44.4%	8.0%	0.0%	4.8%	52.0%	26.9%	34.8%
Some religions supported more than others	3.7%	32.0%	66.7%	23.8%	0.0%	17.3%	30.4%
No unequal treatment	33.3%	56.0%	33.3%	61.9%	32.0%	44.2%	15.2%
N	27	25	6	21	25	52	46

Table 11.2 Religious support in Third World Christian countries

	Denomination		Region			All cases	Western democracies and former Soviet
	Catholic	Other Christian	Asia	Sub-Saharan Africa	Latin America		
Average number of types of religious support	5.15	5.00	5.50	4.81	5.20	5.08	7.59
Engage in at least some religious support (%)	100%	96.0%	100%	95.2%	100%	98.1%	100%
Common types of religious support (%)							
Marriages performed by clergy are given automatic civil recognition	33.3%	12.0%	0.0%	14.3%	36.0%	23.1%	30.4%
Laws that specifically make it illegal to be a homosexual or engage in homosexual intimate interactions	7.4%	68.0%	50.0%	61.9%	12.0%	36.5%	0.0%
Religious education is present in public schools	66.7%	64.0%	83.3%	57.1%	68.0%	65.4%	84.8%
Government funding of religious primary or secondary schools or religious educational programs in non-public schools	37.0%	32.0%	66.7%	19.0%	40.0%	34.6%	65.2%
Official government positions, salaries or other funding for clergy	25.9%	8.0%	0.0%	9.5%	28.0%	17.3%	45.7%
Presence of an official government ministry or department dealing with religious affairs	44.4%	28.0%	66.7%	19.0%	44.0%	36.5%	50.0%
Restrictions on abortions	96.3%	96.0%	100%	90.5%	100.0%	96.2%	28.3%
A registration process for religious organizations exists which is in some manner different from the registration process for other non-profit organizations	70.4%	52.0%	33.3%	57.1%	72.0%	61.5%	71.7%

Notes
No differences in means are statistically significant.

support is in the TWCs, it is significantly less common than in the WFSBCs. In fact, when one compares the results in Table 11.2 to those for the WFSBCs in the previous chapter (Table 10.2), there is no category of states analyzed among the WFSBCs that has less religious support than any of the categories of the TWCs.

Thus, these results definitively prove that among Christian states, religious support is more common in Western and former Soviet states than in the Third World. This is a particularly interesting result as it contradicts a large body of theory that is discussed in more detail in Chapter 2 which argues that the West is secular and that religion is experiencing a resurgence in the Third World. I discuss this finding in more detail later in this chapter.

Table 11.2 also presents the eight most common types of religious support in the TWCs. This list is similar to the common forms of support in the WFSBCs presented in Chapter 10, with five of the items overlapping.

As in the WFSBCs, one of the most common forms of support for religion in the TWCs is religious education in public schools. Thirty-four of the TWCs have religious education in public schools, including a majority in all analyzed categories. As is the case with the WFSBCs, in nearly all cases this education is not mandatory. The one exception is Zambia, which is discussed in more detail later in this chapter.

However, there exists considerable exclusivity in this religious education. In seven states—the Bahamas, Belize, Bolivia, Costa Rica, the Dominican Republic, Panama, and Swaziland—public school religious education is available only in one religion, despite the existence of significant minority populations in all of these countries. All of these countries except Swaziland are in Latin America. Also, in 11 (21.1 percent) of these states, nine of them Catholic, the teachers are clergy or appointed by religious institutions. This is extremely similar to the case in WFSBC states. This indicates a pattern in Catholic-majority states of religious education in public schools controlled by the Catholic Church. Overall, this is present in 22 of 44 Catholic-majority states present in the RAS dataset. This is half of all Catholic-majority states, as against 14.8 percent of all non-Catholic Christian states, 23.4 percent of all Muslim-majority states, and 9.4 percent of states with other religious majorities.

Eighteen of the TWCs also support private religious education, which makes it considerably less common than in the WFSBCs. Perhaps this can be explained by the fact that TWCs tend to be poorer states than those in the WFSBC group and simply have less government funding available for private education in general.

Two facts support this hypotheses regarding funding. The first is that funding for religion in general is considerably rarer in TWCs than in the WFSBCs. While the average WFSBC state engages in 3.52 of the types of financing for religion included in the RAS dataset, the average TWC state engages in 1.25.[2] Thus, it is clear that the financing of religion is considerably less common in the TWCs. The second is that the average GDP per capita for 2008 in the WFSBCs, according to the *UN Statistical Yearbook*, is $35,202, which is almost seven and a half times as high as the $4,731 average GDP per capita in the TWCs.

Given this, it is not surprising that while, other than supporting religious education, four types of religious funding are among the most common forms of government support for religion in the WFSBCs, there is only one type of financial support for religion among the most common types of support in the TWCs. Nine

TWCs, seven of them in Latin America, provide state funding for clergy. This funding is often limited. For example, in Tanzania the government of Zanzibar has made the region's Muslim mufti a public employee. In Haiti, Catholic bishops are nominated by the president and paid by the state. Peru provides salary supplements to the country's 52 bishops as well as those priests whose ministries are located in towns and villages along the country's borders.

As in the WFSBCs, some of the religious support is bureaucratic. Twelve TWCs give religious marriages civil recognition, meaning that marrying under the auspices of a religion brings automatic civil recognition without any necessity to take extra steps to register the marriage with the civil authorities. Thirty-two TWCs have some form of registration process for religion. This means that religious organizations must register in some manner that is unique to religious organizations. In most cases, registration is rarely denied and failure to register does not influence freedom of worship.

However, there are limited exceptions. For example, in the Central African Republic, since 2008 registration of new religious groups has required proof by the religious group that it has at least 1,000 members and leaders who graduated a religious school which the government considers a "well-respected" school. But this legal requirement is rarely enforced. Also, in some cases failure to register has consequences above and beyond being denied the tax privileges that many countries give religions. For example, Burundi's government shuts down all places of worship that fail to register but usually gives a warning and rarely denies registration requests. Equatorial Guinea fines congregations that fail to register, but this penalty is rarely applied and, as in Burundi, applications for registration are usually accepted, though the bureaucratic process can take years. Only Eritrea both restricts registration and limits unregistered religious groups. In May 2002 the government decreed that all religious groups must register, or cease all religious activities. The government also often refuses to register groups such as Jehovah's Witnesses who have no historical ties to the country.

In all, two things must occur for a registration requirement to be a serious barrier to religious practice. First, there must be severe consequences for failure to register. Second, the government must restrict registration. In the TWCs, other than Eritrea, no government takes both measures of this kind. Accordingly, this form of religious support is rarely a barrier to the practice of religion in the TWCs.

Another aspect of bureaucracy common in TWCs is the presence of a government department, ministry, or other body responsible for religious affairs—although these government bodies are not as common as in the WFSBCs.

Also, as in the WFSBCs, legislating religious precepts as law is rare in the TWCs, but there are two exceptions. Both of these exceptions are not overtly religious laws but they are laws that are heavily correlated with religion. That is, religious Christians are much more likely to support these kinds of laws. The first is restrictions on homosexuals. To be clear, this type of law, which is present in 19 TWCs (36.5 percent) does not refer to unequal treatment or rights for homosexuals but, rather, involves the banning of being a homosexual or engaging in a homosexual act. This type of ban is most often found in sub-Saharan Africa among TWCs, and in most cases bans male homosexuality.

The second is a ban on abortion, which is almost universal in TWCs, at least with regard to abortion on demand. Only Cape Verde and South Africa have no ban on abortion on demand in the first trimester, though Guyana allows it in the first eight weeks of a pregnancy. As is shown in Table 11.3, the extent of the ban varies, with 11.5 percent of these states, such as Timor and Chile, limiting abortions even to save the life of the mother. In many cases the laws banning abortion are left over from the colonial era and have not been changed.

REGULATION OF THE MAJORITY RELIGION

As is presented in Table 11.4, just under three-quarters of TWCs regulate the majority religion. Twenty-four of the 29 types of religious regulation measured by the RAS dataset are present in at least one of the TWCs. The average TWC engages in about two of these practices, usually with at least one of them coded as being of more than minimal severity. (As will be recalled, each type of religious regulation can be coded as high as 3.) Except in Asia, this is consistent across different categorizations of states. While it is thus a common practice, it is substantially less common than in the WFSBCs. Three of the six most common practices regulating religion in the TWCs overlap with the most common practices in the WFSBCs.

It is interesting to note that most regulation of religion in the TWCs can be attributed to limitations on religious influence in politics. That is, religious practices and institutions as such are clearly not the target of most of this regulation. Rather, this regulation is meant to protect politics from religious influence. In fact, the three most common types of religious regulation in the TWCs are direct bans on religious political activity.

First, 15 TWCs, 11 of them in sub-Saharan Africa, restrict religious political parties. In many of these cases, including Ghana, Mexico, and the Philippines, the country's constitution specifically bans religious political parties. In others, including Burundi, the Central African Republic, the Republic of Congo, Rwanda, Panama, and Tanzania, the constitution the bans religious political parties but this ban is not limited to religion and rather bans political parties based on a number of types of identification, including religion, ethnicity, nationality, color, sex, and region. Many countries, including Eritrea, Kenya, and Zambia, do not have a constitutional ban but ban religious parties on the basis of laws or government policy. Some bans include both constitutional and law or policy elements. Uganda's constitution states that "membership of a political party shall not be based on sex, ethnicity, religion, or other sectional division." It also has a law banning political parties based on "sex, race, color, ethnic origin, tribal birth, creed, or religion." Such a ban is not clear or total in all TWCs that have one. For example, in Gabon, acts of religious discrimination are punishable by law, as are acts that threaten the "internal or external security of the State or the integrity of the Republic." These laws have been used to outlaw "particularist" parties, which includes parties associated with a particular religious interest and identity (Basedau *et al.*, 2007).

Second, 12 TWCs, 10 of them in Latin America, limit the ability of clergy to run for political office. For instance, article 77 of Honduras' constitution states that

Table 11.3 Restrictions on abortion in Third World Christian countries

	Denomination		Region			All cases	Western democracies and former Soviet
	Catholic	Other Christian	Asia	Sub-Saharan Africa	Latin America		
To save the life of the mother	18.5%	4.0%	16.7%	4.8%	16.0%	11.5%	2.2%
To preserve the physical health of the mother	59.3%	28.0%	50.0%	33.3%	52.0%	44.2%	6.5%
To preserve the mental health of the mother	77.8%	44.0%	66.7%	52.4%	68.0%	61.5%	6.5%
Rape	74.1%	68.0%	100%	71.4%	64.0%	71.2%	10.9%
Incest	81.5%	68.0%	100%	71.4%	72.0%	75.0%	10.9%
Economic reasons	92.6%	84.0%	100%	85.7%	88.0%	88.5%	17.4%
Social reasons	92.6%	84.0%	100%	85.7%	88.0%	88.5%	17.4%
On request	96.3%	96.0%	100%	90.5%	100.0%	96.2%	28.3%

Table 11.4 Regulation of the majority religion or all religions in Third World Christian countries

	Denomination		Region			All cases	Western democracies and former Soviet
	Catholic	Other Christian	Asia	Sub-Saharan Africa	Latin America		
Average number of types of religious regulation	2.22	1.88	1.00	2.52	1.92	2.06	2.63
Average religious regulation score	4.56	3.40	1.67	4.62	4.04	4.00	4.93
Engage in at least some religious regulation (%)	81.5%	64.0%	66.7%	76.2%	72.0%	73.1%	87.0%
Most common types of religious regulation							
Restrictions on religious political parties	22.2%	36.0%	16.7%	52.4%	12.0%	28.8%	15.2%
Restrictions on clergy holding political office	37.0%	8.0%	16.7%	4.8%	40.0%	23.1%	2.2%
Restrictions on religious activities outside of recognized religious facilities	7.4%	16.0%	0.0%	23.8%	4.0%	11.5%	2.2%
Restrictions on clergy and/or religious organizations engaging in public political speech	22.2%	24.0%	0.0%	33.3%	20.0%	23.1%	13.0%
Restrictions on religious-based hate speech	22.2%	16.0%	16.7%	19.0%	20.0%	19.2%	69.6%
State ownership of some religious property or buildings	22.2%	4.0%	0.0%	4.8%	24.0%	13.5%	17.4%

Notes
No differences in means are statistically significant.

"ministers of the various religions may not hold public office nor engage in any form of political propaganda, invoking religious motives or using people's religious beliefs as a means to that end." Article 134 of Nicaragua's constitution does not allow "ministers of any religion" to run for a number of national political offices "unless they have left their ministry at least twelve months prior to the election." Articles 197 and 235 of Panama's constitution similarly ban ministers of religion from running for the national legislature, president, or vice president.

Third, 12 of the TWCs limit political speech and activities by clergy and political organizations. Article 82 of El Salvador's constitution states that "the ministers of any religion . . . may not belong to political parties or opt for elective office. Nor may [they] make political propaganda in any form." Article 130 of Mexico's constitution states that clergy

> shall not consort for political purposes or proselytize in favor of or against any candidate, party or political association. Nor may they, in a public meeting, in the activities of their religion, in religious propaganda or in publications of a religious character, oppose the laws of the country or its institutions, or make an affront to national symbols in any way. . . . Meetings of a political character cannot be held in houses of religious worship.

In Eritrea a 1995 proclamation bans religious organizations from involvement in politics and limits the right of religious media to comment on political matters.

Ten of the TWCs ban religious hate speech. As is the case with similar bans in the WFSBCs, these bans are often found in constitutions and are often parts of general bans on hate speech which are also applied to religion. Seven of the TWCs, six of them in Latin America, own religious property. As part of its constitutional obligation to support the Catholic Church, Costa Rica's government sometimes maintains ownership of the property but allows the church free use. Until 1992 the Mexican constitution nationalized all religious property. In 1992 this specification was amended, but most religious property from earlier than 1992 still belongs to the government.

Six countries, five of them in sub-Saharan Africa, restrict religious activities outside of recognized religious facilities. These restrictions tend to be minor. For example, a 1995 law in Angola bans cult "demonstrations" outside of authorized locations but is rarely enforced. In Zimbabwe the Public Order and Security Act of 2002 requires police notification to hold public gatherings. Although the law is not specifically aimed at religious activities, and even exempts "religious" activities and events, the government has used the law to interfere with religious and civil society groups organizing public prayer rallies, especially in cases where it suspected that the groups would be critical of the government.

RELIGIOUS DISCRIMINATION

As is the case in the WFSBCs, religious discrimination—limitations on the religious practices and institutions of minority religions that are not placed on the majority religion—is common in the TWCs. As is shown in Table 11.5, 44 of 57 of these states engage in at least some discrimination. The average TWC state engages in 2.24 types of discrimination, at least one of them coded as being of more than minimal severity. (As will be recalled, each type of religious discrimination can be coded as high as 3.) Twenty-three of the 30 types of religious discrimination included in the RAS dataset exist in at least one TWC country. Nevertheless, religious discrimination in the TWCs is lower than the average for the WFSBCs in general but similar to the levels for Western democracies and states belonging to the European Union. This is particularly interesting because many of the TWCs are not generally classified as democracies. In fact, 11 of them can be classified as clearly autocratic, as measured by the Polity project. Eight of the 12 least democratic TWCs—the Central African Republic, Equatorial Guinea, Fiji, Gabon, the Republic of Congo, Swaziland, and Tanzania—all score 4 or lower on the discrimination scale, placing them lower than the average scores for Western democracies and EU states. Among these 12 states, only Eritrea scores above 8. This finding further undermines theories discussed in Chapters 2 and 10 predicting that liberal democracies will have the highest level of religious tolerance.

Six of the seven most common forms of religious discrimination in TWCs are also among the most common in the WFSBCs. Interestingly, all six of them are less common than in the WFSBCs. All of this further undermines theories discussed in Chapters 2 and 10 predicting that liberal democracies will have the highest level of religious tolerance.

The most common form of discrimination is the requirement for minority religions to register in some manner not incumbent on the majority religion. As is noted earlier in the chapter, in most TWCs registration is rarely denied and failure to register does not substantially influence the freedom of worship.

Eighteen of the TWCs restrict proselytizing. In the majority of cases the restrictions are limited to minor regulation of foreign missionaries in a way that is not applied to other immigrants or visitors to the country. For example, in Argentina, Colombia, El Salvador, Guatemala, Nicaragua, and Venezuela, missionaries must receive special visas, but these visas are rarely denied. In Belize, foreign missionaries must purchase a religious worker's permit. In Ecuador and Honduras they require special residence permits.

However, in some cases the restrictions are more cumbersome. For example, in Panama the permit requirements are more substantial. Foreign missionaries are granted temporary three-month religious worker visas upon submitting required paperwork, which includes an AIDS test certificate and a police certificate of good conduct. A one-year extension is customarily granted with the submission of additional, less onerous, documentation. Foreign religious workers who intend to remain in Panama more than 15 months must repeat the entire process. However, Catholic and Jewish clergy are given five-year permits. Trinidad and Tobago limits foreign religious workers to 30 per denomination.

In Eritrea, foreign Catholic and Protestant missionaries are active. Some missionaries and representatives of the non-sanctioned religious groups operate in the country but keep a low profile. The government restricts missionary visas. In 2003 it denied visas to representatives of Jehovah's Witnesses and other groups who requested permission to travel to the country to meet with their congregations or

Table 11.5 Religious discrimination in Third World Christian countries

	Denomination		Region			All cases	Western democracies and former Soviet
	Catholic	Other Christian	Asia	Sub-Saharan Africa	Latin America		
Average number of types of religious discrimination	2.37	2.16	1.00	2.57	3.32	2.27	6.09
Average religious discrimination score	3.37	3.52	1.00	4.19	3.40	3.44	10.88
Engage in at least some religious discrimination (%)	85.2%	72.0%	33.3%	81.0%	88.0%	78.8%	84.8%
Most common types of religious discrimination							
Restrictions on public observance of religious services, festivals and/or holidays, including the Sabbath	3.7%	28.0%	0.0%	28.6%	8.0%	15.4%	21.7%
Restrictions on building, leasing, repairing and/or maintaining places of worship	11.1%	12.0%	16.7%	19.0%	4.0%	11.5%	54.3%
Restrictions on formal religious organizations	11.1%	24.0%	0.0%	28.6%	12.0%	17.3%	17.4%
Arrest, continued detention, or severe official harassment of religious figures, officials, or members of religious parties for activities other than proselytizing	7.4%	20.0%	0.0%	23.8%	8.0%	13.5%	30.4%
Restrictions on proselytizing	63.0%	4.0%	16.7%	4.8%	64.0%	34.6%	41.3%
Requirement for minority religions (as opposed to all religions) to register in order to be legal or receive special tax status	51.9%	24.0%	0.0%	38.1%	48.0%	38.5%	60.9%
Restricted access of minority clergy to hospitals, jails, military bases, etc. in comparison to chaplains of the majority religion	18.5%	4.0%	0.0%	4.8%	20.0%	11.5%	39.1%

Notes
No differences in means are statistically significant.

discuss religious freedom issues with government officials. In 2006 a British missionary was detained and later expelled for distributing Bibles. In 2007 the government expelled 13 foreign missionaries from Colombia, Mexico, the Philippines, Italy, and Kenya in "unclear circumstances." The government also restricts fundamentalist forms of Islam. Most foreign preachers of Islam are not allowed to proselytize, and funding of Islamic missionary or religious activities is controlled.

Six TWCs, five of them in Latin America, restrict minority chaplain access to places where majority-group chaplains have free access. For example, in the Dominican Republic the military has only Catholic chaplains. In Peru the police and military similarly have only Catholic chaplains. In addition, a 1999 government decree compelled members of the armed forces and the police, as well as their civilian co-workers and relatives, to participate in Catholic services.

Nine TWCs, six of them in sub-Saharan Africa, place restrictions on minority religious organizations. In Eritrea, as discussed above, such restrictions apply to groups not allowed to register. In 2002, Zaire (the Democratic Republic of Congo) banned the Bundu dia Kongo (BDK) on the grounds of its separatist political beliefs. This ethnically based spiritual and political movement calls for the establishment of an "ethnically pure" kingdom for the Bakongo tribe. In 1977 the Unification Church was banned in Venezuela.

Eight TWCs, six of them in sub-Saharan Africa, restrict the public observance of religion. As is repeatedly noted in this chapter, in Eritrea this applies to religions refused registration, for which public religious observance is illegal. The nature and reasons for the bans vary. Tanzanian police often ban outdoor public religious events that they believe may lead to Muslim–Christian tensions and violence. In Uganda the police also restrict public religious events for security reasons, but these restrictions seem to be universally applied to non-mainstream religions considered cults.

The most common form of ban is on witchcraft. Because groups practicing witchcraft rarely form an organization or institutions, the bans are effectively on the practice of the religion. In Kenya, practicing witchcraft is a criminal offense under colonial-era laws. However, persons are usually prosecuted for this offense only in conjunction with some other offense, such as murder. Witchcraft is also illegal in Zimbabwe but the law is rarely enforced. In 2005 the Bahamas banned Obeah—a form of voodoo—as witchcraft (Paton, 2009). In Malawi, witchcraft prosecutions are more common. The 1911 Witchcraft Act makes it an offense both to claim that another person is practicing witchcraft and to claim that one practices witchcraft oneself. Being a professional witchdoctor or witchfinder is an offense punishable by life imprisonment. The Act assumes that witchcraft does not exist and therefore makes the practice illegal. It states that "any person, who by his statement or actions represents himself to be a wizard or witch or exercising the power of witchcraft, shall be liable to a fine of 50 British Pounds and to imprisonment for 10 years." A report by the Women and Law in Southern Africa Malawi Research and Education Trust found that, in a visit to 11 prisons, there was an average of four witchcraft cases per prison.[3]

Six TWCs, four of them in sub-Saharan Africa, restrict minority religions' places of worship. As is the case in Western democracies, most of these cases, such as in Timor and Rwanda, refer to local governments denying minority religions permission to build places of worship.

Finally, seven TWCs, five of them in sub-Saharan Africa, arrest, detain, or otherwise harass people for engaging in religious activities. In Eritrea this harassment is of unregistered religions. As already noted, in Malawi practitioners of witchcraft are arrested and jailed. In Rwanda, Jehovah's Witnesses are periodically jailed for refusing to participate in government-mandated night patrols. In Mexico's Chiapas region, sometimes local leaders have consented to, or ordered, the harassment or expulsion of individuals belonging largely, but not solely, to Protestant Evangelical groups.

GOVERNMENT POLICIES IN SIX THIRD WORLD COUNTRIES

In this section I examine the government religion policies of six of these countries. I select them to represent all three world regions in which these countries can be found and the different types of policies in each region.

Solomon Islands

Solomon Islands represents the non-former Soviet Asian countries. These countries have low levels of religious discrimination and of government regulation of the majority religion but do have substantial religious support. They also tend to treat all religions equally. This is a good description of the religion policy in the Solomon Islands.

Solomon Islands is a former British protectorate that gained independence in 1976 and in July 2010 had a population of about 560,000.[4] Ninety-two percent of the population belong to various Christian denominations and most of the rest follow indigenous religions. The country's constitution does not address the issue of an official religion but does include a lengthy section on religious freedom.[5] This principle is put into practice since the RAS project codes no religious discrimination against minority religions and no government regulation of the majority religion. There is a registration requirement for religious organizations, but no group has ever been denied registration.

The country engages in several types of support for religion, but in a manner that does not explicitly privilege any one denomination of Christianity. The country allows abortion only in order to save the life of the woman. Sections 160–162 of the penal code make same-sex relations illegal. There is Christian education in public schools but students whose parents do not want them to attend these classes are excused. The government subsidizes church schools and church-run hospitals. It also allows religious groups, Christian and non-Christian, access to airtime on public radio.

Namibia

Namibia is a multiparty democracy that became independent from South Africa in 1988. About 90 percent of the population is Christian, mostly Lutheran and

Catholic. Exact numbers are hard to estimate because many practice a combination of Christian and indigenous beliefs. Article 1 of Namibia's constitution declares the country to be secular and article 21 protects the freedom of religion. While some government officials have expressed preferences for the Anglican, Lutheran, and Roman Catholic denominations, this preference does not translate into government policy. According to the RAS codings, Namibia has no religious discrimination and does not regulate the majority religion. The only form of religious support is in the areas of abortion and homosexuality. Abortion, while legal to save the life or the physical or mental health of the mother, as well as in cases of rape, incest, or fetal impairment, is not allowed for economic reasons, social reasons, or upon request. Same-sex sexual relations are illegal in Namibia for males but not females.[6]

Namibia is representative of a number of Christian countries in sub-Saharan Africa which basically have neutral religion policies. Others include Angola. Cape Verde, the Central African Republic, the Democratic Republic of Congo, Lesotho, the Republic of Congo, South Africa, and Zaire. Collectively, these countries have high levels of separation of state and low levels of religious discrimination that meet or exceed the standards of most Western democracies, though all of them except South Africa still to some small extent legislate for or support religion. This is particularly interesting because according to the Polity project, which provides international measures of democracy, other than Lesotho and South Africa none of these countries meets the democratic standards of Western democracies, and Angola, the Central African Republic, and the Republic of Congo are outright autocracies. This provides further evidence that separation of religion and state and religious freedom are possible under circumstances other than liberal democracy.

Zambia

Zambia is the only sub-Saharan Christian-majority state with an official religion. The country is 50–75 percent Christian, with substantial Muslim and Hindu minorities. The preamble of Zambia's 1996 constitution declares it to be "a Christian nation while upholding the right of every person to enjoy that person's freedom of conscience or religion." Despite this official declaration, government support for religion, regulation of Christianity, and discrimination against minority religions is minimal. While religious groups must register, this registration has never been denied, with one exception that was overturned by the country's Supreme Court. The government provides religious education in Catholicism and Protestantism in public schools but not in the Muslim and Hindu faiths, despite the existence of large populations of both of these religions. In 2007 this education became mandatory for all students. This is the only instance of serious religious discrimination against minority religions in Zambia. Abortion is legal in order to save the life or the mental or physical health of the woman as well as in cases of fetal impairment and for socioeconomic reasons. It is not allowed upon request or in cases of rape or incest. Same sex-sexual relations are illegal for males but not females.

Despite its support for Christianity, the government restricts religion in politics. In 1993 the government banned an Islamic political party but made a specific effort to emphasize that this was because it prohibits all religious political parties. In a similar vein the country's penal code prohibits acts and speech that have the "intent to wound religious feelings."

These examples of Zambia and Namibia are representative of most sub-Saharan African Christian countries. They tend to stay out of religion. When they support it, this support is minimal and, with some exceptions, does not greatly advantage the majority religion. Limitations on religion in politics and on religious hate speech are more common. The only glaring exception to this pattern is Eritrea, which is discussed at several points earlier in this chapter.

Uruguay

Uruguay is one of several countries in Latin America which, like many sub-Saharan Christian countries, have substantial levels of separation of religion and state. and low levels of religious discrimination. The country is about 80 percent Christian, most of the population being Catholics. Article 5 of Uruguay's constitution declares that "the State does not support any religion" but it does give all churches built in the past by the government to the Catholic Church and declares all places dedicated exclusively to worship tax-exempt. The RAS dataset records no discrimination against minority religions and no regulation of Catholicism. In order to gain tax exemptions, religious organizations must apply every five years for recognition of their religious status, but this recognition is rarely denied. Abortion is illegal except to save the life, physical health, or mental health of the mother and in cases of rape or incest.

This minimal intrusion into religion by the government is similarly present in other Latin American and Caribbean Christian-majority countries such as Barbados, Brazil, Ecuador, Guyana, Jamaica, and Paraguay.

Guatemala

Guatemala is about 99 percent Christian, with about two-thirds of these Christians being Catholic. Article 37 of Guatemala's 1986 constitution as amended through 1993 does not declare Catholicism to be the country's official religion but clearly gives it special recognition:

> The juridical personality of the *Catholic Church* is recognized. The other churches, faiths, organizations and associations of a religious character will receive the recognition of legal status under the rules of their institution, and the government cannot deny it except for reasons of public order.
>
> The State will extend to the *Catholic Church*, at no cost, titles to the properties which it currently owns and uses peacefully for its own purposes, provided that they have been part of the heritage of the *Catholic Church* in the past. The affected assets may not be entered in favor of third persons, or assets that the state has traditionally allocated for its services.

Properties owned by religious institutions intended for worship, education and social assistance are exempt from taxes, fees and contributions.[7]

The constitution also limits religion's role in politics. Articles 186, 197, and 207 restrict ministers of religion from holding various political offices, including those of president, vice president, minister, or judge. Article 33 states that "[r]eligious demonstrations outside of churches are permitted and governed by the law." But the constitution also supports religion. It guarantees religious freedom. It allows religious education in public schools while stating that such support should be "without discrimination." It also recognizes marriages performed by clergy.[8]

Non-Catholic religions do not need to register in order to worship but they do need to register in order to be recognized as a legal entity or to own or rent property. Such registration is rarely denied, though the process can take several years. Foreign missionaries must obtain a visa, which must be renewed every three months. These visas require a sponsor who assumes financial responsibility for the missionary while they are in Guatemala. These visas are routinely granted and renewed.

Religious education in public schools is present in most schools but this is determined at the local level. Constitutional guarantees of non-discrimination are observed. The government subsidizes some private schools, including religious schools. Abortion is illegal except to save the life of the woman.

Guatemala is representative of several Christian Latin American countries which unofficially favor a single branch of Christianity, usually Catholicism. They have varying levels of discrimination against minority religions, though usually higher than that of Guatemala. Also, some of them, like Guatemala, restrict political activities by clergy and religious groups. These countries include the Bahamas, Belize, Chile, El Salvador, Haiti, Honduras, Nicaragua, Panama, Paraguay, Peru, and Venezuela.

Costa Rica

About 84 percent of Costa Ricans are Christian, most of them Catholic, but 11.3 percent report having no religious affiliation. Article 75 of Costa Rica's constitution declares that "the Roman Catholic and Apostolic Religion is the religion of the State, which contributes to its maintenance, without preventing the free exercise in the Republic of other forms of worship that are not opposed to universal morality or good customs." However, other parts of the constitution limit the role of religion in politics. Article 28 declares that "clergymen or secular individuals cannot make political propaganda in any way invoking religious motives or making use of religious beliefs." Articles 131, 142, and 159 require that the president, the vice president, ministers, and justices be "laymen."[9]

Costa Rica's Ministry of Foreign Affairs and Religion manages the government relationship with the Catholic Church as well as with all other religions. There is a clear preference for Catholicism in government policy. Until 2004 the government provided an annual subsidy for the Catholic Church. Weddings performed by Catholic priests, and by ministers of other religions, are recognized as valid by the government. The church also performs some semi-official functions. For example, in 2003 the Catholic Church was actively involved in negotiations to end labor strikes. Catholic education is administered in public schools by teachers certified by the Catholic Church Conference. In fact, the law states that the Catholic Church appoints all religion teachers in public schools, and only graduates of Catholic institutions are eligible for the job. In theory, parents can request that their children should not receive this education. In practice, there have been complaints that schools require a letter from the child's clergyperson and that students had to remain in the classroom when Catholic doctrine was being taught, because of a lack of alternative activities. The state subsidizes private schools, including religious ones. Abortion is legal only in order to save the life or health of the woman.

There is no registration requirement for minority religions in order to worship. However, they must register in order to gain residence permits for foreign missionaries and employees, to fundraise, and to gain recognition for their religious holidays. Registration is similar to that for any association and is rarely denied. Until 2003, Catholic chaplains had preferred access to hospitals and prisons in that all other chaplains were placed under the same limits to entry as the general public. Since 2003, non-Catholic chaplains legally have had access, but there are many instances of administrators and staff denying this access. Several non-Catholic churches have been closed by local governments because of noise complaints or other zoning or safety violations. This never happens to Catholic churches. A 2006 law requires that all foreign missionaries belong to a religious organization accredited by the Ministry of Foreign Affairs and Religion. The government has an agreement with the Catholic Church to expedite visa applications for Catholic priests. Also, while the Unification Church has been declared a dangerous sect by the government, its activities do not seem to be limited.[10]

Costa Rica is one of four Latin American countries with official religions. The others are Argentina, Bolivia, and the Dominican Republic. All of these countries are Catholic and reasonably democratic. All of them support Catholicism in practice, though not to a great extent. All of them also place low levels of restrictions on at least some minority religions on a level akin to the restrictions placed by the average Western democracy.

CONCLUSIONS

The Latin American countries highlighted in this chapter show a region where both government support for religion and religious discrimination are lower than in Western democracies. There are some glaring exceptions to this pattern, such as Mexico, which has a distinct anticlerical history. However, overall, it is arguable that Latin America is closer to achieving the liberal values of separation of religion and state and religious freedom than are Western democracies. Many sub-Saharan and non-former Soviet Asian states also fit this description.

Accordingly, the patterns of behavior among the TWCs as compared to the WFSBCs have some interesting implications. As is discussed briefly above, TWCs have lower levels of government support for religion and government interference in religion than do the WFSBCs. Even when one compares the TWCs to the Western democracies, among the WFSBCs the TWCs rarely have more government involvement in religion than do these Western democracies. Yet according to liberal political theory, liberal democracies should have among the highest levels of separation of religion and state in the world. Despite this, the TWCs, many of which are clearly not even democracies, in practice have as much or more separation of religion and state than do Western democracies on nearly all measures.

Clearly, liberal democratic theory cannot explain this. I offer two commonalities among the TWCs that may contribute to an understanding of why these countries have these relatively lower levels of government involvement in religion.

First, as is discussed earlier in the chapter, these are poorer and weaker states. As Anthony Gill (2008) argues, getting involved in religion requires resources. Financing religion uses up scarce funds. Supporting it in other ways, such as enforcing religious laws as state law, also requires resources. As these states have fewer resources in general, they have fewer resources to devote to religion. Second, Christianity is relatively newer in the TWCs, having been brought by Western missionaries and supported by colonial governments. This means that Christianity has had less time to become entrenched in these states. Most of them still have significant populations that continue to practice traditional indigenous and tribal religions, sometimes in a syncretic format that combines Christianity and these indigenous religions.

A second interesting pattern is that most of the restrictions placed on the majority religion or all religions are on religion's political role. That is, many of these states ban or limit some form of political activity by religious groups and clergy. Such restrictions indicate a greater wariness by the political classes in TWCs of the power of religion to influence politics. This wariness concerning religion in politics may provide a cultural-based explanation for the generally high levels of separation of religion and state in many of these countries.

CHAPTER 12

Muslim-Majority States

A common misconception about Islam is that Muslim states are universally religious and all of them strongly support Islam.[1] While this is true of many Muslim states, it is not true of all of them. In fact, as the discussion in this chapter reveals, there is a wide diversity of state religion policies among Muslim states.

To a great extent this diversity is regional. That is, Muslim-majority states located in the same geographic region tend to have similar religion policies. The detailed discussion of the religion policies in former Soviet Muslim-majority states in Chapter 3 shows an example of this. Accordingly, in this chapter I categorize Muslim majority states into the following regions: (1) the Persian Gulf states, (2) the rest of the Middle East and North Africa, (3) sub-Saharan Africa, (4) the former Soviet bloc, and (5) non-Soviet Asia. Yet despite the similarities between state religion policies within these regions, there is still diversity within each region, with no two states having identical policies.

In this chapter I discuss the religion policies of the 47 Muslim-majority states included in the RAS dataset, using the same categories of state religion policy as discussed in Chapter 1 and the previous two chapters: official state religions, religious support, religious regulation, and religious discrimination. I follow this discussion by examining the diversity of state religion policy in Muslim-majority states. Unlike in previous chapters, I do not provide country outlines at the end of the chapter but, rather, rely on more detailed examples throughout the chapter.

A NOTE ON THE "ARAB SPRING"

At the time of this writing, there are a number of active opposition movements in the Middle East that are part of a movement known as the "Arab Spring" which began on December 18, 2010. This movement is a series of uprisings and protests against many of the repressive governments in the Middle East, including, in particular, those of Bahrain, Egypt, Libya, Syria, Tunisia, and Yemen. While these movements have the potential to change many aspects of the regimes in these countries, I do not deal with these uprisings in this chapter, for two reasons.

First, the analysis here is centered on the RAS dataset, which is current only through 2008. Second, at the time of this writing the situation is still unclear. Libya and Syria are essentially in a state of civil war. Bahrain's government remains in power. However, to the extent that the situation is resolving itself, it appears that state support for religion in these countries will increase. In Egypt the Islamic Brotherhood and Salafi parties combined to gain over two-thirds of parliamentary seats in recent elections but have not yet taken power and it is unclear whether they will be allowed to do so. In Tunisia's 2011 elections the Ennahda party, an Islamist party, won the largest number of seats but not a majority. It has formed a caretaker government with leftist parties which is expected to write a new constitution. The opposition movement in Syria is dominated by Islamists, and the civil war in Libya is to a large extent tribal, but Islamist forces will most likely play a large role should a government be formed.

It will likely be several years before the long-term results of the Arab Spring become clear. However, all current indications show that to the extent that change occurs, it will involve governments which adhere more strongly to Muslim fundamentalist ideologies than those that they replace. This indicates a strong likelihood that state support for religion, as well as religious discrimination against minorities, will increase. The increased number of violent attacks on Egypt's Christian Coptic minority certainly supports this prediction.

OFFICIAL RELIGIONS

Official religions are far more common among Muslim-majority states than in any other religious grouping. As is shown in Table 12.1, 25 (53.2 percent) of these 47 states have an official religion. For this reason, in this chapter I use the RAS categorizations of different types of official religions. *Religious states*—Afghanistan, Brunei, Iran, Kuwait, the Maldives, Malaysia, Oman, Pakistan, Qatar, and Saudi Arabia—are states that not only support a majority religion but also make following at least some significant aspects of the religion mandatory for members of the majority religion. While other states also do this, the extent to which these ten states do so is considerably more substantial. In the cases of the Maldives and Saudi Arabia, many Islamic laws are mandatory for all residents, whether or not they are Muslims, though Saudi Arabia enforces this policy much more actively than the Maldives.

This type of state religion policy is found only among Muslim-majority states in the Persian Gulf and Asia. There is no state outside of these regions, whether Muslim

Table 12.1 Official religions in Muslim countries

	Middle East			Non-Middle East				All Muslim states
	Persian Gulf	Other Middle East	All Middle East	Sub-Saharan Africa	Former Soviet	Non-Soviet Asia	All non-Middle East	
Official religion: religious state	55.6%	0.0%	23.8%	0.0%	0.0%	71.4%	19.2%	21.3%
Official religion: state-controlled religion	33.3%	33.0%	33.3%	0.0%	0.0%	0.0%	0.0%	14.9%
Official religion: active support	11.1%	25.0%	19.0%	23.1%	0.0%	14.3%	15.4%	17.0%
One religion supported more than others	0.0%	25.0%	14.3%	15.4%	0.0%	14.3%	11.5%	12.8%
Some religions supported more than others	0.0%	8.3%	4.8%	15.4%	16.7%	0.0%	11.5%	8.5%
Equal treatment, positive attitude	0.0%	0.0%	0.0%	46.2%	0.0%	0.0%	23.1%	12.8%
Hostile	0.0%	8.3%	4.8%	0.0%	83.3%	0.0%	19.2%	12.8%
N	9	12	21	13	6	7	26	47

majority or non-Muslim majority, that enforces the majority religion to this extent. Saudi Arabia is perhaps the most extreme example of such a state, with much of its law being based on Sharia—Islamic law. Article 8 of the country's constitution declares that "government in the Kingdom of Saudi Arabia is based on the premise of justice, consultation, and equality in accordance with the *Islamic Sharia.*" Article 23 declares that "the state protects Islam; it implements its Sharia." Article 48 declares that "the courts will apply the rules of the Islamic Sharia in the cases that are brought before them." Other parts of the constitution directly link family, education, property, capital, labor, human rights, criminal law, and the monarchy to Sharia law or Islamic principles. An advisory body of 20 religious judges, including the Minister of Justice, called the Council of Senior Ulema meets periodically to interpret Sharia and establish state legal principles. There is a separate religious police called the Mutaww'ain which enforces religious dress codes, separation of the sexes, and others violations of Sharia principles.[2]

State-controlled religions are states that strongly support the majority religion but also substantially control its religious institutions. In these states—Bahrain, Egypt, Jordan, Libya, Tunisia, the United Arab Emirates, and Yemen—while religion certainly influences legislation and government policy, the government is clearly dominant over the religion. This type of state religion among Muslim states is found only in the Middle East. It is rare among non-Muslim states, with only Greece following a similar policy. For example, article 2 of Libya's constitution under Qaddafi declares Islam the official religion. Sharia law is the basis for much but not all of Libya's laws. For example, alcohol, pork, and homosexuality are all prohibited. However, all religious activity is under control of the government. The Islam taught and practiced in the country is based on "The Green Book," written by leader Muammar al-Qaddafi. The book outlines Qaddafi's vision and political philosophy. All religious groups are required to conform to these principles and refrain from any political activity that challenges the government. The government directly controls most mosques, including the content of weekly sermons, and the few that are private follow the government-approved interpretations of Islam. The government also controls both the publication and the importation of all religious literature.[3]

This level of control is typical of Muslim-majority states in this category. It is also a much higher level of control than is exerted by Greece, the only non-Muslim-majority country in this category. I discuss the Greek case in more detail in Chapter 10.

Active support for the state religion is the type of official religion present in most non-Muslim states with official religions but is present in only a minority of Muslim-majority states: Algeria, Bangladesh, Djibouti, Iraq, Mauritania, Morocco, Somalia, and the Western Sahara. These states actively support Islam but make less of an effort to regulate and control it than do states in the previous category. For example, Mauritania's constitution declares the country to be Islamic and requires that the president be a Muslim. The country substantially supports Islam, and many of its laws are based on Sharia law, particularly family and criminal law. Yet the religion is not mandatory and the government does not substantially regulate Islam, other than to limit its use in politics, and place limits on what the government considers Islamic extremists, especially if they are foreign backed.[4]

About an eighth (12.8 percent) of Muslim-majority states—Comoros, Guinea, Indonesia, Sudan, Syria, and the government of Turkish Cyprus—have no official religion but in practice support Islam more than any other religion. The policies in these states range from that of states like Indonesia, with levels of support and regulation similar to levels found in governments with state-controlled religion policies, to that of the government of Turkish Cyprus, whose support for religion is considerably lower.

About a third (34.1 percent) of Muslim-majority states do not support Islam exclusively. In 8.5 percent of such countries, such as Lebanon, support is given to several religions more or less equally. Another 12.8 percent, all of them other than Albania located in western sub-Saharan Africa, either support all religions equally or maintain separation of religion and state. An additional 12.8 percent, all of them other than Turkey (through 2008) in the former Soviet bloc, are hostile to religion in general and limit the public influence of Islam. The former Soviet-bloc countries in this category are discussed in more detail in Chapter 3.

RELIGIOUS SUPPORT

As is presented in Table 12.2, religious support is common in Muslim-majority states. All of them have at least some religious support, and, other than in the former Soviet bloc, average levels are considerably higher than in Christian-majority states. However, there is a significant amount of diversity in the extent of religious support. Interestingly, while the Middle East has the reputation for the highest levels of state support for religion in the world, the Muslim-majority non-Soviet Asian states have a higher average level than even the Persian Gulf states. Nevertheless, the state with the highest levels of religious support is Saudi Arabia, a Persian Gulf state. Sub-Saharan African states have levels of religious support considerably lower than other Muslim-majority states in other regions excluding the former Soviet bloc.

Fifty of the 51 types of religious support coded by the RAS dataset exist in at least two Muslim-majority states. Forty-eight types exist in at least five states. The only type that is not present in these states is the granting of diplomatic status to clergy. Thus, religious support not only is common among Muslim majority states but includes nearly the entire range of types of support.

In this section I discuss the ten most common forms of religious support in Muslim-majority states, all of which exist in a majority of these states. Unlike in Christian-majority states, where the funding of religion and government bureaucratic support for religion are the most common forms of religious support, in Muslim-majority states the most common forms of support for religion are the legislation of religious precepts as law. Seven of the top ten forms of religious support fit into this category—though, to be clear, the funding of religion is also quite common. The average Muslim-majority country engages in 3.28 types of the 12 types of funding measured by the RAS dataset, which is actually slightly less than the 3.52 types found in the Christian-majority Western democracies and former Soviet-bloc countries discussed in Chapter 10. However, it is considerably higher than the 1.25 types present in the Third World Christian countries discussed in Chapter 11.

Table 12.2 Religious support in Muslim countries

	Middle East			Non-Middle East				All Muslim states
	Persian Gulf	Other Middle East	All Middle East	Sub-Saharan Africa	Former Soviet	Non-Soviet Asia	All non-Middle East	
Average number of types of religious support	22.44	17.67	19.71[b]	9.08	4.67[c]	26.85[c]	12.85[b]	15.91
Engage in at least some religious support (%)	100%	100%	100%	100%	100%	100%	100%	100%
Common types of religious support (%)								
Restrictions or prohibitions on the sale of alcoholic beverages	88.9%	58.3%	71.4%	30.8%	0.0%	85.7%	38.5%	53.2%
Personal status defined by religion or clergy (i.e. marriage, divorce, and/or burial can only occur under religious auspices)	77.8%	75.0%	76.2%	23.1%	16.7%	71.4%	34.6%	53.2%
Restrictions on interfaith marriages	88.9%	83.3%	85.7%	7.7%	0.0%	85.7%	26.9%	53.2%
Laws of inheritance defined by religion	100%	83.3%	90.5%	38.5%	0.0%	100%	46.2%	66.0%
Laws that specifically make it illegal to be a homosexual or engage in homosexual intimate interactions	77.8%	58.3%	66.7%	61.5%	0.0%	85.7%	53.8%	59.6%
Blasphemy laws or any other restriction on speech about majority religion or religious figures	88.9%	75.0%	81.0%	23.1%	0.0%	100%	38.5%	57.4%
Religious education is present in public schools	100%	83.3%	90.5%	46.2%	0.0%	100%	50.0%	68.1%
Funding for building, maintaining, or repairing religious sites	55.6%	75.0%	66.7%	23.1%	50.0%	85.7%	46.2%	55.3%
Presence of an official government ministry or department dealing with religious affairs	88.9%	83.3%	85.7%	76.9%	100%	100%	88.5%	87.2%
Restrictions on abortion	88.9%	75.0%	81.0%	100%	0.0%	100%	76.9%	77.7%

Notes

a   Significance of marked mean as compared to means for groups in other categories <0.05.
b   Significance of marked mean as compared to means for groups in other categories <0.01.
c   Significance of marked mean as compared to means for groups in other categories <0.001.

Before I begin this description of the most common religious laws in Muslim-majority states, it is important to briefly discuss Sharia (Islamic) law. Sharia potentially encompasses most aspects of life. This body of law is based on the Koran, and on the Sunna, which are sayings and stories attributed to the prophet Muhammad. There are many interpretations of Sharia law, which can results in many practical differences in state policies among states that use Sharia law as a basis for legislation. Yet Sharia law is the source for much of the religious support in Muslim-majority states.

As is shown in Table 12.2, among the most common forms of Sharia law that are passed as state law in Muslim-majority states are laws relating to personal status—essentially, family law and inheritance law. Standard interpretations of Sharia family law generally contain the following types of provisions. Men can divorce their wives with little difficulty and without cause. However, women usually encounter significant difficulty in divorcing their husbands without the husband's consent. In some cases, divorce without the husband's consent is impossible. While Muslim men may marry non-Muslim women, Muslim women are often not allowed to marry non-Muslim men. In cases of divorce in these mixed marriages, the non-Muslim women are rarely given custody of their children. The children are considered Muslims and it is often illegal to raise them as members of another religion. Sharia law allows men to have up to four wives, though many Muslim-majority states prohibit polygamy.

Women are also at a disadvantage in inheritance. They tend to receive smaller shares of their parents' estates than do their brothers. In some cases, when all of the direct heirs are women a male relative is still given much of the inheritance. If a woman is not a Muslim, she often has no right of inheritance from her husband. States that base their family law on Sharia are likely also to base their inheritance law on Sharia. Twenty-three of the 25 Muslim-majority states that base family law on Sharia also base the laws of inheritance on religion, Kyrgyzstan and Gambia being the exceptions. An additional eight Muslim-majority states base their inheritance law but not family law on Sharia. In many cases this application of Sharia law applies only to Muslims, not to members of minority religions. Either minority religions are allowed to use their own family laws or the state legislates a set of secular family laws for non-Muslims.

There are certainly exceptions to this, as not all Muslim-majority states use Sharia law for family law and inheritance, but those that do tend to follow some interpretation of these general principles.

Sharia law also bans alcohol. Twenty-five Muslim-majority states, most of them in the Middle East, enforce this ban with the power of the state. In many states, such as Egypt, Oman, and the United Arab Emirates, alcohol is available to tourists but in others, such as Kuwait and Saudi Arabia, there is no such exemption.

Blasphemy against Islam is banned in 27 of these states. Unlike in Christian-majority states with this type of law, blasphemy laws are typically enforced to some extent, and sometimes very strictly. For example, in Brunei article 189 of the 1984 Religious Council and Kadis Courts law states that

> whoever in any theatrical performance or in any place of public entertainment uses any passage of the Quran or any words having a sacred implication to persons professing the Islamic religion or derides or copies in a derisive manner any act

or ceremony relating to the Islamic religion shall be guilty of an offense: Penalty, imprisonment for one month or a fine of $8,000.[5]

The government strictly enforces this, to the extent that it monitors any Muslim group it considers non-orthodox and usually bans such groups (Black, 2008).

Pakistan's constitution (article 19) grants freedom of speech but specifically limits this right "subject to any reasonable restrictions imposed by law in the interest of the glory of Islam." Pakistan's penal code includes multiple clauses banning blasphemy against Islam. For example, article 295c states that

> [w]hoever by words, either spoken or written, or by visible representation or by any imputation, innuendo, or insinuation, directly or indirectly, defiles the sacred name of the Holy Prophet Muhammad (peace be upon him) shall be punished with death, or imprisonment for life, and shall also be liable to fine.[6]

This is not a case of laws on the books that go unenforced. Blasphemy cases are brought regularly in Pakistani courts, especially against members of minority religions. In fact, criminal blasphemy prosecutions are so common that in 2005 the government passed a law requiring that the police investigate accusations of blasphemy before charges are filed. This reduced such arrests from a rate of 74 a year before the law was passed to 34 a year immediately afterwards.

Twenty-eight of these countries make homosexuality illegal. For example, the Penal Code of the Federal Islamic Republic of Comoros, article 318, states that

> whoever will have committed an improper or unnatural act with a person of the same sex will be punished by imprisonment of between one and five years and by a fine of 50,000 to 1,000,000 francs. If the act was committed with a minor, the maximum penalty will always be applied.
>
> (Ottosson, 2009)

Article 144 of Gambia's 1965 Criminal Code, as amended in 2005, similarly states that

> any person who has carnal knowledge of any person against the order of nature . . . or permits any person to have carnal knowledge of him or her against the order of nature is guilty of a felony, and is liable to imprisonment for a term of 14 years . . . carnal knowledge of any person against the order of nature includes . . . committing any . . . homosexual act with the person.
>
> (Ottosson, 2009)

Morocco's 1962 penal code states that

> any person who commits lewd or unnatural acts with an individual of the same sex shall be punished with a term of imprisonment of between six months and three years and a fine of 120 to 1,000 dirhams, unless the facts of the case constitute aggravating circumstances.
>
> (Ottosson, 2009)

Thirty-eight of these countries restrict abortion. However, unlike in Christian-majority countries, the policies are consistent. Nearly all of the countries that restrict abortion on demand also restrict it in cases of rape and incest, and for economic and social reasons. However, only three Muslim-majority countries—Indonesia, Lebanon, and Somalia—restrict it when necessary to save life of the mother. Even in these countries, abortions to save the life of the mother, while restricted, are possible. In Indonesia, for example, according to a 1992 law an abortion to save a woman's life must be based upon advice from medical experts, requires consent from the woman and her husband or family, and must be performed by an obstetrician or gynecologist.

Thirty-two Muslim-majority countries support religious education in public schools. In nine countries—Brunei, Iran, Kuwait, Libya, Qatar, Saudi Arabia, Sudan, Tunisia, and Yemen—it is available only in Islam and mandatory for all students, whether or not they are Muslim. In an additional 14 countries, education in Islam is mandatory in public schools for at least some members of minority religions. Finally, 37 of these countries have government departments that deal with religion, and 26 financially support the building and maintenance of mosques. These final three forms of government support for religion are also common in Christian countries.

REGULATION OF THE MAJORITY RELIGION

While Muslim-majority countries heavily support Islam, they also heavily regulate it. As is shown in Table 12.3, the average levels of regulation among Muslim-majority states are almost four times the levels found in Christian states and are high in all categorizations of Muslim-majority states other than those in sub-Saharan Africa. All 29 types of religious regulation included in the RAS dataset are present in at least two Muslim-majority states, and 22 of them are present in at least five of these states.

The patterns of religious regulation by region show an interesting diversity. Within the Middle East, the non-Persian Gulf states have the most regulation of religion, but both Persian Gulf and non-Persian Gulf Middle Eastern states have average levels that are near the mean. Outside of the Middle East, the former Soviet states and the non-Soviet Asian states have extremely high levels of religious regulation, while levels in sub-Saharan Africa are relatively low.

While it is often difficult to discern motivations from actions, in this case it is arguably possible to do so. The seven most common types of religious regulation, shown in Table 12.3, indicate that this regulation is likely motivated to a great extent, though not exclusively, by a desire to control the impact of Islam as a potential political opposition force.

Nearly all of these seven most common forms of government regulation of Islam have political importance. That 27 of these states restrict Muslim political parties is a case in point. This number is actually low, because many of these countries, such as Oman, Qatar, and Saudi Arabia, do not allow any political parties at all, and this variable was coded only if political parties were allowed but religious parties were banned or restricted.

Table 12.3 Religious regulation in Muslim countries

	Middle East			Non-Middle East				All Muslim states
	Persian Gulf	Other Middle East	All Middle East	Sub-Saharan Africa	Former Soviet	Non-Soviet Asia	All non-Middle East	
Average number of types of religious regulation	6.33	8.42	7.52	2.92[c]	12.33[b]	10.29	7.08	7.28
Average religious regulation score	14.78	18.25	16.76	6.77[c]	29.17[b]	23.57	16.46	16.60
Engage in at least some religious regulation (%)	88.9%	91.7%	90.5%	85.7%	100%	100%	92.3%	92.5%
Common types of religious regulation (%)								
Restrictions on religious political parties	33.3%	75.0%	57.1%	61.5%	83.3%	28.6%	57.7%	57.4%
The government restricts or harasses members and organizations that are affiliated with the majority religion but operate outside of the state-sponsored or recognized ecclesiastical framework	22.2%	75.0%	52.4%	38.5%	83.3%	100%	65.4%	59.6%
Restrictions or monitoring of sermons by clergy	88.9%	83.3%	85.7%	15.4%	83.3%	57.1%	42.3%	61.7%
Restrictions on clergy and/or religious organizations engaging in public political speech	33.3%	41.7%	38.1%	23.1%	50.0%	42.9%	34.6%	36.2%
Restrictions on or regulation of religious education in public schools	77.8%	66.7%	71.4%	7.7%	0.0%	85.7%	26.9%	46.8%
Restrictions on or regulation of religious education outside of public schools, or general government control of religious education	33.3%	33.3%	33.3%	7.7%	83.3%	85.7%	46.2%	40.6%
The government appoints or must approve clerical appointments, or somehow takes part in the appointment process	44.4%	50.0%	47.6%	15.4%	50.0%	71.4%	38.5%	42.6%

Notes

a   Significance of marked mean as compared to means for groups in other categories <0.05.
b   Significance of marked mean as compared to means for groups in other categories <0.01.
c   Significance of marked mean as compared to means for groups in other categories <0.001.

Egypt before the "Arab Spring" provides a good example of this and the other four types of restrictions on Islam, which are clearly intended to limit its political impact. Article 4 of Egypt's constitution states that "no political activity shall be exercised nor political parties established on a religious referential authority." Thus, both religious political parties and the involvement of clergy and religious organizations in politics are banned. The government appoints and pays the salaries of most imams. Whether or not they are on government salary—as imams in "unauthorized" mosques are not among those appointed by the government—the government monitors their sermons, primarily for political content. The Muslim Brotherhood, Egypt's largest opposition group, and comprising radical Islamists, has officially been outlawed since 1954; its members are routinely detained and harassed (Guindi, 2006). However, in the wake of the "Arab Spring" protests in Egypt it emerged as the largest political party elected to Egypt's parliament in the 2011–2012 elections.

Syria also provides an interesting example. While not declaring Islam the official religion, article 3 of Syria's constitution states that "the religion of the President of the Republic has to be Islam [and] Islamic jurisprudence is a main source of legislation." This support for Islam is present in policy. For example, Sharia law guides family law for Muslims and inheritance laws for all Syrians other than Catholics. As in Egypt, the government funds mosques but appoints the imams and monitors their sermons for political content. The government severely restricts radical Islam. It considers militant Islam a threat and closely monitors the practice of any known militant groups. The regime bans Islamist political parties, and membership in the Muslim Brotherhood is technically a capital offense, though this penalty is rarely applied. Beginning in 2008 the government began "moving forcefully to curb the influence of Muslim Conservatives." It has "fired Imams and asked others to provide recordings of their Friday sermons." This crackdown began in 2008 but gained steam in the summer of 2010. All of this predates the protests of the "Arab Spring" of 2011.[7]

The regulation of religious education in public and private schools, which is present in 22 and 19 Muslim-majority states respectively, does not refer to bans on religious education. It refers to government control of the content of that education. This policy can be attributed, at least in part, to controlling the spread of forms of radical Islam that can be a political threat to the state. For example, in Malaysia the government sets the curriculum for Islamic education in public schools. The teachers of these courses require government approval. Private schools can receive funding from the government, but this funding is contingent upon the acceptance of government supervision and the implementation of a government-adopted curriculum, including the curriculum for religious studies. Even when a private school is not funded, the government monitors it and has required teachers to retire or be fired for unspecified reasons. In addition, the government closes schools considered too radical.[8]

In some cases, such as that of Saudi Arabia, this control of religious education also has clear aspects of maintenance of doctrinal orthodoxy. Education in Saudi Arabia's Wahhabi interpretation of Sunni Islam is mandatory in all public schools, even those attended by Shiite Muslims. The public school curriculum as a whole is a reflection of the country's interpretation of Islam. Anything that may be perceived as "un-Islamic" is prohibited. Also prohibited are the study of evolution, Western philosophy, Freud, Marx, and Western music.[9]

RELIGIOUS DISCRIMINATION

Religious discrimination against minority religions is also high in Muslim majority states. As is shown in Table 12.4, with the exception of Muslim-majority states in sub-Saharan Africa, all categories of Muslim-majority states engage in levels of religious discrimination that are considerably higher than those in Christian states. All 30 types of religious discrimination—which again refers to limitations on the practices or institutions of a minority religion that are not placed on the majority religion—are present in at least two Muslim-majority states. Twenty-five of them are present in at least ten of these states. Among the ten most common forms of religious discrimination, seven restrict the practice of religion. This is different from what is found in Christian states, where the more common restrictions focus on religious institutions.

The overall pattern shows religious discrimination being higher in the Middle East but, as is the case with religious support and regulation, this is deceptive. Overall, in Muslim-majority states religious discrimination is highest in the Gulf region and non-Soviet Asia, which have similar levels of discrimination. The non-Gulf Middle Eastern states and the Muslim-majority states of the former Soviet bloc have levels similar to each other. However, the Muslim-majority states in sub-Saharan Africa have levels of religious discrimination that are not just relatively low compared to other Muslim-majority states but only slightly higher than those in Western democracies. I discuss these patterns and trends in more detail later in the chapter.

Limitations on the practice of religion

The most common form of religious discrimination in Muslim-majority states is limits placed on proselytizing. For example, in Yemen proselytizing is considered apostasy under Sharia law and is punishable by death, though this sentence is rarely, if ever, imposed. However, those who proselytize are arrested. In Jordan there is no official edict against proselytizing but government policy in practice restricts efforts to proselytize to Muslims. Sharia courts have the authority to prosecute proselytizers. In addition, foreign missionary groups must refrain from all forms of public proselytizing. Similarly, in Mauritania there is no specific prohibition against proselytizing by non-Muslims. However, the government prohibits such activities by its interpretation of article 5 of the Constitution, which says, "Islam shall be the religion of the State and the people." The government also uses article 11 of the Press Act to prevent the distribution of any material that could be used for proselytizing.

In other countries the bans are more limited yet substantial. Some countries focus on limiting the entry of foreign missionaries. For example, in Bangladesh foreign missionaries require special missionary visas which must be renewed annually. Missionaries often have trouble renewing these visas, especially if they are perceived to be converting Muslims. Azerbaijan simply bans all proselytizing by foreigners and requires domestic proselytizers to obtain authorization from the government for all materials they hand out (Wilhelmsen, 2009).

Twenty-six of these states go beyond bans on missionaries and proselytizing by restricting conversion away from Islam. An extreme example of this is Sudan.

Table 12.4 Religious discrimination in Muslim countries

	Middle East			Non-Middle East				All Muslim states
	Persian Gulf	Other Middle East	All Middle East	Sub-Saharan Africa	Former Soviet	Non-Soviet Asia	All non-Middle East	
Average number of types of religious discrimination	14.11	11.08	12.38ᵃ	3.62ᶜ	10.33	14.57ᵇ	8.12ᵃ	10.00
Average religious discrimination score	30.11	20.75	24.76	7.46ᵇ	19.33	31.71ᵇ	16.46	20.17
Engage in at least some religious discrimination (%)	100%	100%	100%	57.1%	100%	100%	76.9%	87.2%
Common types of religious discrimination (%)								
Restrictions on public observance of religious services, festivals and/or holidays, including the Sabbath	77.8%	58.3%	66.7%	15.4%	50.0%	85.7%	42.3%	53.2%
Restrictions on building, leasing, repairing, and/or maintaining places of worship	88.9%	83.3%	85.7%	23.1%	50.0%	71.4%	42.3%	61.7%
Restrictions on formal religious organizations	33.3%	58.3%	47.6%	15.4%	16.7%	57.1%	26.9%	36.2%
Restrictions on religious schools or education	77.8%	41.7%	57.1%	7.7%	66.7%	14.3%	23.1%	38.3%
Mandatory education in the majority religion	88.9%	58.3%	71.4%	15.4%	0.0%	85.7%	30.8%	48.9%
Arrest, continued detention, or severe official harassment of religious figures, officials, or members of religious parties for activities other than proselytizing	33.3%	58.3%	47.6%	23.1%	83.3%	57.1%	46.2%	46.8%
Restrictions on religious publications	77.8%	58.3%	66.7%	23.1%	50.0%	100%	50.0%	57.4%
Restrictions on conversion to minority religions	76.8%	66.7%	71.4%	23.1%	50.0%	71.4%	55.3%	55.3%
Restrictions in proselytizing	100%	83.3%	90.5%	47.2%	83.3%	100%	59.2%	78.7%
Requirement for minority religions (as opposed to all religions) to register in order to be legal or receive special tax status	44.4%	91.7%	71.4%	15.4%	50.0%	16.7%	26.9%	46.8%

Notes

a Significance of marked mean as compared to means for groups in other categories <0.05.
b Significance of marked mean as compared to means for groups in other categories <0.01.
c Significance of marked mean as compared to means for groups in other categories <0.001.

Sudan's 1991 Criminal Act forbids conversion away from Islam.[10] Armed forces enlistees, including non-Muslims, are given indoctrination in Islam. In prisons and juvenile detention facilities, government officials pressure inmates to convert, often promising incentives and benefits. People in the government-created camps for displaced persons have reported being pressured to convert to Islam. There are also reports of children in camps for vagrant minors being required to study the Koran and pressured to convert.

In Malaysia, those seeking to convert away from Islam must receive the approval of a Sharia court. This approval has never been granted except in cases of non-Muslims who had converted to Islam for marriage and were trying to return to their original religion after divorce. Anyone else who attempts to covert away from Islam can be subject to mandatory "rehabilitation." This rehabilitation takes place in rehabilitation centers that teach government-approved Islamic practices so people can be brought back to the "true path of Islam." Children of mixed marriages, which are never legally recognized, are often taken away from their parents pending the results of these rehabilitation efforts.

Yemen detains those who convert away from Islam and holds them until they recant their conversion.[11] In Afghanistan, Iran, and the United Arab Emirates, conversion away from Islam is punishable by death, though in practice this penalty is rarely applied.

Twenty-five Muslim-majority states restrict the public observance of religious services, festivals, and/or holidays, including the Sabbath. In Saudi Arabia and the Maldives these restrictions are near-absolute for all minority religions. Saudi Arabia prohibits the public practice of any religion other than Islam. Religious symbols such as crosses and Bibles are banned. Churches, synagogues, and other houses of worship are forbidden. Similarly, in the Maldives the public practice of any religion other than Islam is prohibited. In both cases private worship is in theory allowed but in practice often restricted. For example, Saudi Arabia's religious police often raid non-Muslim religious gatherings on private property. These raids usually lead to arrests, detainment, deportation, and seizure of religious items such as Bibles or Hindu shrines. In some cases the worshipers are also physically assaulted.[12]

In most other cases the restrictions vary according to the religious minority in question. For instance, in Tunisia Jews and Christians can worship publicly but the Baha'i faith is considered a heretical sect and the public practice of the religion is prohibited. In 1994 Oman passed a law restricting public gatherings which has been invoked to significantly restrict public non-Muslim religious celebrations. Similarly, in 1998 Uzbekistan passed a new religious registration law which makes illegal religious activities by unregistered groups.

Twenty-three states make education in Islam mandatory in public schools, and 17 restrict the religious education of minority religions. For example, in Kuwait, Islam is a required topic in all public schools for all students, and in all private schools that have one or more Muslim students. Organized religious education for other religions is prohibited, although this law is not rigidly enforced. The government does not interfere with private, informal religious instruction, but the *Awqaf* ministry occasionally inspects public and private schools to ensure that non-Islamic religious instruction is not taking place.[13]

However, other than Kuwait, Saudi Arabia, and Brunei, most Muslim-majority countries are not quite so strict. For instance, in Jordan Muslim education is mandatory in public schools for Muslim children. Christian children are allowed to leave the classroom during this portion of the curriculum. However, state mid-term and final exams in social studies that are administered in both public and private schools include questions on Islamic poetry and Koranic verses in Arabic.[14] While article 31 of Pakistan's constitution requires religious education in public schools, article 22 states that "no person attending any educational institution shall be required to receive religious instruction, or take part in any religious ceremony, or attend religious worship, if such instruction, ceremony or worship relates to a religion other than his own." While this is usually observed, violations are common. Many teachers compel non-Muslim students to study in the Islamic religion classes. Also, there is no religious education in minority religion in Pakistan's schools. Religious education in minority religions in private schools is not restricted by Pakistan's government.

Twenty-seven states restrict religious publications. Twenty-five of these restrict the ability to write, publish, and disseminate religious literature, 21 restrict their importation, and 9 restrict them even for personal use. The banning of the publication of religious materials is harshest in the Persian Gulf, with Kuwait, Oman, Qatar, and Saudi Arabia banning it altogether and with all of the other states other than Bahrain placing some restrictions on importation. For example, in Kuwait non-Islamic publishing companies are forbidden. Only one company, The Book House Company Ltd., is permitted to import Christian religious materials into the country, including Bibles, videos, and CDs, for use by the country's recognized churches. All imported material requires approval by government censors. Occasionally customs officials confiscate non-Islamic religious material from private citizens upon their arrival.

Outside of the Gulf, only Comoros, Mauritania, and the Maldives place a near-total ban on publishing non-Muslim religious materials. In the Maldives, religious minorities are also forbidden from importing any non-Muslim religious materials, including symbols, statues, and publications. Prohibited materials are taken and destroyed, usually by customs officials. However, non-Muslims are allowed to bring personal copies of religious books into the country for personal use only.

Malaysia limits the use in non-Islamic publications of certain words that are considered to be under the sole jurisdiction of Islam. While this restriction is enforced sporadically, use of words such as *Allah*, *Baitullah* (House of God), *Solat* (prayer), *al-Kitab* (Bible), *wayhu* (revelation), and *doa* (prayer) can result in the banning of a non-Muslim religious publication (Harding, 2002; Martinez, 2001; Yousif, 2004). In Morocco there is no official law against banning non-Muslim religious literature. However, the importation and display of Bibles in French, English, and Spanish is generally tolerated, while Arabic versions are not.

Most countries that restrict the importation of religious publications are among those that ban publication, though the restrictions on importation are sometimes less strict, as is the case with Kuwait. Bans on religious publications for personal use—which usually involves individuals bringing items such as a Bible with them as they enter the country—are rarer. In most cases a ban is the result of arbitrary behavior by customs or law enforcement officials, who sometimes confiscate these materials and sometimes do not. For example, the official policy in Saudi Arabia is that foreign workers of other religions are allowed to bring in personal religious materials and to worship privately in their homes. However, as is noted earlier in the chapter, there are multiple cases of religious police breaking up such meetings and confiscating personal religious materials.

Twenty-three Muslim-majority countries arrest, incarcerate, and otherwise harass religious minorities. The Iranian government's treatment of Baha'is is an extreme example of this phenomenon. Many Baha'is are targeted for arrest and imprisonment because of their faith, which is illegal in Iran. They are often charged with violating penal code articles relating to activities against the state and spreading falsehoods. Most Baha'is who are detained are released after paying large fines or posting large sums as bail. For example, in 2006, 54 Baha'is were arrested while teaching under-privileged children. They were charged for "indirectly" teaching the Baha'i faith, a crime in Iran.

In Comoros the government periodically arrests and convicts Christians on charges of "anti-Islamic activity," and police regularly threaten and sometimes detain practicing Christians. Usually the authorities have held those detained for a few days and often attempted to convert them forcibly to Islam. Most countries are not quite as extreme. Yemen, as noted above, detains only those who are proselytizing, those found in possession of religious literature for distribution, and those who convert away from Islam.

This type of behavior is not limited to the Middle East. For example, in Azerbaijan police routinely detain and question members of religious minorities, especially members of "non-traditional" groups such as Baptists and Jehovah's Witnesses. Authorities also interrupt religious meetings both in places of worship and in private homes and, when doing so, confiscate religious articles and literature.

Limitations on religious institutions

Among the top ten most common forms of religious discrimination in Muslim-majority states, three involve limitations in religious institutions. As is the case in Christian-majority countries, the requirement for minority religions to register is common in Muslim-majority states. While 31 of these states require registration, eight of them never deny such registration and, accordingly, are not coded as being discriminatory about registration. Twelve of these countries significantly restrict religions that are unable or unwilling to register, and all these 12 deny registration to at least some minority religions. For example, in Egypt unregistered groups are subject to detention, prosecution, and punishment. Registering in Egypt is difficult. To register, a religious group must apply to the Religious Affairs Department, which then determines whether the group poses a threat to security or national unity. The department also consults the leaders of the Muslim and Coptic communities before taking the request to the president. The government last recognized a new religious group in 1990. Malaysia also requires all religious groups to register. Under the terms of the 1966 Societies Act, groups that fail to register may not operate.[15] While Malaysia usually grants registration, it does not do so in all cases.

Seventeen Muslim-majority states restrict the formal religious organizations of at least some minority religions. Only Saudi Arabia and the Maldives ban all minority religious organizations altogether. The other 15 Muslim-majority countries that ban minority religions ban only some. For instance, as already noted, Iran bans Baha'i organizations, as do Mali and Tunisia. Jordan bans Baha'i and Druze organizations.

Finally, 29 Muslim-majority states restrict the ability to build maintain or repair places of worship. Three of these countries—the Maldives, Saudi Arabia, and Somalia—allow no minority places of worship at all. The others place varying levels of restrictions on them. Several effectively limit minority places of worship to those that already exist. For example, most existing churches in Tunisia date back to the eighteenth or nineteenth century. Egypt's Christian Coptic community can in theory build or renovate churches, but in practice it is rarely allowed to do so. Building a new church requires a presidential decree, and repairing an existing one requires the approval of the regional government, both of which are rarely forthcoming. For example, Ministry of Interior regulations specify ten conditions that must be met before any new non-Muslim place of worship can be constructed, including the requirements that a church must be at least 100 meters away from the nearest mosque, and the neighboring Muslim community must approve of any church to be built in the area. In Malaysia the restrictions come mostly from local governments. State government approval is required for building a new place of worship. Permits are granted very slowly, if at all. Local governments often use restrictive zoning and construction codes to stop the construction. Furthermore, official zoning policies for the cities allow non-Muslim places of worship to be built at a ratio of 1:4,000 worshipers, whereas for mosques the ratio is 1:800 worshipers.[16]

Many of the countries that engage in these restrictions do so less comprehensively or selectively. For example, Jordan restricts only Druze and Baha'i places of worship as part of its general ban on these religions. In Indonesia there is no law against building minority places of worship but in some localities it is still difficult to do so. Some local governments regularly deny permits to build. Even when permits are forthcoming, religious minorities can encounter problems. For example, a North Jakarta Christian community's church was destroyed in 2001 by rioters. The police refused to intervene or investigate. On other occasions the minority community received official approval to build but outside activists used petitions to oppose the building and succeeded in getting the authorities to cancel the building permit (Crouch, 2006, 2010).

PATTERNS AND TRENDS

As I note earlier in the chapter, the Muslim-majority states within each of the various regions exhibit similar policies. That is, each region has distinctive characteristics that define the religion policies of most of the states in the region. Yet there are exceptions to each of these patterns. Table 12.5 compares the patterns.

The nine Persian Gulf states exhibit a pattern of high levels of support for Islam with low tolerance for minority religions. Declaration of Islam as the official religion is universal to these states, and five of them—Iran, Kuwait, Oman, Qatar, and Saudi

Table 12.5 Patterns and trends in Muslim-majority states

	Official religions	Religious support	Religious regulation	Religious discrimination
Persian Gulf	All states have official religions. Five of them are classified as "religious states"	*High*, with the exceptions of Bahrain and Iraq, which have relatively moderate levels	All states other than Iraq and Qatar have *moderate* to *high* levels	*High* overall. Extremely high (30+) in Iran, Kuwait, Qatar, and Saudi Arabia. High in the UAE and Yemen. Moderate in Bahrain, Iraq, and Oman
Other Middle East	All but two states have official religions or support Islam more than any other religion	Most states have *high levels* but not as high as the Persian Gulf or Asia. Three have moderate levels. Turkish Cyprus has low levels	All states other than Lebanon and Turkish Cyprus have *moderate* to *high* levels	*High* overall. Extremely high (30+) in Egypt and Sudan. Moderate in Lebanon and Syria. Low in Turkish Cyprus. High elsewhere
Sub-Saharan Africa	Nearly half of these states treat all religions equally	Seven have *low* levels. Six have *moderate* levels	*Lowest* overall among Muslim-majority states. Seven have low levels. Six have moderate levels	*Lowest* overall among Muslim-majority states. None in Burkina Faso, Gambia, Niger, Senegal, and Sierra Leone. These are the only Muslim-majority states in the world with no discrimination. Ranges from low to high elsewhere
Former Soviet Bloc	Five of these states are hostile to religion; Albania is mostly supportive of religion in general	*Lowest* overall among Muslim-majority states. All states have low levels	*Highest* among Muslim-majority states. All states other than Albania have high levels	*Moderate* average but with high variation. Extremely high (30+) in Turkmenistan and Uzbekistan. High in Azerbaijan. Low in Albania, Kyrgyzstan, and Tajikistan
Non-Soviet Asia	Six states have official religions, with five classified as "religious states." Indonesia has no official religion but supports Islam	*Highest* overall among Muslim-majority states. Bangladesh has a relatively moderate level of religious support	*High* in six states. *Moderate* in Bangladesh	*Highest* overall among Muslim-majority states. Extremely high (30+) in Brunei, Malaysia, Maldives, and Pakistan. High in Afghanistan and Indonesia. Low in Bangladesh

Arabia—are classified as "religious states" by the RAS dataset. This means that not only do they support Islam, but the religion can be said to have a significant influence on state policy. Given this, it is not surprising that most of these states have high levels of religious support. These states also engage in moderate to high levels of regulation of Islam. Thus, while the religion influences these governments, these governments are also heavily involved in regulating the religion.

There is a high level of variation in the levels of religious discrimination against minority religions. Saudi Arabia engages in the highest levels of religious support of any state in the RAS dataset, scoring a 71 (out of a possible 90) overall. This score is 18 points more than the next-highest country, the Maldives. Saudi Arabia also engages in 29 of 30 types of religious discrimination. The thirtieth—the requirement of minority religions to register—is moot because minority religions are banned. But, as is noted in Table 12.5, Bahrain, Iraq, and Oman engage in moderate levels of discrimination.

Post-Saddam Hussein Iraq is very much the odd man out in this region. As noted, it has moderate levels of religious discrimination, which are lower than in some Western democracies such as Austria, Belgium, France, and Greece. Nor does it regulate Islam. It has 15 types of religious support, but this is considerably lower than the Persian Gulf average, with only Bahrain scoring lower. This exception can be attributed to two factors: First, even under Saddam Hussein, Iraq was never a religious state; Islam was supported, but closely controlled by the government. Second, in the post-Saddam era the United States has had a significant influence on Iraq's government. Bahrain, too, does not fit the pattern of this region, with no more than moderate levels of support, regulation, and discrimination. This exception can be attributed to the policies of the country's monarchy.

The other Middle Eastern states support Islam but not to the extent of the Persian Gulf states. A large minority of these states do not declare Islam to be the official religion, and none of them is a religious state. Most of these states are supportive of Islam. Most states without official religions in practice support Islam, though Lebanon can be better described as multicultural and Turkey has historically been an ideologically secular state, though this is beginning to change. These states provide less religious support and show less discrimination than the Persian Gulf states but regulate Islam more. The only government included in this region that breaks this pattern is the government of Turkish Cyprus. This government is an exception in many respects, including the fact that while effectively having ruled for decades, it has no international recognition. Egypt is not precisely an exception, but it stands at an extreme in this range, with the highest levels of religious support and discrimination of any state in this category. In fact, it has higher levels of religious support, regulation, and discrimination than most Persian Gulf states and would not be out of place in that region, other than that the government is firmly in control of Islamic institutions, with Islam having less of an influence in policy than in most Persian Gulf states. Again, should the government elected in the 2011–2012 electrons take power, the position could change.

Overall, the sub-Saharan African states have the most moderate religion policies, though there are clear exceptions to this. These states can be combined into two categories. First, Burkina Faso, Gambia, Mali, Niger, and Sierra Leone all show low levels of government support for Islam. All of them treat most religions equally, either with full separation of religion and state or relatively equal levels of support for most religions. Other than Mali, none of them engages in religious discrimination. None of them has more than six of the types of religious support included in the RAS dataset. Other than Niger, they all engage in low levels of regulation of Islam. These moderate Muslim-majority states are all clustered geographically in the northwest portion of sub-Saharan Africa. Given this, it is a reasonable conclusion that these moderate Muslim states are influenced by regional culture.

The other sub-Saharan African states all support Islam either as an official religion or in practice, though Chad supports other religions and Nigeria has a complicated arrangement whereby its northern states support Islam but its southern states support Christianity. They have low to moderate levels of religious regulation, support, and discrimination. The only exception to this is Comoros, which scores 30 on discrimination against minority religions. (For the purposes of this chapter, Sudan is included in the Middle East non-Gulf region.)

Non-Soviet Asia, which is all countries in Asia that were never part of the Soviet bloc, competes with the Persian Gulf region's support for Islam. Five of these seven states are classified as religious states. Only Indonesia has no official religion, but otherwise behaves as if Islam is the official religion. This region has the highest average levels of religious support among Muslim-majority states, with all states other than Bangladesh showing high levels of religious support (though Saudi Arabia has the highest individual religious support score). Religious regulation is higher than in Persian Gulf states, with only Bangladesh having moderate levels. Religious discrimination is, on average, the highest among all Muslim-majority states, with again Bangladesh being the exception. Thus, the cluster of Muslim states that most strongly privilege Islam are not in the Middle East but, rather, in Asia.

The states of the former Soviet bloc are very different from the other Muslim-majority states. As is discussed in more detail in Chapter 3, most of them consider Islam a potential threat to the state and seek to control and limit it in order to mitigate this threat. All of these countries other than Albania fit into this pattern. None of them has an official religion, with all of these states other than Albania being classified by the RAS dataset as hostile to religion. Religious support is low in all of these states. Other than in Albania, regulation of Islam is high. Treatment of minority religions varies for low to extremely high levels.

As noted, Albania is the exception. It has no official religion but maintains supportive bilateral agreements with the Orthodox, Bektashi, Muslim, and Catholic communities. These agreements guarantee the communities' official recognition, tax exemptions, prioritized property restitution from Communist-era seizures, and state financial support for the restoration and reconstruction. Other than some restrictions on small non-indigenous religions, there is little religious discrimination. This can be attributed to the fact that Albania is the only one of the Muslim-majority former Soviet-bloc states that was never part of the Soviet Union. It is also geographically separated from the five Muslim former Soviet states, all of which, other than Kyrgyzstan, border on more radical Muslim states such as Afghanistan and Iran.

Given all of this, it is clear that Islam's influence in state religion policy is not at all monolithic. It appears to be greatly influenced by regional culture and interpretations of Islam. Even within geographic regions, there remains diversity and outright exceptions to regional trends. Thus, Islam can inspire the most draconian of theocratic regimes such as those in Saudi Arabia, Iran, and the Maldives. But it can also be the majority religion in states that treat all religions equally, and rarely discriminate against religious minorities, such as Burkina Faso, Gambia, Mali, Niger, and Sierra Leone, countries that can be said to have higher levels of separation of religion and state than does the average Western democracy.

The religious culture and policies in these West African states break the stereotype of intolerant Islam. The fact that, on average, non-Soviet Asia Muslim states score higher on all of the combined measures than do even the Gulf States of the Middle East similarly breaks the assumption that the Middle East is the main source of religious radicalism among Muslims. Thus, stereotypes must yield to a more nuanced and multifaceted view of Islam and politics.

CHAPTER 13

Other Religions

Grouping a diverse set of religions, including Buddhism, Hinduism, Judaism, Animism, and Shinto, among others, into a single category is unsatisfying.[1] Yet only 32 of the countries included in the RAS dataset, which includes all countries with populations of 250,000 or more, have neither Christian nor Muslim majorities. This relatively small number of states without Muslim or Christian majorities is even more pronounced when, as shown in Table 13.1, Muslims, Christians, or both are among the largest groups in all 13 states that have no majority religions, and another state, Cuba, while being classified as communist, can be said to have a Catholic majority. Thus, only 18 countries in the world can be said to have a majority religious group that is neither Christian nor Muslim. This is especially startling considering that Muslims and Christians together account for about 54 percent of the world's population.[2] Perhaps part of the explanation is that the world's two most populous states, China and India, while both having large Muslim minorities, are among those states whose majority is neither Christian nor Muslim. These two states combined have a population of over 2.5 billion.[3]

Clearly, combining these diverse groups into a single chapter is problematic, but there is no other manageable way to combine these groups within the context of this book. This use of the "other" category is common in the social sciences despite this type of problem, because often there is no other workable option. Also, unlike in previous chapters it is difficult to divide these groups into categories based on a single majority religion, as there are too many groups that would not fit into a category large enough to analyze seriously. However, for purposes of discussion I divide the groups into three categories: countries with a single majority religion, countries with no

Table 13.1 "Other"-majority countries

Country	Region	Majority religion
Benin	Sub-Saharan Africa	Animist
Bhutan	Asia	Buddhist
Bosnia	Former Soviet	Mixed Christian and Muslim
Botswana	Sub-Saharan Africa	Mixed Christian and Animist
Burma	Asia	Buddhist
Cambodia	Asia	Buddhist
Cameroon	Sub-Saharan Africa	Mixed Christian, Islam, and Animist
China	Asia	Communist/Confucian
Cuba	Latin America	Communist/Catholic
Ethiopia	Sub-Saharan Africa	Mixed Christian, Islam, and Animist
Guinea-Bissau	Sub-Saharan Africa	Mixed Christian, Islam, and Animist
India	Asia	Hindu
Israel	Middle East	Jewish
Ivory Coast	Sub-Saharan Africa	Mixed Christian, Islam, and Animist
Japan	Asia	Shinto
Kazakhstan	Former Soviet	Mixed Christian and Islam
Laos	Asia	Buddhist
Liberia	Sub-Saharan Africa	Mixed Christian, Islam, and Animist
Madagascar	Sub-Saharan Africa	Animist
Mauritius	Sub-Saharan Africa	Mixed Christian, Islam, and Hindu
Mongolia	Asia	Buddhist
Mozambique	Sub-Saharan Africa	Animist
Nepal	Asia	Hindu
North Korea	Asia	Communist/personality cult
Singapore	Asia	Mixed Buddhist, Christian, Islam, and Taoist
South Korea	Asia	Mixed Christian and Buddhist
Sri Lanka	Asia	Buddhist
Suriname	Latin America	Mixed Christian, Islam, and Hindu
Taiwan	Asia	Mixed Buddhist, Confucian, and Taoist
Thailand	Asia	Buddhist
Togo	Sub-Saharan Africa	Animist
Vietnam	Asia	Buddhist

majority religion, and communist countries. While the latter are only three countries, their behavior is significantly different from that of the others, to the extent that they cannot be combined with another category without skewing the results. I also examine these countries on the basis of world region.

Also, as this is the final chapter surveying religion policies across the world, I compare the results for all religions.

OFFICIAL RELIGIONS

As is shown in Table 13.2, only 9.4 percent of these states have official religions, and another 18.8 percent support one religion more than others, totaling 28.2 percent; 37.5 percent treat all religions equally, and 15.6 percent are hostile to religion. The "denomination" categorization is strongly associated with patterns of state support for religion. Only countries with a single denomination in the majority have official religions, and other than Ivory Coast, which supports Christianity despite the fact that Christians make up only 32.8 percent of the population,[4] only these countries support a single religion more than others. Countries with no majority religion, other than Ivory Coast, all either treat all religions equally or support two or more religions more than others. For example, Bosnia's two governments (one Christian and the other Muslim) support Serbian Orthodoxy, Roman Catholicism, Judaism, and Islam. The three communist states, China, Cuba, and North Korea, are all ideologically hostile to religion.

Overall, these states have the lowest level of support for official religions or unofficial support for a single religion. However, when one looks only at those states with a single majority religion, 50.1 percent have official religions or support one religion more than others. This is similar to the rate for Western democracies. Thus, much of this result is driven by the demographically mixed and communist states.

RELIGIOUS SUPPORT

As is shown in Table 13.3, all of these states support religion to at least some small extent. Taiwan and Japan have two types of religious support; the rest have at least three types. The average state has about six and a half types of religious support, as based on the RAS dataset categories. Demographics play a role in this, as states with a majority religion undertake more religious support than states with no majority religion. Thirty-nine of the 51 types of religious support are present in at least one of these states.

The most common forms of religious support are all types that were included in previous chapters. Eleven of these states, nine of them in sub-Saharan Africa, have laws banning homosexuality. The laws are usually part of the penal codes and tend to ban sexual relations with persons of the same sex, or unnatural acts. The punishment is usually imprisonment, sometimes accompanied by a fine.

Twenty-two of these states restrict abortion on demand. While such a restriction is more common in states with a single majority religion than in states with no majority religion, it is universal among these states in sub-Saharan Africa. In most of these sub-Saharan African states the abortion laws were inherited from their European colonizers and have not been changed significantly. Only Laos places any restrictions on abortions to save the life of the mother; such abortions require specific approval from the Ministry of Health before they can be performed. Twenty states restrict abortion for social and economic reasons. Thirteen restrict it in cases of rape and incest, and to protect the mental health of the woman. Ten of these countries restrict it even when the physical health of the woman is at risk.

Twelve of these states have religious education in the public schools. As common as this is among the countries analyzed in this chapter, this type of religious support is not as common as it is among Christian- and Muslim-majority states. In most of these states the religious education is egalitarian. None of them makes it mandatory, without any possibility of minority students opting out. It is available in multiple religions in all of these countries other than Bhutan, Burma, and Cambodia, all Buddhist-majority states in Asia.

Table 13.2 Official religions in "other" countries

	Denomination			Region			All cases
	Single religion	Mixed	Communist	Sub-Saharan Africa	Asia	Other	
Official religion	18.8%	0.0%	0.0%	0.0%	12.5%	20.0%	9.4%
One religion supported more than others	31.3%	7.7%	0.0%	9.1%	31.3%	0.0%	18.8%
Some religions supported more than others	12.5%	30.8%	0.0%	36.4%	0.0%	40.0%	18.8%
Equal treatment	25.0%	61.5%	0.0%	54.5%	31.3%	20.0%	37.5%
Hostile	12.5%	0.0%	100%	0.0%	25.0%	20.0%	15.6%
N	16	13	3	11	16	5	32

Table 13.3 Religious support in "other" countries

	Denomination			Region			All cases
	Single religion	Mixed	Communist	Sub-Saharan Africa	Asia	Other	
Average number of types of religious support	8.00	5.31	4.33	5.36	6.56	9.20	6.56
Engage in at least some religious support (%)	100%	100%	100%	100%	100%	100%	100%
Common types of religious support (%)							
Laws that specifically make it illegal to be a homosexual or engage in homosexual intimate interactions	25%	53.8%	0.0%	72.7%	18.8%	0.0%	34.3%
Religious education is present in public schools	43.8%	38.5%	0.0%	36.4%	31.3%	60.0%	37.5%
Funding for building, maintaining, or repairing religious sites	37.5%	30.8%	66.7%	9.1%	50.0%	60.0%	37.5%
Presence of an official government ministry or department dealing with religious affairs	50.0%	23.1%	66.7%	18.2%	50.0%	60.0%	40.6%
Restrictions on abortions	81.3%	69.2%	0.0%	100%	56.3%	40.0%	68.8%
A registration process for religious organizations exists which is in some manner different from the registration process for other non-profit organizations	75.0%	61.5%	66.7%	81.8%	56.3%	80.0%	68.8%

Notes
No differences in means are statistically significant.

Twelve of these states fund the building, maintaining, or repair of religious buildings or sites. In Africa, only Ivory Coast does so, by funding the building of Catholic cathedrals as well as shrines for other religions. Interestingly, both China and North Korea fund religious buildings as part of their state-controlled religious systems, which are discussed in more detail in the next section.

Twenty-two of these states have registration processes specific to religion. In addition to the three communist states, seven of these states—Botswana, Kazakhstan, Laos, Madagascar, Mongolia, Singapore, and Vietnam—sometimes deny registration and restrict unregistered religions. I discuss this in more detail in the religious minorities section of this chapter.

Finally, 13 of these countries have departments or offices that deal specifically with the issue of religion. Interestingly, such departments are considerably less common among sub-Saharan African states, with only Ivory Coast's and Mozambique's governments having this type of department. This category is also common among Christian- and Muslim-majority states.

REGULATION OF THE MAJORITY RELIGION

Overall, religious regulation in the non-Muslim non-Christian states is higher than the world average, as is shown in Table 13.4, but this can be mostly attributed to the extremely high levels in the three communist states included in this group. Among the other states covered in this chapter, religious regulation is relatively low at 4.23 in states with no majority religion and just under the world average in states with a majority religion. All 29 types of religious regulation included in the RAS dataset are present in at least one of these countries.

In this chapter, rather than discuss the specifics of the religious regulation in most of the countries covered here, I discuss the efforts at regulation by the three communist regimes. On the one hand, the most common forms of regulation in the region overlap with those discussed in the previous chapters. On the other, these three governments engage in extremely high levels of regulation of the majority religion. North Korea and China have the highest levels of any state in the world, scoring 48 and 54 respectively on the RAS measure, out of a potential 87. Cuba's levels of regulation, while still high, score 23, a level similar to that of many other states.

China has five officially recognized religions: Buddhism, Taoism, Islam, Catholicism, and Protestantism. Each of these five faiths has a government-affiliated association that monitors, registers, and supervises all religious activities for the faith. Religious activity is allowed for any citizen within the context of these associations, which are funded by the government and include, according to a 1997 government White Paper, over 100,000 places of worship. Clergy are monitored especially closely and must register with the government. Religious activity outside these associations, while not technically illegal, is often more heavily restricted (Carlson, 2005; Edelman and Richardson, 2005; Nichols, 2007).

North Korea is more restrictive than China. It engages in the most extreme forms of 16 of the 29 types of regulation of the majority religion included in the RAS dataset. In place of a religion in the accepted sense of the word, the regime has created

Table 13.4 Religious regulation in "other" countries

	Denomination			Region			All cases
	Single religion	Mixed	Communist	Sub-Saharan Africa	Asia	Other	
Average number of types of religious regulation	5.19	1.85[a]	16.00	1.91[a]	6.81	5.00	4.84
Average religious regulation score	10.88	4.23[b]	41.67	4.45[b]	16.06	9.60	11.06
Engage in at least some religious regulation (%)	81.2%	69.2%	100%	63.6%	87.5%	80.0%	78.1%
Common types of religious regulation (%)							
Restrictions on religious political parties	56.2%	30.8%	33.3%	54.5%	31.2%	60.0%	43.7%
Restrictions on formal religious organizations other than political parties	31.2%	7.7%	100%	0.0%	37.5%	60.0%	28.1%
Restrictions or monitoring of sermons by clergy	25.0%	7.7%	66.7%	9.1%	25.0%	40.0%	21.9%
Restrictions on clergy and/or religious organizations engaging in public political speech	43.7%	0.0%	66.7%	27.3%	31.2%	20.0%	28.1%
Restrictions on religious-based hate speech	43.7%	38.5%	0.0%	18.2%	50.0%	40.0%	37.5%
Restrictions on or regulation of religious education outside of public schools, or general government control of religious education	31.2%	23.1%	100%	9.1%	50.0%	40.0%	34.4%

Notes
a Significance of marked mean as compared to means for groups in other categories <0.05.
b Significance of marked mean as compared to means for groups in other categories <0.01.
c Significance of marked mean as compared to means for groups in other categories <0.001.

an alternative ideology called *Juche* (translated as "self-reliance"). The core principle of the ideology is that man is master of everything and decides everything. It focuses on three separate principles: independence in politics (*chaju*), self-sustenance in the economy (*charip*), and national self-defense (*chawi*). This ideology focuses on the person of leader, instilling him as the spiritual head of the nation. The leader becomes a "god," and citizens are constantly exhorted to glorify Kim Jong-il and his father. The people are constantly indoctrinated in the ideology to ensure their loyalty to the regime and its authority, and are required to display absolute loyalty. The practice of this "religion" or ideology is manifested in numerous ways. For example, a 21-meter-high statue of Kim Il-sung has been built in Pyongyang. Sculptures and pictures are found everywhere in offices, factories, homes, and streets, and citizens are supposed to bow to these objects. People must also wear lapel pins with the images of both Kim Il-sung and Kim Jong-il, and hang portraits of both of them in their homes. Citizens also frequently make visits to "pilgrimage" sites relating to Kim Il-sung and Kim Jong-il.[5] With the death of Kim Jong-il in 2011, this glorification has passed to his son and successor, Kim Jong-un.

There exist government-controlled religious organizations, including the Christian League, the Buddhist League, the Catholic Association, the Chondogyo Central Guidance Committee, and the Association of Religious Practitioners. However, it is questionable whether the free practice of religion is possible under the auspices of these organizations. Witnesses and defectors from the country say that the official churches were simply "just buildings" used for show to create a pretense of religious freedom. Foreigners who have met with representatives of such groups report that the members are genuinely religious but appear to know very little about religious dogma or teaching. Those who visited the churches noted that services appeared to be staged and often contained political content supportive of the regime in addition to the regular religious materials. Oftentimes, congregations arrived and departed from services on tour buses, usually without any children. Foreigners were not permitted to have any contact with the citizen congregants.[6]

About 85 percent of Cuba's population was nominally Roman Catholic before Fidel Castro's 1959 communist revolution. Catholicism is still the largest organized religion in Cuba, but over 50 years of atheist communist rule has managed to create a culture where most young people are not religious and know little about the religion. Cuba's Ministry of the Interior controls and monitors the country's religious institutions, with tactics including surveillance, infiltration, and harassment of religious professionals and laypersons. While worship is allowed at government-approved sites, the worshipers are subject to harassment and surveillance. Members of the households of members of the armed forces may not engage in religious practices, with the exception of "elderly" relatives. The government allows religious groups to publish newspapers and magazines but monitors their content and closes publications when it disapproves of the content, usually through pressure on the editors and by blocking access to the equipment and materials necessary for publishing. The government also controls all access to the internet and denies such access to groups it does not trust. Churches are often pressured to expel pro-democracy and human rights activists. In fact, the activities of government agents who infiltrate religious services have recently been shifting their attention to activists rather than attendees in general.

There has been some relaxing of this regulation over time. Since 1991, persons who openly declare their religious faith have been admitted as members to the Communist Party, but they rarely gain senior positions in the government. However, this may be changing. In January 2008, four religious leaders became National Assembly members. Since 1999 it has become easier for registered religious groups to import religious publications, such as the Bible. While in theory new churches may be built, the process for obtaining approval is lengthy and difficult. Once a building has been approved, the process for obtaining the materials to build the church is lengthy, difficult, and expensive, though since 2008 this has eased somewhat.

Since 2008, when Raúl Castro effectively began his rule in Cuba, restrictions have been easing further. Political activities such as prayers for prisoners have been tolerated, though using the names of specific prisoners in these prayers is still out of bounds. Restrictions on importing religious publications and religious official traveling abroad have been eased further. Churches have been granted radio time for broadcast on early Sunday mornings. In 2009 the Cuban government began to allow Roman Catholic Mass and Protestant services inside prisons. Nevertheless, the Cuban government still maintains high levels of regulation of religion.

RELIGIOUS DISCRIMINATION

Religious discrimination among these states is just above the world average. However, as is shown in Table 13.5, as in the case of religious regulation the three communist states engage in unusually high levels of religious discrimination. Removing them from the equation drops this average considerably. Also, as in the case of religious regulation, discrimination is considerably lower in states with no majority religion than in states with a majority religion. All 30 types of religious discrimination monitored by the RAS dataset are present in at least one of these states.

The types of religious discrimination that are most common among these states are similar to those listed in previous chapters as being more common in Muslim- and Christian-majority states. All seven of them are present to some extent in Laos, a Buddhist-majority state. Laos is ruled by a single political party, the Laos People's Revolutionary Party (LPRP). There are four officially recognized religions: Buddhism, Christianity, Islam, and the Baha'i faith. Recognized Christian groups include the Catholic Church, the Laos Evangelical Church (LEC), and the Seventh-day Adventist Church. All other religions must register, and registration is usually denied. This is in part because all Protestants seeking to register must do so under the auspices of the LEC or the Seventh-day Adventists. Technically it is illegal for unregistered groups to practice their religion, but in practice they usually can worship without harassment.

The Laos Front for National Construction (LFNC), a body of the LPRP, controls all religious activity. In fact, all religious activity requires the permission of the LFNC, giving the government a legal tool to ban any religious activity it sees fit. Local officials have used this to harass the LEC, despite its being a legal body in Laos. Forms of harassment have included church closings, arrests, and bans on the observance of religious holidays such as Christmas, both in homes and in houses of worship. In the north of Laos, local authorities similarly restrict the Catholic Church. In 2006 the

Table 13.5 Religious discrimination in "other" countries

	Denomination			Region			All cases
	Single religion	Mixed	Communist	Sub-Saharan Africa	Asia	Other	
Average number of types of religious discrimination	7.75	3.00[b]	18.00	1.73[c]	9.56[a]	9.00	6.78
Average religious discrimination score	13.38	4.85[b]	39.00	2.55[c]	18.19[a]	15.00	12.31
Engage in at least some religious discrimination (%)	87.5%	53.8%	100%	54.5%	87.5%	80.0%	75.0%
Common types of religious discrimination (%)							
Restrictions on public observance of religious services, festivals and/or holidays, including the Sabbath	43.7%	23.1%	66.7%	9.1%	50.0%	60.0%	37.5%
Restrictions on building, leasing, repairing and/or maintaining places of worship	43.7%	23.1%	66.7%	9.1%	43.7%	80.0%	37.5%
Restrictions on formal religious organizations	37.5%	23.1%	66.7%	9.1%	50.0%	40.0%	34.4%
Arrest, continued detention, or severe official harassment of religious figures, officials, or members of religious parties for activities other than proselytizing	37.5%	23.1%	100%	18.2%	43.7%	60.0%	27.5%
State surveillance of minority religious activities not placed on the majority	37.5%	15.4%	66.7%	27.3%	37.5%	20.0%	31.2%
Restrictions on proselytizing	68.8%	30.8%	100%	27.3%	75.0%	60.0%	56.3%
Requirement for minority religions (as opposed to all religions) to register in order to be legal or receive special tax status	31.2%	30.8%	66.7%	26.4%	25.0%	60.0%	34.4%

Notes

a Significance of marked mean as compared to means for groups in other categories <0.05.
b Significance of marked mean as compared to means for groups in other categories <0.01.
c Significance of marked mean as compared to means for groups in other categories <0 001.

government began to require religious groups other than Buddhists and Catholics to periodically report membership information to the Religious Affairs Department of the LFNC. The government regularly arrests and incarcerates Protestants for proselytizing or for engaging in religious activities such as holding services in private homes. The charges are often unauthorized assembly, sedition, and treason. The government does not allow Bibles to be printed in Laos and severely limits their importation, as it does with most non-Buddhist religious literature. Foreigners may not proselytize; those caught doing so are arrested and deported. However, foreign NGOs with religious affiliations are permitted to work in the country.[7]

Building a house of worship requires government approval, which is rarely granted. This results in the majority of Christian congregations worshiping in house churches. Government regulators often close these house churches on the grounds that they should be replaced with designated structures, creating a catch-22 situation. Between 1999 and 2001, local authorities closed over 80 Protestant churches throughout the country. Since 2002 this policy has eased and many of these churches have been allowed to reopen, but several remain closed and local authorities still occasionally close churches.

Sometimes the government goes beyond this policy of arrest and harassment. There have been periodic campaigns by local authorities to force Christians to renounce their faith. Similarly, some authorities have occasionally attempted to force Christian communities to adhere to Buddhist practices by working on Sundays or resting on Buddhist holy days. Both of these types of campaigns tend to be localized and sporadic. This is also the case with other forms of harassment, such as the with-holding of government documents, including identity cards and travel documents, and the banning of Christian children from schools.[8]

Laos is an extreme case. Other than China, no non-Muslim, non-Christian state engages in more religious discrimination, as measured by the RAS dataset. On the other side of the coin, many of these states, including Benin, Mozambique, Cameroon, Guinea-Bissau, Liberia, South Korea, Suriname, and Taiwan, engage in no religious discrimination against minorities. Interestingly, all of these states have no majority religion or an Animist majority. Buddhist-majority states, other than Laos, engage in levels of discrimination that range from low (e.g. Cambodia and Mongolia) to high (Bhutan, Myanmar, and Vietnam). Among the no religious majority states, only those outside of sub-Saharan Africa—Kazakhstan and Singapore—engage in more than low levels of religious discrimination.

WORLD TRENDS AND COMPARISONS

In this chapter and the previous three, I summarize the religion policies of 177 governments across the world. Overall, 43 have official religions, and another 42, while not declaring an official religion, support one religion more than others. Thus, 48.0 percent of these countries favor a single religion. Another 18.7 percent favor some religions over others, and a further 4.5 percent support religion in general, giving no preference to any one religion. Thus, a total of 126 of these 177 countries have general frameworks that support religion. With only 16 countries (9 percent) being classified as hostile to religion and 35 (19.8 percent) as being mostly neutral on the issue of religion, this means that the overwhelming majority of the world's countries support religion, and usually do so on a preferential basis for one or more religions.

However, within the general trend of support for religion there is considerable diversity, as is displayed in Table 13.6. Within the Christian world, Third World Christian-majority countries intervene less in religion than do those in the West and former Soviet bloc, as is discussed in more detail in Chapters 10 and 11. Muslim-majority countries are more likely to have official religions, and engage in more religious support, regulation of the majority religion, and discrimination against minority religions than do non-Muslim majority states. Yet as is discussed on Chapters 10–13 there is a significant amount of diversity within each of these religious groupings. The countries most likely to have an official religion are Muslim-majority states in the Persian Gulf and non-Soviet Asia. The ones least likely are states in the former Soviet bloc, regardless of their majority religion, and Christian states in non-Soviet Asia.

Religious support is highest in Muslim-majority states in the Middle East and non-Soviet Asia. It is lowest in communist states, Third World Christian states, and states with no majority religion. Yet it is common to the point where only South Africa has none of the 51 forms of religious support included in the RAS dataset, and Albania is the only country with only one type of religious support, as measured by the RAS dataset. Neither of these are states one would expect to have the strongest levels of separation of religion and state if one is among those who predict that it will be strongest among Western liberal democracies.

Religious regulation is low in Christian states in general, as well as states with no majority religion. It is highest in Communist states and Muslim-majority states other than those in sub-Saharan Africa. All but 31 countries (17.5 percent) engage in at least some religious regulation.

Religious discrimination is lowest in countries with no majority religion and Third World Christian states. It is highest in communist states and Muslim-majority states other than those in sub-Saharan Africa. All but 31 countries (17.5 percent) engage in at least some religious discrimination.

There are also several more specific interesting trends and patterns worthy of note and reiteration:

- Third World Christian-majority states are closer to having separation of religion and state than are those outside of the Third World, including the Western states that are the source of the liberal doctrines supporting separation of religion and state. These levels of separation of religion and state are even higher than in Third World countries with no majority religion. This can be attributed to the fact that Third World governments have fewer resources to devote to religion policy, and to the more recent introduction of Christianity into these countries.
- Religious denomination plays an important role in religion policy among Christian states. Catholic states are more likely to support religion than are non-Catholic-majority states, with the exception of Orthodox Christian-majority states.

Table 13.6 Overall comparisons between all countries

Country grouping	Official religion	Support for single religion	Official + single religion support	Religious support (mean)	Religious regulation (mean)	Religious discrimination (mean)
All countries	24.3%	23.7%	48.0%	8.88	8.86	11.11
All Christian countries	15.3%	30.6%	45.9%	6.26	4.44	6.37
Christian countries in the West and former Soviet bloc.	19.6%	34.8%	54.4%	7.59	4.93	10.88
Catholic	11.8%	47.1%	58.9%	7.12	2.35	5.65
Orthodox	15.4%	61.5%	76.9%	7.38	9.54	19.84
Other Christian	31.3%	0.0%	31.3%	8.25	3.94	5.69
Western democracies	30.8%	19.2%	50.0%	7.46	3.38	6.04
Former Soviet bloc	5.0%	55.0%	60.0%	7.75	6.95	14.40
Non-European Union	21.1%	42.1%	63.2%	6.32	6.21	12.52
European Union	18.5%	29.6%	48.1%	8.48	4.04	7.67
Christian countries in the Third World	11.5%	34.8%	46.3%	5.08	4.00	2.27
Catholic	18.5%	44.4%	62.9%	5.15	4.56	3.37
Other Christian	4.0%	8.0%	12.0%	5.00	3.40	3.52
Asia	0.0%	0.0%	0.0%	5.50	1.67	1.00
Sub-Saharan Africa	9.5%	4.8%	14.3%	4.81	4.62	4.19
Latin America	16.0%	52.0%	68.0%	5.20	4.04	3.40
Muslim countries	53.2%	17.0%	70.2%	15.91	16.60	20.17
Muslim Middle Eastern countries	76.1%	14.3%	90.4%	19.71	16.76	24.76
Persian Gulf	100%	0.0%	100%	22.44	14.78	30.11
Other Middle East	58.0%	25.0%	83.0%	17.67	18.25	20.75
Muslim non-Middle Eastern countries	34.7%	11.5%	46.2%	12.85	16.46	16.46
Sub-Saharan Africa	23.1%	15.4%	38.5%	9.08	6.77	7.46
Former Soviet bloc	0.0%	16.7%	16.7%	4.67	29.17	19.33
Non-Soviet Asia	85.7%	0.0%	85.7%	26.85	23.57	31.71
All other countries	9.4%	18.8%	28.2%	6.56	11.06	12.31
Single religion	18.8%	31.3%	50.1%	8.00	10.88	13.38
Mixed	0.0%	7.7%	7.7%	5.31	4.23	4.85
Communist	0.0%	0.0%	0.0%	4.33	41.67	39.00
Sub-Saharan Africa	0.0%	9.1%	9.1%	5.36	4.45	2.55
Asia	12.5%	31.3%	43.8%	6.56	16.06	18.29
Other world region	20.0%	0.0%	20.0%	9.20	9.60	15.00

- States located in northwest sub-Saharan Africa are a glaring exception to the general rule of strong support for Islam and high levels of discrimination against minority religions in Muslim-majority states.
- On the basis of religious support, regulation, and discrimination, non-Soviet Asia's Muslim-majority states are, on average, the strongest supporters of Islam and the most repressive against religious minorities. This is true even when compared to the Muslim-majority states of the Persian Gulf and the rest of the Middle East. This undermines the stereotype of Arabs being the least tolerant and supporting the most religious states among Muslims.
- Within each religious grouping, sub-Saharan African states generally have the highest levels of separation of religion and state. The only exception is former Soviet Muslim-majority states with regard to support for a single religion and religious support.
- The liberal democracies of the West do not have the highest levels of separation of religion and state. Nor do they have the lowest levels of religious discrimination. This undermines both stereotypes and modern liberal thought on the nature of state religion policy and religious freedom in Western democracies.

Given all of this, both world region and the majority religion of a state matter. These two factors alone are sufficient to allow one to make a good guess on the general parameters of a state's religion policy. However, to each rule there are exceptions. Also, every state is unique in that no two governments have exactly the same policy toward religion. Nevertheless, each state is unique in that its religion policy is different from that of every other state. While there are discernible patterns in state religion policy, each pattern includes diversity and outright exceptions.

CHAPTER 14

Conclusions

LINKING THEORY AND PRACTICE

The purpose of this book is to provide an overview of religion and politics both in theory and in practice. Religion and politics is a diverse topic and it is not possible to discuss every possible issue and every possible case. While Chapters 10–13 include an analysis of 177 states, not all of them are discussed specifically in this volume. Furthermore, state religion policy, while a critical aspect of religion and politics, is certainly not the only one. A book like this one could have focused on the impact of religious institutions such as the Catholic Church, violent religious movements such as Al-Qaeda, religious political parties, or many other types of religious actors and religious influences on politics. As I note earlier, I chose this topic matter for the empirical portion of this book because it is an important topic, and one with which I am familiar. I also have a unique resource—the RAS dataset—which greatly facilitated the empirical discussion.

In Chapters 2–9 I discuss what I believe to be the major theories, trends, and literatures that are relevant to the study of religion and politics. I have no doubt that someone else writing a volume like this one might have selected differently. Yet the examination of state religion policies across the world shows that all of the theories and literatures I discuss in Chapter 2–9 are relevant and significant.

Chapter 2 discusses secularization theory—the predictions of religion's demise as a relevant political and social factor—and how it has influenced scholarship on religion. The state religion policies of 177 countries demonstrate at least two things that are important to the debate over secularization theory: First, despite these predictions, religion remains relevant in politics. Nearly every state supports, finances, enforces, or restricts religion, and many of them do more than one of these. Support for religion, financial or otherwise, along with restrictions on minority religions, are perhaps the most common, but regulation of the majority religion is also extremely common. Most states can be said to have a policy that is supportive of religion, but even those that do not, prove religion's importance. Regulating and limiting religion would not be necessary if it were not important and relevant. If religion was emasculated and disappearing, countries like China and North Korea would not need to invest massive resources into limiting and controlling it. In fact, the sociological argument discussed in Chapter 7, known as the supply side argument, specifically argues that when religion is left alone, it thrives.

Second, state religion policies across the globe show that religion is not just present in politics, but a contentious issue. Secular forces seek to limit its role while religious forces seek to increase it. Furthermore, different religions and even advocates of different interpretations of the same religion seek to change state religion policy in favor of their preferred outcome. This can be seen both domestically and in international movements. Al-Qaeda, for example, seeks to change state policies across the globe in conformance with its interpretation of Islam. Numerous human rights organizations seek to increase religious freedom in the world. Every country in the world is in play in this complex international multiplayer contest. While this conflict most often plays out through normal political channels, it can become violent. Thus, the theories in Chapter 9 on religion and conflict are particularly relevant.

All of this also describes a dynamic that is not at all consistent with the predictions of secularization theory. Even the more recent versions, such as differentiation theory, which allow for religion's continued presence and significance do not really describe a world where religion is so central and contentious an issue. In addition, in analyses not presented here, religious support, regulation, and discrimination—as measured by the RAS dataset—are all increasing significantly. Thus, at least in the realm of state religion policy, the predictions of secularization theory are not accurate.

The religious institutions discussed in Chapter 6 are very much part of this process. In state after state they advocate on both sides of this contest. As is noted in Chapter 7, majority religions tend to seek to push the state into supporting them as a religious monopoly. While few true religious monopolies exist today, nearly half the world's states have a single religion that is given preference over other religions. On the other side of the coin, religious minorities tend to push for separation of religion and state, because this creates a more even playing field where they are more likely to thrive.

Religious identity, discussed in Chapter 3, is also relevant. Nearly half of the world's countries identify officially or unofficially with a single religion. Many countries that engage in religious discrimination do so against some religious groups but not others. Given all of this, one's religious identity has a significant impact on the ability to practice one's religion freely, and in some cases even on one's citizenship status in a country.

It is difficult to explain the presence of religious support and discrimination without resorting to the issues of religious worldviews, beliefs, doctrines, and theologies discussed in Chapter 4. Much of this support enacts or enforces elements of these worldviews, beliefs, doctrines, and theologies into law. Other aspects support the institutions and education that propagate and maintain these beliefs. This support is present, at least to a small extent, in every country in the world save one, South Africa (as measured by the RAS dataset). Religious discrimination—limitations place on the religious practices and institutions of minority religions not placed on the majority religion—is an expression that some beliefs, theologies, and doctrines are beyond the pale. In many countries, levels of discrimination against religious minorities are higher precisely against those groups whose beliefs are considered more abhorrent to the doctrines of the dominant religion. Religious fundamentalists, as discussed in Chapter 8, are a specific manifestation of religious worldviews that follow this same pattern, but because of their higher perceived threat level are likely to do so more vigorously.

Another possible motivation for the presence of support for religion in a state is religious legitimacy, discussed in Chapter 5. Supporting a religion can be part of an arrangement of mutual support that benefits the state. As is noted in Chapter 7, religious legitimacy can lower the costs of ruling. Supporting a state religion that upholds the legitimacy of the state can be both more effective than coercion, and less expensive.

Religion is a complex, multifaceted phenomenon. This is certainly true of its influence on politics. This book seeks to provide a framework for a more ordered understanding of what can seem like a chaotic topic. While the topics discussed here are complex and overlapping, they also provide a distinct set of categories of religion's influence on politics that can aid in understanding the role of religion and politics. They also, I argue, provide a toolbox that can allow us to understand religion's many political manifestations that can be applied in a wide variety of contexts.

A THEORETICAL FRAMEWORK TO COMPREHEND RELIGION AND POLITICS

You may ask why I have placed a theoretical framework to comprehend religion and politics at the end of this book rather than the beginning. I did so because religion's interaction with the political is complicated. The concepts I use in this framework are those I develop at length throughout the book. I also assume that the academic study of religion and politics will be a new topic to many readers. Thus, without the information contained throughout the book, many readers would find the framework I present here difficult to fully assimilate.

This book essentially cuts religion and politics up into manageable pieces based on theoretical perspective, religion's many facets, world region, and major religious traditions. Such a division is unavoidable because religion is an incredibly complicated topic that requires vast amounts of knowledge which cover a wide range of topics before one can begin to comprehend it. This is also true of the more limited topic of religion and politics. I make no claim to provide an all-encompassing description and explanation for religion and politics in this book. However, I do attempt to provide a means to begin the process of comprehending religion and politics in a format that links the major intersections between religion and politics into a single framework. I begin with the tools to understand religion I develop in Part 1, and in this last portion of this book I attempt to demonstrate that the various facets of religion and politics contained in these tools fit into such a unified framework.

Before I begin this process, I want to emphasize that this book is intended to provide a theoretical toolbox for those who wish to understand religion's intersection with the political. I fully expect that readers will have their own perspective on how and when to use each of these tools. That is, each of us has our own perspective on which theories and aspects of religion and politics are more important and useful than others. I do not expect that everyone's perspective will match mine. This discussion is intended to relate my perspective on this issue.

I begin with the ideas in Chapter 4 on religious belief systems, frameworks, doctrines, and theologies. The concept of religious beliefs motivating behavior is, from my perspective, the most central element of religion's influence on politics. It is, in effect, the font from which all of religion's other influences upon politics spring.

Without these beliefs and the communities they create, religion would likely not exist. Without this there would be no religious identity (Chapter 3). These beliefs are what make religion legitimate (Chapter 5). That is, what makes religion legitimate is its connection to morality, a higher truth, and a source of knowledge greater than our own, all of which are contained in religious belief systems. Without these beliefs, religion's mechanism for legitimating political actions would have no engine and little fuel. Similarly, without religious beliefs there would be no religious institutions (Chapter 6). Certainly, religious institutions and leaders can have legitimacy in and of themselves due to historical inertia, good works in the community, their charisma, and perceived qualities as moral and upstanding individuals. But these sources of legitimacy are weak and transient compared to their access to religious belief systems, theologies, and doctrines.

While some perspectives described in Chapter 7 see religion as the creation and tool of other social and political forces, I see it as something with an independent existence based on religious beliefs that can also serve and interact with other social forces. Certainly, rational calculations are involved in these interactions. This is how political actors behave and how many clergy and religious institutions behave when seeking to achieve their political goals. Politicians will seek to use religious identity, institutions, ideologies, and legitimacy to serve their own ends, just as religious institutions and clergy will seek to use politicians to achieve the goals inspired by their religious beliefs, theologies, and doctrines. But this use of religion would not be possible if it did not have an independent existence that includes a strong foundation in society and the ability to motivate behavior. Thus, religion being a tool is an important part of the framework, but the tool itself is not always a tool, has an independent existence, and is often an independent political actor.

Thus, religion's influence in politics is driven by belief, doctrine, and theology but heavily influenced by religious identity, institutions, legitimacy, and the rational calculations of religious and secular actors.

Yet religion and politics are also heavily influenced by secular belief systems. As is noted in Chapter 2, religion clashes with secularism in every political setting. The current status of this clash is unique in each of the 177 countries examined here, but the presence of this contest between religion and secularism is universal to all of them. Thus, it is not possible to understand religious politics in modern times without understanding this interaction between the religious and the secular. I graphically present this set of relationships in Figure 14.1.

Despite the apparent simplicity of this framework for understanding religion and politics, the devil is in the details. Each of these factors represents a complex and diverse set of interactions between multiple religious and secular actors. For example, there are many religious belief systems in the world. Most of them include complex and diverse theologies that are subject to multiple interpretations, even within a single religious tradition. No country has a population with completely homogeneous religious beliefs. Most have substantial religious minorities, disagreements over interpretations of the majority religion, and those who support secularism, or at least a more secular political system. These secularists do not agree over the specifics of how

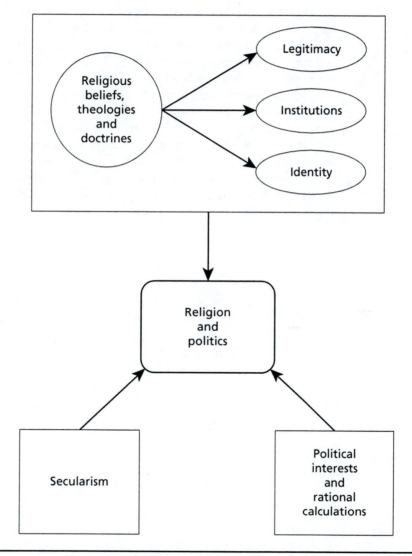

Figure 14.1 Framework for understanding religion and politics.

religion should be separated from politics and society. Thus, it may be simple to say that religious beliefs influence political behavior, but in practice the number of ways in which this influence can play out is so large that it might as well be infinite. This is true for each of the factors that are included in Figure 14.1. Also, even in the most autocratic and repressive of regimes, religion and politics is a multiplayer political contest.

Thus, while this framework is capable of providing an understanding of the larger picture, it is better seen as an overview that simplifies a far more complex reality. It describes the larger relationships that exist, but each case must be examined in detail in order to provide a workable understanding. The framework helps to identify which factors and relationships must be examined, but the examination itself will likely reveal a far more complex reality.

Religion is likely to remain an active and significant political issue for the foreseeable future. It is my hope that this book will help introduce students of religion and politics to the many theories, literatures, and perspectives on religion and politics and how these theories, literatures, and perspectives relate to each other. I also hope to provide an understanding of how all of this plays out in practice, with special attention to state religion policy. The theories, perspectives, trends, examples, and analyses contained in this volume are all intended to further these goals.

All of the theories and perspectives are constantly evolving and state religion policies worldwide are in a state of flux. Religion is a multifaceted phenomenon that is dynamic and constantly evolving, as is religion's interaction with politics. This book is a snapshot of the state of affairs at the time of this writing. But it also contains the tools a student of religion and politics will need to understand religion and politics as this relationship continues to evolve.

Appendix

RAS data collection procedures

This appendix is an edited excerpt from Jonathan Fox, "Building Composite Measures of Religion and State" Interdisciplinary Journal of Research on Religion, *7 (8), 2011, 1–39 (www.religjournal.com).*

▎ BUILDING THE INDEXES

The three indexes used in this book and described in Chapter 1 (religious support, religious regulation, and religious discrimination) were created as follows: In round 1 of the data collection (RAS1), which the period covered 1990–2002 and included a total of 60 variables in this index combined, the project developed a listing of components for each index based on what the project staff, in consultation with numerous colleagues,[1] expected to find. In the early stages of the RAS1 data collection process, variables were added as research assistants uncovered government behaviors that had not been anticipated. However, about one-third of the way into the project, the code sheet was closed to changes because of the logistical difficulties of adding components, which involved redoing much of the coding work that had already been done. Nevertheless, as new information was uncovered it was incorporated into a working code sheet for the current round of coding (RAS2). Thus, as RAS1 was completed, a new code sheet had already been developed for RAS2 that included all relevant government behaviors that are present in at least several states. The process for coding RAS2 revealed no additional codable behaviors that were present in a sufficient number of states to justify adding a variable to any of the indexes. Each index also includes at least one "other" variable for behaviors that are deemed important and relevant enough to be coded but also sufficiently rare or unique that they do not warrant a separate component variable. In each case the coder provided a description of the unique behavior on the code sheet.

This means that the components that are included in the RAS2 indexes are not based on any theoretical assessment of what ought to be coded. Rather, they are based on a ground-up comparative project that uncovered all relevant practices and placed each of them in the appropriate index. As a result, these indexes include all known government actions regarding state religion policy taken by at least several governments anywhere in the world. No other data collection can make this claim.

DATA COLLECTION PROCEDURES

All 175 countries that were included in RAS1 are included in RAS2. Timor and Montenegro were added because they had recently gained independence, so 177 countries were included in RAS2.[2]

In RAS2, as was the case in RAS1, each country was assigned to a research assistant (RA) who wrote a report based on the country. These reports cover 2003–2008 and are meant to supplement and update the RAS1 reports, which cover 1990–2002. These reports used the following sources:

- Primary sources such as constitutions and the texts of legislation and government policy papers regarding religion. In cases in which laws were not available in a language that the RA understood, Google Translate was used. A sampling of constitutions and laws that were available both in translation and in the original language were tested to see whether the Google Translate results matched the human translation. Although the texts were rarely identical, the Google Translate texts did not result in any inaccuracies that would have influenced the codings.
- News articles, mostly from a search of the LexisNexis database but also obtained from other sources.
- Academic resources such as journal articles and books.
- Government and intergovernmental organization reports such as the US State Department IRF reports and the United Nations Abortion Policies reports, among others.
- Reports by non-governmental advocacy groups and academic organizations such as Human Rights without Frontiers and Amnesty International, among many others.

As project director I vetted all RAS2 reports and often required several rounds of revisions. Each report used all available sources. While sources were more common for some countries than others, there was sufficient information to code all cases. In general, even among undeveloped peripheral countries, when general reports such as the US State Department International Religious Freedom reports indicated that there was significant religious discrimination, regulation, or support, there tended to be significant amounts of information in other primary, academic, media, and advocacy group sources. The research that was involved in writing the reports inad-

vertently revealed that religion is a sufficiently important topic that various organizations devote considerable resources to documenting governments that either
support or restrict religion anywhere in the world. Thus, there do not seem to be
any informational backwaters where states either restrict or strongly support religion.

While this additional information provides considerable advantages over relying
on a single source, some of the sources, such as non-governmental organizations'
human rights reports and press coverage, are published only sporadically. This raises
the issue of whether the information that is available is partially determined by
international attention. Although it is impossible to fully discount this issue, the
advantages of multiple sources outweigh relying on a single source that consistently
covers nearly all countries, such as the US State Department International Religious
Freedom reports.[3] This is true for several reasons.

First, additional sources brought in additional information that increases the
accuracy of the data. I argue that this alone is sufficient to justify the practice.

Second, using multiple sources allows cross-checking for accuracy. There was a
high level of consistency of information between sources and very few cases of
contradicting sources. In cases of contradicting sources, the RAs sought additional
sources and performed a reliability assessment of all of the sources in question.

Third, international attention seems to be highly correlated with the presence of
government activity in the field of religion. In cases in which the general sources
(those that prepared a report on all countries regardless of their policy) indicated large
amounts of religious discrimination, regulation, and/or support, there tended to be
considerably more information in the other sources than there was when the general
sources indicated lower levels of religious support, discrimination, and regulation.
That is, in cases that the general sources showed to be important, researchers were
more likely to find more academic, media, and advocacy group sources. This demonstrates both a consistency in coverage among sources and that international attention
tends to be attracted when governments take codable actions. This was true even of
countries that would otherwise be considered peripheral and less likely to attract
media and nongovernmental organizational attention. In other words, the squeaky
wheels seem to be getting the grease. Because the project is seeking out squeaky
wheels, this is arguably an advantage. The general sources provided a good description
of a state's policy, but in most cases the additional sources provided details that were
not included in the general sources.

Fourth, the legitimacy of any single source can be challenged. Many of the sources
used to collect the data can be criticized for being produced by organizations or
individuals that have an agenda. By this I mean that it is possible to make such an
accusation, not that the accusations are necessarily justified. Nevertheless, such
criticisms can gain acceptance among at least a portion of the academic community
even if they are not accurate. Thus, the issue in this case can often be one of perception
rather than fact. Using multiple sources effectively neutralizes this issue by showing
agreement among different sources that have no common agenda.

The RAS2 report, along with the RAS1 report (which was collected by using the
same methodology), provided the basis for filling out the code sheets. I reviewed all
code sheets to ensure that the code sheets were filled out accurately and that all RAs
were using the same interpretation of the code sheet. No matter how specifically

worded, items on the code sheet can be subject to multiple interpretations. This policy of a single individual reviewing all code sheets is, among other things, intended to reduce the influence of differing interpretations on the codings. Differences between countries in codings need to be based on real differences rather than on differences in interpretations of similar actions by different coders. Overall, 14 RAs worked on the project, and they coded between 1 and 42 cases each.

This system had an additional advantage: In many cases, I questioned specific codings and received an illuminating reply from the RA. That is, the RA would give an answer that revealed information that was not clear in the report. In these cases the RA was instructed to clarify the report; the result was a more accurate report. This also emphasizes the reason behind the project policy that the RA who wrote the report is the one to fill out the code sheet. The one who invested tens of hours in researching a case will have more insight into the details of the case than will someone who only reads the report.

The variables were coded according to the following rules:

1 "If there was a relevant national law. In cases where this law was on the books but rarely enforced (a relatively rare occurrence), this was taken into account in the scaling of the variable when possible but always coded unless there is clear and positive information that the law has not been enforced at all for at least several decades."

2 "If there was a relevant national policy. For example, if there was no law against proselytizing, yet by official or unofficial policy those who proselytize were arrested or otherwise harassed, this would have been coded."

3 "If there is no national policy or law but a significant plurality of local or regional governments had such policies or laws, the relevant variable was coded. In such cases the proportion of the country's population which was under the rule of these regional or local governments was taken into account both with regard to whether the variable was coded and, when relevant, how high a coding on the scale was assigned."

4 "The project codes only actions taken by government and their representatives. Societal actions are not coded. This is not because societal attitudes and actions are unworthy of study; it is simply not within the purview of the RAS project. As a result, the RAs are not searching for information on religion on society in the reports, which means that any codings based on the RAS reports that focus on religion in society may be based on incomplete information."[4]

5 Courts with effective judicial review powers are part of the legislation and policy-making process. Accordingly, laws, policies, or activities that were overturned or banned by a country's court system were not coded from the point at which they were overturned unless the government ignored the court's ruling and continued engaging in the codable action or policy. In cases in which the action, policy, or law was overturned (and the court's ruling was enforced) shortly after the action was taken or the law or policy came into force, it was not coded at all.

The reasoning behind coding both laws and policies is as follows: The purpose of the project is to code state religion policy. This policy can take the form of laws, policies that have some format other than a law, and actual practice. Take, for example, limits on proselytizing. If one were to code only laws, states with such laws on the books that are enforced weakly would be coded, while a state that has no such law but in practice arrests and deports all foreign missionaries would not be coded. Thus, ignoring policies, both official and unofficial, would lead to a less accurate coding of the true religion policy of a government. Laws are not the only way in which states make policy; to ignore this would be to provide a less accurate representation of a state's true policy.

Similarly, it can be argued that laws that are not enforced should not be coded. While this is a valid point, laws that have not been repealed still have import, if only because repealing them might be politically difficult. However, the coding rules are clear that if there is positive and reliable information that a law has not been enforced at all for decades, it is not coded. Cases of laws discovered by the RAs that met this standard for lack of enforcement were rare. I speculate that there might be more such laws on the books but that the lack of enforcement has resulted in their not being recorded in any of the sources uncovered by the RAs.

Notes

1 INTRODUCTION

1 Detailed information on the dataset, including how it was collected and a listing of information on each country included in the dataset, is available at Fox (2008) and the project website at www.religionandstate.org. The dataset itself is also available at this address. Also see this book's appendix.

2 The following are the general sources for the RAS project which are the basis for the examples and case studies used in this book: Morigi *et al.* (2000); Amore (1995); Barrett *et al.* (2000); Fox (2008); the Religion and State dataset at www.religionandstate.org; the US State Department's yearly Reports on International Religious Freedom at www.state. gov/g/drl/irf/rpt/; European Studies on Religion and State Interaction at www.euresis net.eu/Pages/Default.aspx; Human Rights Without Frontiers at www.hrwf.net; Amnesty International at www.amnesty.org; the Religion and Law Consortium at www.relig law.org/countryportal.php; Forum 18 at www.forum18.org/index.php; the International Christian Concern at http://persecution.org; the International Coalition for Religious Freedom at www.religiousfreedom.com; Freedom House Freedom in the World Report at www.freedomhouse.org/template.cfm?page=15; United Nations Abortion Reports at www.un.org/esa/population/publications/abortion; the AWW Abortion report at www.guttmacher.org/pubs/AWWfullreport.pdf; Ottosson (2009); "Religious Freedom in the Majority Islamic Countries: Aid to the Church in Need" www.alleanzacattolica. org/acs/acs_english/acs_index.htm (downloaded January 1, 2008); "Handbook on Religious Liberty Around the World" http://religiousfreedom.lib.virginia.edu/rihand; and Library of Congress Country Studies at http://lcweb2.loc.gov/frd/cs/cshome.html. These sources are not noted further in this book's references but other country-specific sources are noted when used. Also, unless otherwise noted, constitutional clauses are taken from www.thearda.com/internationalData/index.asp.

2 SECULARIZATION AND SECULARISM

1 Peter Berger "A Bleak Outlook on Religion" *New York Times*, February 25, 1968.
2 See Nietzsche (1966, 2011).
3 See Freud (1989).
4 See Durkheim (1964, 1975) and Weber (1930, 1963).
5 For a full discussion of this theory and its critics, see Fox (2004). As to the impact of the theory on thinking on religion's resurgence, see Eisenstadt (2000a), Esposito and Voll (2000), Tibi (2000), and Toft (2007: 99).
6 See also Crouch (2000), Halman and Draulans (2006), Kaspersen and Lindvall (2008), and Voicu (2009).
7 For examples of sociologists who openly expressed secularization as an ideology, see Hadden (1987b).
8 For a discussion of what types of state support for religion can violate the principle of state neutrality toward religion, see Driessen (2010) and Mazie (2006). For a review of the Western intellectual history of the concept of separation of religion and state, see Laycock (1997) and Witte (2006).

3 RELIGIOUS IDENTITY

1 RAS project data, available at www.religionandstate.org.
2 This examination is separate from the general RAS dataset. There is some discrepancy in the statistics for religion in constitutions and religion in state policy in the RAS dataset. This is because many states establish significant portions of their religion policy in a context other than constitutions.
3 For more on Jewish, Christian, and Muslim fundamentalism as a constructed religious identity, see Eistenstadt (2000b), Lawrence (1989: 27), Sadowski (2006: 220), and Soloveitchik (1994).
4 For a discussion on how primordialism, instrumentalism, and constructivism can be used to understand religion in an international relations context, see Hasenclever and Rittberger (2000). See also Fox (2008).
5 All governments restrict and regulate religious practices and institutions. In an extreme example, human sacrifice—while a part of some religions—is universally illegal because it is also murder. Most states also require that religious institutions register or incorporate in some manner in order to be recognized as a legal entity. The key issue here is whether minority religious practices or institutions are somehow regulated or limited in a way that does not apply to the majority religion or its institutions.
6 For further discussion on the issue of Islamic thought on religious minorities and a wide range of opinions on the issue of the treatment of religious minorities by Muslims, see Abou El Fadal (2000), Asani (2003), Furman (2000), Kedourie (1992), and Yousif (2000).
7 A previous version of this section was published as Jonathan Fox, "Muslim Hypocrisy: On the Violation of Religious Freedoms" BESA Center Perspectives Paper 120, November 14, 2010, available at www.biu.ac.il/SOC/besa/perspectives120.html. This version is edited to fit the format of this book.
8 The additional seven Middle Eastern Muslim-majority states that place restrictions on churches are Algeria, Iran, Kuwait, Libya, Oman, the United Arab Emirates, and Yemen.
9 See, for example, Lijphart (1977), Esman (1973), and Nordlinger (1972).
10 For a full discussion of all aspects of the debate over this theory, see Fox (2004).

4 RELIGIOUS WORLDVIEWS, BELIEFS, DOCTRINES, AND THEOLOGIES

1 See the 1984 Religious Council and Kadis Courts Law and the 2000 Syariah Courts Act, among other laws. English-language copies of these laws are available at www.lexadin.nl/ wlg/legis/nofr/oeur/lxwebri.htm.

2 1984 Religious Council and Kadis Courts Law. www.lexadin.nl/wlg/legis/nofr/oeur/ lxwebri.htm.

3 Article 48 of the 1984 Religious Council and Kadis Courts Law is very clear that these are Muslim-only courts when it states that "no decision of the Court of the Chief Kadi or a Kadi shall affect any rights of any non-Muslim." www.lexadin.nl/wlg/legis/nofr/oeur/ lxwebri.htm. Some of the laws for non-Muslims include the 2000 Married Women Act and the 1992 Dissolution of Marriage Act. Both are available at www.lexadin.nl/ wlg/legis/nofr/oeur/lxwebri.htm. See also Haji Nabil Daraina Badaruddin "Challenges to Legal Education in a Changing Landscape—Brunei." www.aseanlawassociation.org/docs /w3_brunei.pdf, 94.

4 Richard Edwards "Sharia Courts Operating in Britain" *Telegraph* (London), September 14, 2008; Abul Taher "Revealed: UK's First Official Sharia Courts" *Sunday Times* (London), September 14, 2008; Steve Doughty "Britain Has 85 Sharia Courts" *Mail Online*, June 29, 2009.

5 Niki Kitsantonis "Muslims in Athens Build Their Own Mosque" *New York Times*, July 6, 2007; Anthee Carassava "The Faith That Has No Place" *Time* magazine, April 23, 2006; "ECHR Convicts Greece for Violating Religious Rights" *New Anatolian*, July 14, 2006; Boussiakou (2008).

6 ReligLaw Document Library "Document No. 19: The Basic Viewpoint and Policy on the Religious Question during Our Country's Socialist Period" Central Committee of the Communist Party of China, March 31, 1982, www.religlaw.org/document.php? DocumentID=789.

7 Senegal, 2001 Constitution, religlaw.org/countryportal.php.

8 An English translation of this report is available at www.cftf.com/french/Les_Sectes_ en_France/cults.html.

9 "France Moves to Outlaw Cults" *BBC News Europe*, June 22, 2000; Ontario Consultants on Religious Tolerance, www.religioustolerance.org/rt_franc.htm; "Religious Discrimination in France: CAP submission regarding the appointment of Mr. Georges Fenech as President of MIVILUDES" *Human Rights Without Frontiers*, October 7, 2008, www. osce.org/odihr/34105; "MIVILUDES 2006 Report to the Prime Minister" http:// carolineletkeman.org/sp/index.php?option=com_content&task=view&id=1266.

10 "Institute Report to UN Details Systematic Religious Discrimination in Belgium" International Christian Concern, www.persecution.org.

5 RELIGIOUS LEGITIMACY

1 Genesis 9: 20–27. In Samson Raphael Hirsch *The Pentateuch Translated and Explained*, trans. Isaac Levy, Gateshead, UK: Judaica Press, 1976.

2 An English translation of the German constitution is available at the International Constitutional Law database at www.servat.unibe.ch/icl/.

3 An English translation of the Polish constitution is available at the International Constitutional Law database at www.servat.unibe.ch/icl/.

4 For others who make similar arguments, see Appleby (2000: 106), Kunovich (2006: 437), Selinger (2004: 530–531), Sahliyeh (1990), Shupe (1990), and Thomas (2005: 40–41). For others who make this argument specifically with respect to Islam, see Azzam (2006: 1120), Esposito (1998), Monshipouri (1998: 26), Nasr (1998), Sadowski (2006: 223–225), and Zubadia (2000: 60).

5 An English translation of the Danish constitution is available at the International Constitutional Law database at www.servat.unibe.ch/icl/.

6 Jane Macartney "China Says Missing Panchen Lama Gendun Choekyi Myima Is Living in Tibet" *Sunday Times*, March 8, 2010.

7 A copy of this law is available at www.cecc.gov/pages/virtualAcad/index.phpd?show single=98772.

6 RELIGIOUS INSTITUTIONS AND POLITICAL MOBILIZATION

1 Steve Twomey "Thousands Rally for Israel" *Washington Post*, April 16, 2002; Jodi Enda and Peter Boylan "At Rally, Broad Support for Israel" *Philadelphia Inquirer*, April 16, 2002; Philip Dine "Pro-Israel Rally in Washington Draws Thousands of Supporters" *St. Louis Post-Dispatch*, April 16, 2002; Diana Jean Schemo "Mideast Turmoil: Demonstrators; Thousands Hold Rally in Capital to Back Israel" *New York Times*, April 16, 2002.

2 For a survey of the general mobilization literature, see Tilly (1978), McCarthy and Zald (1976), and Rule (1988).

3 Christopher Toothaker "Maverick Priests Found Pro-Chavez Church, Angering Catholic Hierarchy" *Associated Press*, July 1, 2008.

4 "Sticking Up for Chávez: A New Church Fuels Debate" *New York Times*, August 1, 2008.

5 Simon Romero "Sympathetic to Chávez, a New Church Draws Fire" *New York Times*, August 1, 2008; Christopher Toothaker "Maverick Priests Found Pro-Chavez Church, Angering Catholic Hierarchy" *Associated Press*, July 1, 2008.

6 1949 constitution of Costa Rica as amended through 2003. www.servat.unibe.ch/icl/.

7 1983 Constitution of El Salvador as amended through 2009. http://pdba.georgetown. edu/Constitutions/ElSal/elsalvador.html.

7 RATIONAL AND FUNCTIONAL RELIGION

1 "Saudi Arabia; Warrants for 47 terror suspects" *Los Angeles Times*, January 10, 2011; "Militants Linked to al-Qaeda arrested" *Telegraph* (London), November 27, 2010; Robert F. Worth "Saudi Arabia Arrests 149 Qaeda Suspects, Many with Ties to Yemen, over 8 Months" *New York Times*, November 27, 2010; Hugh Tomlinson "Saudis Arrest 98 al Qaeda Members Planning Attack" *The Times* (London), March 25, 2010.

2 "Rare Arrests in Iran" *The Dominion Post* (Wellington), December 31, 2010.

3 For more on China's house church movement, see Cheng (2003) and "Karrie Koesel on House Churches in China," a podcast at http://www.researchonreligion.org/church-organization/koesel-on-house-churches-in-china.

4 This discussion of the supply side theory of religion is based on McCleary and Barro (2006b), Finke and Iannaccone (1993), Fox and Tabori (2008), Iannacconne (1995a, b), Stark and Iannaccone (1994), and Stark and Finke (2000).

5 There are some notable exceptions to this such as Chaves and Cann (1992) and Chaves *et al.* (1994)

6 For a survey of the literature critiquing the supply side theory, see Bruce (2000), Ellison (1995), Fox and Tabory (2008), Demerath (1995), and Froese (2004).

8 RELIGIOUS FUNDAMENTALISM

1 The discussion in this chapter is based primarily on Almond *et al.* (2003), Appleby (2000, 2002), Eisenstadt (2000b), Emerson and Hartman (2006), Gellner (1992), Juergensmeyer (1993, 2008), Lawrence (1989), Marty and Appleby (1991, 1993, 1994), Miztal and Shupe (1992), and Swatos (1993).

9 RELIGION AND CONFLICT

1 These statistics are from the National Abortion Federation website at http://prochoice. org/about_abortion/violence/index.html.

2 Isabel Kershner "Religious-Secular Fight Rages for Jerusalem's Soul; Opening of Parking Lot leads to New Round of City's 'Sabbath Wars'" *International Herald Tribune*, September 4, 2009.

3 Philip Shenon "Standoff in the Gulf; Out of Saudi View, U.S. Force Allows Religious Their Rites" *New York Times*, December 21, 1990.

4 See, for example, Little (1991), Laustsen and Wæver (2000), and Seul (1999).

5 For similar arguments see Abu-Nimer (2001), Gopin (2000, 2002), and Toft *et al.* (2011).

10 CHRISTIAN-MAJORITY STATES 1: WESTERN DEMOCRACIES AND THE FORMER SOVIET BLOC

1 As previously noted, the RAS project general sources, listed at the end of Chapter 1, are not cited in the examples used in this chapter. These citations list only country-specific sources beyond the project's general sources.

2 Cornell University Law School, Supreme Court Collection. www.law.cornell.edu/ supct/html/00-1751.ZS.html and www.law.cornell.edu/supct/html/98-1648.ZS.html.

3 A copy of the relevant clause in the 1964 Education act is available at www.legislation. govt.nz/act/public/1964/0135/latest/DLM357868.html#DLM357868.

4 Constitution of Belgium. www.dekamer.be/kvvcr/pdf_sections/publications/constitution/ grondwetEN.pdf.

5 T.R. Reid "Sweden Separates Church, State" *Washington Post*, December 30, 2000.

6 Law on Religious Organizations, adopted by the Parliament on September 7, 1995 and signed by President G. Ulmanis on September 26, 1995, as amended on June 17, 1996, February 27, 1997, February 19, 1998, and July 19, 2000 (Latvia). Translation by Latvia's Religious Affairs Board.

7 "Swedish Government Funds Malmö Mosque Repair" *The Local: Sweden's News in English*, March 27, 2006. http://www.thelocal.se/3392/20060327/; Andrew Higgins "In Europe, God is (Not) Dead" *Wall Street Journal*, July 14, 2007.

8 Karagiannis (2009); Anthee Carassava "Greek Church Struggles to Quell Raft of Scandals Involving Clergy" *New York Times*, February 5, 2005.

9 Religious Denominations Act, adopted by the National Assembly of the Republic of Bulgaria, 39th National Assembly on December 20, 2002; original Bulgarian version published in *State Gazette*, issue no. 120 of December 29, 2002 (Bulgaria). Translation by Kalina Miller.

10 www.religlaw.org.

11 "Polish Priests Are Refused Work Permits in Belarus" *Ecumenical News International*, January 12, 2010.

12 "Meeting for Bible Instruction Raided in St. Petersburg" Jehovah's Witnesses Office of Public Information, October 8, 2009.

13 Nicholas Wood "Macedonian Church Guards Its Identity: Bishop's Struggle Reflects Wider Balkan Rift" *New York Times*, November 3, 2004; Branko Bjelajac "Orthodox Archbishop Jailed without the Gospels" Forum 18 News Service, July 27, 2005, www.forum18.org/Archive.php?article_id=618&pdf=Y; Drasko Djenovic "Macedonia: New Religion Law Perpetuates Discrimination" Forum 18 News Service, March 31, 2008, www.forum18.org/Archive.php?article_id=1107; Beth Kampschror "Jailed Priest Pushes for Religious Freedom" *Christian Science Monitor*, April 12, 2006.

14 For additional versions of this argument, see, among others, Demerath (2001: 2) and Shah (2000).

15 Constitution of Spain, www.senado.es/constitu_i/indices/consti_ing.pdf.

16 "The Closing of the Church Door; The Catholic Church Was Once Central to Spanish Life. But Spain Is Changing—Just Like Its Neighbors" *Newsweek*, May 19, 2008; "As Spaniards Lose Their Religion, Church Leaders Struggle to Hold On" *New York Times*, June 26, 2005; "Church and State Clash, Noisily, in Spain" *New York Times*, October 4, 2004; "For Vatican, Spain Is a Key Front in Church–State Battle" *New York Times*, January 6, 2009.

17 Martinez-Torron (2005); "Spanish Bishops Win Fight to Put Religion Back in Schools" *Independent* (London), June 21, 2003; "New Law Requires Roman Catholicism Classes in Spain's Schools" *New York Times*, December, 2003; "Catholic squeeze; Spain", *The Economist*, September 18, 2004.

18 "Church and State Clash, Noisily, in Spain", *New York Times*, October 4, 2004; "For Vatican, Spain Is a Key Front in Church–State Battle" *New York Times*, January 6, 2009; "Spanish Catholics Mount Opposition to Socialist Education Reform" *Christian Science Monitor*, November 18, 2005; "The Closing of the Church Door; The Catholic Church Was Once Central to Spanish life. But Spain Is Changing—Just Like Its Neighbors" *Newsweek*, May 19, 2008.

19 Constitution of Greece, www.hellenicparliament.gr/en/Vouli-ton-Ellinon/To-Politevma/Syntagma/.

20 Anderson (2003); Karagiannis (2009); Anthee Carassava "Greek Church Struggles to Quell Raft of Scandals Involving Clergy" *New York Times*, February 5, 2005; "Church Responsible for Bias in Greece, Says Report" *Hurriyet Daily News*, September 15, 2009.

21 European Court of Human Rights, *Alexandridis* v. *Greece*, http://sim.law.uu.nl/SIM/CaseLaw/hof.nsf/233813e697620022c1256864005232b7/9a779bb197d792f6c12573f5003a9cee?OpenDocument.

22 Anderson (2003); Efstathiou *et al.* (2008); Karagiannis (2009); Altana Filos "Greece: Religious Freedom—the Achilles Heel" Forum 18 News Service, May 17, 2004; European Commission Against Racism and Intolerance, ECRI Report on Greece, April 2, 2009, www.coe.int/t/dghl/monitoring/ecri/Country-by-country/Greece/GRC-CbC-IV-2009-031-ENG.pdf; Caroline Moorhead "Jehovah's Witnesses Jailed in Greece for Proselytism" *Independent* (London), September 28, 1992.

23 Anderson (2003); Caroline Moorhead "Jehovah's Witnesses Jailed in Greece for Proselytism" *Independent* (London), September 28, 1992.

24 Iris Boussiakou "Greece: The Case of the Muslim Minority in Western Thrace" London School of Economics and Political Science, December 2008, www2.lse.ac.uk/european Institute/research/hellenicObservatory/pdf/GreeSE/GreeSE21.pdf; "ECHR convicts Greece for Violating Religious Rights" *New Anatolian* (Ankara), July 14, 2006.

25 Niki Kitsantonis "Muslims in Athens Build Their Own Mosque" *New York Times*, July 6, 2007; Anthee Carassava, "The Faith That Has No Place" *Time* magazine, April 23, 2006.

11 CHRISTIAN-MAJORITY STATES 2: THE THIRD WORLD

1 As previously noted, the RAS project general sources, listed at the end of Chapter 1, are not cited in the examples used in this chapter. These citations list only country-specific sources beyond the project's general sources.

2 The significance of the difference between these two means is 0.000.

3 "Witchcraft Act Review Programme: Issues Paper" Malawi Law Commission, Lilongwe, Malawi, April 2009, www.lawcom.mw/docs/ip_witchcraft.pdf; Pilirani Semu-Banda "Witchcraft and Mob Justice in Malawi" Women's International Perspective, May 21, 2008, www.thewip.net/contributors/2008/05/mob_justice_in_malawi_accused.html; "A Shadow Report to the Malawi Government Sixth Periodic Report on the Implementation of the Convention on the Elimination of all Forms of Discrimination" submitted to the CEDAW Committee's 45th Session, 15 January—2 February 2010 by the Women and Law in Southern Africa Research and Educational Trust (WLSA Malawi) and the Malawi

NGO Gender Coordination Network, December 2009. This report quotes Seodi White, Emmily Kamwendo, and Wezi Malonda (2009) "Poor, Invisible and Excluded: Women in State Custody in Malawi" WLSA Malawi, Limbe, Malawi. www2.ohchr.org/english/bodies/cedaw/docs/ngos/WLSAMalawi45_session.pdf.

4 CIA World Factbook, www.cia.gov.

5 Constitution of Solomon Islands, www.paclii.org/sb/legis/consol_act/c1978167/.

6 "Religion and the Namibian Secular State" *Africa News*, June 8, 2007.

7 Constitution of Guatemala, www.religlaw.org/countryportal.php.

8 Constitution of Guatemala, www.religlaw.org/countryportal.php.

9 Constitution of Costa Rica, www.servat.unibe.ch/icl//.

10 International Coalition for Religious Freedom, Costa Rica (2009) www.religiousfreedom.com/index.php?option=com_content&view=article&id=122&Itemid=29 (downloaded January 1, 2010).

12 MUSLIM-MAJORITY STATES

1 As previously noted, the RAS project general sources, listed at the end of Chapter 1, are not cited in the examples used in this chapter. These citations list only country-specific sources beyond the project's general sources.

2 Brian Hershorin "The Separation of Church and State: Have We Gone Too Far?" (2003) www.expertlaw.com/library/misc/first_amendment-2.html#O.

3 World Health Organization, Substance Abuse, Alcohol, Libya, www.who.int/substance_abuse/publications/en/libyan_arab_jamahiriya.pdf.

4 Zelezeck Nguimatsa Serge "Researching the Legal System and Laws of the Islamic Republic of Mauritania" *Globalex* (August 2009), www.nyulawglobal.org/Globalex/Mauritania.htm#_edn14; Mauritania 1983 Penal Code, www.nyulawglobal.org/Globalex/Mauritania.htm#legislations.

5 Brunei 1984 Religious Council and Kadis Courts Law, www.lexadin.nl/wlg/legis/nofr/oeur/lxwebri.htm.

6 Pakistan Penal Code, www.unhcr.org/refworld/country,LEGAL,,LEGISLATION,PAK,4562d8cf2,485231942,0.html.

7 Kareem Fahim "In Reversal, Syria Turns Cold against Its Islamists" *Herald Tribune*, September 4–5, 2010; Marc Perelman "With Islamic Militancy Rising, Syria's Baath Regime Finds Religion" *Forward*, May 25, 2007, www.forward.com/articles/10792/.

8 Rabasa (2005); Yousif (2004); Malaysia 1996 Education Act, www.commonlii.org/my/legis/consol_act/ea1996104/; "Malaysian Government Shoots Down Minister's Proposal to Keep Religion out of State Schools" *Associated Press Worldstream*, May 3, 2005.

9 Robert Sedgwick "Education in Saudi Arabia" *World Education News and Reviews*, November/December 2001, www.wes.org/ewenr/01nov/Practical.htm; Robert F. Worth "For Saudi Liberals, a Ripple of Hope in a Sea of Tradition" *New York Times*, March 3, 2009; Dana Moss and Zvika Krieger "A Tipping Point in Saudi Arabia" *Christian Science Monitor*, August 15, 2007.

10 Sudan 1991 Criminal Act, www.ilo.org/dyn/natlex/natlex_browse.details?p_lang=en&p_country=SDN&p_classification=01&p_origin=SUBJECT.

11 "Official: Yemen Detains 9 People for Converting to Christianity" *Fox News*, August 19, 2008, www.foxnews.com/story/0,2933,406142,00.html.

12 "Saudi Arabia: End Secrecy, End Suffering" *Amnesty International*, www.amnesty.org/en/library/info/MDE23/016/2000; Human Rights Without Frontiers, "Persecution of Christians Grows under New King Abdullah" August 2005, www.assistnews.net/Stories/2005/s05080105.htm.

13 "Catholics Free to Worship in Kuwait, Says Bishop" *Catholic News Agency*, June 22, 2007, www.catholicnewsagency.com/new.php?n=9701; "Today's Education in Kuwait" *Kuwait Cultural Office*, Washington, DC, www.kuwaitculture.com/About%20Us/today.htm.

14 "Jordanian Minister Denies External Pressure behind Curricula Changes" *Al-Sharq al-Awsat*, November 30, 2004.

15 Malaysia, 1966 Societies Act, www.commonlii.org/my/legis/consol_act/sa1966198 7191/.

16 Martinez (2001); "Update: Indigenous Church Group Sues over Demolished Church" Compass Direct/International Christian Concern, January 24, 2008, www.persecution. org/2008/01/26/update-indigenous-church-group-sues-over-demolished-church/; "Malaysian Hindus Urge King to Stop Temple Destruction" *Agence France Presse*, June 21, 2006.

13 OTHER RELIGIONS

1 As previously noted, the RAS project general sources, listed at the end of Chapter 1, are not cited in the examples used in this chapter. These citations list only country-specific sources beyond the project's general sources.

2 www.adherents.com/Religions_By_Adherents.html. Statistics are for 2007 (downloaded July 3, 2011).

3 UN Population, latest available census and estimates report current through June 9, 2011, http://unstats.un.org/unsd/demographic/products/vitstats/ (downloaded July 3, 2011).

4 CIA World Factbook, https://www.cia.gov/library/publications/the-world-factbook/ fields/2122.html#iv (downloaded January 5, 2011).

5 Yoon (2003); Christian Caryl and B. J. Lee "Houses of the Hidden" *Newsweek*, September 24, 2007; Peter Harmsen "Kim Worship Makes North Korea One of World's Most Religious Societies" *Agence France Presse*, February 19, 2003; M. S. G. Proctor "*Juche:* The State Religion of the Democratic People's Republic of Korea: A Predictive Analysis of the Impact of Religion in the Korean Theater of Operations" *News from the Front*, http://call.army.mil.

6 *2009 White Paper on Religious Freedom in North Korea.* Seoul, South Korea: Database Center for North Korean Human Rights, 2009, www.uscirf.gov/index.php?option= com_content&view=article&id=3454; "Life inside North Korea" Senate Foreign Relations Committee Subcommittee on East Asian and Pacific Affairs Hearing, June 5, 2003, www.uscirf.gov/north-korea.html; "North Korea: Faith and Famine" *Washington Times*, October 8, 2008; Kim Hyung-jin "Does Genuine Religious Freedom Exist in Communist North Korea?" *Yonhap News*, May 18, 2007; Uwe Siemon-Netto "Covert Church in North Korea Growing" *United Press International*, February 21, 2002.

7 "Laos Says Christmas Arrest of Christians for Possessing 'Poisons'" Associated Foreign Press, January 12, 2004; "Two Christians Sentenced to Three Years in Prison" *AsiaNews*, July 19, 2005; "Laos: 11 Christians Arrested in Laos for Celebrating Christmas, 3 Remain in Custody" *AsiaNews,* January 12, 2011; "Violence against Christians in Vientiane and Luang Phrabang" *AsiaNews*, September 7, 2004.

8 Alex Spillius "Christians in Laos are Forced to Drink Blood and Renounce Faith" *Telegraph* (London), July 15, 2001; "Laos Officials Seize, Slaughter Christians' Livestock" *Compass News Direct*, July 10, 2009; "Christians Denied Food, Water in Laos at 'Critical Stage'" *Compass News Direct*, February 25, 2011.

APPENDIX: RAS DATA COLLECTION PROCEDURES

1 Although I did not keep precise records, I estimate that at least 25 colleagues were consulted. This includes 14 who commented on the grant proposals for the research, another 5 who commented on articles submitted to journals describing the proposed format for the research, and at least 6 who were consulted on a less formal basis and were specifically asked whether they could think of any variables that should be included but

were not on the list. This pool expanded considerably after the completion of round 1 to include referees for publications based on RAS1, audiences at presentations based on the data, and colleagues who showed an interest in the data collection.

2 This section is based on the RAS2 codebook, which is available online at the Religion and State project webpage, www.religionandstate.org.

3 The one country that is glaringly absent from the US State Department reports is the United States itself.

4 The first four rules are taken directly from the RAS2 codebook.

References

Abou El Fadl, Khaled *The Place of Tolerance in Islam*. Boston: Beacon, 2000.

Abu-Nimer, Mohammed "Conflict Resolution, Culture, and Religion: Toward a Training Model of Interreligious Peacebuilding" *Journal of Peace Research*, 38 (6), 2001, 685–704.

Achterberg, Peter, Dick Houtman, Stef Aupers, Willem de Koster, Peter Mascini, and Jerome van der Waal "A Christian Cancellation of the Secularist Truce? Waning Christian Religiosity and Waxing Religious Deprivatization in the West" *Journal for the Scientific Study of Religion*, 48 (4), 2009, 687–701.

Albright, Madeleine *The Mighty and the Almighty: Reflections on America, God, and World Affairs*, New York: Harper Perennial, 2007.

Almond, Gabriel, R. Scott Appleby, and Emmanuel Sivan *Strong Religion: The Rise of Fundamentalism around the World*, Chicago: University of Chicago Press, 2003.

Ammerman, Nancy T. "Accounting for Christian Fundamentalisms: Social Dynamics and Rhetorical Strategies" in Martin E. Marty and R. Scott Appleby eds. *Accounting for Fundamentalisms: The Dynamic Character of Movements*, Chicago: University of Chicago Press, 1994, 149–170.

Amore, Abdelfattah "Implementation of the Declaration on the Elimination of All Forms of Intolerance and of Discrimination Based on Religion or Belief" United Nations Economic and Social Council Commission on Human Rights, 1995.

Anderson, John *Religious Liberty in Transnational Societies: The Politics of Religions*, New York: Cambridge University Press, 2003.

Appleby, R. Scott *Religious Fundamentalisms and Global Conflict*, New York: Foreign Policy Association, 1994.

Appleby, R. Scott *The Ambivalence of the Sacred: Religion, Violence, and Reconciliation*, Lanham, MD: Rowman & Littlefield, 2000.

Appleby, R. Scott "History in the Fundamentalist Imagination" *Journal of American History*, 89 (2) September 2002, 498–511.

Apter, David ed. *Ideology and Discontent*, New York: Free Press, 1964.

Asani, Ali S. "'So That You May Know One Another': A Muslim American Reflects on Pluralism and Islam" *Annals of the American Academy of Political and Social Science*, 588 (1), 2003, 40–51.

Ayers, John W. and C. R. Hofstetter "American Muslim Political Participation following 9/11: Religious Belief, Political Resources, Social Structures, and Political Awareness" *Politics and Religion*, 1 (1), 2008, 3–26.

Azzam, Maha "Islamism Revisited" *International Affairs*, 86 (6), 2006, 1119–1132.

Barkun, Michael "Religious Violence and the Myth of Fundamentalism" *Totalitarian Movements and Political Religions*, 4 (3), 2003, 55–70.

Barnhart, Joe "The Incurably Religious Animal" in Emile Sahliyeh ed. *Religious Resurgence and Politics in the Contemporary World*, New York: State University of New York Press, 1990, 27–32.

Barrett, D. B., G. T. Kurian, and T. M. Johnson *World Christian Encyclopedia*, 2nd ed. Oxford: Oxford University Press, 2001.

Barro, Robert J. and Rachel M. McCleary "Religion and Economic Growth across Countries" *American Sociological Review*, 68 (5), 2003, 760–781.

Basedau, Mathias, Matthijs Bogaards, Christof Hartmann, and Peter Niesen "Ethnic Party Bans in Africa: A Research Agenda" *German Law Journal*, 8 (6), 2007, 617–634.

Baumgartner, Jody C., Peter L. Francia, and Jonathan S. Morris "A Clash of Civilizations? The Influence of Religion on Public Opinion of U.S. Foreign Policy in the Middle East" *Political Research Quarterly*, 61 (2), 2008, 171–179.

Beckford, James A. "The Insulation and Isolation of the Sociology of Religion" *Sociological Analysis*, 46 (4), 1985, 347–354.

Beit-Hallahmi, Benjamin "The Return of Martyrdom: Honour, Death, and Immortality" *Totalitarian Movements and Political Religions*, 4 (3), 2003, 11–34.

Bellin, Eva "Faith in Politics: New Trends in the Study of Religion and Politics" *World Politics*, 60 (2), 2008, 315–347.

Ben-Dor, Gabriel and Ami Pedahzur "The Uniqueness of Islamic Fundamentalism and the Fourth Wave of International Terrorism" *Totalitarian Movements and Political Religions*, 4 (3), 2003, 71–90.

Berger, Peter L. "Secularism in Retreat" *The National Interest*, Winter 1996/1997, 3–12.

Berger, Peter L. "Epistemological Modesty: An Interview with Peter Berger" *Christian Century*, 1145, 1997, 972–975.

Berger, Peter L. *The Desecularization of the World: Resurgent Religion in World Politics*, Grand Rapids, MI: Wm. B. Eerdmans, 1999.

Berger, Peter L. "Faith and Development" *Society*, 46 (1), 2009, 69–75.

Beyer, Peter "Secularization from the Perspective of Globalization: A Response to Dobbelaere" *Sociology of Religion*, 60 (3), 1999, 289–301.

Beyerlein, Kraig and Mark Chaves "The Political Activities of Religious Congregations in the United States" *Journal for the Scientific Study of Religion*, 42 (2), 2003, 229–246.

Black, Ann "Ideology and Law: The Impact of the MIB Ideology on Law and Dispute Resolution in the Sultanate of Brunei Darussalam" *Asian Journal of Comparative Law*, 3(1), 2008.

Boussiakou, Iris "Greece: The Case of the Muslim Minority in Western Thrace" *Hellenic Observatory Papers on Greece and Southeast Europe*, paper 21, 2008.

Bowen, John, R. *Why the French Don't Like Headscarves: Islam, the State, and Public Space*, Princeton, NJ: Princeton University Press, 2007.

Bruce, Steve "The Supply Side Model of Religion: The Nordic and Baltic States" *Journal for the Scientific Study of Religion*, 39 (1), 2000, 32–46.

Bruce, Steve *God Is Dead: Secularization in the West*, Malden, MA: Blackwell, 2002.

Bruce, Steve "Secularization and Politics" in Jeffrey Haynes ed. *Routledge Handbook of Religion and Politics*, London: Routledge, 2009, 145–158.

Canetti, Daphna, Stevan E. Hobfoll, Ami Pedahzur, and Eran Zaidise "Much Ado about Religion: Religiosity, Resource Loss, and Support for Political Violence" *Journal of Peace Research*, 47 (5), 2010, 575–587.

Carlson, Eric "China's New Regulations on Religion: A Small Step, not a Great Leap, Forward" *Brigham Young University Law Review*, 747, 2005, 747–797.

Cavalcanti, Tiango V., Stephen L. Parente, and Rui Zhao "Religion in Macroeconomics: A Quantitative Analysis of Weber's Thesis" *Economic Theory*, 32, 2007, 105–123.

Charters, David A. "Something Old, Something New . . . ? Al-Qaeda, Jihadism, and Fascism" *Terrorism and Political Violence*, 19 (1), 2007, 65–93.

Chaves, Mark "Secularization as Declining Religious Authority" *Social Forces*, 72 (3), March 1994, 749–774.

Chaves, Mark and David E. Cann "Religion, Pluralism, and Religious Market Structure" *Rationality and Society*, 4 (3), 1992, 272–290.

Chaves, Mark, Peter J. Schraeder, and Mario Sprindys "State Regulation of Religion and Muslim Religious Vitality in the Industrialized West" *Journal of Politics*, 56 (4), 1994, 1087–1097.

Cheng, May M. C. "House Church Movements and Religious Freedom in China" *China: An International Journal*, 1 (1), 2003, 16–45.

Chiozza, Giacomo "Is There a Clash of Civilizations? Evidence from Patterns of International Conflict Involvement, 1946–97" *Journal of Peace Research*, 39 (6), 2002, 711–734.

Cohen, Stuart A. "The Changing Jewish Discourse on Armed Conflict: Themes and Implications" *Terrorism and Political Violence*, 17 (3), 2005, 353–370.

Coleman, James S. "Commentary: Social Institutions and Social Theory" *American Sociological Review*, 55, 1990, 333–339.

Crouch, Colin "The Quiet Continent: Religion and Politics in Europe" *Political Quarterly*, 71 (Supplement 1), 2000, 90–103.

Crouch, Melissa "The Proselytisation Case: Law, the Rise of Islamic Conservatism and Religious Discrimination in West Java" *Australian Journal of Asian Law*, 8(3), 2006, 322–337.

Crouch, Melissa "Implementing the Regulation on Places of Worship in Indonesia: New Problems, Local Politics and Court Action" *Asian Studies Review*, 34, 2010, 403–419.

Dahl, Robert A. *Polyarchy: Participation and Opposition*, New Haven, CT: Yale University Press, 1971.

Dalacoura, Katarina "Unexceptional Politics? The Impact of Islam on International Relations" *Millennium*, 29 (3), 2000, 879–887.

Davie, Grace *Religion in Modern Europe: A Memory Mutates*, Oxford: Oxford University Press, 2000.

Dawkins, Richard, *The God Delusion*, New York: Mariner Books, 2008.

De Juan, Alexander "A Pact with the Devil? Elite Alliances as Bases of Violent Religious Conflict" *Studies in Conflict and Terrorism*, 31 (12), 2008, 1120–1135.

De Soysa, Indra and Neumayer, Eric "Disarming Fears of Diversity: Ethnic Heterogeneity and State Militarization, 1998–2002" *Journal of Peace Research*, 45 (4), 2008, 497–518.

Demerath, N. J. III "Rational Paradigms, A-Rational Religion, and the Debate over Secularization" *Journal for the Scientific Study of Religion*, 34 (1), 1995, 105–112.

Demerath, N. J. III *Crossing the Gods: World Religions and Worldly Politics*, New Brunswick, NJ: Rutgers University Press, 2001.

Djupe, Paul A. and Christopher P. Gilbert "Politics and Church: Byproduct or Central Mission?" *Journal for the Scientific Study of Religion*, 47 (1), 2008, 45–62.

Dobbelaere, Karel "Secularization: A Multi-dimensional Concept" *Current Sociology*, 29 (2), 1981, 1–153.

Dobbelaere, Karel "Secularization Theories and Sociological Paradigms: A Reformulation of the Private–Public Dichotomy and the Problem of Societal Integration" *Sociological Analysis*, 46 (4), 1985, 377–387.

Dobbelaere, Karel "Some Trends in European Sociology of Religion: The Secularization Debate" *Sociological Analysis*, 48 (2), 1987: 107–137.

Dobbelaere, Karel "Towards an Integrated Perspective of the Processes Related to the Descriptive Concept of Secularization" *Sociology of Religion*, 60 (3), 1999, 229–247.

Don-Yehiyah, Eliezer "The Book and the Sword: The Nationalist Yeshivot and Political Radicalism in Israel" in Martin E. Marty and R. Scott Appleby eds. *Accounting for Fundamentalisms: The Dynamic Character of Movements*, Chicago: University of Chicago Press, 1994, 264–302.

Driessen, Michael D. "Religion, State, and Democracy: Analyzing Two Dimensions of Church–State Arrangements" *Politics and Religion*, 3 (1), 2010, 55–80.

Durham, W. Cole Jr. "Perspectives on Religious Liberty: A Comparative Framework" in Johan D. van der Vyver and John Witte Jr. *Religious Human Rights in Global Perspective: Legal Perspectives*, The Hague: Kluwer Law International, 1996, 1–44.

Durkheim, Emile *The Elementary Forms of Religious Life*, trans, Joseph Ward Swain, London: George Allen & Unwin, 1964.

Durkheim, Emile "Concerning the Definition of Religious Phenomena" in W. S. F. Pickering *Durkheim on Religion: A Selection of Readings with Bibliographies*, London: Routledge & Kegan Paul, 1975, 74–99.

Ebaugh, Helen R. "Return of the Sacred: Reintegrating Religion in the Social Sciences" *Journal for the Scientific Study of Religion*, 41 (3), 2002, 385–395.

Edelman, Bryan and James T. Richardson "Imposed Limitations on Freedom of Religion in China and the Margin of Appreciation Doctrine: A Legal Analysis of the Crackdown on the Falun Gong and Other 'Evil Cults'" *Journal of Church and State*, 47 (2), 2005, 243–267.

Efstathiou, Ioannis, Fokion Georgiadis, and Apostolos Zizimos "Religion in Greek Education in a Time of Globalization" *Intercultural Education Journal*, 19 (4), 2008, 325–336.

Eisenstadt, S. N. "The Reconstruction of Religious Arenas in the Framework of 'Multiple Modernities'" *Millennium*, 29 (3), 2000a, 591–611.

Eisenstadt, S. N. "The Resurgence of Religious Movements in Processes of Globalisation: Beyond End of History or Clash of Civilisations" *International Journal on Multicultural Societies*, 2 (1), 2000b, 4–15.

Eisenstein, Marie A. *Religion and the Politics of Tolerance: How Christianity Builds Democracy*, Waco, TX: Baylor University Press, 2008.

El Fadal, Khalid A. "The Rules of Killing at War: An Inquiry into Classical Sources" *The Muslim World*, 89 (2), 1999, 144–157.

Ellingsen, Tanja "The Relevance of Culture in UN Voting Behavior" Paper presented at the International Studies Association Forty-third Annual Conference, New Orleans, March 2002.

Ellison, Christopher G. "Rational Choice Explanations of Individual Religious Behavior: Notes on the Problem of Social Embeddedness" *Journal for the Scientific Study of Religion*, 34 (1), 1995, 89–97.

Emerson, Michael O. and David Hartman "The Rise of Religious Fundamentalism" *Annual Review of Sociology*, 32, 2006, 127–144.

Enders, Walter and Todd Sandler "Distribution of Transnational Terrorism among Countries by Income Class and Geography after 9/11" *International Studies Quarterly*, 50 (2), 2006, 367–393.

Esbeck, Carl H. "A Typology of Church–State Relations in American Thought" *Religion and Public Education*, 15 (1), 1988, 43–50.

Esman, Milton "The Management of Communal Conflict" *Public Policy*, 21, 1973, 49–78.

Esposito, John L. "Religion and Global Affairs: Political Challenges" *SAIS Review of International Affairs*, 18 (2), 1998, 19–24.

Esposito, John L. and James P. Piscatori "Democratization and Islam" *Middle East Journal*, 45 (3), 1991, 427–440.

Esposito, John L. and John O. Voll "Islam and the West: Muslim Voices of Dialogue" *Millennium*, 29 (3), 2000, 613–639.

Farr, Thomas F. "Diplomacy in an Age of Faith: Religious Freedom and National Security" *Foreign Affairs*, 87 (2), 2008.

Fawcett, Liz *Religion, Ethnicity, and Social Change*, Basingstoke, UK: Palgrave Macmillan, 2000.

Fein, Helen "Genocide: A Sociological Perspective" *Current Sociology*, 38 (1), Spring 1990, 1–126.

Fink, Simon "Politics as Usual or Bringing Religion Back In? The Influence of Parties, Institutions, Economic Interests, and Religion on Embryo Research Laws" *Comparative Political Studies*, 41 (2), 2008, 1631–1656.

Finke, Roger and Laurence R. Iannaccone "Supply-Side Explanations for Religious Change" *Annals of the American Association of Political and Social Sciences*, 527, May 1993, 27–39.

Fisch, M. Steven "Islam and Authoritarianism" *World Politics*, 55 (1), 2002, 4–37.

Fitzhugh, George *Cannibals All! Or, Slaves without Masters*, Bedford, MA: Applewood Books, 1857.

Fox, Adam and Trang Thomas "Impact of Religious Affiliation and Religiosity on Forgiveness" *Australian Psychologist*, 43 (3), 2008, 175–185.

Fox, Jonathan *Religion, Civilization, and Civil War: 1945 through the New Millennium*, Lanham, MD: Lexington Books, 2004.

Fox, Jonathan "Paradigm Lost: Huntington's Unfulfilled Clash of Civilizations Prediction into the 21st Century" *International Politics*, 42 (4), 2005, 428–457.

Fox, Jonathan "The Increasing Role of Religion in State Failure: 1960–2004" *Terrorism and Political Violence*, 19 (3), 2007, 395–414.

Fox, Jonathan *A World Survey of Religion and the State*, New York: Cambridge University Press, 2008.

Fox, Jonathan and Shmuel Sandler *Bringing Religion into International Relations*, New York: Palgrave Macmillan, 2004.

Fox, Jonathan and Ephraim Tabory "Contemporary Evidence regarding the Impact of State Regulation of Religion on Religious Participation and Belief" *Sociology of Religion*, 69 (3), 2008, 245–271.

Fradkin, Hillel "Does Democracy Need Religion?" *Journal of Democracy*, 11 (1), 2000, 87–94.

Freud, Sigmund *The Future of an Illusion*, New York: W. W. Norton, 1989.

Friedrichs, Robert W. "The Uniquely Religious: Grounding the Social Scientific Study of Religion Anew" *Sociological Analysis*, 1985, 46 (4), 361–366.

Froese, Paul "After Atheism: An Analysis of Religious Monopolies in the Post-Communist World" *Sociology of Religion*, 65 (1), 2004, 57–75.

Froese, Paul and F. Carson Mencken "A U.S. Holy War? The Effects of Religion on Iraq War Policy Attitudes" *Social Science Quarterly*, 90 (1), 2009, 103–116.

Frykenberg, Robert Eric "Accounting for Fundamentalisms in South Asia: Ideologies and Institutions in Historical Perspective" in Martin E. Marty and R. Scott Appleby eds. *Accounting for Fundamentalisms: The Dynamic Character of Movements*, Chicago: University of Chicago Press, 1994, 591–618.

Fukuyama, Francis "Social Capital, Civil Society, and Development" *Third World Quarterly*, 22 (1), 2001, 7–20.

Fuller, Graham E. "The Future of Political Islam" *Foreign Affairs*, 81 (2), 2002, 48–60.

Furman, Uriah (2000) "Minorities in Contemporary Islamist Discourse" *Middle Eastern Studies*, 36 (4), 2000, 1–20.

Garvey, John H. "Introduction: Fundamentalism and Politics" in Martin E. Marty and R. Scott Appleby eds. *Fundamentalisms and the State: Remaking Polities, Economies, and Militance*, Chicago: University of Chicago Press, 1991, 13–27.

Geertz, Clifford "Religion as a Cultural System" in Michael Banton ed. *Anthropological Approaches to the Study of Religion*, London: Tavistock, 1966, 1–46.

Geertz, Clifford *The Interpretation of Culture*, New York: Basic Books, 1973.

Geertz, Clifford "Centers, Kings and Charisma: Reflections on the Symbolics of Power" in J. Ben-David and C. Nichols Clark eds. *Culture and Its Creators*, Chicago: University of Chicago Press, 1977, 150–171.

Gellner, Ernest *Postmodernism, Reason and Religion*, London: Routledge, 1992.

Gill, Anthony *Rendering unto Caesar: The Catholic Church and the State in Latin America*, Chicago: University of Chicago Press, 1998.

Gill, Anthony "Religion and Comparative Politics" *Annual Review of Political Science*, 4, 2001, 117–138.

Gill, Anthony "The Political Origins of Religious Liberty: A Theoretical Outline" *Interdisciplinary Journal of Research on Religion*, 1 (1), 2005, 1–35.

Gill, Anthony *The Political Origins of Religious Liberty*, New York: Cambridge University Press, 2008.

Glynn, Patrick "Racial Reconciliation: Can Religion Work Where Politics Has Failed?" *American Behavioral Scientist*, 41 (6), 1998, 834–841.

Goldewijk, Berma K. ed. *Religion, International Relations, and Cooperation Development*, Wageningen, the Netherlands: Wageningen Academic Publishers, 2007.

Gopin, Marc *Between Eden and Armageddon: The Future of World Religions, Violence, and Peacemaking*, Oxford: Oxford University Press, 2000.

Gopin, Marc *Holy War, Holy Peace: How Religion Can Bring Peace to the Middle East*, New York: Oxford University Press, 2002.

Gorski, Philip S. and Ate_ Altınordu "After Secularization?" *Annual Review of Sociology*, 24, 2008, 55–85.

Greenawalt, Kent *Religious Convictions and Political Choice*, Oxford: Oxford University Press, 1988.

Guillermo, Trejo "Religious Competition and Ethnic Mobilization in Latin America: Why the Catholic Church Promotes Indigenous Movements" *American Political Science Review*, 103 (3), 2009, 323–342.

Guindy, Adel "The Islamization of Egypt" *Middle East Review of International Affairs*, 10 (3), 2006. http://meria.idc.ac.il/journal/2006/issue3/jv10no3a7.html (accessed February 1, 2012).

Guiso, Luigi, Paola Sapienza, and Luigi Zingales, L. "People's Opium? Religion and Economic Attitudes" *Journal of Monetary Economics*, 50 (1), 2003, 225–282.

Gurr, Ted R. "War, Revolution, and the Growth of the Coercive State" *Comparative Political Studies*, 21 (1), April 1988, 45–65.

Gurr, Ted R. *Minorities at Risk*, Washington, DC: United States Institute of Peace, 1993.

Gurr, Ted R. "Peoples against the State: Ethnopolitical Conflict and the Changing World System" *International Studies Quarterly*, 1994, 38 (3), 347–377.

Hadden, Jeffrey K. "Religious Broadcasting and the Mobilization of the New Christian Right" *Journal for the Scientific Study of Religion*, 26 (1), 1987a, 1–24.

Hadden, Jeffrey K. "Toward Desacralizing Secularization Theory" *Social Forces*, 65 (3), 1987b, 587–611.

Hadden, Jeffrey K. and Anson Shupe *Prophetic Religion and Politics: Religion and the Political Order*, vol. 1, New York: Paragon, 1986.

Hallward, Maia Carter "Situation the 'Secular': Negotiating the Boundary between Religion and Politics" *International Political Sociology*, 2 (1), 2008, 1–16.

Halman, Loek and Veerle Draulans "How Secular Is Europe?" *British Journal of Sociology*, 57 (2), 2006, 263–288.

Hardacre, Helen "The Impact of Fundamentalisms on Women, the Family, and Interpersonal Relations" in Martin E. Marty and R. Scott Appleby eds.

Fundamentalisms and Society: Reclaiming the Sciences, the Family, and Education, Chicago: University of Chicago Press, 1993, 129–150.

Harding, Andrew "The Keris, the Crescent and the Blind Goddess: The State, Islam and the Constitution in Malaysia," *Singapore Journal of International and Comparative Law*, 6, 2002, 154–180.

Harris, Fredrick C. "Something Within: Religion as a Mobilizer of African-American Political Activism" *Journal of Politics*, 56 (1), 1994, 42–68.

Hasenclever, Andreas and Volker Rittberger "Does Religion Make a Difference? Theoretical Approaches to the Impact of Faith on Political Conflict" *Millennium*, 29 (3), 2000, 641–674.

Hashimi, Sohail H. "Saving and Taking Life in War: Three Modern Views" *The Muslim World*, 89 (2), 1999, 158–180.

Haynes, Jeff "Religion, Secularisation, and Politics: A Postmodern Conspectus" *Third World Quarterly*, 18 (4), 1997, 709–728.

Haynes, Jeff *Religion in Global Politics*, Harlow, UK: Longman, 1998.

Haynes, Jeffrey ed. *Routledge Handbook of Religion and Politics*, New York: Routledge, 2009.

Hefner, Robert H. "Public Islam and the Problem of Democratization" *Sociology of Religion*, 62 (4), 2001, 491–514.

Hehir, J. Bryan "Expanding Military Intervention: Promise or Peril?" *Social Research*, 62 (1), 1995, 41–50.

Henderson, Errol A. "Culture or Contiguity: Ethnic Conflict, the Similarity of States, and the Onset of War, 1820–1989" *Journal of Conflict Resolution*, 41 (5), October 1997, 649–668.

Henderson, Errol A. "The Democratic Peace through the Lens of Culture, 1820–1989" *International Studies Quarterly*, 42 (3), September 1998, 461–484.

Henderson, Errol A. "Mistaken Identity: Testing the Clash of Civilizations Thesis in Light of Democratic Peace Claims" *British Journal of Political Science*, 34, 2004, 539–563.

Henderson, Errol A. "Not Letting the Evidence Get in the Way of Assumptions: Testing the Clash of Civilizations with More Data" *International Politics*, 42 (4), 2005, 458–469.

Henderson, Errol A and Richard Tucker "Clear and Present Strangers: The Clash of Civilizations and International Conflict" *International Studies Quarterly*, 45 (2), 2001, 317–338.

Hilary, Gilles and Kai Wai Hui "Does Religion Matter in Corporate Decision Making in America?" *Journal of Financial Economics*, 93 (3), 2009, 455–473.

Hill, Kim Q. and Tetsuya Matsubayashi "Church Engagement, Religious Values, and Mass–Elite Policy Agenda Agreement in Local Communities" *American Journal of Political Science*, 52 (3), 2008, 570–584.

Hitchens, Christopher *God Is Not Great: How Religion Poisons Everything*, New York: Warner Twelve, 2007.

Hjelm, Titus "To Study or Not to Study Religion and Society: The Institutionalization, Fragmentation and Marginalization of Sociology of Religion in Finland" *Acta Sociologica*, 51 (2), 2008, 91–102.

Hoffman, Bruce "'Holy Terror': The Implications of Terrorism Motivated by a Religious Imperative" *Studies in Conflict and Terrorism*, 18, 1995, 271–284.

Horowitz, Donald L. *Ethnic Groups in Conflict*, Berkeley: University of California Press, 1985.

Horowitz, Michael C. "Long Time Going: Religion and the Duration of Crusading" *International Security*, 34 (2), 2009, 162–193.

Hunsberger, Bruce and Lynne M. Jackson "Religion, Meaning, and Prejudice" *Journal of Social Issues*, 61 (94), 2005, 807–826.

Huntington, Samuel P. "The Clash of Civilizations?" *Foreign Affairs*, 72 (3), 1993, 22–49.

Huntington, Samuel P. *The Clash of Civilizations and the Remaking of the World Order*, New York: Simon & Schuster, 1996.

Hurd, Elizabeth S. "The Political Authority of Secularism in International Relations" *European Journal of International Relations*, 10 (2), 2004a, 235–262.

Hurd, Elizabeth S. "The International Politics of Secularism: US Foreign Policy and the Islamic Republic of Iran" *Alternatives*, 29 (2), 2004b, 115–138.

Hurd, Elizabeth S. *The Politics of Secularism in International Relations*, Princeton, NJ: Princeton University Press, 2007.

Hurd, Ian "Legitimacy and Authority in International Politics" *International Organizations*, 53 (2), 1999, 379–408.

Iannaccone, Laurence R. "Voodoo Economics? Reviewing the Rational Choice Approach to Religion" *Journal for the Scientific Study of Religion*, 34 (1), 1995a, 76–89.

Iannaccone, Lawrence R. "Second Thoughts: A Response to Chaves, Demerath, and Ellison" *Journal for the Scientific Study of Religion*, 34 (1), 1995b, 113–120.

Jaggers, Keith and Ted R. Gurr "Tracking Democracy's Third Wave with the Polity III Data" *Journal of Peace Research*, 32, (4), 1995, 469–482.

Jelen, Ted G. "The Political Consequences of Religious Group Attitudes" *Journal of Politics*, 55 (1), 1993, 178–190.

Johnston, Douglas "The Churches and Apartheid in South Africa" in Douglas Johnston and Cynthia Sampson eds. *Religion, the Missing Dimension of Statecraft*, Oxford: Oxford University Press, 1994, 177–207.

Johnston, Hank and Jozef Figa "The Church and Political Opposition: Comparative Perspectives on Mobilization against Authoritarian Regimes" *Journal for the Scientific Study of Religion*, 27 (1), 1988, 32–47.

Jones-Correa, Michael A. and David L. Leal "Political Participation: Does Religion Matter?" *Political Research Quarterly*, 54 (4), 2001, 751–770.

Juergensmeyer, Mark "Sacrifice and Cosmic War" *Terrorism and Political Violence*, 3 (3), 1991, 101–117.

Juergensmeyer, Mark *The New Cold War?* Berkeley: University of California Press, 1993.

Juergensmeyer, Mark "Terror Mandated by God" *Terrorism and Political Violence*, 9 (2), Summer 1997, 16–23.

Juergensmeyer, Mark "Christian Violence in America" *Annals of the American Academy of Political and Social Sciences*, 558, July 1998, 88–100.

Juergensmeyer, Mark *Terror in the Mind of God: The Global Rise of Religious Violence*, Berkeley: University of California Press, 2000.

Juergensmeyer, Mark *Global Rebellion: Religious Challenges to the Secular State, from Christian Militias to Al Qaeda*, Berkeley: University of California Press, 2008.

Kalyvas, Stathis N. "Democracy and Religious Politics: Evidence from Belgium" *Comparative Political Studies*, 31 (3), 1998, 292–320.

Kalyvas, Stathis N. "Commitment Problems in Emerging Democracies: The Case of Religious Parties" *Comparative Politics*, 22 (4), 2000, 379–398.

Kamil, Omar "Rabbi Ovadia Yosef and His 'Culture War' in Israel" *Middle East Review of International Affairs*, 4 (4), 2000, 22–29.

Karagiannis, Evangelos "Secularism in Context: The Relation between the Greek State and the Church of Greece in Crisis" *European Journal of Sociology*, 50 (1), 2009, 122–167.

Kaspersen, Kars B. and Johannes Lindvall "Why No Religious Politics? The Secularization of Poor Relief and Primary Education in Denmark and Sweden" *Archives of European Sociology*, 49 (1), 2008, 119–143.

Keane, John "Secularism?" *Political Quarterly*, 71 (Supplement 1), 2000, 5–19.

Kedourie, Elie *Politics in the Middle East*, London: Frank Cass, 1992.

Kennedy, Robert "Is One Person's Terrorist Another's Freedom Fighter? Western and Islamic Approaches to 'Just War' Compared" *Terrorism and Political Violence*, 11 (1), 1999, 1–21.

Kim, Myunghee "Spiritual Values, Religious Practices, and Democratic Attitudes" *Politics and Religion*, 1 (2), 2008, 216–236.

Kimball, Charles *When Religion Becomes Evil*, New York: HarperCollins, 2002.

Kokosalakis, Nikos "Legitimation, Power and Religion in Modern Society" *Sociological Analysis*, 1985, 46 (4), 367–376.

Kowalewski, David and Arthur L. Greil "Religion as Opiate: Church and Revolution in Comparative Structural Perspective", *Journal of Church and State*, 32 (3), 1990, 511–526.

Kramer, Martin "Hizbullah: The Calculus of Jihad" in Martin E. Marty and R. Scott Appleby eds. *Fundamentalisms and the State: Remaking Polities, Economies, and Militance*, Chicago: University of Chicago Press, 1991, 539–556.

Künkler, Mirjam and Julia Leininger "The Multi-faceted Role of Religious Actors in Democratization Processes: Empirical Evidence from Five Young Democracies" *Democratization*, 16 (6), 2009, 1058–1092.

Kunovich, Robert M. "An Exploration of the Salience of Christianity for National Identity in Europe" *Sociological Perspectives*, 49 (4), 2006, 435–460.

Kuran, Timur "Fundamentalism and the Economy" in Martin E. Marty and R. Scott Appleby eds. *Fundamentalisms and the State: Remaking Politics, Economies, and Militance*, Chicago: University of Chicago Press, 1991, 289–301.

Kuru, Ahmet T. *Secularism and State Policies toward Religion: The United States, France, and Turkey*, New York: Cambridge University Press, 2009.

Lambert, Yves "Religion in Modernity as a New Axial Age: Secularization or New Religious Forms" *Sociology of Religion*, 60 (3), 1999, 303–333.

Laustsen, Carsten Bagge and Ole Wæver "In Defence of Religion: Sacred Referent Objects for Securitization" *Millennium*, 29 (3), 2000, 705–739.

Lawrence, Bruce B. *Defenders of God: The Fundamentalist Revolt against the Modern Age*, San Francisco: Harper & Row, 1989.

Laycock, Douglas "The Underlying Unity of Separation and Neutrality" *Emory Law Journal*, 46, 1997, 43–75.

Lechner, Frank A. "The Case against Secularization: A Rebuttal" *Social Forces*, 69 (4), June 1991, 1103–1119.

Lechner, Frank A. "Global Fundamentalism" in William H. Swatos Jr. ed. *A Future for Religion? New Paradigms for Social Analysis*, Newbury Park, CA: Sage, 1993, 19–36.

Lewis, Bernard "Introduction" in *Islam: From the Prophet Muhammad to the Capture of Constantinople, vol. 1: Politics and War*, ed. and trans. Bernard Lewis, New York: Oxford University Press, 1987.

Lewis, Bernard *Islam and the West*, Oxford: Oxford University Press, 1993.

Lewis, Bernard "License to Kill: Usama bin Ladin's Declaration of Jihad" *Foreign Affairs*, 77 (6), 1998, 14–19.

Lewis, Bernard *What Went Wrong? The Clash between Islam and Modernity in the Middle East*, New York: Harper Perennial, 2003.

Lewy, Guenter *Religion and Revolution*, New York: Oxford University Press, 1974.

Lijphart, Arend *Democracy in Plural Societies*, New Haven, CT: Yale University Press, 1977.

Lincoln, Bruce ed. *Religion, Rebellion and Revolution*, London: Macmillan, 1985.

Lincoln, Bruce *Holy Terrors: Thinking about Religion after September 11*, Chicago: University of Chicago Press, 2003.

Linz, Juan J. *The Breakdown of Democratic Regimes: Crisis, Breakdown, and Reequilibration*, Baltimore: Johns Hopkins University Press, 1978.

Little, David *Ukraine: The Legacy of Intolerance*, Washington, DC: United States Institute of Peace Press, 1991.

Luttwak, Edward "The Missing Dimension" in Douglas Johnston and Cynthia Sampson eds. *Religion, the Missing Dimension of Statecraft*, Oxford: Oxford University Press, 1994, 8–19.

Lynch, Cecelia "Dogma, Praxis, and Religious Perspectives on Multiculturalism" *Millennium*, 29 (3), 2000, 741–759.

Madeley, John T. S. "European Liberal Democracy and the Principle of State Religious Neutrality" *West European Politics*, 26 (1), 2003, 1–22.

Manor, James "Organizational Weakness and the Rise of Sinhalese Buddhist Extremism" in Martin E. Marty and R. Scott Appleby eds. *Accounting for Fundamentalisms: The Dynamic Character of Movements*, Chicago: University of Chicago Press, 1994, 770–784.

Marquand, D and R. L. Nettler "Foreword" *Political Quarterly*, 71 (Supplement 1), 2000, 1–4.

Martin, David A. *A General Theory of Secularization*, Oxford: Basil Blackwell, 1978.

Martin, J. Paul "The Three Monotheistic World Religions and International Human Rights" *Journal of Social Issues*, 61 (94), 2005, 827–845.

Martin, Richard C. "The Study of Religion and Violence" in David C. Rapoport and Yonah Alexander eds. *The Morality of Terrorism: Religious and Secular Justifications*, 2nd ed., New York: Columbia University Press, 1989, 349–373.

Martinez, Patricia A. "The Islamic State or the State of Islam in Malaysia" *Contemporary Southeast Asia*, 23 (3), 2001. http://findarticles.com/p/articles/mi_hb6479/is_3_23/ai_n28886555/ (accessed February 1, 2012).

Martinez-Torron, Javier "School and Religion in Spain" *Journal of Church and State*, 47 (1), 2005.

Marty, Martin E. and R. Scott Appleby eds. *Fundamentalisms and the State: Remaking Polities, Economies, and Militance*, Chicago: University of Chicago Press, 1991.

Marty, Martin E. and R. Scott Appleby eds. *Fundamentalisms and Society: Reclaiming the Sciences, the Family, and Education*, Chicago: University of Chicago Press, 1993.

Marty, Martin E. and R. Scott Appleby eds. *Accounting for Fundamentalisms: The Dynamic Character of Movements*, Chicago: University of Chicago Press, 1994.

Mazie, Steven V. "Rethinking Religious Establishment and Liberal Democracy: Lessons from Israel" *Brandywine Review of Faith and International Affairs*, 2 (2), 2004, 3–12.

Mazie, Steven V. *Israel's Higher Law: Religion and Liberal Democracy in the Jewish State*, New York: Lexington, 2006.

McCarthy, John D. and Mayer N. Zald "Resource Mobilization and Social Movements: A Partial Theory" *American Journal of Sociology*, 82 (6), 1976, 1212–1241.

McCleary, Rachel M. and Robert J. Barro "Religion and International Economy in an International Panel" *Journal for the Scientific Study of Religion*, 45 (2), 2006a, 149–175.

McCleary, Rachel M. and Robert J. Barro "Religion and Economy" *Journal of Economic Perspectives*, 20 (2), 2006b, 49–72.

Mendelsohn, Everett "Religious Fundamentalism and the Sciences" in Martin E. Marty and R. Scott Appleby eds. *Fundamentalisms and Society: Reclaiming the Sciences, the Family, and Education*, Chicago: University of Chicago Press, 1993, 23–41.

Midlarsky, Manus I. "Democracy and Islam: Implications for Civilizational Conflict and the Democratic Peace" *International Studies Quarterly*, 42 (3), 1998, 458–511.

Miles, Jack "Religion and American Foreign Policy" *Survival* 46 (1), 2004, 23–37.

Mill, John S. "Considerations on Representative Government" in John S. Mill, *Utilitarianism, Liberty, and Representative Government*, New York: E. P. Dutton, 1951. (Originally published in 1861.)

Minkenberg, Michael "Religion and Public Policy: Institutional, Cultural, and Political Impact on the Shaping of Abortion Policies in Western Democracies" *Comparative Political Studies*, 35 (2), 2002, 221–247.

Minkenberg, Michael "The Western European Right as a Collective Actor: Modeling the Impact of Cultural and Structural Variables on Party Formation and Movement Mobilization" *Comparative European Politics*, 1, 2003, 149–170.

Minkenberg, Michael "Religion and Euroscepticism: Cleavages, Religious Parties and Churches in EU Member States" *West European Politics*, 32 (6), 2009, 1190–1211.

Misztal, Bronislaw and Anson Shupe eds. *Religion and Politics in Comparative Perspective: Revival of Religious Fundamentalism in East and West*, Westport, CT: Praeger, 1992.

Moghadam, Assaf "Motives for Martyrdom: Al-Qaida, Salafi Jihad, and the Spread of Suicide Attacks" *International Security*, 33 (3), 2008–2009, 46–78.

Mol, Hans *Identity and the Sacred: A Sketch for a New Social-Scientific Theory of Religion*, Oxford: Basil Blackwell, 1976.

Monshipouri, Mahmood "The West's Modern Encounter with Islam: From Discourse to Reality" *Journal of Church and State*, 40 (1), 1998, 25–56.

Morigi, Andrea, Vittorio Emanuele Vernole, and Chiara Verna, *Report 2000 on Religious Freedom in the World*, Rome: Aid to the Church in Need, Italian Secretariat, 2003.

Müller, Tim "Religiosity and Attitudes towards the Involvement of Leaders in Politics: A Multilevel-Analysis of 55 Societies" *World Values Research*, 2 (1), 2009, 1–29.

Nasr, Seyyed Vali Reza "Religion and Global Affairs: Secular States and Religious Oppositions" *SAIS Review of International Affairs*, 16 (2), Summer–Fall 1998, 32–37.

Nelsen, Brent F., James L. Guth, and Cleveland R. Fraser "Does Religion Matter? Christianity and Public Support for the European Union" *European Union Politics*, 2 (2), 2001, 191–217.

Nichols, Joel "Dual Lenses: Using Theology and International Human Rights to Assess China's 2005 Regulations on Religion" *Pepperdine Law Review*, 105, 2007, 105–121.

Nietzsche, Friedrich *Beyond Good and Evil*, trans. Helen Zimmern, New York: Vintage Books, 1966.

Nietzsche, Friedrich *Thus Spake Zarathustra*, trans. Thomas Common, Calgary, Alberta: Theophania Publishing, 2011.

Noland, M. "Religions, islam et croissance économique: l'apport des analyses empiriques" *Revue Française de Gestion*, 171, 2007, 97–118.

Nordlinger, Eric *Conflict Regulation in Divided Societies*, Cambridge, MA: Harvard University Press, 1972.

Norris, Pippa and Ronald Inglehart *Sacred and Secular: Religion and Politics Worldwide*, New York: Cambridge University Press, 2004.

Oldmixion, Elizabeth and William Hudson "When Church Teachings and Policy Commitments Collide: Perspectives on Catholics in the U.S. House of Representatives" *Politics and Religion*, 1 (1), 2008, 113–135.

Oldmixion, Elizabeth A., Beth Rosenson, and Kenneth D. Wald "Conflict over Israel: The Role of Religion, Race Party, and Ideology in the U.S. House of Representatives, 1997–2002" *Terrorism and Political Violence*, 17 (3), 2005, 407–426.

Olson, Mancur Jr. *The Logic of Collective Action*, Cambridge, MA: Harvard University Press, 1971.

Ottosson, Daniel *A World Survey of Laws Prohibiting Same Sex Activity between Consenting Adults*, Brussels: International Lesbian, Gay, Bisexual, Trans and Intersex Association, 2009. http://ilga.org/historic/Statehomophobia/ILGA_State_Sponsored_Homophobia_2009.pdf (accessed February 1, 2012).

Pape, Robert A. "The Strategic Logic of Suicide Terrorism" *American Political Science Review*, 97 (3), 2003, 343–361.

Paton, D. "Obeah Acts: Producing and Policing the Boundaries of Religion in the Caribbean" *Small Axe*, 13 (1), 2009, 1–18.

Patterson, Eric "Different Religions, Different Politics? Religion and Political Attitudes in Argentina and Chile" *Journal for the Scientific Study of Religion*, 43 (3), 2004, 354–362.

Penning, James M. "Pat Robertson and the GOP: 1988 and Beyond" *Sociology of Religion*, 55 (3), 1994, 327–344.

Peterson, Steven A. "Church Participation and Political Participation: The Spillover Effect" *American Politics Research* 20 (1), 1992, 123–139.

Philpott, Daniel "The Religious Roots of Modern International Relations" *World Politics*, 52, 2000, 206–245.

Philpott, Daniel "The Challenge of September 11 to Secularism in International Relations" *World Politics*, 55 (1), 2002, 66–95.

Philpott, Daniel "Explaining the Political Ambivalence of Religion" *American Political Science Review*, 101 (3), 2007, 505–525.

Philpott, Daniel "Has the Study of Global Politics Found Religion?" *Annual Review of Political Science*, 12, 2009, 183–202.

Pickering, W. S. F. *Durkheim on Religion: A Selection of Readings with Bibliographies*, London: Routledge & Kegan Paul, 1975.

Pickering, W. S. F. *Durkheim's Sociology of Religion: Themes and Theories*, London: Routledge & Kegan Paul, 1984.

Piekalkiewiez, Jaroslaw, "Poland: Nonviolent Revolution in a Socialist State" in Jack A. Goldstone, Ted Robert Gurr, and Farrokh Moshiri eds. *Revolutions of the Late Twentieth Century*, Boulder, CO: Westview, 1991, 136–161.

Piscatori, James "Accounting for Islamic Fundamentalisms" in Martin E. Marty and R. Scott Appleby eds. *Accounting for Fundamentalisms: The Dynamic Character of Movements*, Chicago: University of Chicago Press, 1994, 361–373.

Polkinghorn, Brian and Sean Byrne "Between War and Peace: An Examination of Conflict Management Styles in Four Conflict Zones" *International Journal of Conflict Management*, 12 (1), 2001, 23–46.

Pollack, Detlef "Religious Change in Europe: Theoretical Considerations and Empirical Findings" *Social Compass*, 55 (2), 2008, 168–186.

Pollack, Detlef and Gett Pickel "Religious Individualization or Secularization? Testing Hypotheses of Religious Change in Eastern and Western Germany" *British Journal of Sociology*, 58 (1), 2007, 603–632.

Presser, Stanley and Mark Chaves "Is Religious Service Attendance Declining?" *Journal for the Scientific Study of Religion*, 46 (3), 2007, 417–423.

Rabasa, Angel "Islamic Education in Southeast Asia" *Current Trends in Islamist Ideology*, 2, 2005. www.currenttrends.org/research/detail/islamic-education-in-southeast-asia (accessed February 1, 2012).

Ransler, Karen and William R. Thompson "Looking for Waves of Terrorism" *Terrorism and Political Violence*, 21 (1), 2009, 28–41.

Rapoport, David C. "Fear and Trembling: Terrorism in Three Religious Traditions" *American Political Science Review*, 78 (3), 1984: 658–677.

Rapoport, David C. "Messianic Sanctions for Terror" *Comparative Politics*, 20 (2), January 1988, 195–213.

Rapoport, David C. and Yonah Alexander, eds. *The Morality of Terrorism: Religious and Secular Justifications*, 2nd ed. New York: Columbia University Press, 1989.

Rawls, John *Political Liberalism*, New York: Columbia University Press, 1993.

Raz, Joseph *The Morality of Freedom*, Oxford: Oxford University Press, 1986.

Robbers, Gerhard *Church Autonomy: A Comparative Survey*, Frankfurt am Main: Peter Lang, 2001.

Robertson, Roland "Beyond the Sociology of Religion?" *Sociological Analysis*, 46 (4), 1985, 355–360.

Roof, Wade C. "American Presidential Rhetoric from Ronald Regan to George W. Bush: Another Look at Civil Religion" *Social Compass*, 56 (2), 2009, 286–301.

Rubin, Barry "Religion and International Affairs" in Douglas Johnston and Cynthia Sampson eds. *Religion, the Missing Dimension of Statecraft*, Oxford: Oxford University Press, 1994, 20–34.

Rule, James B. *Theories of Civil Violence*, Berkeley: University of California Press, 1988.

Russett, Bruce, John R. Oneal, and Michaelene Cox "Clash of Civilizations, or Realism and Liberalism Déjà Vu? Some Evidence" *Journal of Peace Research*, 37 (5), 2000, 583–608.

Sadowski, Yahya "Political Islam: Asking the Wrong Questions?" *Annual Review of Political Science*, 9, 2006, 215–240.

Sahliyeh, Emile ed. *Religious Resurgence and Politics in the Contemporary World*, New York: State University of New York Press, 1990.

Sala-i-Martin, X., Doppelhofer, G., and Miller, R. I. "Determinants of Long-Term Growth: A Bayesian Averaging of Classical Estimates (BACE) Approach" *American Economic Review*, 94(4), 2004, 813–835.

Schanda, Balázs "Religious Freedom Issues in Hungary" *Brigham Young University Law Review*, 2002, 405–433.

Schoenfeld, Eugen "Militant and Submissive Religions: Class, Religion and Ideology" *British Journal of Sociology*, 43 (1), 1992, 111–140.

Selinger, Leah "The Forgotten Factor: The Uneasy Relationship between Religion and Development" *Social Compass*, 51 (4), 2004, 523–543.

Seul, Jeffrey R. "'Ours Is the Way of God': Religion, Identity and Intergroup Conflict" *Journal of Peace Research*, 36 (3), 1999, 553–569.

Shah, Timothy S. "Making the Christian World Safe for Liberalism: From Grotius to Rawls" *Political Quarterly*, 71 (s1), 2000, 121–139.

Shani, Giorgio "Transnational Religious Actors and International Relations" in Jeffrey Haynes ed. *Routledge Handbook of Religion and Politics*, New York: Routledge, 2009, 308–322.

Sherkat Daren E. and Christopher G. Ellison "Recent Development and Controversies in the Sociology of Religion" *Annual Review of Sociology*, 25, 1999, 363–394.

Shields, John A. "Between Passion and Deliberation: The Christian Right and Democratic Ideals" *Political Science Quarterly*, 122 (1), 2007, 89–113.

Shupe, Anson "The Stubborn Persistence of Religion in the Global Arena" in Emile Sahliyeh ed. *Religious Resurgence and Politics in the Contemporary World*, New York: State University of New York Press, 1990, 17–26.

Silberman, Israella "Religion as a Meaning System: Implications for the New Millennium" *Journal of Social Issues*, 61 (4), 2005, 641–663.

Smith, Anthony D. "Ethnic Election and National Destiny: Some Religious Origins of Nationalist Ideals" *Nations and Nationalism*, 5 (3), 1999, 331–355.

Smith, Anthony D. "The Sacred Dimension of Nationalism" *Millennium*, 29 (3), 2000, 791–814.

Smith, Donald E, *Religion and Political Development*, Boston: Little, Brown, 1970.

Smith, Donald E. ed. *Religion, Politics and Social Change in the Third World*, New York: Free Press, 1971.

Smith, Donald E. ed. *Religion and Political Modernization*, New Haven, CT: Yale University Press, 1974.

Soloveitchik, Haym "Rupture and Reconstruction: The Transformation of Contemporary Orthodoxy" *Tradition*, 28 (4), 1994, 64–130.

Spiro, Melford E. "Religion: Problems of Definition and Explanation" in Michael Banton ed. *Anthropological Approaches to the Study of Religion*, London: Tavistock, 1966, 85–126.

Sprinzak, Ehud "Models of Religious Violence: The Case of Jewish Fundamentalism in Israel" in Martin E. Marty and R. Scott Appleby eds. *Fundamentalisms and the State: Remaking Polities, Economies, and Militance*, Chicago: University of Chicago Press, 1991, 462–490.

Sprinzak, Ehud "Extremism and Violence in Israel: The Crisis of Messianic Politics" *Annals of the American Academy of Political and Social Sciences*, 555, January 1998, 114–126.

Stark, Rodney "Secularization, R.I.P." *Sociology of Religion*, 60 (3), 1999, 249–273.

Stark, Rodney, *For the Glory of God*, Princeton, NJ: Princeton University Press, 2003.

Stark, Rodney and William Bainbridge, *The Future of Religion: Secularization, Revival, and Cult Formation*, Berkeley: University of California Press, 1985.

Stark, Rodney and Roger Finke *Acts of Faith: Explaining the Human Side of Religion*, Berkeley, CA: University of California Press, 2000.

Stark, Rodney and Lawrence R. Iannaccone "A Supply Side Reinterpretation of the 'Secularization' of Europe" *Journal for the Scientific Study of Religion*, 33 (3), 1994, 230–252.

Stepan, Alfred "Religion, Democracy, and the 'Twin Tolerations'" *Journal of Democracy*, 11 (4), 2000, 37–56.

Stepan, Alfred and Graeme B. Robinson "An 'Arab' More than 'Muslim' Electoral Gap" *Journal of Democracy*, 14 (3), 2003, 30–44.

Stern, Jessica *Terror in the Name of God: Why Religious Militants Kill*, New York: HarperCollins, 2003.

Stulz, René M. and Rohan Williamson "Culture, Openness, and Finance" *Journal of Financial Economics*, 70(3), 2003, 313–349.

Svensson, Isak "Fighting with Faith: Religion and Conflict Resolution in Civil Wars" *Journal of Conflict Resolution*, 51 (6), 2007, 930–949.

Swatos, William H. Jr. *A Future for Religion? New Paradigms for Social Analysis*, Newbury Park, CA: Sage, 1993.

Taylor, Charles *A Secular Age*, Cambridge, MA: Harvard University Press, 2007.

Thomas, Scott M. "Taking Religious and Cultural Pluralism Seriously: The Global Resurgence of Religion and the Transformation of International Society" *Millennium*, 29 (3), 2000, 815–841.

Thomas, Scott M. *The Global Resurgence of Religion and the Transformation of International Relations: The Struggle for the Soul of the Twenty-first Century*, New York: Palgrave Macmillan, 2005.

Thomas, Scott M. "Outwitting the Developed Countries? Existential Insecurity and the Global Resurgence of Religion" *Journal of International Affairs*, 61 (1), 2007, 21–45.

Tibi, Bassam "Post-Bipolar Disorder in Crisis: The Challenge of Politicized Islam" *Millennium*, 29 (4), 2000, 843–859.

Tilly, Charles *From Mobilization to Revolution*, Reading, MA: Addison-Wesley, 1978.

Tocqueville, Alexis de *Democracy in America*, Cambridge, MA: Sever & Francis Press, 1863.

Toft, Monica Duffy "Getting Religion? The Puzzling Case of Islam and Civil War" *International Security*, 31 (4), 2007, 97–131.

Toft, Monica D., Daniel Philpott, and Timothy S. Shah *God's Century: Resurgent Religion and Global Politics*, New York: W. W. Norton, 2011.

Turner, Brian S. *Religion and Social Theory*, 2nd ed. London: Sage, 1991.

Tusicisny, Andrej "Civilizational Conflicts: More Frequent, Longer, and Bloodier?" *Journal of Peace Research*, 41 (4), 2004, 485–498.

van der Brug, Wouter, Sara B. Hobolt, and Claes H. de Vreese "Religion and Party Choice in Europe" *West European Politics*, 32 (6), 2009, 1266–1283.

van der Vyver, Johan D. "Religious Fundamentalism and Human Rights" *Journal of International Affairs*, 50 (1), 1996, 21–40.

Ver Beek, K. A. "Spirituality: A Development Taboo" in Deborah Eade ed. *Development and Culture: Selected Essays from Development in Practice*, Oxford: Oxfam GB, 2002, 58–75.

Voicu, Malina "Religion and Gender across Europe" *Social Compass*, 56 (2), 2009, 144–162.

Voye, Liliane "Secularization in a Context of Advanced Modernity" *Sociology of Religion*, 60 (3), 1999, 275–288.

Wald, Kenneth D. and Clyde Wilcox "Getting Religion: Has Political Science Discovered the Faith Factor?" *American Political Science Review*, 100 (4), 2006, 523–529.

Wald, Kenneth D., Adam L. Silverman, and Kevin S. Fridy "Making Sense of Religion in Political Life" *Annual Review of Political Science*, 8, 2005, 121–143.

Wallace, Anthony F. C. *Religion: An Anthropological View*, New York: Random House, 1966.

Warr, Kevin "The Normative Promise of Religious Organizations in Global Civil Society" *Journal of Church and State*, 41 (3), 1999, 499–523.

Weber, Max *The Protestant Ethic and the Spirit of Capitalism*, trans. Talcott Parsons, London: Allen & Unwin, 1930.

Weber, Max *Sociology of Religion*, Boston: Beacon Press, 1963.

Welch, Michael R., David Sikkink, Eric Sartain, and Carolyn Bond "Trust in God and Trust in Man: The Ambivalent Role of Religion in Shaping Social Trust" *Journal for the Scientific Study of Religion*, 43 (3), 2004, 317–343.

Wentz, Richard *Why People Do Bad Things in the Name of Religion*, Macon, GA: Mercer, 1987.

Westhus, Kenneth "The Church in Opposition" *Sociological Analysis*, 37 (4), 1976, 299–314.

Wilcox, Clyde, Sharon Linzey, and Ted G. Jelen "Reluctant Warriors: Premillennialism and Politics in the Moral Majority" *Journal for the Scientific Study of Religion*, 30 (3), 1991, 245–258.

Wilhelmsen, Julie "Islamism in Azerbaijan: How Potent?" *Studies in Conflict and Terrorism*, 32 (8), 2009, 726–742.

Williams, Rhys H. "Movement Dynamics and Social Change: Transforming Fundamentalist Ideology and Organizations" in Martin E. Marty and R. Scott

Appleby eds. *Accounting for Fundamentalisms: The Dynamic Character of Movements*, Chicago: University of Chicago Press, 1994, 785–833.

Willis, Aaron P. "Shas–The Sephardic Tora Guardians: Religious 'Movement' and Political Power" in Asher Arian and Michal Shamir eds. *Elections in Israel*, Albany, NY: State University of New York Press, 1995.

Wilson, Bryan R. *Religion in Sociological Perspective*. Oxford: Oxford University Press, 1982.

Wink, Paul, Michele Dillon, and Adrienne Prettyman "Religiousness, Spiritual Seeking and Authoritarianism: Findings from a Longitudinal Study" *Journal for the Scientific Study of Religion*, 46 (3), 2007, 321–335.

Witte, John Jr. "Facts and Fictions about the History of Separation of Church and State" *Journal of Church and State*, 48 (1), 2006, 15–45.

Wong, Sonia "Of Religious Freedom and Economic Well-Being" Master's thesis, University College London, 2006.

Woodhead, Linda and Paul Heelas eds. *Religion in Modern Times: An Interpretive Anthology*, Oxford: Oxford University Press, 2000.

Wuthnow, Robert and Valerie Lewis "Religion and Altruistic U.S. Foreign Policy Goals: Evidence from a National Survey of Church Members" *Journal for the Scientific Study of Religion*, 47 (2), 2008, 191–209.

Yamane, David "Secularization on Trial: In Defense of a Neosecularization Paradigm" *Journal for the Scientific Study of Religion*, 36 (1), 1997, 109–122.

Yoon, Dae-Kyu "The Constitution of North Korea: Its Changes and Implications" *Fordham International Law Journal*, 27 (4), 2003, 1289–1305.

Yousif, Ahmad "Islam, Minorities and Religious Freedom: A Challenge to Modern Theory of Pluralism" *Journal of Muslim Minority Affairs*, 20 (1), 2000, 29–41.

Yousif, Ahmad "Islamic Revivalism in Malaysia: An Islamic Response to Non-Muslim Concerns" *American Journal of Islamic Social Sciences*, 21(4), 2004, 30–56.

Zaidise, Eran, Daphna Canetti-Nisim, and Ami Pedahzur "Politics of God or Politics of Man? The Role of Religion and Deprivation in Predicting Support for Political Violence in Israel" *Political Studies*, 55 (3), 2007, 499–521.

Zubadia, Sami "Trajectories of Political Islam: Egypt, Iran and Turkey" *Political Quarterly*, 71 (Supplement 1), 2000, 60–78.

Index